Developments in British Politics 9

Developments in British Politics 9

Edited by

Richard Heffernan

Philip Cowley

and

Colin Hay

palgrave
macmillan

First published 2011 by
PALGRAVE MACMILLAN

Palgrave Macmillan in the UK is an imprint of Macmillan Publishers Limited, registered in England, company number 785998, of Houndmills, Basingstoke, Hampshire RG21 6XS.

Palgrave Macmillan in the US is a division of St Martin's Press LLC, 175 Fifth Avenue, New York, NY 10010.

Palgrave Macmillan is the global academic imprint of the above companies and has companies and representatives throughout the world.

Palgrave® and Macmillan® are registered trademarks in the United States, the United Kingdom, Europe and other countries

ISBN-13: 978–0–230–22173–4   hardback
ISBN-10: 0–230–22173–4   hardback
ISBN-13: 987–0–230–22174–1   paperback
ISBN-10: 0–230–22174–2   paperback

This book is printed on paper suitable for recycling and made from fully managed and sustained forest sources. Logging, pulping and manufacturing processes are expected to conform to the environmental regulations of the country of origin.

A catalogue record for this book is available from the British Library.

A catalog record for this book is available from the Library of Congress.

10 9 8 7 6 5 4 3 2 1
19 18 17 16 15 14 13 12 11 10

Printed and bound in Great Britain by MPG Books Group, UK

Contents

List of Boxes, Figures and Tables

Boxes

Figures

Tables

Acknowledgements

For this ninth edition of *Developments in British Politics* Patrick Dunleavy, the last of the founding editors, has stepped down from the editorial team. We thank Pat for his splendid contributions over the 27 years *Developments* has been up and running.

As always, the list of authors is entirely new. We are entirely in the debt of all our contributors for their expertise and insights and especially for their forbearance in the face of the numerous and no doubt exacting demands made of them. Our grateful thanks to them all. The timetable for this edition of *Developments* was unusually elongated owing to the need to commission chapters before – and to publish the book after – Gordon Brown called a general election, something he first contemplated doing in September 2007. The move towards five-year fixed-term parliaments, whatever its political and democratic impact, will make it easier to plan the schedule of future editions. We have especially to thank, as ever, our excellent publisher, Steven Kennedy. Steven, as his Palgrave politics authors and editors know only too well, kept us on our toes. He did so by email and telephone. We are glad he has yet to use Facebook or Twitter.

Richard Heffernan
Philip Cowley
Colin Hay

Notes on the Contributors

Richard J. Aldrich is Professor of International Security at Warwick University and is the author of several books including *GCHQ: The Uncensored Story of Britain's Most Secret Intelligence Agency*. He is currently directing the AHRC project 'Landscapes of Secrecy: The Central Intelligence Agency and the contested record of American Foreign Policy, 1947–2001'.

Rosie Campbell is Senior Lecturer in politics at Birkbeck, University of London. She has written widely on gender and British politics, focusing on voting behaviour, representation and political participation. She has co-authored a number of reports including the Electoral Commission's 'Gender and Political Participation' and the Hansard Society's *Women at the Top*. Her book *Gender and the Vote in Britain* was published by the ESRC press in 2006.

Andrew Chadwick is Professor of Political Science and Co-Director of the New Political Communication Unit in the Department of Politics and International Relations at Royal Holloway, University of London.

Philip Cowley is Professor of Parliamentary Government at the University of Nottingham. He is the co-author of *The British General Election of 2010* (Palgrave).

David Denver is Emeritus Professor of Politics at Lancaster University. A new edition of his text *Elections and Voters in Britain* (co-authored on this occasion with Rob Johns and Christopher Carman) is scheduled to appear in 2011.

Antony Field is a Research Fellow at the University of Warwick. He has published in a number of journals including *Review of International Studies*. His current research is concerned with the degree of continuity and change in the organisation of terrorist groups and its implications for the responses of intelligence and security agencies in the context of globalisation.

Andrew Gamble is Professor of Politics and Head of the Department of Politics and International Studies at the University of Cambridge. He is joint editor of *The Political Quarterly* and a Fellow of the British Academy.

Cathy Gormley-Heenan is Senior Lecturer in the School of Criminology, Politics and Social Policy and Director of the Institute for Research in Social Sciences (IRiSS) at the University of Ulster. Her most recent book is *Political Leadership and the Northern Ireland Peace Process* (Palgrave-Macmillan, 2007).

Colin Hay is Professor of Political Analysis and Director of the Political Economy Research Centre at the University of Sheffield. Among his recent books are *New Directions in Political Science* (Palgrave, 2010); *The Role of Ideas in Political Analysis* (with Andreas Gofas, Routledge, 2010); *The Oxford Handbook of British Politics* (with Matthew Flinders, Andrew Gamble and Michael Kenny, Oxford University Press, 2009) and *Why We Hate Politics* (Polity, 2007 – winner of the WJM Mackenzie Prize). *European Welfare Capitalism in Hard Times* (with Daniel Wincott) will be published by Palgrave later this year.

Richard Heffernan is Reader in Government at the Open University and a Visiting Professor at the University of Notre Dame.

Alexandra Kelso is Lecturer in Politics at the University of Southampton. She is author of *Parliamentary Reform at Westminster* (Manchester University Press, 2009) and co-author, with Peter Dorey, of *House of Lords Reform Since 1911: Must The Lords Go?* (Palgrave, 2011).

David Richards is Professor of Politics at the University of Sheffield. He is the author of *New Labour and the Civil Service: Reconstituting the Westminster Model* (Palgrave, 2008) and of *British Politics* (Oxford University Press, 2006 with Dennis Kavanagh, Martin Smith and Andrew Geddes).

Meg Russell is Reader in British and Comparative Politics at University College London, where she is also Deputy Director of the Constitution Unit. She is author of *Reforming the House of Lords: Lessons from Overseas* (Oxford University Press, 2000), and *Building New Labour: The Politics of Party Organisation* (Palgrave, 2005).

Roger Scully is Professor of Political Science and Director of the Institute of Welsh Politics at Aberystwyth University. His research focuses on political representation in the European Union and the United Kingdom; he is currently completing a major study of politics in Wales (co-authored with Richard Wyn Jones). He is also Co-Director of the ESRC-sponsored 2011 Welsh Election Study.

James Stanyer is Senior Lecturer in Communication and Media Studies in the Department of Social Sciences, Loughborough University. He is co-editor of *The Political Communication Reader* (Polity, 2007) and author of *Modern Political Communication* (Polity, 2007).

Gerry Stoker is Professor of Politics and Governance and the Director of the Centre for Citizenship, Globalisation and Governance at the University of Southampton.

Lori Thorlakson is an Associate Professor of Political Science at the University of Alberta in Canada. Her work on party competition, European Union politics and multilevel systems has been published in *West European Politics*, the *European Journal of Political Research*, *Journal of European Public Policy*, *Journal of Common Market Studies* and *Party Politics*.

Richard Wyn Jones is Professor of Welsh Politics and Director of the Wales Governance Centre at Cardiff University.

Chapter 1

Introduction: A Landscape without a Map? British Politics after 2010

PHILIP COWLEY, COLIN HAY AND RICHARD HEFFERNAN

It is far too early to tell if the general election of 2010 will prove a defining moment in British politics. Few elections by themselves herald a radical or abrupt change of direction. The roads both to and from the watershed election of 1945 were as important as the election itself. The same could be said of another election, 1979, which saw the election of the first Thatcher government and from which a different form of politics eventually emerged.

Yet the election of 2010 is likely to earn its place in the history books, regardless of what follows. It resulted in only the second hung parliament in 80 years, and the first since 1974 in which no one party could command a majority or form a single-party government. The resulting Conservative–Liberal Democrat government is Britain's first peacetime coalition since 1931. Given the electoral arithmetic, many commentators had expected a hung parliament but one from which a Conservative minority government would eventually emerge, with a second election, held within a year, to decide matters, similar to what occurred in 1974. Few predicted a full coalition between the Conservatives and the Liberal Democrats, not least because it was thought unlikely it would seem desirable to the parties themselves.

The majority of European countries have a multiparty system and are governed by some kind of coalition. Such coalitions presently comprise at least a centre-right conservative party and a centrist liberal party. The British Conservative and Liberal Democrat coalition is, for some, an indication that Britain, so long the exception, might be in the process of entering the European 'mainstream', and that 2010 marks another yet nail in the coffin of the 'Westminster model'. Moreover, if the coalition is able to deliver on its promise of widespread political reform, it may well come to have a significant impact on both the way our politics is conducted and the means by which it is enacted.

The coalition agreement specified a five-year term. If it is to last that long, however, the coalition has to overcome some significant hurdles. The most obvious is the economic. Having claimed early in the 2005 parliament that they would seek to 'share the proceeds of growth', the Conservatives moved fully behind fiscal retrenchment as the extent of Britain's budget deficit became clear. Indeed, in the long pre-election campaign the Conservatives went so far as to project themselves as the guardians of Britain's (in their view) much needed return to austerity after a decade of excess. Their own polling data, however, suggested that this did not play well with broad swathes of the public. Voters, it seemed, were happy to accept that some fiscal rebalancing was required but one that affected others, not them personally. Thus, when it came to the campaign itself, the deficit was rather downplayed, becoming something of the elephant in the room.

The Liberal Democrats undoubtedly scored many points in the coalition negotiations despite bringing only a relatively small number of seats to the table. But the tenor of the new government's economic agenda was set by the Conservatives. True to their manifesto commitment, George Osborne's first 'emergency' budget took place scarcely a month after the election itself. It was very much an austerity budget – with substantial increases in taxation and the promise of drastic reductions in public spending to come – but it was also very short of substantive detail about where the axe would ultimately fall and the single greatest tax-raising measure (the increase in VAT from 17.5 to 20 per cent) was deferred until January 2011. The emergency budget was as much as anything a signal – to both the financial markets and the electorate – of the painful fiscal rebalancing to come. More detail came in the Comprehensive Spending Review in October 2010 when it was announced that unprotected departments (those other than health and international development) would face an average real cut of around 25 per cent over four years. Welfare reform, which many consider likely to put the coalition under strain, is at the centre of the government's approach to fiscal retrenchment. The welfare shakeup announced in the budget will save the country only a minimum of £11 billion by 2014/15, but additional, significant savings are being canvassed. Ministers have made it clear that the greater the size of the cut in the welfare budget, the lower the cuts will be elsewhere.

Labour allege that this policy is a 'gamble'. It is certainly risky. If it takes Britain back into recession – a so-called double-dip recession – as Labour charged, then it will be seen to have failed even by its own standards. Were this to arise, it would almost certainly serve to discredit the government's economic policy at a time of mounting political opposition and unrest. It is not difficult to see how that in turn might lead to a slide in the opinion polls, exacerbating differences within and between the coalition partners and perhaps even prompting a vote of no confidence and an early election.

Yet even if that does not happen, the consequences will be considerable. The government's cuts, the most significant reductions in public spending since 1945, will have an enormous impact on the quality of life in almost every household in Britain. They involve political risk, further compounded by the deeply uneven impact. For those parts of the British economy in which the public sector is the largest – Northern Ireland, the North-East of England, and urban Scotland and Wales in particular – are likely to see far steeper rises is unemployment from both public and private sector redundancies. It is, in short, difficult not to see the coalition as facing a series of profound economic challenges in the years ahead.

But the political challenges are also considerable. Opinion polls during the 2010 election found that the British public were not as afraid of hung parliaments as many of its politicians assumed; the idea of politicians working 'together' appealed. However, whether the coalition's particular blend of policies and personnel appeal as much as the principle of coalition government remains to be seen. By forming their coalition, the Conservatives and the Liberal Democrats can claim to have won the election. Together they can boast the support of 59 per cent of the voting public. No single-party government has won over 50 per cent of the vote at any post-war election. Yet no elector voted for the coalition that emerged from within the hung parliament. The internal functioning of the Cameron–Clegg-led coalition government – *qua* executive – appeared initially to be relatively smooth, despite the lack of any experience of coalition on the part of its key players. Any problems that did exist were as likely to intra-party as they were inter-party. Yet tensions within the parties outside of government were evident relatively early on – both from the Liberal Democrat left and the Conservative right. The former were exacerbated by the electoral costs of the coalition, which appeared to be being born almost entirely by the Lib Dems, who seemed to be taking the blame for the unpopular policies of the coalition while gaining none of the credit.

The 'official' coalition's narrative for the parliament goes something like this:

The parties govern for a full five-year term, as promised. They experience unpopularity as a result of the spending cuts, but gain credit for taking hard decisions, which eventually translates into rising levels of support as the economy picks up (and voters realise that the cuts were not as severe as people were claiming). As a result of being in government, the Conservative brand is further 'detoxified'; the Lib Dems' period in government makes people see them as a grown-up party of government, rather than merely a spittoon for disgruntled voters. They then fight the election as two separate parties.

There are, however, all sorts of alternative scenarios, of which the following are just the most obvious.

1   The parties manage to govern for a full five-year term, and experience rising popularity, but the process of governing as a coalition results in the parties fighting the next election with some form of joint arrangement. This could range from a full-blown joint ticket (in which there are coalition candidates), to ad hoc arrangements not to contest certain seats or even just an understanding that they will pull their punches, not putting any significant resource into seats that the other needs to hold or win.

2   The compromises required of the Lib Dems – as well as the effect government has had on their poll ratings (which contrary to their hopes, do not improve) – exacerbate tensions in the party to such an extent that it splits, but with 'coalition Lib Dems' remaining in government, and the government lasting most or all of the five years. The coalition Lib Dems fight the next election in some pact or arrangement with the Conservatives, but facing a separate rump Liberal Democrat Party. Over time, the coalition Liberals merge with (or are, in reality, subsumed into) the Conservatives.

3   As 2, but rather than splitting, the Liberal Democrats withdraw from the coalition en masse, and attempt to rebuild support in opposition, probably electing a new leader as they do so, and disowning much of the Clegg-era. The Conservatives attempt to govern as a minority administration for a short period, before calling an election.

4   The Conservative right – disgruntled by the coalition from the beginning, and increasingly frustrated by the compromises which the leadership are giving to the Lib Dems to keep them on board – stage a series of rebellions against the leadership. These increase tensions within the coalition so much that it collapses before the end of the five-year term, triggering an early election.

5   The Conservative leadership sees an opportunity to capitalise on any rise in its opinion poll ratings to govern alone, and contrive to break the coalition apart, hoping to gain an outright Commons majority of their own.

All of these scenarios are possible but some seem more likely than others. Any scenario in which the Conservative leadership pulls the coalition down to try to stage a snap election is extremely risky (both because they have to justify it, but also because if it fails to secure an outright Commons majority, they have no would-be coalition partner with which to work). Similarly, it seems likely that if there are tensions within the coalition which prevent it lasting a full five years, then those are more likely to come from the Liberal Democrats than from the Conservative right. And, in addition, poor poll ratings are just as likely to hold the coalition together – no one will want an early election if polling badly – as pull it apart. But none of us are fortune tellers, and all these scenarios are possible, as are many variants of them.

The broader political map remains equally unclear. The 2010 election campaign was the most closely fought since 1992. Unlike 1997 and 2001, when Labour's strong poll leads heralded enormous Labour majorities, and 2005 when it was widely assumed that Labour would be re-elected with a smaller majority, the outcome of the 2010 election was always in doubt. It was the most exciting and unpredictable of recent decades. Yet in spite of such a close race, turnout, the percentage of the eligible electorate voting in the election, at 65 per cent, saw only a small increase on the 61 per cent of 2005. These recent figures are some way off the 75 per cent post-war average. Britain's low turnouts are perhaps an indication of an underlying problem with our electoral politics. While the refusal of the apathetic citizen to vote should not be a surprise, the failure of the angry or alienated citizen, those turned off of politics and suspicious of all politicians, to do so should sound some alarm.

A conventional Lib Dem response to political disengagement has long been to argue for political – and especially constitutional – reform, and the coalition agreement secured a referendum on electoral reform, among other reforms. Yet the system proposed – the Alternative Vote (AV) – was not a proportional one, and not one that the Lib Dems backed previously. Its use in the referendum was a compromise between the Lib Dem desire for the Single Transferable Vote and the Conservative desire for the status quo. Indeed, it is one of the ironies of the coalition that the only party which promised a referendum on AV in its manifesto was Labour (which promptly went and voted against the legislation implementing it). The coalition agreement specified that both the Conservatives and the Liberal Democrats, having put the question of changing the electoral system from the present single member plurality system to AV, would be free to campaign for their own preferences. Almost all Conservatives backed the status quo, and the coalition parties divided on the question put to the electorate. Labour was also divided on the question of electoral reform. The referendum on changing the electoral system, which took place in May 2011, resulted in an overwhelming rejection of AV, by more than 2:1. But even if it had passed, to what extent can political reform of this sort – or the coalition's other proposal – generate substantial political renewal? The experience of the Blair/Brown era is not a positive one: a whole series of political reforms were introduced by the Labour governments, yet they generated little or no rise in political engagement; indeed, many appeared to have made things worse. The reality of government might also make us at least initially sceptical about the success of the 'big society' – the Conservatives' underpinning philosophy at the 2010 election – or the coalition's much-vaunted bonfire of quangos (a policy which is always easier to promise, than to deliver).

It is, as we begin to survey the past election and the early stages of the new government, imprudent to anticipate future developments. But the 2010 election brought to an end New Labour's 16-year domination of British politics; the Blair, Brown and Mandelson generation passed into history; it brought about the return of the Conservatives to government; and it seemed to mark the final, long anticipated demise of the two-party system under which government had been entirely monopolised by either Labour or the Conservatives since 1945. We wait to see if further changes to the British party system emerge in the coming period. If AV had replaced the single member plurality system, then future elections might have become more competitive, election outcomes more volatile, and coalition or minority government more likely. But even without AV, the likelihood of future hung parliaments remains high as a result of the way that the British electoral system currently functions. Labour or the Conservatives, having not been able to win on their own at the 2010 election, might not be able to do so at a future election. We wait to access the work of the coalition and to see how Labour responds under a new, untested leader to being in opposition. We are only just beginning to uncover the meanings of the last election and the new government. Britain has found itself in unchartered electoral and political waters. These are fascinating times to be studying British politics.

Chapter 2

Constitutional Politics

MEG RUSSELL

One of the clearest legacies of Labour's extended period in government between 1997 and 2010 is its programme of constitutional reform. Vernon Bogdanor, a leading constitutional historian, has described it as 'the most radical programme of constitutional reform that Britain has seen since 1911 or 1832' (Bogdanor 2001: 143). Yet, despite this, the Conservative–Liberal Democrat coalition government formed in May 2010 arrived with a large constitutional reform agenda of its own, demonstrating that Labour's reforms were not universally accepted: having been criticised variously for going either too far, or not far enough.

This chapter looks backwards at the recent history of constitutional reform, and forwards to its likely future. It seeks to make a balanced assessment of reform under Labour 1997–2010. What will be that period's lasting legacy, and to what extent were its critics correct? It also sets a context for developments under the coalition, both past and future, and how the 'settlement' left by Labour is likely to be further reformed.

In what follows developments during 1997–2010 are first summarised in terms of the early period under Blair and the later period under Brown: Tony Blair presided over extensive reform despite having little interest in it, while Gordon Brown was profoundly interested yet his legacy is almost nil. Why was this? Next the chapter looks at the criticisms of the reform programme – coming broadly from two groups (characterised respectively as 'conservative' and 'radical' critics), and focusing on three main criticisms: that the reforms were incoherent, ineffective and liable to be unstable. It then explores in greater detail the implementation and effects of reforms in several key areas, to see how well these criticisms stack up, concluding that Labour's programme was both more coherent and more radical than many give it credit for. Finally, the chapter turns to the new constitutional agenda, suggesting that the new government will find it equally difficult to deliver coherent reforms, and therefore to placate the critics.

Blair: the reluctant radical

Labour came to power in 1997 on a manifesto promising wide-ranging constitutional reform. By the end of the government's first term in 2001 a whole range of measures had been approved, as summarised in Box 2.1. These included the creation of new devolved institutions in Scotland, Wales, Northern Ireland and London, reform of the House of Lords to remove the great majority of hereditary peers, new Human Rights and Freedom of Information Acts, and new rules governing the funding of political parties. In addition the government established an Independent Commission on the Voting System to consider electoral reform for the House of Commons, though its recommendations were not put into effect. In the second term reform slowed down, but included the Constitutional Reform Act 2005, which created a new Supreme Court to replace the top judges in the House of Lords, and a referendum on devolution to the North-East of England, which was defeated. In the third term, before Gordon Brown took over in June 2007, the main measure was a Bill giving greater powers to the Welsh Assembly. Most of these measures are discussed in more detail below.

On the basis of these events it would be natural to assume that Tony Blair was a keen constitutional reformer. But in fact he was never a great enthusiast for reform. Even in Labour's first term his principal focus was on other domestic matters, such as welfare reform and public services. After 2001 he became more distracted by international affairs, particularly in Iraq and Afghanistan. He spoke only rarely about the party's achievements on the constitution, and had a tendency to be cautious or even disinterested when it came to decisions in this area.

Three key explanations can be found for the mismatch between Blair's attitude and the achievements of his governments:

- First, Blair inherited most of the constitutional reform commitments enacted in the first term from his predecessor as Labour party leader, John Smith. Smith was a more convinced reformer but died suddenly in 1994, leaving this legacy to Blair. By then many reforms were difficult to resile from. For example the commitment to create a Scottish Parliament was the response to years of pressure from a large grassroots devolution movement in Scotland, which culminated in a Scottish Constitutional Convention. Backing away from such commitments would have alienated key elements of Labour's electoral support base.
- Second, having been in opposition since 1979 and lost repeated general elections, Labour was not confident before 1997 that it could form a government alone. Hence it entered discussions with the

Box 2.1   Key action on constitutional reform 1997–2010

Legislation	Non-legislative action
First term: 1997–2001	

Referendums (Scotland and Wales) Act 1997
Scotland Act 1998
Government of Wales Act 1998
European Communities Amendment Act 1998
Bank Of England Act 1998
Human Rights Act 1998
Northern Ireland Act 1998
Regional Development Agencies Act 1998
Greater London Authority Act 1998
Registration of Political Parties Act 1998
House of Lords Act 1999
Freedom of Information Act 2000
Local Government Act 2000
Political Parties, Elections and Referendums Act 2000

House of Commons Modernisation Committee 1997–2010
Independent Commission on the Voting System (Jenkins Commission) 1997–98
Royal Commission on the Reform of the House of Lords (Wakeham Commission) 1999–2000

Second term: 2001–5

Regional Assemblies (Preparations) Act 2003
Constitutional Reform Act 2005

Commission on the Powers and Electoral Arrangements of the National Assembly for Wales (Richard Commission) 2002–4

Third term: 2005–10

Government of Wales Act 2006
Parliamentary Standards Act 2009
Constitutional Renewal and Governance Act 2010

Commission on Scottish Devolution (Calman Commission) 2007–09
Select Committee on Reform of the House of Commons (Wright Committee) 2009

Liberal Democrats in order to prepare for a possible hung parliament and/or coalition government. Unlike Labour, the Liberal Democrats had always considered constitutional reform a high priority. The inter-party ('Cook–Maclennan') agreement resulting from these talks set out a series of proposals. Although Labour went on to win a large majority in 1997, and so in the end did not need the Liberal Democrats in order to govern, it had already made public commitments to many of the reforms.

- Third, Labour in opposition was determined to appear economically responsible, and made a public commitment to match Conservative spending plans for the first two years post-1997, which ruled out major budget increases. Other big reforms such as to public services or welfare benefits would be expensive, so could not be fully implemented straightaway. Constitutional reform, by contrast, both looked radical and required little public spending.

These three factors explain why Labour, despite its leader's ambivalence, ended up implementing wholesale constitutional reform particularly in its early years. However, this context also helps us to understand why, as discussed later, some reforms were perhaps implemented half-heartedly, and others not implemented at all.

Brown 2007–10: the frustrated radical

Fresh impetus might have been expected after Gordon Brown took over the premiership. While Blair did not give a single speech on constitutional reform when he was prime minister, Brown had written and spoken in favour of it over many years. During his leadership campaign he said that he aimed to 'build a shared national consensus for a programme of constitutional reform' and that 'one of my first acts as Prime Minister would be to restore power to Parliament in order to build the trust of the British people in our democracy'. Within a week of taking office he made a major parliamentary statement setting out his plans in this area.

Yet when he left office, almost three years later, Brown's constitutional legacy was very slight: well short of Blair's, and of his own earlier rhetoric. As shown in Box 2.1, the only significant legislative initiatives during his premiership were a bill on parliamentary standards (previously unplanned), and the Constitutional Renewal and Governance Bill. The second of these was limited in scope, and key elements were dropped when it ran out of parliamentary time before the 2010 general election.

Once again we are faced with a paradox: while Blair was ambivalent but implemented very significant reforms, Brown appeared passionate about the constitution but achieved little. Again, three principal factors can explain the mismatch between prime ministerial intent and action:

- First, Brown arrived in office after Blair had been there 10 years, by which time the most easily implementable major reforms had already occurred. It was no accident that the bits of 'unfinished business' still on the agenda – most obviously further Lords reform and change to the electoral system for the House of Commons – had not been implemented earlier. Tony Blair's scepticism about these issues was shared by many other within his party, and progress was therefore bound to be difficult. Brown then introduced further ideas – notably moving Britain to a written constitution – which were even more challenging and ambitious.
- Second, Prime Minister Brown became a victim of events. Within months of his taking office there was a global financial crisis, and all attention turned to stabilising the economy. As a former Chancellor Brown played a pivotal role, both in Britain and internationally, which distracted from less urgent elements of his domestic agenda. Then within the constitutional sphere he also had to manage a second crisis, caused by the revelations in the *Daily Telegraph* about abuses of MPs' expenses (as discussed in Chapter 4 in this volume). This resulted in the Parliamentary Standards Bill and creation of the Independent Parliamentary Standards Authority, which diverted both officials and ministers from other reforms.
- Third, however, Brown's own character was also to blame. As Prime Minister he demonstrated two key flaws: indecisiveness and an inability to delegate. His Constitutional Renewal and Governance Bill was endlessly delayed, initially being published in draft in March 2008, but then not in its final form until June 2009, and ultimately being held up by further dithering over whether to add new clauses on electoral reform. The bill was criticised by many as a damp squib, given Brown's rhetoric: it comprised mainly small tidying-up measures, such as allowing retirements from the House of Lords. Its passage was then mismanaged, due to constant meddling from Number 10, and some of these clauses had to be dropped.

With respect to both Blair and Brown we therefore see that prime ministers can be significantly driven by their inheritance and by events outside their control. Their abilities to shape matters according to their own policy preferences are more limited than we might assume. The constitutionally cautious Blair was constrained by previous commitments to carry out reform, while the reform-minded Brown was constrained in ways that prevented it. This holds important lessons for the 2010 coalition government, as discussed later in the chapter.

Critiques of the Labour legacy

Labour's constitutional reform has sparked a large literature, with many scholars and commentators analysing both the merits of the reform programme and its effects. Although some of this commentary has been broadly neutral, much has been highly critical. The strongest critics may be broadly characterised as falling into two camps: conservatives and radicals.

Though some conservative critics were also 'large c' Conservatives, many were not, including numerous sceptical Labour MPs. The starting point for these critics was an adherence to the basic contours of the 'old' constitution. This constitution centred on the 'Westminster model', based on parliamentary sovereignty, a two-party system and a strong centralised executive (Lijphart 1999). Academic examples include Philip Norton (2007) and Nevil Johnson (2004). In contrast the starting point for radical critics is largely the reverse: they believed that the old constitution was too centralised and in need of major changes, and their fundamental problem with Labour's programme was that it was too cautious. Scholars taking this view include Matthew Flinders (2005, 2009), David Judge (2006) and Patrick Dunleavy (2005, 2006). Many constitutional campaign groups also shared this position (e.g. Power Commission 2006). As with any classification system there are also some candidates who do not fit neatly either camp: Anthony King (2007) and Vernon Bogdanor (2009) share some analyses with conservative critics while also advocating radical positions. Andrew Gamble (2003b) takes a more neutral view.

Although the positions taken by conservative and radical critics differ, there are three broad criticisms made of Labour's reform programme, two of which are shared between them. The principal criticisms are that the reforms were:

- **Incoherent.** Both conservative and radical critics make this claim, arguing that the government carried out a large-scale programme of reform but rarely if ever articulated an overall vision of what it was seeking to achieve. Even generally sympathetic commentators suggested that the government did 'its utmost to avoid the impression that there [was] a coherent programme of reform or to claim credit for it' (Gamble 2003: 18). Instead the impression was of a series of piecemeal reforms driven by individual pragmatic concerns.

- **Ineffective.** This is principally an allegation made by radical critics, who claim that many of the reforms were half-hearted and did not go as far as they should have. For example, both devolution and the Human Rights Act were carefully designed to retain Westminster parliamentary sovereignty, rather than giving ultimate power away. The Freedom of Information Act did not go as far as its advocates had hoped and the promised 'stage two' of Lords reform never happened. Radical critics wanted to see a fundamental shift from the old centralised constitution towards a more pluralistic 'consensus' model of democracy (Lijphart 1999) where power was more widely shared. Instead, these critics suggest, power relations in the new constitution are relatively little changed.
- **Unstable.** Again this criticism is shared by both conservatives and radicals. Conservatives suggest that the old constitution is 'in danger of being unravelled' (Norton 2007: 273), and that 'the glue provided by the customary constitution binding people and institutions together has been seriously eroded' (Johnson 2004: 287). The result was the destruction of something simple and elegant with 'mess' (King 2007: 345). Radicals agree that Britain is now left with a sort of halfway house and that the desirable, and perhaps inevitable, outcome is to continue moving towards the more pluralistic constitution that they seek.

Most of this criticism relates to the rights and wrongs of moving from a centralised, majoritarian or 'power-hoarding' constitution to a pluralised, consensus or 'power-sharing' one. But, as Hazell (2008b) points out, there are other directions in which the constitution may move. He suggests that there are two perpendicular axes: concentration versus dispersal of power is one, while the other leads from a 'political' to a 'legal' constitution. Traditionally Britain had a political constitution, meaning issues were principally resolved by politicians, thanks to the sovereignty of parliament and the relatively simple structure of power. But more is now codified, and the arrival of new actors and institutions also makes legal interpretation and adjudication more important, giving judges a potentially greater role. This trend concerns some of those critics cited above, and also others, including legal scholars (e.g. Bellamy 2007, Tomkins 2002, Oliver 2009). The 'judicialisation' of the constitution may on the one hand help protect minority rights, but can also be seen as weakening democratic accountability, as it removes power from elected politicians, giving it to unelected actors instead.

A step-by-step assessment

Many critics weighed in relatively early in the reform process. Now that we have the benefit of greater hindsight, how well do their criticisms stand up to more considered scrutiny? The short sections below analyse the effectiveness of the key reforms in terms of the pluralisation of power, stability of reform, and, where relevant, contribution to judicialisation. The section ends with a general assessment, including of the overall coherence of the reforms.

Devolution

Devolution was one of the first and most important constitutional reforms enacted by Labour, resulting in a new parliament in Scotland, and elected Assemblies in Northern Ireland and Wales (all following referendums in 1997–8). The devolution 'settlement' has been subject to all three criticisms cited above. It certainly appears untidy, and therefore somewhat incoherent, and has also been criticised for not devolving enough power. Both problems may contribute, in turn, to instability.

The 'asymmetric' nature of the devolution settlement, with different powers devolved to Scotland, Wales and Northern Ireland, and no parallel arrangements for England, can be explained by pragmatic concerns at the outset. Scottish campaigners demanded a strong parliament, while attitudes in Wales were far more ambivalent and the referendum only narrowly passed. Meanwhile the Northern Irish arrangements were part of a delicate peace settlement across a sectarian divide. In more recent years there has been some minor convergence between the three devolved areas: the Richard Commission in Wales proposed that further powers should be devolved. Some were granted through the Government of Wales Act 2006, and the Assembly gained primary legislative powers following a second referendum in 2011. But devolution is always likely to be 'lopsided'.

In all three devolved areas the legislation formally protected traditional Westminster parliamentary sovereignty by retaining the UK parliament's ultimate right to legislate if it so wished. This has not led to Westminster interference in Scottish and Welsh affairs (though in Northern Ireland local problems resulted on several occasions in arrangements reverting back temporarily to 'direct rule'). But it fuelled some commentators' claims that devolution did not represent a meaningful dispersal of power. Johnson (2004: 305) concluded that '[n]one of the constitutional measures of recent years, including those providing for devolution, has done much to push responsibilities outwards and downwards'. This scepticism was further fuelled by the fact that Labour initially formed governments in both Scotland and Wales, as well as

London: resulting in limited policy divergence, and systems of intergovernmental relations that were largely informal. But this all changed following the devolved assembly elections in 2007, which resulted in a Scottish National Party (SNP) government in Scotland and a coalition in Wales including the Welsh nationalists Plaid Cymru. In 2010 partisan interests diverged further with the election of the Conservative–Liberal Democrat coalition at Westminster. Gradually, therefore, devolution has become far more meaningful in terms of creating distinct institutions representing the views of voters in Scotland and Wales. This potential was acknowledged by some radical critics, notably Flinders (2005, 2009) and Judge (2006), who considered devolution to be the most significant move that had occurred away from the old Westminster model.

As for instability, the initial 'settlement' has already been changed in Wales following the Richard Commission. In Scotland the 2009 Calman Commission report proposed greater fiscal autonomy for the parliament, and this is promised by the UK government. But changes so far have been largely consensual. In future intergovernmental relations between the three areas could become more strained, both as a result of conflicting partisan control and spending cuts at the UK level. Under the 2007 SNP minority government pressure for Scottish independence was contained, but the party gained a majority in 2011 so this is likely to change. Another significant territorial instability relates to England, as discussed in Chapter 7 in this volume.

Parliament

One of the most glaring failures by Labour to adhere to its constitutional promises was on parliamentary reform. The 1997 manifesto pledged that the House of Lords would be reformed in two stages: the first to remove the hereditary peers (who inherited their seats in the chamber and made up the majority of its members), the second to create a 'more democratic and representative' second chamber. The first stage was (more or less) implemented through the House of Lords Act 1999, which removed all but 92 hereditaries, and left a chamber made up largely of life peers. But the second stage was never reached, despite the establishment of a royal commission on the matter, and publication of various government White Papers, parliamentary committee reports, and proposals from outside bodies (most of which supported creating at least a partly elected second chamber). For many reformers the government's record on Lords reform was therefore a severe disappointment.

Instinctively it might be assumed that Lords reform made little difference, particularly in terms of constraining executive power. The chamber remained unelected and continued to suffer legitimacy problems in challenging the government and House of Commons. At the outset it was feared, particularly by conservative critics but also by some radicals, that 'first stage' Lords reform could actually weaken the chamber against a Labour government – since the departing hereditary peers were disproportionately Conservatives. Hence Flinders (2005), applying Lijphart's (1999) models of majoritarian and consensus democracy, concluded that bicameralism would constrain the executive less than before.

Yet in practice the reformed House of Lords presented a significantly greater challenge to government than its predecessor. Post-reform, government defeats in the chamber became more common, and the Lords was less prone to back down in confrontations than it had been previously (Russell 2010). The key reason for this perhaps surprising outcome was that the change in the Lords' party balance did not give Labour a majority. Unlike in the Commons, the Lords' membership was relatively proportional to vote shares, resulting in the Liberal Democrats and independents holding the balance of power. This created opportunities for new coalitions to form against Labour, putting the third party, in particular, in a strong position. At the same time, removing Conservative bias gave peers greater confidence to mount challenges against the government, enabling some of this potential to be realised. Hence the numerous ensuing government defeats, but just as importantly the government's greater responsiveness to Lords' demands in order to avoid defeats occurring (Russell 2010). Most authors (for example Bogdanor 2009, Cowley 2006, King 2007, Russell 2010) have therefore concluded that the second chamber actually strengthened under Labour, and Flinders (2009) later changed his view. Relations between the Commons and the Lords are a good example of how measuring the impact of constitutional change is difficult, and focusing on confrontation can be misleading.

Radical critics thus largely agree that 'stage one' Lords reform was a step in the right direction, albeit an inadequate one. The chamber may be more legitimate and powerful, but for them this has not gone far enough. The next step is thus for the second chamber to be elected. However it is precisely the fear of a much more legitimate and interventionist second chamber that split both main parties and prevented the second stage of reform during 1999–2010. Brown, unlike Blair, declared himself in favour of a largely or wholly elected second chamber and a White Paper was finally published to this effect in 2008. All three parties are now officially committed to this position, and the coalition published proposals in May 2011. The makeup of the Lords therefore appears unstable, but many obstacles to reform still remain (Russell 2009).

As well as the Lords, Commons reform was often on the agenda under Labour. In 1997 a new Modernisation Committee was established and proposed numerous procedural reforms. Some of these, such as 'programming' of legislation, and shorter parliamentary sitting hours, were seen by critics as simply having enhanced the 'efficiency' of parliament from the executive's point of view. But other reforms are seen as having enhanced the 'effectiveness' of the Commons in keeping the executive in check (Kelso 2007b). These include greater resources for select committees, the prime minister appearing regularly in front of the Liaison Committee of select committee chairs, and the establishment of public bill committees which hear outside evidence on government bills. It is common to hear both conservative and radical critics bemoaning the decline of parliament. But Flinders has concluded that '[o]verall, developments in Britain during 1997–2005 appeared to contradict the decline of Parliament thesis' (2006: 399).

This became even more true after 2005. In June 2009, in the wake of the MPs' expenses crisis, Gordon Brown established a new select committee (the 'Wright committee') on Commons reform. It proposed that in future both chairs and members of select committees would be elected, thus diminishing the influence of the whips, and that the Commons should be given greater control over its own agenda. These key recommendations were agreed shortly before parliament broke up for the 2010 election, and operate in the new parliament. Most agree that they will boost parliament's effectiveness, and indeed they may represent the most important package of Commons reforms since the departmental select committees were created in 1979. They were not government proposals, and were put through on a free vote, but ironically could prove to be the biggest constitutional legacy of the Brown era.

Electoral systems

Labour's reforms resulted in the widespread introduction of new electoral systems for the European elections, the devolved institutions, the Greater London Assembly and Scottish local government. Yet the biggest disappointment of all to radical critics was Labour's failure to introduce electoral reform for the House of Commons. This is the key to majoritarian politics at the UK level, from which many other consequences flow: most obviously the historical fact of two-party politics and single-party cabinets (Lijphart 1999), although both are now challenged by the Conservative/Liberal Democrat coalition. Labour's 1997 manifesto had promised a referendum on moving to proportional representation (PR), and the Independent ('Jenkins') Commission on the Voting System proposed an alternative system, but there was great resistance in Labour's own senior ranks to putting this to a referendum. The prospect of reform remained in the 2001 and 2005 manifestoes, albeit with the pledge watered down.

But no further action followed until Prime Minister Brown, in the dying days of his government, announced a determination to hold a referendum on the Alternative Vote (AV) system. This is a more genuinely 'majoritarian' system than traditional British 'first past the post', which is in fact a 'plurality' system (meaning that the candidate with the largest number of votes is elected locally even if they have not won a majority). AV instead uses preferential voting, and requires each MP elected to have support from at least 50 per cent of local voters. Had Brown proposed this when he took office in 2007 he might have been able to implement it. But his conversion came so late that it simply resulted in amendments to the Constitutional Reform and Governance Bill which helped it run out of time before parliament dissolved in 2010.

Given the absence of reform, questions of effectiveness do not apply, although there are concerns both about incoherence and about the instability of what resulted. In terms of coherence, the adherence to Westminster's plurality electoral system was out of step with reforms that Labour implemented elsewhere. Hence Labour appeared to support traditional majoritarianism at Westminster but a more pluralistic or consensual form of politics elsewhere. This could be seen as a further example of piecemeal – or indeed even positively confused – thinking. Judge (2006) used this to accuse Labour of having a 'blind spot' when it came to reform at Westminster, while Flinders (2009) described the result as 'bi-constitutionality', with two different and inconsistent logics employed at national and sub-national level. There were, however, pragmatic explanations. Labour supported non-plurality for the devolved institutions partly as a means of avoiding divisive or separatist politics, hoping to prevent (unsuccessfully, as it turned out) a majority SNP government in Scotland. The Scottish local government decision to adopt PR was forced by the Liberal Democrats as part of a coalition deal. Labour's leadership thus never really embraced this kind of pluralist politics from principle, although a minority strand in the party did.

Claims of instability in this sphere have been most clearly put by Dunleavy and appear to be borne out by the 2010 general election result. Dunleavy (2005) suggests that the use of PR outside Westminster changed party allegiances, voting behaviour and party systems. Now that voters everywhere in the UK can vote in at least one proportional election they are more likely to switch to third, fourth and minor parties, which puts the dominance of the top two parties in general elections under increasing strain. In 2010 the proportion of votes cast for Labour and Conservatives indeed reached an all time low of 65 per cent: compared to over 90 per cent for the two 'main' parties up to 1970, and around 75 per cent up to 2001. In these circumstances, Dunleavy claims, the first-past-the-post system becomes both normatively indefensible and also more likely to lead to chaotic and unexpected election results. In 2010 it delivered the first coalition government since the Second World War, which gave the Liberal Democrats a platform to press for electoral reform. Although this failed (as discussed below) it may in the long term prove impossible to maintain different logics of representation at national and devolved levels in a 'bi-constitutional' system.

The Human Rights Act and the judges

The passage of the Human Rights Act (HRA) 'brought home' the rights in the European Convention on Human Rights, making them justiciable in UK courts, rather than only through appeal to the European Court of Human Rights in Strasbourg. Again the government implemented this reform in a way that, at least formally, protected traditional parliamentary sovereignty. Unlike in many jurisdictions with rights protection, such as Germany or the US, judges were not given the power to annul Westminster legislation found to breach the HRA. Instead they could merely issue a 'declaration of incompatibility', which left parliament to decide whether to amend it accordingly. The new arrangements also required the government to certify whether new bills were compatible with the HRA before introducing them to parliament. A new parliamentary committee, the Joint Committee on Human Rights, was created to scrutinise all bills for compliance with the Act. But this committee was given an advisory function only and no veto power.

Radical critics could again argue that this reform did not go as far as it might have done. The government could still in principle ignore court rulings under the HRA and propose new legislation that breached it (though remaining in both cases ultimately answerable to the Strasbourg court). In other countries human rights are often protected by constitutional documents which have a higher status than ordinary law, significantly constraining executives. This makes the sanctions in Britain look rather 'soft'.

Opinion has been mixed on the effectiveness of the HRA. Vernon Bogdanor (2009: 53) has described it as the 'cornerstone of the new constitution'. But other critics have judged it 'futile' (Ewing and Tham 2008). Radical critics were very troubled by some aspects of Labour government policy on individual rights and freedoms, for example on anti-terrorist legislation and ID cards, which were introduced despite the Act.

Since its introduction the HRA and its effects have been the subject of study by many specialist scholars, both in Britain and overseas. But such assessments are very difficult. At the simplest level, data collected by Francesca Klug and Helen Wildbore at LSE showed that by May 2010 only 18 declarations of incompatibility had been agreed by the courts, and in almost all cases government had responded by asking parliament to bring legislation into line with the Act. It thus appears that the courts were being cautious, but that parliament was keen to comply. Notably there was just one occasion when government explicitly proposed legislation contradicting rights in the Act. Hence while the HRA may have served as a constraint, it was not an absolute one. But, as with Lords reform, specialists note that it is too simplistic to measure the effectiveness of such arrangements by seeking instances of conflict. In fact, the greater impact of rights provisions, especially under the kind of parliamentary model adopted in Britain, may come through 'anticipated reactions', whereby government chooses not to act in a way that breaches rights. There may also be cultural change, through encouraging greater 'dialogue' between government, parliament and the courts (Klug and Starmer 2005). The HRA itself, and the Joint Committee on Human Rights, may therefore have helped create a new 'culture of rights' or 'culture of compliance' with rights in Westminster and Whitehall (Nicol 2004).

In terms of limiting executive action it is thus very hard to measure the effectiveness of the HRA. But some of its other consequences are clearer. Most agree that it has brought the judges closer into policy-making. This judicial activism may increase further over time, thanks to the Supreme Court, which created a clearer separation between parliament, government and judiciary by taking the top judges out of the House of Lords. It is also clear that the human rights settlement is unstable, at least to some extent. The HRA has been controversial with right-wing newspapers such as the *Daily Mail*, which claim that it principally protects unpopular minorities such as immigrants and suspected terrorists. It has therefore not come to be widely loved by the British public. Consequently all three main political parties entered the 2010 election with a commitment to create a 'British Bill of Rights' which would add to or replace the HRA.

Transparency

A less discussed aspect of Labour's reforms is the move towards greater government transparency. The most obvious example is the introduction of the Freedom of Information Act. This placed new requirements on public authorities to make information available on request. Other measures included numerous new forms of regulation of the political process and creation of 'constitutional watchdog' bodies. For example party-funding regulation and creation of the Electoral Commission in 2000, creation of the House of Lords Appointments Commission that same year, and the Parliamentary Standards Act and establishment of the Independent Parliamentary Standards Authority during Brown's premiership.

The Freedom of Information Act was seen as disappointing by radical critics. This was in part a question of contrast: the government's initial White Paper *Your Right to Know*, published in 1997, would have created one of the most open regimes in the world. But the subsequent bill watered down these proposals, which some more conservative critics at the time believed went too far. David Judge (2006: 379) thus complains that the FoI regime included 'significant limitations on disclosure' and it is true that the Act stated 27 exemptions to the public's right to information. But in practice most of these exemptions are subject to a public interest test, which has been interpreted generously by the Information Commissioner, the watchdog who decides these matters. Thus, for example, despite the exemption on 'advice to ministers', much such information has been released. The government does retain a veto, and has twice vetoed publication of Cabinet papers against the Commissioner's advice. But such vetoes exist in other FoI jurisdictions such as Ireland and Australia, and their use in the UK has been limited in comparative terms.

Those who have monitored the impact of FoI conclude that this has been greater than many sceptics initially expected (Hazell *et al.* 2010). It has opened up government, at least to some extent, and may have caused 'anticipated reactions' in terms of better government behaviour. But what these arrangements plainly have not done is enhance public trust in the political system, as some hoped they would. The most high-profile consequence of FoI was the release of information on MPs' expenses, which led to many outraged newspaper headlines, ended numerous political careers, and ultimately resulted in a new expenses regime. Negative impacts on public trust have also followed from other transparency measures, including on political party funding and revelations of 'cash for peerages'.

The new transparency regime has thus been relatively effective in holding politicians to account, and also appears relatively stable. But perhaps its most notable effect is adding to the 'legalisation' or 'judicialisation' of the constitution, through the creation of new rules and watchdogs. As with the judges, these watchdogs remove discretion from elected politicians, handing it to bodies which are more 'independent' and 'expert', but which raise concerns about *democratic* accountability: leading some to express concern about 'the rise of the unelected' (Vibert 2007).

A surprisingly new constitution?

The accounts above indicate how assessing the impact of constitutional change is not straightforward. The full effects must be considered over a long period, while Labour's reforms still remain relatively new. Yet over longer periods there can be many confounding factors, such as parallel social, economic or political developments which make it hard to distinguish the specific contribution made by institutional change. In addition the impact of reform is often not direct or easily visible, but instead may primarily come through subtle changes in the behaviour and attitudes of political actors.

But, in sum, what can we conclude about the criticisms of conservative and radical critics? It appears that some of their criticisms have force, but the picture is complex and mixed. In places the complaints of the critics are mutually contradictory.

Ineffectiveness?

In terms of assessing effectiveness in pluralising power away from the famously centralised British executive, the most complete 'whole system' analysis is that of Flinders (2005, 2009). Flinders measures the reforms against Lijphart's (1999) models of majoritarian and consensus democracy, concluding that the only significant move from majoritarianism resulted from devolution. This shifted Britain away from Lijphart's 'unitary and centralised government' in the direction of 'federal and decentralised government'. Flinders also notes moderate change away from 'legislative supremacy', towards the judges having more power (as a result of the Human Rights Act and new Supreme Court). But in most respects he sees no change, and in some even a drift to greater majoritarianism. Hazell, however, judges the changes to be more important than that, suggesting that 'the UK executive is becoming significantly more constrained and the political system less majoritarian' (2008a: 286). This is not just thanks to devolution and the judges, but also changes in parliament and the growing power of 'non-majoritarian' constitutional watchdogs. Using his aforementioned axes, he suggests that the British constitution has become both more plural, and more legal.

As already indicated, final assessments are difficult, but on the basis of the evidence presented here there do appear to be weaknesses in Flinders' analysis. These largely originate from Lijphart himself. First there is a measurement problem, of a kind common in political science. Several of the reforms explicitly retained parliamentary sovereignty (and thus in practice UK executive discretion), rather than unconditionally giving power away. That is, they retained some of the traditions of the 'political' constitution. The likely response to this was greater dialogue, and behind-the-scenes changes to government behaviour and culture, rather than outright confrontation. Reforms initially received as disappointing may thus have constrained the executive in important hidden ways. Lijphart – and therefore Flinders – focus principally on the legal aspects of constitutional constraint, which risks overlooking political constraints that can be equally important. In short, if we use formal legal power – because it is more measurable – as a proxy for actual political power, we may misjudge the importance of reform.

The second difficulty is one of focus. As Flinders (2009) points out, Lijphart's analysis concentrates on the *national* level, taking no account of the political cultures and rules applying *sub-nationally*: and in a 'bi-constitutional' system this provides an incomplete picture. Lijphart's framework also overlooks reforms such as freedom of information, and important changes in parliament. It did not capture the more proportional makeup of the House of Lords, which introduced greater pluralism within Westminster itself post-1999 (nor indeed the potential weakening of the Lords since the 2010 election, due to the coalition holding more Lords seats than Labour). And the procedural changes within the House of Commons, which have further strengthened parliament against the executive, occurred at a level beneath Lijphart's radar.

All in all an assessment of the effectiveness of Labour's reforms is clearly difficult. But where things did change it was generally in a pluralising or 'power-sharing' direction. Had the Conservatives formed a single-party government after the 2010 election they would have found themselves significantly more constrained that their predecessors. In the 1980s Margaret Thatcher got the controversial 'Poll Tax' through the House of Lords, and trialled it initially in Scotland. Neither of these things would be possible now. Of course that scenario did not occur, but Prime Minister Cameron instead faces new and additional kinds of constraint thanks to being in a coalition government.

Incoherence?

What of the near-universal criticism of incoherence in Labour's constitutional reforms? The examples above demonstrated that there is some truth in this claim. The government never issued a White Paper or similar indicating what the overall constitutional reform programme was all about. Neither was this convincingly addressed in ministerial speeches. The reforms themselves appeared piecemeal. But there are at least partial defences to both of these points.

First, ministers may not have articulated the purpose of the programme, but it did have an underlying logic: to pluralise power. As the 18 years of Conservative rule post-1979 wore on, activists on the left became increasingly concerned about the extent of central executive power. This fed demands for devolution, human rights, freedom of information, parliamentary and electoral reform. These were articulated and driven in particular by the campaign group Charter 88 (Erdos 2009), and supported by the Liberal Democrats in the Cook–Maclennan talks. Even if the politicians implementing the reforms later were sometimes unclear of their purpose, therefore, their original proponents' aims were largely coherent.

Second, as we have seen, there were often pragmatic explanations for the piecemeal and sometimes apparently contradictory ways in which reform was implemented. Ironically, this resulted in part from seeking to reconcile the positions of radical and conservative critics at the time. Large-c Conservatives opposed most of the reforms, and were partly accommodated, as were small-c conservatives on Labour's own parliamentary benches. The outcome was a compromise which suited neither them, nor the radicals (including Liberal Democrats) who sought more far-reaching reform. It is hard for a constitution to look – or indeed be – elegant when this is the process through which it emerges. Wholesale constitutional reform in other states usually has followed war or revolution, and employed a distinct process to 'normal' politics. It of course also benefits from starting with a blank piece of paper. Perhaps it is unfair to expect constitution-making outside times of state crisis to be equally coherent.

Instability?

The third charge, that the new constitutional arrangements are unstable, finds support both above and in recent events. The coalition entered government in 2010 with significant plans for further reform. In some cases, such as devolution, these result from reform having developed a momentum of its own. Elsewhere the biggest pieces of unfinished business, both of which the coalition has sought to tackle, are electoral reform for the Commons and further House of Lords reform. Britain's period of constitutional reform is therefore clearly not over yet. But while the charge of instability may be correct, the extent to which this condition is new can be overstated. The British constitution has always been famously 'flexible' and responded to pressures over time. In the early twentieth century there was enormous instability in terms of both territorial politics and bicameralism, which resulted in pragmatic reforms that proved surprisingly durable. The Lords spent most of the twentieth century in a 'semi-reformed' state, while electoral reform also periodically reached the political agenda. A certain level of instability – and discontent with present arrangements – may therefore be considered the British norm (and to some extent exists in other countries as well). Though demands for reform in recent years do appear to have become more aggressive, this seems more related to changes in political style than to concrete evidence of growing public concern about constitutional matters.

A more legal constitution?

Finally, there is also clear evidence that the British constitution is moving from a 'political' to a more 'legal' model. This comes most notably through the Human Rights Act and Supreme Court, but also through the growth in constitutional 'watchdogs' and regulation, and the need to adjudicate between the greater number of actors in what has become a more complex political system. Nonetheless the constitution remains flexible because there is no formal legal entrenchment of any of its provisions: all only have the status of ordinary law. The only exception is where some degree of 'political entrenchment' exists: for example through the referendums in Scotland and Wales. The overall settlement thus falls far short of a typical written constitution – in the sense of a single, legally superior document – of the kind that Gordon Brown claimed to want. But the changes have nonetheless further enhanced the role of judges and other non-political actors in policy-making, which had already been increasing for some decades before (King 2007).

The constitution under Cameron and Clegg

The coalition government formed in 2010 thus inherited a set of constitutional arrangements that were more plural, and more legal, than those prior to 1997 and which also included elements of inherent instability. All three of these trends were reinforced by the arrival of the coalition. The inclusion of two parties in government itself adds to pluralism, in terms of distinct voices with influence in government. It consequently also leads to greater formalisation of arrangements, requiring inter-party agreements rather than depending on established relationships between party colleagues. Hence the publication of a new Cabinet Manual, setting out relationships and responsibilities, and the decline of the 'sofa government' style characteristic of Tony Blair. Finally, the coalition itself adds to constitutional instability, as both governing parties arrived with constitutional reform ideas of their own, strongly contrasting to what had gone before.

Constitutional and political reform issues were central to the coalition agreement that the two parties published in May 2010. This was largely due to the Liberal Democrats' historic commitments in this area: returning in part to policies that they had pressed pre-1997. But important aspects were also the legacy of Conservative manifesto policies. Liberal Democrat leader Nick Clegg, as Deputy Prime Minister, was given overall responsibility for political and constitutional reform. In an early speech he boldly promised a government 'unlike any other', which would 'transform [British] politics' in the 'biggest shakeup of [British] democracy since 1832'. As the experience of Gordon Brown shows, however, high rhetoric on constitutional reform does not necessarily translate into significant policy change, and some formidable obstacles exist to reform.

The Liberal Democrats' central constitutional demand in forming the coalition was electoral reform for the House of Commons. The party has long favoured proportional representation (ideally using the Single Transferable Vote system), while the Conservative manifesto stated the party's firm commitment to maintaining 'first past the post'. Ironically, the compromise that the two parties reached was the policy contained in Labour's manifesto: to hold a referendum on the (non-proportional) Alternative Vote system. This is a 'majoritarian' single-member constituency system, but by allowing voters to express preferences for their second, third and subsequent choice parties, could have resulted in the Liberal Democrats and (maybe minor parties) winning greater numbers of seats. The coalition agreement explicitly stated that while both parties would support a bill for a referendum, they would be free to campaign in the referendum on opposite sides. The referendum was held on 5 May 2011, and the proposal for the Alternative Vote was heavily defeated. This was the first UK-wide referendum since that held on membership of the European Community in 1975, but in a sense the question was fairly trivial. Voters were asked only whether they wished to rank candidates '1, 2, 3...' rather than place a single 'X' against one candidate. The campaign excited relatively little interest, in part because many campaigners and voters would have preferred a wider choice. But the Conservatives were against a referendum on moving to a proportional system. The defeat in the referendum was a major blow to Nick Clegg and his credibility within the government. The campaign also saw him pitted directly against David Cameron, which seemed to end their initially cosy relationship.

Another source of tension for the coalition is a key policy area where the Conservatives won concessions from the Liberal Democrats: that of Europe. Here many Conservatives are Eurosceptic, while most Liberal Democrats are the reverse. The coalition agreement included a commitment that referendums should be held before any future transfer of power to Brussels (this similarly could result in referendums on relatively trivial matters).

The Conservative manifesto had also sought to assert greater national sovereignty over human rights, with a commitment to replace the Human Rights Act with a British Bill of Rights. The Liberal Democrats also supported a new Bill, but for quite different reasons. Their instincts would be to expand the Human Rights Act, while many Conservatives would prefer to limit those rights. The coalition promised to refer this to a commission, which faces difficulty reconciling the two approaches.

Similarly, the coalition promised a commission on the 'West Lothian Question' (or 'English question') created by devolution, where the two parties have traditionally taken very different views. There was more agreement on immediate measures in Scotland and Wales, where the coalition proceeded with the referendum on devolving legislative power in Wales (held in March 2011), and introduced a Scotland Bill to implement the recommendations of the Calman Commission on Scottish funding. Relations between the governments in London and Edinburgh looked set to become more difficult following the election of a majority SNP administration in May 2011. The First Minister Alex Salmond will push for the Scotland Bill to go further, and plans a referendum on Scottish independence.

As with the British Bill of Rights, the two coalition partners ostensibly held similar views on Lords reform before the 2010 election: both favouring a largely or wholly elected second chamber. In May 2011 proposals were published for an 80 per cent elected second chamber, with 240 members elected by proportional representation, plus 60 appointed non party-political members and 12 Church of England bishops (down from the present 26). But Lords reform remains difficult (Russell 2009). Many Conservative MPs, and particularly peers, are strongly opposed to election, and many more oppose the use of proportional representation. There will also be arguments about the terms of office for elected members, electoral boundaries, the continued inclusion of bishops, and most importantly of all the powers of the second chamber (which the coalition proposes to leave unchanged, but which most expect an elected chamber would use far more assertively). As occurred under Labour, the coalition is therefore likely to find that the devil is in the detail, and that proclaiming support for reform is a great deal easier than actually making it happen. In fact, there were probably more MPs on the government benches under Labour who supported Lords reform than there are under the coalition. In addition, many Conservatives resented the idea that reform was being driven by Nick Clegg, whose popularity declined sharply during the first year of the coalition, and whose political capital – and therefore leverage powers – slumped further after the AV referendum defeat. In the meantime, the coalition government is in a stronger position with respect to the Lords than Labour because, with the Liberal Democrats in government, government peers significantly outnumber opposition (Labour) peers. While 1999 brought greater party pluralism to parliament through the Lords, we see that it is possible for pluralism in the Commons to neutralise it (at least to some extent) by reducing the creative tension between the chambers (Russell 2008). However some defeats continued to occur, due to greater activism by independent Crossbench peers.

Finally in terms of big reforms, the two coalition parties were united in their commitment to shrink the size of the House of Commons by reducing the number of MPs. This commitment in the coalition agreement therefore appeared more genuinely consensual. Nonetheless, it faced significant parliamentary resistance. Labour strongly opposed the bill to introduce this change, first because it saw it as 'gerrymandering' to favour the Conservatives, and second because the legislation was rushed and subject to little consultation. Concerns about undue haste and ill-thought-through proposals were also raised with respect to the coalition's plan to introduce fixed-term parliaments of five years. All of this caused the Constitution Committee in the House of Lords to launch an inquiry on the process of constitutional reform in the UK, as many believed that there should be greater constraints on government putting forward such large changes at short notice and with little public debate.

Is it possible to determine a clear direction in which the coalition government will take the British constitution in the years ahead? In part due to its composite nature, the answer appears to be no. The Liberal Democrats favour moving Britain further towards a plural, 'power-sharing' or 'consensus' democracy (which, perhaps not coincidentally, would see them more often having a share of power). However their early attempts faced major obstacles, not least because Conservatives remain largely committed to a more traditional British 'power-hoarding' constitution and the retention of, or return to, greater British sovereignty. For reasons outlined above, both visions are independently difficult to achieve, but risk being mutually contradictory when combined in a single 'partnership' government. In any case, as Labour demonstrated during 1997–2010, compromise certainly does not result in simple or elegant constitutional design. In practice reform proposals are always liable to be amended. They depend on circumstances as they develop and there are various directions in which they may be blown off course altogether. The likeliest direction of progress in this parliament is therefore more 'muddling through' with respect to constitutional reform. In short, the constitution will almost certainly continue to be decided by politics, rather than grand visions and plans. The impression one is perhaps left with is that this is simply the British way.

Chapter 3

Changing Patterns of Executive Governance

DAVID RICHARDS

The Westminster model, it is said, has long enabled Britain's governing party to form a strong, stable and authoritative government by virtue of its House of Commons majority and to govern, making full use of parliamentary sovereignty to enact its legislation, subject to it being held accountable by the electorate at a subsequent election. This model of executive power, the once dominant organising perspective of British politics, offered substantial authority to an incumbent government, a feature which neither Labour nor the Conservatives, when in office, had seen as being in their interests to abandon. So despite the radicalism of Thatcherism in pursuing economic and social reform, the Thatcher and Major governments of 1979–97 showed little reforming zeal when it came to constitutional issues or challenging the Westminster model. Similarly, the Blair and Brown governments of 1997–2010 regularly invoked the rhetoric of devolving power away from Whitehall, but, Scottish and Welsh devolution aside, were never willing properly to empower actors and organisation beyond the core of the central state. Between 1979–2010, then, the governing code of ministers and civil servants continued to draw from the Westminster model and displayed a degree of continuity in their respective patterns of executive government. It remains to be seen if the Conservative–Liberal Democrat coalition government which emerged in 2010 will mark a disjuncture from the past and deliver on its claims to have embraced a 'new politics' by offering a different type of executive government.

The core executive and the comfort blanket of the Westminster model

The longevity of the Westminster model can mainly be explained by the fact that the two dominant parties in British politics, Labour and Conservative, have been willing to subscribe to and sustain it. As Evans

(2003: 18) observes: 'the Westminster model forms the basis of the British Political Tradition and in the course of the nineteenth and twentieth centuries became the political orthodoxy of British government'. The model presents an image of parliament as sovereign, but in practice, the growth of the party system and bureaucracy over the last 150 years has led to executive or cabinet sovereignty.

Crucially, the key normative element of the model is that political power is located within the executive and inside the domain of Westminster and Whitehall. This is part of what is referred to as the British Political Tradition (see Birch 1964; Beer 1965; Greenleaf 1983a, 1983b, 1987). It is premised on:

- a limited, liberal notion of representative democracy, encapsulating the view that it is the government that governs in the interests of the nation and therefore power should rest with the government;
- a conservative notion of responsibility. A crucial element is the convention of ministerial responsibility which in practice leads to 'executive government' by placing responsibility for decision-making within the hands of ministers. However, this notion is also useful to legitimise elite rule because it justifies the concentration of power in central government generally and Whitehall departments particularly; and
- an emphasis on the need for responsible government which is willing and able to take strong, decisive, necessary action, even when opposed by a majority of the population.

In practice, the Westminster model presents a top-down view that 'government knows best', where governing is essentially a process of 'one-way traffic', from those governing (the government) to those being governed (society). Politics is seen as a zero-sum game with the prime minister dominating ministers, ministers dominating civil servants and central government (the core executive) dominating the wider policy arena. This reinforces the notion of Britain as a strong, unitary state in which the power vested in central government remains largely unfettered. While it is recognised that the Westminster model, as with all models, is only intended to represent an 'ideal type' and so oversimplifies the reality of how British politics operates, it nevertheless captures a number of essential characteristics of the British system of government.

In recent decades, various forces in politics have emerged that challenge the notion of power being hermetically sealed in Westminster. New patterns of governance have emerged that have affected the strategic capacity of the central, core executive (see Rhodes 1997; Marsh *et al.* 2001). Crucially, as we see below, the response of government to this dynamic has been to rhetorically defend the Westminster model, using it as a 'legitimising mythology' to defend its asymmetric position of power in the British system of government.

Challenges to the Westminster model in an era of governance

In the last 40 years, the state's capacity to control or direct policy and the extent to which the institutions of central government retain a monopoly on political power have become a keenly debated topic. Crucially, changing relationships between the state and society have brought into question whether Britain remains a strong unitary state (see Saward 1997; Holliday 2000; Marinetto 2003; Richards 2008) or has seen its powers increasingly eroded and fragmented (see Rhodes 1997; Pierre and Peters 2000; Jessop 2004; Bevir and Rhodes 2006). Central to this debate are a range of factors that have been identified as undermining the assumptions of the Westminster model:

- The unity of the state being compromised by growing regionalist feeling and the process of devolution in Scotland, Wales and Northern Ireland.
- Territorial integrity being eroded by the increasing Europeanisation and globalisation of a range of policies with power being seen to drain from Westminster and Whitehall.
- This has been compounded by the increasing fragmentation and segmentation of the state through such forces as agencification, privatisation and the pluralisation of public service delivery agents which collectively have been seen to undermine the capacity of the central state.
- Lines of accountability have become blurred by the fragmentation of the central state. For example, ministers have been accused of deflecting responsibility for policy failings onto chief executives of agencies, rather than being accountable themselves.
- Ministerial accountability rarely seems to work in the way that it should. In the last 40 years, few ministers have resigned for reasons of accountability and the notion of collective cabinet and individual ministerial responsibility is little more than a myth.
- Whitehall's public service ethos has been challenged by managerial reforms which presume officials could be conditioned by market criteria. Ministers and officials often act in secret to protect their own interests rather than the public good.

These factors have led some to suggest that the Westminster model no longer reflects the realities of the British political system (see Rhodes

1997; Marsh *et al.* 2001). New narratives on the nature of the British state have emerged under the umbrella term of 'governance', understood as an approach identifying the changing nature of the policy process in recent decades. It highlights the increasing variety of terrains and actors involved in the making of public policy. Governance demands that we consider all the actors and locations involved in the policy-making process and suggests central government has become only one among many actors involved. In so doing, it suggests that in recent decades, the mode of governing has shifted from one of hierarchy and command by central government to a more pluralistic mix of hierarchies, networks and markets (see Bevir and Rhodes 2003). The governance narrative then, clearly offers a direct challenge to the view of power presented by the Westminster model. It is of course important to recognise that the views presented within the governance literature concerning state transformation and the perceived emasculation of the strategic capacity of central government are contested (see Richards 2008). But crucially, key characteristics associated with governance, that of fragmentation, segmentation, the pluralisation of the policy-making arena and with it, to coin a key phrase, the 'hollowing-out' of central government, became crucial elements contributing to Labour's interpretation of the state it inherited in 1997. In opposition, key figures at the heart of the New Labour project argued that the pathology of governance had compromised the government's ability to operate in a unified and coordinated manner (see Blair 1996; Mandelson and Liddle 1996; Gould 1998). This conclusion subsequently shaped the path the Labour government, first under Tony Blair and then Gordon Brown, chose to pursue when establishing its own pattern of executive government.

New Labour's pattern of executive government: from Blair to Brown

When in government, one of the key hallmarks of both the Blair and Brown era was the need to strengthen ministerial power, particularly at 'the centre' of British government to respond to the pathology of governance and in so doing reassert control over what was perceived as an increasingly fragmented polity. Throughout Labour's 13 years of governing, ministers constantly spoke of their frustration when the policy ambitions they were pursuing in Whitehall were not being implemented in the way they expected. Drawing from the governance narrative, Labour's analysis of the changing nature of the policy arena was that central government's authority, autonomy and power had been eroded. Under Blair, the diagnosis to this issue was to argue for the need to try to 'wire the system back up', by pursuing a strategy of 'joined-up government', contingent on bolstering the coordinating units right at the centre of the British political system – most notably Number 10, the Cabinet Office and the Treasury. The claim here was this would allow for the reassertion of central control over an increasingly fragmented system. Later, the hallmark of the Brown approach, which as we see below had been honed when he was Blair's chancellor of the exchequer, was a fixation with control, rather than a willingness to delegate or trust other actors. This culminated in an increasing emphasis on micro-policy management by Number 10 that contributed to the undermining of Brown's power base in government.

The Blair approach

Tony Blair's model of leadership was revealed at the outset of his premiership in a speech to the Newspaper Society in March 1997, where he declared that everyone should be aware: 'that we will run from the centre and govern from the centre' (see Richards 2008: 105). 'Control-freakery' and 'presidentialism' became some of the familiar tags to be associated with his style of executive government. The popular perception of the Blair style of government was one based on strong central control, the engine room of which was the Blair inner circle – a coterie of trusted ministers and advisers – who undertook key government decisions, in private, with limited, if any, broader consultation. Such an approach was regarded by some, including figures in Blair's own Cabinet as being unhealthy, undemocratic and leading to poor policy (Mowlam 2002; Cook 2003; Short 2004). Similar sentiments were made by Richard Wilson (2002), Robin Butler (2004) and Michael Quinlan (2004), all former senior civil servants, who regarded Blair's informal style of working which ignored traditional Whitehall practices, as eroding the principles of Cabinet government and undermining effective decision-making. Lord Butler in particular, following his inquiry into the intelligence surrounding the decision to go to war in Iraq, was surprisingly forthright in his criticism of Blair's 'sofa style of government' (2004).

Despite the compelling image associated with the Blair years, that all government business was simply emanating from Number 10 and dispensed to departments to act on, the reality of how government actually works, as Blair discovered, was markedly different. Blair recognised that the nature of the British political system ensures that it is Whitehall departments, not the centre, that are institutionally strong. The response was a process of central capacity enhancement, based on a programme of institution-building to augment the existing coordinating and controlling powers located at the centre. Crucially, such an approach was working with, not against the grain of both the Westminster model and the British Political Tradition. Key innovations included:

- the enhanced role of the Policy Unit (later know as the Policy Directorate), a policy think-tank unit in Number 10, which almost doubled in size. It operated in a style that aimed to ensure that departments were aware of the Blair agenda and deliver policy in line with Number 10's wishes;
- the Performance and Innovation Unit, later known as the Strategy Unit, was formed to improve the centre's capacity to address strategic, cross-cutting issues (such as social exclusion, teenage pregnancies and homelessness) and promote innovation;
- the Prime Minister's Delivery Unit (PMDU) was created to: 'ensure the delivery of the Prime Minister's top public service priority outcomes' (Barber 2005). The Unit reported directly to Blair over the core policy priorities of health, education, crime and transport;
- challenging Whitehall's traditional monopoly on policy advice to ministers. Here, three institutional changes, mainly driven by Number 10, led to a pluralisation in policy advice: first, the creation of an array of ad hoc bodies, labelled 'task forces', with the aim of crossing departmental boundaries and providing a range of sources of advice. Their numbers grew to over 200 drawing on individuals from the private, public and voluntary sector; second, the introduction of 'Tsars', an eclectic mix of outside appointments, who reported to the prime minister to address specific issues of concern; third, an increased role for special advisers (SpAds) party political appointments to Whitehall departments who offered ministerial advice and promoted the work of government. Their numbers more than doubled during the Labour years.

A key executive problem to emerge during the Blair years and which persisted under Brown concerned effective policy delivery. Under both prime ministers there was a tendency to impose targets in a top-down, hierarchical manner. Frameworks of national standards had been established across different public services, but even clearly defined standards imposed from the centre did not necessarily translate further down the policy chain. This issue was compounded by the extent to which departments continued to challenge the wishes of the centre. Throughout the Labour years, the age-old problem of 'departmentalism' prevailed, with departments continuing to follow their own interests and agendas. Cumulatively, the reforms pursued under Blair at Number 10 saw a substantial increase in the institutional capacity of the Prime Minister's

Office. But, these changes tell only half a story. As important was the pattern of executive governance based on control and secrecy, established in the Treasury under Gordon Brown, elements of which re-emerged during his time at Number 10.

Gordon Brown: from chancellor to prime minister

Brown's approach to governing when in Number 10 bore familiar trademarks to his time in the Treasury. Command and control, particularly over the ambitions of Whitehall departments, had been central to Brown's strategy as chancellor of the exchequer. This approach was underpinned by the increasing use of targets and audit mechanisms to impose a form of Treasury control not just over Whitehall, but also the extended state of multiple agencies involved in delivering public services. This institutional mechanism pre-dated Brown's arrival at the Treasury, but its rationale was to shift power away from service providers to consumers. Under Brown, it became the dominant Treasury tool, an explicit process of auditing the public sector through the publishing of performance lists for public services such as schools, hospitals, and universities.

The other discernible element to emerge during Brown's time as chancellor was the increasing policy activism of the Treasury. This was a facet which Brown also took with him to Number 10. It partly reflects the dynamics between Blair and Brown and a *de facto* agreement that the latter would be given the autonomy to determinate key spheres of government economic, industrial and social policy. Contingency, of course, is important. As Blair's government tried to grapple with the various ramifications stemming from the decision to invade Iraq, Brown increasingly dominated large swathes of domestic policy. This led one observer to conclude that by the end, Blair and Brown's:

> oscillating relationship is a fine example of the politics of political space. Brown commanded much domestic political space forcing Blair almost by default into overseas adventures...Recognition of Brown's authority requires us to shift from tales of a Blair presidency to stories of at least a dual monarchy. (Rhodes 2006: 677)

The barely concealed divisions between these two principal actors had a fundamental impact on the pattern of governance to emerge between 1997–2007. In Whitehall circles, outbreaks in the dysfunctional relationship between Number 10 and the Treasury were euphemistically referred to as 'the TBGBies' (Seldon 2008; Rawnsley 2010; Mandelson 2010). But this dysfunctionality, predominantly based on distrust, meant each actor set about enhancing his own fiefdom, creating a ratchet-like effect in their grab for power. The legacy of this dualism conditioned Labour's programme of public service reform. New Labour's 'Third Way' rhetoric spoke of the need to abandon the Westminster model's characteristics of statist, top-down government and a one-size-fits-all approach to public services and instead pursue a path of devolution, pluralisation, delegation and greater autonomy for the multiple actors beyond Whitehall. But retrospectively the baronial-like battle that unfolded between the Treasury and Number 10 meant that such devolutionary instincts were overshadowed by the ensuing power struggle. The outcome of course was the reversion to a well-established, though rarely harmonious, pattern of state-centric control employed by the centre's duumvirate that fits within the contours of the British Political Tradition.

The Brown administration and executive government

Brown's long wait to become prime minister led to a resolve to be seen to offer a distinct break from the governing patterns established by his predecessor. But his experience in the Treasury, his tendency to operate in a controlling and secretive manner, bouncing departments with directives rather than engaging in dialogue and consultation, coupled to the informal, socialising effect of the Westminster model on how politics is conducted, from the outset raised questions over whether meaningful reform was likely to follow. Luck also was not on Brown's side. For much of his time as prime minister, a brief honeymoon period aside, 'crises' of various kinds loomed large. Both the economic crisis that unfurled from autumn 2008, combined 12 months later with the parliamentary scandal surrounding the misuse of MPs' expenses, for which Labour as the incumbent government bore a sizeable chunk of the public opprobrium, dominated the agenda. Governments overwhelmed by crisis management often turn in on themselves as the defensive mechanism of choice. This was certainly the case for the period 2007–10. Rather than challenging the Westminster model, Brown and his government increasingly embraced it, as they attempted to retain their position of governing authority.

It is ironic then, that Brown had initially used the rhetoric of reform and called for a 'new constitutional settlement' based on the devolution of power away from the centre. As Blick and Jones (2010: 11) observe, Brown made a number of announcements each of which had the potential to render a 'decentralising effect'. They included:

• More frequent and longer Cabinet meetings, to allow for the reassertion of the principle of collective Cabinet government.

- The reduction in the size of Number 10, particularly in terms of the number of special advisers alongside, the removal of managerial powers over permanent Whitehall staff given to certain special advisers through a 1997 Order in Council.
- The relocation of the PMDU from Number 10 to the Treasury.
- Bolstering the Ministerial Code and in so doing, curtailing some of the extensive powers enjoyed by the executive.
- Introducing a constitutional reform package, in the guise of the Green Paper *The Governance of Britain* (2007), increasing the powers of parliament over the executive and also relinquishing some of the executive powers available to the prime minister, notably in relation to public appointments, management over the civil service and the right to dissolve and recall parliament.

Of course, it should be pointed out that none of these reforms were about challenging or offering a distinct break from the Westminster model. Instead, they were an attempt by Brown to be seen to be operating differently to Blair. In practice, Brown's strategy appeared to be a reversion to a more 'traditional', rather than 'new' style of governing, so demonstrating that the much criticised 'sofa-style' associated with his predecessor had gone. For example, the desire to be seen to abandon the use of an inner coterie of unelected advisers determining government policy was heralded by the appointment of a new post of permanent secretary to Number 10, filled by a Whitehall 'lifer' Jeremy Heywood. The Heywood appointment should be understood as a broader response by the new Brown administration to address what it accepted had in the past been at times an antagonistic relationship between the three coordinating bodies at the centre of British government – Number 10, the Cabinet Office and the Treasury. But evidence from elsewhere contests the view that it marked a reversion to a more traditional model of government. Brown's Number 10 was seen as particularly dysfunctional and ineffective, something Brown himself recognised as he sought, unsuccessfully, to rectify the problem with several changes in key personnel. Brown's Treasury model of working did not translate to being prime minister (Mandelson 2010). Former trusted, key staffers such as the Eds Balls and Miliband struck out on their own as ministers, others, such as Spencer Livermore and Douglas Alexander, fell out with Brown following political disagreements, while the public support Brown received from some of his most senior Cabinet members, notably Alistair Darling and David Miliband, was at times little more than lukewarm (Rawnsley 2010; Seldon 2010). Attempts by No.10 to sustain the notion of a cordial team still operating together during the latter stages became increasingly less persuasive, as ministers' own personal, political ambitions and the sectional interests of departments no longer remained hidden. Brown's reputation as a strong and dominant chancellor was not repeated during his time at No.10. Nor was his aim of leading a government from the centre that operated in a unified and coordinated manner ever properly realised.

Weaknesses at the centre and the less than harmonious Cabinet relations under Brown led him, like Blair before, to rely on almost double the number of SpAds than previous governments. Indeed, the longer Brown remained in Number 10, the more reliant he became on these actors. The issue of SpAds was one that rumbled on throughout the Blair and Brown governments. It had spawned a shrill, but in many ways misplaced debate on their role within the Westminster system of government. Accusations of creeping politicisation, of Labour pursuing a US 'spoils' system or a French *cabinet* system based on the systematic appointment of large numbers of party political appointees were misplaced. As the former Head of the Civil Service, Richard Wilson, rightly suggested, it is hard to believe that 70 or 80 special advisers are likely to 'swamp' the 3,000 or so senior career civil servants responsible for advising ministers (2002: 10). Put another way, even with the doubling in SpAd numbers since 1997, proportionately their numbers remained small compared to the overall size of Whitehall.

Elsewhere, other changes introduced by Brown to improve coordination in British government focused on institutional modifications to enhance the process of policy-making and the security/intelligence function. For example, advisers to the prime minister on 'European and Global Issues', 'Foreign and Defence Policy' and 'Domestic Policy' were all moved from Number 10 to the Cabinet Office to improve relations at the centre. Another key innovation aimed at bolstering coordination and stemming from the economic crisis was the creation of a new Cabinet Committee, the National Economic Council, in October 2008. Its remit was to 'frame and coordinate the appropriate departmental and cross-Governmental policy responses'. Crucially, none of these changes were concerned with devolving power away from the centre.

Retrospectively, the Brown government's legacy bore no discernible testament to resolving the 'coordination issue' or rendering a significant shift in the decentralisation of power in British government. Why? What cannot be overlooked is the degree to which these rhetorical aspirations were hampered both by events and the response by Brown, manifested in both his public and private style of leadership. The net effect was to see him trying, often failing, to operate in similar style as prime minister to that of his time in the Treasury; embedding himself in Number 10, surrounded by confidants and failing to nurture key networks of support, particularly within the Cabinet and more broadly the Party that all prime ministers crucially depend on to sustain them in office.

After 2008 Brown's style of executive governance was influenced by two key environmental factors. First, the emasculating effect of the economic crisis that became the dominant issue throughout. Ironically, Brown, particularly on the international stage, won plaudits for both his and his government's swift handling of the crisis, but the cumulative and residual effect of the economic downturn was to undermine Labour's and in particular Gordon's Brown's much vaunted claims as the established party of both prudence and economic competence. There was no coincidence in the correlation between the ongoing economic crisis and the subsequent and sustained downturn in Labour's opinion poll ratings. Second, the MPs' expenses scandal that emerged in the summer of 2009 which was to have a devastatingly caustic effect on the whole parliamentary class, but in particular, the incumbent government and its claims of legitimacy to govern. The scandal was not of Brown's making, but part of a broader, firmly embedded culture in Westminster borne out of the politically explosive debate over how much MPs should be paid. Nevertheless, it had a debilitating effect on him, both in terms of the time it consumed, but more importantly, in eroding a sense of trust that all prime ministers rely on to present themselves as statesmen and leaders. These political problems were made worse by Brown's own inability to comfortably settle into a job he had for so long coveted. Much is made of the qualities required to be a successful prime minister. Two of his recent predecessors, Margaret Thatcher and Tony Blair, while both experiencing fluctuations in their authority and standing, were nevertheless portrayed as dominant leaders. Similar sentiments were rarely directed at Brown. Disgruntlement within the parliamentary Labour party over his lack of leadership qualities first publicly emerged following the perceived vacillation over calling an early election in the autumn of 2007. The subsequent stream of media stories discussing Brown's 'psychological flaws', his indecisiveness, temper tantrums, policy wavering and at times paranoia became increasingly hard to dismiss as just the usual Westminster tittle-tattle.

Crucially though, it was the perceived lack of a sense of policy renewal under Brown which most disappointed his own members. After ten years of government and with a change in prime minster, the Party's heightened expectations of political rejuvenation were not met, as the Brown government dealt both with the faltering economy and the political fall-out from the expenses scandal. To compound matters, the government was placed on the back foot over a number of avoidable, micro-policy issues, notably the abolition of the 10 pence income tax band, opposing the right to settlement in the UK for Ghurkha soldiers and resisting a hike in the level inheritance tax (and subsequent accusations by the opposition of a Labour Death Tax of 10 percent to fund a National Care Service for the elderly) that did little to enhance its declining popularity in the polls. Collectively, these events eclipsed the much vaunted 'progressive agenda' that Brownites in the Party had claimed would become the bedrock of their leader's term in office and secure a fourth, historic electoral victory.

In the light of these episodes, it is unsurprising that during the course of Brown's brief incumbency there occurred some very public, but unsuccessful attempts to depose him. What was particularly humiliating for the prime minister was that public challenges to his leadership were not from stalking-horse on the margins of the Party, but key new Labour actors. Some were unsurprising, with former ministers like Charles Clarke and Frank Field snipping at the prime minister from the backbenchers, but much more damaging was James Purnell's high-profile resignation in June 2009 as Work and Pension Secretary following Brown's refusal to publicly address the need for cuts in welfare spending. In January 2010 a final attempt to unseat Brown by two more former Blairite ministers, Patricia Hewitt and Geoff Hoon, who called for a secret ballot of MPs on the Labour leadership, fizzled out when others in the Party quickly (many reluctantly) distanced themselves from what was retrospectively a bodged coup attempt.

Brown held onto office because publicly at least, he retained the backing, if in a rather lukewarm fashion, of the majority of his Cabinet colleagues. Their caution over change was driven first by a desire not to be portrayed as being disloyal to the Party, but also because of the close proximity of the general election. A change of leader at such a late stage in the electoral cycle was unpalatable. Nevertheless, the net effect was to further erode Brown's credibility as a leader and feed his own insecurities. The need to turn inwards and seek the support from his closest confidants was understandable, but these were not the actions of a strong or dominant prime minister. The increasing media portrayal was that of a bunker-mentality, with Brown hunkered down within the confines of Number 10 still trying to pull the levers of government. Talk of collegiality, a government of all the talents and an outward-looking and pluralistic style of governance faded. Instead, the comfort blanket of security presented by the Westminster model and, in theory at least, the extended power it offered to actors at the centre of British government was one that Brown enveloped himself in to shore up his own authority.

New Labour's governance legacy

If, then, the Brown style of governing could be located within a traditional approach that offered little evidence of a departure from the

Westminster model, was there any evidence of the emergence of a new governing settlement after 2007? One means of addressing this question resides in the passage of *The Governance of Britain* (2007) onto the statue books in March 2010. *The Constitutional Reform and Governance Act* (2010) exposed a gap between the rhetoric of reform and the politics of contingency and compromise. The Act was effectively a reworking of the Westminster model, containing scant evidence of any new, more participatory or delegative forms of politics that would signal a break from the existing elitist, representative model of government. Instead, there were a number of cursory attempts to improve parliament's ability to hold the executive to account, a minor liberalisation in the culture of secrecy protecting the executive with the shift from a 30- to a 20-year rule concerning the publication of key government documents, the placing of the civil service onto a statutory footing and legislative change to the powers and functions of the Independent Parliamentary Standards Authority to assist it in implementing the report by the Committee on Standards in Public Life on MPs' expenses. Cumulatively, these reforms did little to challenge either the increasing asymmetry of centralised power that the core executive commanded or, concomitantly, suggest a repudiation of the British Political Tradition (Political Studies Association 2007; Richards *et al.* 2008).

During the final year of the Brown administration, four separate reports from various, contrasting bodies each delivered their verdict on both the Brown and more broadly the Labour administration's approach to executive government. A commonality of themes emerged from their conclusions organised round a set of concerns over:

- a growing democratic deficit between the government and its subjects; the lost of trust in the political elite;
- the continued accruing of power at the centre of British government;
- and a lack of effective checks and accountability mechanisms within the existing system (see Regulatory Policy Institute 2009; Institute for Government 2010; Better Government Institute 2010; House of Lords Select Committee on the Constitution 2010).

Each of these reports commanded attention, as they drew heavily on evidence given by both 'insiders' and 'outside experts' who had closely tracked the New Labour administration. What becomes apparent is that the institutional and organisational reforms it introduced to address the various pathologies associated with the turn to governance had themselves led to a series of often unforeseen and unintended consequences. The key trends identified can be summarised as:

- An asymmetric shift in resources within and beyond the core executive. The reforms between 1997–2010, particularly at the heart of Whitehall, most notably in Number 10 and the Treasury led to a shift in resources from departments to the centre and changed the focus of the civil service and the multiple public service delivery agents from process to outcomes.
- The greater involvement by the centre in detailed policy-making and its impact on the relationship with departments. Capacity-building at the centre, in particular the PMDU, altered the relationship between Number 10, the Cabinet Office and the Treasury, but more particularly led to policy being driven much more from the centre.
- The impact of the change in the balance of resources between the centre and departments and the centre and locality. The centre had for the first time direct contact with street-level bureaucrats but perhaps more importantly it developed alternative information resources which give it leverage over departments. In the past, the Cabinet Office and Number 10 were largely dependent on departments for information. Reforms and capacity-building at the centre changed the nature of this relationship.
- Increased complexity at the centre. The marked increase in central capacity based on a programme of creating more units at the centre exacerbated the complexity at the heart of the core executive. This process originated during the Blair era, but continued during the Brown years. Its impact was to leave those in the traditional government departments unsure over which power centre to engage with to secure their own departmental goals.
- The changing nature of power and accountability. In any liberal democratic system, but particularly an elitist-style one associated with the UK's representative model of government, the effectiveness of its accountability mechanisms are crucial. Structures of accountability should mirror structures of power. The asymmetric change in the pattern of executive governance within the core executive under New Labour was not accompanied by an adequate enhancement in either transparency or accountability mechanisms.

Despite appealing to the rhetoric of reform, the *modus operandi* of both the Blair and Brown years reflected an ongoing commitment to the Westminster model. In confronting the various issues associated with the governance era, Labour regarded such problems as localised, not systemic. There was a belief that solutions could be found from within, not beyond the existing Westminster model of government. Labour's approach of state-centric control through the use of targets, regulation and other similar management tools demonstrated an ambition to pursue a mode of governing concerned with top-down command and control. It is an approach that sits comfortably within the British Political Tradition, rather than embracing alternatives predicated on, for example participatory, pluralistic, devolved or delegative models of power and democracy. As a former senior Cabinet minister mused, Labour's governance reforms:

> continues a long tradition of the political class – both ministers and civil servants – operating as staunch defenders of the key principles of the Westminster model and protecting their asymmetric position of power...The government appears to have learnt little about the critical nature of reform...Does sustaining the Westminster model of government – a model forged in a bygone era – remain the only option? (Richards *et al.* 2008: 497)

How, then, does Brown's style of executive governance compare with that of his Labour predecessor? While, for most of the Blair era, labels such as 'control-freakery' could be brushed aside and neatly presented as a virtue under the heading of 'strong leadership', for Brown they were popularly portrayed as a vice, bordering on obsession. Here context is crucial. As has been argued above, the three years of his premiership for the most part were conditioned by various forms of crisis management notably on the economic, parliamentary and leadership fronts. Brown's response was to become increasingly insular and inward looking. But like his predecessor, his default setting was shaped by the contours of the British Political Tradition and its top-down code of governing based on control. So, while throughout his time in office, Brown retained a desire to be seen to be in command, presenting an image of strong leadership, the combination of the crises faced during his incumbency and his own personality, in practice materialised as indecisiveness, borne of an obsession to detail, leading to policy oscillation and micro-management. As one informed commentator suggested, Brown: 'remained pathologically determined to run every bit of Government himself' (Rawnsley 2010: 545), while a very close political adviser concluded:

> The preparation that went into his leadership positioning [of the Party] should have equipped him well when he at last succeeded Tony Blair, and in his first few months he exceeded expectations. But all too quickly he stopped listening...He retreated into his No. 10 bunker – the dream home had become a prison. Turning to a succession of flavour-of–the-month advisers, chopping and changing as he went, he gave the impression of drift and lack of direction. (Mattinson 2010: 79)

The coalition government: establishing new patterns of governance?

In itself, the formation of a Conservative–Liberal Democrat coalition government, the first time Britain has not been governed by a single-party government in peacetime since the 1930s, threatens to rework – in some way – the Westminster and Whitehall rulebook. As a coalition, the new government is likely, by definition, to be less strong and stable than a single-party government. Should, however, the governing partnership of the Conservatives and the Liberal Democrats hold together, then, by virtue of its House of Commons majority, it will, by intra-party agreement, be able to enact its legislation and govern, subject, as ever, to its being held accountable by the electorate at a subsequent election.

To understand the potential emergence of new patterns of governance in the aftermath of the May 2010 election and with it the establishment of a Conservative–Liberal coalition government, this section considers two broad areas – the state and the parliamentary system. The potential for a real and sustained shift in the way British government operates needs to be located within a debate over the extent to which reform challenges both the British Political Tradition and in so doing offers a distinct break from the Westminster model. It is this latter question that the conclusion to this chapter then considers.

Reforming the state

Even prior to the 2010 election, the Conservative party and the Liberal Democrats had declared themselves committed to devolving power away from the centre of government. In opposition, each had offered a critique of Labour's years in government, claiming that the strategy pursued during the Blair–Brown era was predicated on an excessive accumulation of power at the heart of Whitehall. Their sharpest barbs of criticism centred on the 'unit building' that went on in and around Number 10 and more broadly Labour's excessive use of centrally imposed targets and auditing across the public services. When in opposition, both parties had regularly attacked Labour's statist approach collectively arguing that 'the old top-down, big-government approach has failed' (Cameron 2010a). Their criticisms, drawing from different, but not mutually exclusive, ideological strands of liberalism were that such an approach had stifled the capacity of actors beyond the central state effectively to shape and deliver services for the public good. Following the 2010 election, the coalition government was quick to claim it was in the business of offering a new state settlement predicated on the notion of promoting a: 'radical devolution of power and greater financial autonomy to local government and community groups' (Conservative–Liberal Democrat Coalition, 2010: 4). The Deputy Prime Minister, Nick Clegg, whose ministerial responsibilities included leading the government's programme of constitutional and political reform, argued that:

> This government is going to break up concentrations of power and hand power back to people. I'm not talking about a few new rules for MPs; not the odd gesture or gimmick to make you feel a bit more involved. I'm talking about the most significant programme of empowerment by a British government since the great enfranchisement of the 19th Century. The biggest shake up of our democracy since 1832. (2010)

In addition, the notion of the 'Big Society' developed by the Conservative party in opposition, but which the coalition government subsequently presented as a key narrative round which to organise the legislative programme for its term in office, presented a challenge to the well-worn aphorism that 'the man [sic] in Whitehall knows best'. The themes associated with the Big Society could be seen as a critique of the previous Labour government's failure to deliver on its rhetorical commitments to devolve power away from the centre. It argued that the ideas associated with 'stakeholding' and 'communitarianism' that the Labour party flirted with in opposition during the mid-1990s, were not properly pursued when in government (see Blond 2010; Conservative Party 2010). Labour's crucial failing was portrayed as its inability to build partnerships of trust with appropriate actors drawn from civil society and so devolve power beyond the central state, instead resorting to an executive pattern of 'big government' via state expansion and top-down control. Crucially, then, the claim of the Big Society is an:

> alternative to big government...a society with much higher levels of personal, professional, civic and corporate responsibility; a society where people come together to solve problems and improve life for themselves and their communities; a society where the leading force for progress is social responsibility, not state control. (Conservative Party 2010: 37)

The practical manifestation of the Big Society narrative by the coalition can be identified in its moves to alter the relationship between the central sate, non-state actors and front-line service deliverers. This includes changes to the role of:

- The civil service – the introduction of new departmental boards across Whitehall involving non-executive board members drawn from outside of the civil service with experience of running large companies. Accompanied by a shift from what the government refers to as a culture of 'bureaucratic accountability' to one of 'democratic accountability' in Whitehall. Crucially, George Osborne's first emergency budget in June 2010 signalled wholesale cuts across Whitehall departments on a scale estimated to be between 25–40 per cent, parallels here being drawn with similar cuts in Canada made by Jean Chrétien's Liberal government between 1993–6.
- The third and private sector – crucial to the coalition's narrative of a smaller state coupled to a Big Society approach to governing – is to foster a 'new culture of voluntarism, philanthropy, social action' (Cameron 2010b). This requires a more extensive role for the private and third sectors (such as the voluntary sector, charities, not-for-profit organisations). The government's strategy in this area is predicated on three core ambitions: 'Make it easier to run a charity, social enterprise or voluntary organisation... Get more resources into the sector-social investment, giving and philanthropy...Make it easier for sector organisations to work with the State' (Cabinet Office 2010a). The coalition's 2010 Public Bodies Bill sought to reduce the size of the state through its cull of non-elected, publicly funded quangos such as the Qualifications and Curriculum Development Agency, the body responsible for designing the school curriculum, and the Food Standards Agency.

Reform of the extended state fits with the coalition's wider agenda of reducing government spending, while claiming to protect front-line services, and relatedly the size of the public sector, alongside greater fiscal accountability through the creation, ironically, of a new agency, the 'independent' Office for Budget Responsibility. The coalition's argument for a need to shift from bureaucratic to democratic accountability in many ways encapsulates the government's critique of Labour's approach to executive governance while signposting what its own intentions are. In his first major speech to the civil service David Cameron (2010c) argued that:

Where [Labour] went wrong with reform was the techniques they used. Top-down. Centralising...We want a new system of democratic accountability – accountability to the people, not the government machine... We want to turn government on its head, taking power away from Whitehall and putting it into the hands of people and communities...through transparency, local democratic control, competition and choice...From politician power to people power.

The coalition government identified four examples – Eden Valley in Cumbria, Windsor and Maidenhead, Sutton and Liverpool (which later withdrew from the pilot) as nascent, but contrasting versions of the 'Big Society' already in action, claiming them to be 'vanguard communities' (Cameron 2010b). Elsewhere, examples of the potential impact of these reforms in policy terms include: in education, the establishment of more academy schools independent of local education authorities, alongside greater flexibility over the curriculum; policing with the introduction of much greater accountability at the local level through the oversight by a directly elected individual; and in housing and planning with the devolution of control away from Whitehall to the local level.

Reforming the parliamentary system

Beyond debates about the type of state that the coalition government aspires to, the other key theme that also has the potential to render a long-term effect on future patterns of governing stems from the pressure to reform the existing parliamentary system. In many ways, the train of events set in motion after May 2010 were the culmination of two different forces conjoining as a potential catalyst for change.

The first set of longer-term forces can be grouped under the banner, discussed above, of growing disillusionment with the existing parliamentary system. Specifically, these relate to criticisms over various pathologies associated with key elements of the Westminster model including: the emphasis on a representative and so elitist, rather than participatory approach to governing; a perceived 'unfairness' of the single member plurality electoral system (SMPS); and a culture of self-regulation, secrecy and 'club government' underpinning practices in Westminster and Whitehall that directly relate to various scandals over the last two decades – 'cash for questions', 'MPs' expenses' and the 'lobbying of ministers for hire'. The second shorter-term, but not mutually exclusive, force is the repercussions stemming from the establishment of a coalition government. Again, this involves a number of elements. In terms of the electoral system, SMPS no longer appears to be delivering, in terms of producing an outright winner and with it a strong government with a mandate to govern. In 2010, for the second election in a row, the two largest parties – Conservative and Labour – collectively mustered less than 70 per cent of the total vote. The last time a similar outcome occurred was in 1923, another era of three-party politics, with the slow decline of the former Liberal party and the emergence of a new political force, the Labour party. The coalition negotiations after 2010 led the coalition to agree to a referendum on the Alternative Vote (AV) system for Westminster. Crucially, though, it is important to recognise that AV is still a majoritarian, rather than a fully proportionate model that would signal the outright end to single-party government that has for so long been the mainstay of the Westminster model. For example, modelling by the Electoral Reform Society of the 2010 general election suggested that using AV the Liberal Democrats would only see an increase in the number of seats won from 57 to 79 compared to a more proportional system such as the single transferable vote that would have led to 162 MPs (Electoral Reform Society 2010).

Reforms pursued elsewhere include: moves towards proportional representation for an elected House of Lords; a reduction in the number of MPs from 650 to 600; reform of the workings of the Houses of Parliament, in particular over how business should be determined; the right to recall MPs guilty of serious wrongdoing; and the introduction of fixed-term parliaments.

Conclusion: the Westminster model under Cameron's coalition

British governments, of all political persuasions, have long operated from within the top-down and elitist framework captured in the Westminster model. It follows that a coalition government, once it is united on its programme, can be expected to do likewise. Crucial to the Westminster model is the British Political Tradition and its emphasis on a limited, liberal notion of representative democracy and a conservative notion of responsibility, emphasising strong government. The Labour governments of both Blair and Brown, while appealing to the rhetoric of establishing a new pattern of governance, most notably in a shift towards pluralism, never really abandoned the model, nor relinquished the centralising tendencies associated with it. Does the 2010 change in government suggest a new paradigm in British politics is to be established?

The coalition's putative programme of reforms for both the state and parliament offer tentative evidence of its commitment to a shifting power from the centre. But to argue that the coalition will deliver on a 'new politics' framed by a clear break from the previous Westminster model of government is premature. Both the recent and longer term trends in executive patterns of government reveal reluctance by Britain's political elites to pursue a more pluralistic or devolved model of governance. While the Conservatives agreed to the Liberal Democrats demand to hold a referendum on the existing electoral system, the disproportionate SMPS, the Conservatives' position, espoused by David Cameron, was to retain the status quo. Moreover, the agreement to opt for the majoritarian

Alternative Vote electoral system rather than a more proportional system such as proportional representation or a mixed system such as the Additional Member System (AMS, used in elections to the Scottish parliament and the Welsh Assembly where it promotes coalition government) was itself a compromise. Even if the May 2011 referendum had supported the change to AV then the electoral system in operation at the general election provisionally set for 7 May 2015, were it AV instead of SMPS would not have undermined the key characteristic of representative delegation so crucial to the Westminster model.

Yet the tendency of British governments to accumulate power at the epicentre of the core executive, most notably in Number 10, the Cabinet Office and the Treasury, in order to drive their respective political projects forward is harder to pursue in a coalition government. Collegiality and consensus become an imperative to sustain such a government in power by binding two different and autonomous parties together. As Prime Minister David Cameron has to work with his Deputy Prime Minister the Liberal Democrat leader Nick Clegg. Both Cameron and Clegg – and their fellow ministers – have to ensure that broad, network–coalitions of support between the Conservatives and the Liberal Democrats are nurtured, for they are fundamental to retaining the Cameron government's authority and, ultimately, its Commons majority. When the coalition encounters rough political waters, any moves towards an insular, inward-looking, Number 10 bunker mentality, akin to that of Brown, are no longer an option for survival. Cameron has always to reach out to, and work with, the Liberal Democrats. There is, thus, an opportunity for a reappraisal of the expectations placed on the prime minister, which may help to further expose the myth surrounding the presidentialisation of the post of prime minister (Foley 2000, 2002; Hennessy 2000; Heffernan 2003, 2005). The prime minister never was, nor never can be a ubiquitous all-powerful figure. Rather than always seeming to be answerable for the actions of all elements of the government's work and the dominant focal point on which the political media feeds off, Cameron has instead an opportunity to defer questions beyond his compass to the relevant Cabinet minister and, in certain policy areas, notably constitutional reform, to Nick Clegg. In many ways, then, for the coalition to work it requires, by definition, a reassertion of a core characteristic of the Westminster model, that of collective Cabinet or ministerial government. This was a practice that remained part of the operation of British government up until the late 1970s until it was called into question by both Margaret Thatcher and Tony Blair.

The coalition government, itself a remarkable change from established practice in both Whitehall and Westminster, has undoubtedly led to a discernible and ongoing change in the political discourse in those circles.

Nevertheless, the weight of history suggests that, in the longer term, it is unlikely to lead to the abandonment of the British Political Tradition. In a climate of austerity following on from economic recession, the pressures for strong, powerful, potentially unpopular, political leadership based on command and control loom large. In this regard it is not impossible, should they have the support of their party lieutenants, that Cameron and Clegg, following Blair and Brown, might well see the need to strengthen ministerial power, particularly at 'the centre' of British government. Command and control are all key characteristics of the Westminster model's informal code of governing and one the coalition government may well find hard to resist. Clearly, the potential exists for the coalition to emulate their Blair/Brown predecessors by initially appealing to the rhetoric of radical reform, of pluralism and the devolving of power away from the centre, but only then to envelope itself in the comfort blanket of asymmetric executive power that the Westminster model has for so long provided British governments.

Chapter 4

New Parliamentary Landscapes

ALEXANDRA KELSO

There have been some remarkable developments in British parliamentary politics in the past few years. The most visible development was the hung parliament caused by the outcome of the 2010 general election; with no single party gaining an overall majority in the House of Commons, the importance of parliament as an institutional arena came to the fore, with the parties spending several days after the election in negotiations establishing how they might work together in order to secure the Commons control necessary before state power could be effectively wielded. Those negotiations quickly produced another remarkable development, with the new coalition government agreeing to give up its power to call the next general election at a time of its choosing, and instead to institute a system of fixed, five-year parliaments.

These two developments – a post-election hung parliament and the move away from executive control of parliamentary duration – took place in the context of yet another crucial event. One of the defining issues in British politics as the 2010 general election approached was the parliamentary expenses scandal of 2009, which seemed to confirm the worst assumptions about politicians as a class and parliament as an institution. The scale of this crisis, and the wide-ranging nature of the reforms suggested to remedy it, made it one of the key political issues of recent times, one which raised difficult questions about what we expect from parliament and those who represent voters there. It produced an obvious desire to introduce new regulation and oversight of MPs, where very little had existed before, in order to prevent such abuse of position happening again. But it also generated examination of how parliament might be reformed more broadly, in order to reshape it into a more effective institution capable of engaging with rigorous oversight of government. To understand recent parliamentary developments, we must explore particular aspects of the reform trajectory unleashed by the expenses scandal, and probe what they reveal about our expectations about parliament within the British political system.

We also need to look beyond Westminster, to include the Scottish Parliament at Holyrood, the National Assembly for Wales in Cardiff, and the Northern Ireland Assembly at Stormont (not to mention the London

Assembly, which, while not serving as a 'national' arena, nevertheless represents a population almost equal to that of Scotland and Wales combined). Each of these legislative institutions performs a range of representative and accountability roles which, when taken together, were supposed to enhance the functioning of democratic politics in the UK, one of the key underpinning justifications of the devolution process made by the Labour government. More than a decade has passed since these new institutions were established, and we are now in a position to draw some conclusions about key developments within them.

The devolved bodies are also interesting in terms of their impact on the Westminster parliament (which still provides for the direct governing of some 85 per cent of the UK population). Recent institutional developments at Westminster, in terms of coalition government, legislative capacity and public engagement strategies, facilitate interesting comparison and contrast with the devolved institutions. Indeed, because of the asymmetrical nature of UK devolution, the accompanying legislative arenas are markedly

---

Box 4.1　Key developments in the MPs' expenses crisis

2004	Parliament begins releasing information about individual MPs' allowances, in order to conform to the Freedom of Information Act 2000 (FOI).
2005	Campaigners lodge series of FOI requests about MPs' allowances. The House of Commons authorities, under the leadership of Speaker Michael Martin, appeal against these requests to the Information Commissioner.
2007	MPs unsuccessfully attempt to amend Freedom of Information Act to exclude parliament from its competence.
May 2007	Report published by the *Sunday Times* claims Derek Conway MP paid his son as a researcher from parliamentary staffing allowances although he was in full-time university education; matter later investigated by Commons Standards and Privileges Committee which questioned whether payments were acceptable.
March 2008	FOI campaigners force publication of the Commons 'John Lewis list', used by House authorities to guide MPs on allowance expenditures.
May 2008	High Court rules that House of Commons must produce the information about MPs' allowances requested by the FOI campaigners.

→

different in terms of competence, character and complexion. These differences not only illuminate interesting insights into the institutional development of the devolved parliaments, and the various demands that have been made with respect to expanding legislative competence, but increasingly impact on how Westminster itself seeks to manage its own business.

The expenses crisis and its consequences

The events of May 2009, which followed the publication by the *Daily Telegraph* of a series of Westminster parliamentary expenses revelations, constituted one of the most serious crises in recent British political history. The story dominated news and media agendas for close to a month, shifting from initial coverage of the specifics of MPs' expense claims to demands for heads to roll (as they did in the resignation of the House of Commons Speaker, Michael Martin, the first Speaker to be forced out in 300 years) and

→	
July 2008	Members Estimate Committee publishes review of allowances.
March 2009	Committee on Standards in Public Life announces inquiry into MPs' allowances.
April 2009	Prime minister announces, on YouTube, cross-party agreement on allowances reform, although none exists.
May 2009	*Daily Telegraph* begins printing expenses revelations in advance of Commons publication of redacted expense claims.
19 May 2009	Speaker of House, Michael Martin, resigns over criticism of his role in expenses crisis.
20 July 2009	Reform of the House of Commons Committee established.
21 July 2009	Parliamentary Standards Act 2009 passed, creating the Independent Parliamentary Standards Authority to regulate and administer system of MPs' allowances.
Oct 2009	Sir Thomas Legg writes to MPs required to pay back expenses claims.
Nov 2009	Committee on Standards in Public Life, chaired by Sir Christopher Kelly, reports on MPs' expenses and allowances, and recommends substantial changes to regime.
Jan–May 2011	David Chaytor becomes first former MP to be convicted over the MPs' expenses scandal, and is sentenced to 18 months in jail; Eric Illsley sentenced to one year in prison for similar offences; Jim Devine sentenced to 16 months for false accounting; Elliot Morley convicted of the same offence and sentenced to 16 months in jail.

then onto broader discussions about the state of parliamentary politics in Britain and the need for wide-ranging constitutional changes. The *Telegraph*'s revelations sparked a debate which fundamentally questioned the trustworthiness of MPs, the extent to which taxpayer monies were being effectively used to support them, and the possibility that the system of parliamentary democracy had been irredeemably undermined.

We are not usefully detained here by recounting at length the entire sordid expenses episode, populated as it is by depressing stories of house flipping, moat cleaning and duck houses. Box 4.1 provides a useful overview of the key events, and further discussion can be found in Kelso (2009a).

One of the first key developments in the immediate aftermath of the expenses revelations involved the system by which MPs' expenses were handled and made public. David Cameron declared that full details about Conservative MPs' expenses would be examined by a party Scrutiny Committee and made available online, while the Labour party leadership appointed a Star Chamber to look at the most serious cases of expenses irregularities on its side and, if need be, prevent MPs from seeking re-election. As a result of the *Telegraph* expose, and the internal party inquiries held, around 149 MPs, a post-war record, eventually announced their intention not to seek re-election, contributing to a significant turnover in Commons membership in the May 2010 general election, and the eventual arrival at Westminster of a large new cohort of MPs with no previous parliamentary experience.

The scale of public anger over the revelations left politicians with little alternative but to reform the system (or at least appear to be reforming it), and a fundamental shift occurred away from traditional self-regulation among MPs and towards external independent statutory regulation. Two separate inquiries were launched by the prime minister in summer 2009, one by Sir Thomas Legg, which reviewed MPs' expense claims and issued requests for repayment where necessary, and the second by Sir Christopher Kelly, which explored what a new system of independent regulation of pay and allowances should look like. The Commons passed the Parliamentary Standards Act in June 2009, which was rushed through the legislative process on the eve of the Westminster summer recess. Although stripped of some important regulatory tools, particularly an all-encompassing Statutory Code of Conduct for MPs, the legislation created a new Independent Parliamentary Standards Authority (IPSA), whose work would be structured by the various recommendations of the Kelly Inquiry published in November 2009 (and summarised in Box 4.2). Of crucial importance, IPSA now has the authority to set MPs' salary and allowance rates without recourse to Commons approval. Although IPSA did not adopt all of the recommendations of

---

Box 4.2   Main recommendations of the Kelly Inquiry

- Ending of allowances for mortgage interest on second homes, and ending of property 'flipping'; capital gains accumulated during transition period to be surrendered to taxpayer.
- MPs should only be reimbursed for hotel/rent costs associated accommodation away from their constituency address.
- No support for cleaning, gardening or furnishings associated with additional accommodation away from main constituency address.
- Practice of employing family members should be ended within five years.
- Abolition of MPs' communication allowance.
- Removal of resettlement grant paid to those who step down from parliament.
- Receipts required for all expenses.

---

the Kelly Inquiry, most were incorporated into the new regulatory regime, and the new constraints it imposed represents a significant change in the way in which MPs' work is resourced and audited. IPSA's longevity is not, however, guaranteed: MPs have consistently questioned IPSA's utility and value for money, and calls were already being heard for its reform or replacement within a year of its creation.

Westminster is, however, not the only legislature in the UK to have been hit by problems over the way it funds parliamentarians, and there are interesting comparisons and contrasts to be made between what happened at Westminster in 2009 with earlier developments in the Scottish Parliament. In 2005, David McLetchie, leader of the Scottish Conservative party, became embroiled in a scandal regarding claims for taxi expenses that were argued not to have had anything to do with his parliamentary work. The episode resulted in McLetchie's resignation, along with a substantial reorganisation of the way in which expenses information was made available, including a shift to placing details of all MSP expenses online on a monthly basis (Kelso 2009a). The goal was to make the system more transparent, in order to condition the behaviour of MSPs towards the expenses available to them, as well as to engender public trust through the accessibility of the information. A similar online system was launched in the National Assembly for Wales in spring 2009. However, none of these systems provide access to the kind of detailed information about individual expenses that some freedom of information campaigners argue is of fundamental importance for transparency.

One revealing aspect of the Westminster expenses crisis was the trend which developed in the print media for identifying MPs with low expense claims and lionising them as 'saints', while MPs with higher claims were singled out as 'sinners', a strategy which obscured the hugely complex basis of the various expenses regimes and their goals (Kelso 2009a). Parliamentary democracy costs money, and MPs who make a minimal claim on the public purse are not necessarily better representatives than others. In fudging the issue of the cost of democracy, MPs failed to formulate a convincing account of the work of a parliamentarian and the resource implications of that work. In the post-expenses political climate, it has become even harder for MPs to claim that individual Members specifically, and parliament more generally, require increased resources in order to function properly. Yet the resources of government vastly outweigh those of parliament, and for parliament to fulfil its functions of scrutinising the executive and holding it to account, it needs to be sufficiently resourced.

In addition, the monies spent by MPs must be acknowledged as public money, rather than MPs' money to spend as they wish. In terms of accommodation expenses, for example, IPSA will now only cover the costs of hotel rooms or rent, not mortgage interest payments, bringing Westminster in line with existing practice at Holyrood and with recent changes instituted in Cardiff (National Assembly for Wales 2009). Significantly, however, the Kelly Inquiry recommended that the MP communication allowance, designed to allow MPs to send information to their constituents, be abolished, in direct contrast to the practice in Scotland and Wales, where the emphasis is on increasing this kind of parliamentary expenditure and improving the way it is spent. IPSA subsequently preserved the communication expenditure category, although the rules surrounding how this money is used may now be more robustly enforced to prevent such funds being used for partisan purposes.

The expenses scandal also prompted a more general reassessment of some aspects of how the Westminster parliament operates, its value in the political system, and its contribution to democratic governance. Despite talk about the need to respond to the expenses crisis by way of constitutional change – such as completion of House of Lords reform, electoral reform, political party funding reform, a written constitution, and so on – most of these sorts of things were totally unachievable in the dying months of an exhausted Labour government. It did, however, result in the creation of a committee on the reform of parliament, under the chairmanship of the Labour backbencher Dr Tony Wright MP, a long-standing champion of parliamentary reform.

Gordon Brown claimed that Wright's Committee would 'take forward urgent modernisation of the procedures of the House of Commons' (HC

Debs., 10 June 2009, col. 797). The description of modernisation as an 'urgent' matter was interesting, if only because the government had set up a Modernisation Committee for this very purpose when it came to office in 1997, and Brown's announcement thus illustrated the limitations of what had been achieved in that 12-year period. Nonetheless, with a new reform-oriented Commons Speaker (John Bercow) in place, the various recommendations from the Wright Committee, summarised in Box 4.3, were made in a reasonably receptive political environment. These reform proposals covered the three key areas that the defunct Modernisation Committee had struggled with since 1997, and which were viewed as significant in 'reinvigorating' parliament.

We will return to these three central recommendations throughout this chapter. Crucially, however, each of these proposals, in their own way, pointed to the need for a broader debate which went beyond the relatively narrow issue of expenses, and focused on substantially larger questions about the purpose and role of the Westminster parliament within British politics.

Box 4.3 Main recommendations of Wright Committee

Select committees
Chairs of select committees should be elected by the whole House through a secret ballot using the alternative vote; all other members should be elected from within the party groups by secret ballot.

Organisation of House business
Non-government business to be organised through a Backbench Business Committee, which must then liaise with a House Business Committee (comprising representatives of government and opposition parties) to agree a draft agenda that would be submitted to whole House for approval; better access to the House agenda for select committee business and for backbenchers to raise matters of concern.

Engagement with the public
Urgent discussions on creating an e-petitions system; House of Commons Procedure Committee also to act as a temporary Petitions Committee for a trial period; greater significance for written petitions in House proceedings.

Data from: First Report from the Select Committee on Reform of the House of Commons, *Rebuilding the House* (HC 1117, 2009), London: TSO)

What is parliament for?

The reform agenda quickly expanded beyond correcting the obvious faults associated with the expenses regime to encompass broader issues about parliamentary capacity within the political system. The default position of many Westminster observers is to complain that government is too strong while parliament is too weak. This is a narrative of substantial historical pedigree, rehearsed in earnest since at least the beginning of twentieth century, when the executive first began to expand its capacity for action and alter the resource dependencies inside parliament (in terms of legislative procedures and access to time) in its own favour (Flinders and Kelso 2011; Kelso 2009b). Parliament has an erratic record of influencing government policy making, and, on the whole, the executive tends to secure its legislation without too much parliamentary interference (Cowley 2006; Norton 2005), irrespective of the substantive quality of that legislation. This evidence is often used to argue that parliament is in decline, resulting in an over-powerful government and a dysfunctional democracy.

We should take care before making such arguments. As Cowley (2006) noted in the previous edition of this volume, parliamentary power does not just equate with the willingness of the Commons to defeat the government on legislative divisions. Its power and influence flow from a whole range of far less obvious (and far less easily measurable) sources. A more nuanced view of the House of Commons sees it, not as a contest between government and opposition, but as a set of potentially tense intra-party relationships, and it is in fact the relationships between members of the governing party that underpins much of the 'power' or influence of parliament (King 1976). This point is even more crucial in the context of the Conservative–LibDem coalition government formed in May 2010: the relationships between members of the constituent governing parties, and the management of conflict between and among them when it arises, will be key to the coalition's success. Parliament's influence on government policy-making substantially involves its role as a politically significant arena through which government backbenchers can pressurise the executive into making changes to its legislation on the basis that they may well use that arena to vote against the government if need be. In most instances, governments will prefer to resolve such policy differences where possible and avoid potentially damaging and embarrassing rebellions from their own backbench MPs (Cowley 2002, 2005). Consequently, the absence of government defeats does not equate with a lack of parliamentary power and influence, but points instead to the desire of the executive to keep internal policy disagreements away from the oxygen of publicity afforded by the Commons chamber. This was demonstrated soon after the 2010 election when the new prime minister, David Cameron, attempted to exert control over his MPs by giving Conservative ministers the right to vote on the influential backbench 1922 Committee, as a way of diffusing internal concerns within the parliamentary party about its coalition arrangements with the Liberal Democrats. The failure of Cameron to secure this control, and the ability of senior backbenchers to rebuff this manoeuvre, illustrates that the intra-party tensions created by coalition government are intimately related to the parliamentary arena that facilitates such government in the first place.

Parliament's fundamental resource is that it alone can confer legitimacy on government and its legislation (Judge 1993). This was again perfectly illustrated following the 2010 general election which produced a hung parliament in which no single party was able to seize the levers of state power: only when the parties had worked together to create a coalition which could command a majority in the House of Commons was it possible for the change in government to happen. Parliament, then, far from being irrelevant, remains central in determining how governing happens in the UK.

This point is similarly illustrated in the context of the devolved legislatures. When we talk about the power of the Scottish Parliament or the Welsh or Northern Ireland Assemblies, we are not talking necessarily about their respective policy competences under the devolution settlement. Instead, we are talking about the nature of the relationship between the executive and the legislature, and how this impacts on processes of governing and on policy outcomes. Consequently, when contrasting the institutions at Westminster, Holyrood, Cardiff and Stormont, the fallacy of equating parliamentary power with ability and willingness to defeat the executive becomes fully apparent. The Westminster parliament provides for strong and responsible government (Birch 1964) specifically because the single member plurality electoral system (SMPS) is designed with that outcome in mind, and usually produces majorities in the House of Commons for the winning party quite out of proportion to its actual share of the vote (although, as we saw in 2010, it does not guarantee this outcome). The devolved institutions, by contrast, are elected through mixed member systems which produce more proportional results than SMPS, and in each case, the outcome has tended to be, by design, a hung parliament, resulting in minority or coalition government. In other words, it is manifestly easier in the devolved institutions for the executive to be defeated on its legislation. Yet, in those settings, any persistent failure of those executives to secure their legislation would not necessarily mean that we could claim the respective legislatures were strong, but, rather, that something had gone horribly wrong with the system of representative government. The devolved parliaments and assemblies do not demonstrate their influence and power by thwarting executive legislation, but through other less obvious mechanisms and processes, just as at Westminster.

Consequently, seeking to assess the 'power of parliament' fundamentally asks the wrong kind of question. We best understand parliaments, at Westminster or elsewhere, when we conceptualise them in terms of resource dependencies and interdependencies in relation to the executive and to the parties which comprise them, because only in this way can we generate the insights required to take account of the complex ways in which they influence political outcomes and shape the nature of representative democracy in twenty-first-century Britain.

New legislative mechanisms

A key role of any parliament is to subject the government's legislation to scrutiny and provide a forum through which policy can be turned into law. One of the most interesting developments in British parliamentary politics in recent years has been the introduction of new legislative scrutiny mechanisms designed to make that scrutiny more focused and rigorous.

For much of the twentieth century, detailed scrutiny of government bills in the House of Commons took place in standing committees. These typically comprised a government minister from the department in charge of the bill, an opposition spokesperson, party whips and a number of backbench MPs from across the parties, with the membership reflecting that of the chamber. As a result there was (usually) a government majority, which meant that almost the only legislative amendments that were accepted were those the government approved. Standing committees were routinely criticised on the grounds that they were adversarial and did not engage in any meaningful scrutiny, with much of the real parliamentary influence on government legislation taking place away from the committee and through informal processes which were difficult to observe and assess.

The new public bill committees, introduced in 2006 following the recommendations of the Modernisation Committee (HC 1097, 2005–6), sought to address some of these concerns. Whilst their structure remains the same as that of standing committees, they have the new power to take evidence on the bills before them. By mirroring the practice of evidence-taking used in select committees, the aim is that the adversarial nature of the committee environment may be dampened, and that expert evidence might be more fully brought to bear.

The new procedures came into operation at the start of the 2006–7 session, and, with time, may engender a different approach to the scrutiny of government bills, where cooperation between different legislative actors becomes far more important than in the past, and where the outcome of the process is a body of usefully 'improved' legislation (Levy 2010). The creation of the public bill committee mechanism is an interesting institutional innovation for Westminster, in the context of its increasing attempts to constrain partisan influences in work that is conducted away from the chamber.

Quite different legislative mechanisms are in place at Holyrood, Cardiff and Stormont. Perhaps the most crucial difference is that, in each of the devolved institutions, legislation can be proposed not only by the executive and by individual members, as at Westminster, but also by the parliamentary committees, with time specifically allocated for the consideration of committee bills. This is possible because the devolved parliaments are far more oriented around a committee-based approach to work, an approach which was incorporated into their institutional fabric from their inception. The Scottish Parliament has a system of permanent subject committees, which is not only the starting-point for bills going through the legislative process but also the forum for detailed executive scrutiny like that conducted by Westminster select committees. The subject committees were empowered to take evidence on bills from their creation. In this respect, we can see how some aspects of legislative practice in the devolved institutions have come to be fused at Westminster with its existing evidence-taking select committee system, demonstrating how processes of reflexive learning can emerge in a context where different legislatures do things in different ways.

There have also been key developments in the Welsh Assembly legislative process since the Government of Wales Act 2006, which expanded the legislative competence of the Assembly, meaning that each of the devolved institutions at Holyrood, Cardiff and Stormont now has the authority to make primary legislation (broadly) commensurate with a Westminster Act of Parliament. In a referendum in Wales in March 2011, just over 63 per cent of those who voted supported enabling the National Assembly for Wales to pass Acts of the Assembly without first seeking the agreement of the UK parliament, thus calling time on the previously confused terminology of Assembly Legislative Competence Orders and Assembly Measures. This further refinement of the Welsh Assembly's powers marks not just a new stage in the devolution process but also a new era in Welsh legislative politics.

Beyond the issue of the specific institutional format through which legislation is secured, there is also the important question of who controls parliamentary time in the first place. A key criticism of the

House of Commons is that the government has too much control over the time available, and backbenchers too little. Time is a significant institutional resource, and the government's domination of it has long been a sore point for reformers. Consequently, one of the recommendations from the 2009 Wright Committee was that a new system be introduced to manage House time (see Box 4.3). This would provide for more backbench control over non-government time, and also give backbenchers a bigger role in deciding how government business time should be used. The Commons approved these plans for new management of House time just before the general election, and the new coalition government included in its coalition agreement a pledge to fully enact these measures over the course of its time in office. The promised Backbench Business Committee was established in June 2010, and enables backbenchers to decide together how they should spend the parliamentary time allocated specifically to them, rather than having to liaise with government business managers. A key question for the future will be the extent to which this new control enhances backbench autonomy inside the Commons. Early indications regarding the topics for debate chosen by the committee – such as that on prisoner voting rights at a time when the government was under pressure following various court rulings against it – suggest that time is being used creatively to help highlight the variety of backbench opinion which exists on various topic.

Scrutiny and oversight

Legislative scrutiny is only part of the role of a parliament; it also engages in scrutiny of executive policies and activities. Since 1979, the House of Commons has done this primarily through its system of departmental select committees, which conduct inquiries, take evidence and publish reports on various aspects of government policy and administration, and which comprise backbench MPs from across the parties, with a government majority. They organise their work along all-party lines, in which partisan struggle is less pronounced, and MPs themselves acknowledge that the committees cannot work if they are overly divided by party battle. In 2002, the select committees went through a process of moderate reform, in which their chairpersons were paid for the first time (in an attempt to create an alternative career path for parliamentarians to that of frontbench service), and they gained increased resources and staffing, particularly through the creation of a dedicated Scrutiny Unit to support their work (Kelso 2003). In time, the select committees have grown into their scrutiny task, and now enjoy reasonable levels of media exposure. Their reports feature regularly on Radio 4 news and current affairs programming, but with their increasing attention to high-profile public policy matters, they also appear more regularly in television news and in the press. In February 2009, for example, the Treasury Select Committee, under the chairmanship of Labour's John McFall, conducted an inquiry into the banking crisis, and hauled before it the 'disgraced' former chief executives of some of the banks which had been part-nationalised in order to prevent them from collapsing (HC 144–I, 2008–9). The importance of the issue meant that the evidence sessions enjoyed top-billing in many television news programmes. The hearings demonstrated exactly how parliament, through its committees, can provide a rigorous forum for exploring important issues of public interest, and the questioning employed by its members illustrated just how far the committees have come from the somewhat unsystematic and deferential inquiry styles of their earlier years.

Yet institutional constraints on committee capacity persisted, most particularly in terms of the extent to which the party whips could determine their memberships and chairs, with this widely viewed as delimiting the quality of scrutiny performed. A key Wright Committee recommendation was that the select committee chairs should be chosen by election, and that other members be elected by a party ballot (Box 4.3). These key proposals were designed to remove the whips from the organisation of select committees, and help make them more independent of government and better positioned to engage in quality scrutiny. The proposal addressed the long-standing concern of reformers that those being scrutinised should not have a determining influence on those who perform the scrutiny. Select committee chairs were elected by the whole House for the first time in June 2010, while the remaining members had to seek support from their party colleagues in internal elections to secure their positions.

The Commons now also scrutinises the prime minister for over two hours twice a year before the Liaison Committee, a group of senior and experienced backbenchers. The prime minister is aware of the broad areas to be covered by questions, but not the detailed questions. This innovation, introduced in 2002, was designed to provide for better scrutiny of the head of government than could be obtained through prime minister's questions, which arguably generates more heat than light. As with the select committees, these sessions seek to remove partisan point-scoring from the scrutiny framework, facilitating in-depth questioning into key matters of government policy and strategy over which the prime minister is in charge. It has taken time for the Liaison Committee members to develop systematic approaches to this task, and to devise inquiry tactics that can deliver the best scrutiny. The key point here is not that the prime minister leaves the sessions broken, beaten and bested by parliamentary interrogators, but that the sessions provide a strategic institutional arena in which executive arguments are tested, defences explored and governance problems examined. Yet these sessions have not been wildly successful illustrations of parliamentary scrutiny, and that the format requires further tweaking in order to maximise its potential.

Perhaps because much of the partisan heat has been removed from the Liaison Committee sessions, they have not attracted much media attention, despite marking another notable institutional innovation for Westminster, and one which has attracted attention from the devolved institutions. The National Assembly for Wales sought to replicate the format by creating a Committee for the Scrutiny of the First Minister in 2005, and went on to hold three evidence sessions with Rhodri Morgan. Subsequently, the sessions fell into some disuse after the Welsh elections in 2007, not least because of problems in finding capacity within a small Assembly of 60 members, and they did not resume until late in 2009. This demonstrates that the arena has not become as embedded as at Westminster, where the practice continued across the 2005 and 2010 general elections, and through the change in prime minister from Tony Blair to Gordon Brown. In 2007, the Scottish Labour party committed to holding regular sessions between the First Minister and the Committee Convenors, in a similar format to that developed at Westminster (Scottish Labour Party 2007: 98), but as the SNP went on to form a minority administration, the idea was never put into practice, and there has been no such process at Stormont either. Once more, therefore, we see the contrasting styles and practices which have developed in the different parliamentary settings, and the ways in which some institutional approaches are imported and exported between them, while others are not.

Facilitating public engagement

The expenses scandal brought in its wake a growing interest in how parliament can better communicate with the public and involve it in its work, as part of an effort to remedy such disengagement and enhance the functioning of democratic institutions.

This was not a new debate, however. Recent years have seen no shortage of discussion about the need to reinvigorate the Westminster parliament's approach to engaging with the public it represents. In 2004, the Modernisation Committee published a report entitled *Connecting Parliament with the Public* (HC 368, 2003–4), which aimed to 'better reconcile the necessary purpose of Parliament with the reasonable expectation of the people to have access to the processes by which we govern ourselves' (p. 3). The report recommended plans for improved information on parliament, increased engagement with young people, and improved media relations. Reports from the Hansard Society Commission on the Communication of Parliamentary Democracy (Hansard Society 2006) and the Power Commission Inquiry into Britain's Democracy (2005) both made much of the need for parliament to better involve the public in its various processes.

Ideas about how Westminster engages with the public are underpinned by the development of an institution predicated on representative government rather than democratic participation (Judge 1993). The Westminster parliament has struggled with the task of how to enhance its participatory and deliberative credentials without undermining the representative basis on which it is founded (Kelso 2007), a struggle illustrated by debates over the issue of public petitioning.

Petitioning is one of the least energy-intensive forms of political engagement, generally requiring little more than a signature on a form circulated by other concerned citizens and it remains one of the most popular forms of political participation in Britain. A recent Audit of Political Engagement estimated that around 36 per cent of the population signed a petition across a three-year period, far more than participated in other kinds of non-voting activities (Hansard Society 2009). However, public petitions presented to MPs generally disappear into a procedural black hole: MPs have only a limited opportunity to present the arguments of the petition in the chamber (Blackburn and Kennon 2003: 380), and at times when there is little chance of generating much interest. If parliament is supposed to be the focus for public concerns, and if petitions are a key vehicle through which many people express them, then parliament is largely failing in its duty to highlight matters of public concern expressed through this mechanism.

The rudimentary nature of the procedures at Westminster is now in stark contrast to the practice elsewhere. The Scottish Parliament was established with a structured petitioning process built into its institutional design. At Holyrood 'petitioning the Scottish Parliament is one of the principal means through which members of the public can have a direct influence and role in the policy development process' (Scottish Parliament 2008), and the Scottish Parliament has a dedicated Public Petitions Committee (PPC) for this job, which incorporates the first parliamentary e-petitioning system in the world. The PCC can invite petitioners to give oral or written evidence, and decide whether the petition should be referred to the relevant Holyrood subject committee for consideration, or whether parliamentary time is required for a debate on the petition. This petitioning process has facilitated a substantial public impact on parliamentary work, and although we should be cautious when judging the 'success' of petitions (Carman 2005), there have been many outcomes as a result of petitions that may not have been secured otherwise, ranging from increased political attention for some topics (particularly through parliamentary debates and committee investigations) to substantive changes to legislation and government action in others. Following an inquiry by the PPC in 2008, which highlighted gaps in public knowledge about petitioning (SP 300, 2009), further efforts were made to enhance the petitioning process in 2009 incorporating Web 2.0, blogs, podcasting and videoconferencing, all embedded on the PPC website.

The National Assembly for Wales operates a very similar petitioning system to that at Holyrood, utilising the services of a Petitions Committee with powers of referral and evidence-taking. An e-petitions system has also operated since April 2008, adopted on the evidence of the success at Holyrood, and while it comprises an e-forum for debating petitions along with email informational support to petitioners, it has yet to expand into the kind of ICT territory being explored at Holyrood.

The Northern Ireland Assembly, by contrast, has no substantially developed petitions mechanism, with the procedure bearing considerable resemblance to that of Westminster. Yet Stormont at least has a good excuse for its lacklustre approach to petitions, in that its institutional development has been substantially constrained by the suspension of devolution after 2002. Westminster has no such excuse, and fell massively out of step with the developing systems of public engagement being pursued in the devolved parliaments, as well as with processes adopted by other UK-level political actors: 10 Downing Street has operated a massively popular e-petitions system since November 2006, which has arguably, and problematically, supplanted Westminster's fundamental role as the focus for the articulation of public concerns.

In 2007 the Commons Procedure Committee recommended improvements to accessibility, mechanisms to make it easier to debate petitions, and a shift towards e-petitioning, with these recommendations stemming directly from observations of the Holyrood practice (HC 513, 2006–7, paras. 9–14). But the Committee rejected the idea of a Petitions Committee for Westminster, on the grounds that this would break the traditional MP-constituent 'bond'. Proposals for an e-petitioning system were further outlined in 2008 (HC 136, 2007–8), which also stopped far short of the comprehensive nature of the Scottish or Welsh systems, essentially advocating replicating the existing Commons procedure but on an electronic platform. No action followed these recommendations, and the Labour government stepped back from its commitment to facilitate the creation of an e-petitions system, largely on grounds of cost (House of Commons Library 2009).

The 2009 Wright Committee proposals were also restrained on this issue, recommending further discussion on an e-petitions system, the creation of an experimental Petitions Committee, and some streamlining of how petitions are handled procedurally. The new coalition government pledged to implement plans to allow popular petitions (with more than 100,000 signatures) to be formally debated in parliament, and in some cases for such petitions to form the basis of a parliamentary bill. Again, therefore, the developments in the field of parliamentary petitioning demonstrate the extent to which processes of institutional learning go on, albeit slowly.

More dramatic still was a pledge of the Conservatives following the expenses scandal, which went on to form part of the coalition agreement, that the public should be able to exert more control over wayward MPs by having the power, through recall petitions, to force by-elections when there is the support of 10 per cent of constituents, albeit only where there is evidence of wrongdoing. This may be a crucial public tool once implemented, in terms of democratic control, and could reshape the way that MPs engage and communicate with their constituents in order to prevent such recalls occurring in the first place.

House of Lords reform

Yet another impact of the expenses crisis was that the question of second chamber reform also rose up the political agenda. A Commons vote in March 2007 had demonstrated that there was significant support among MPs for either a wholly or substantially elected second chamber, a result which was not only a snub to the outgoing prime minister, Tony Blair, a dogged supporter of an appointed chamber who resisted wholesale Lords reform throughout his premiership, but which also laid down a gauntlet for the incoming prime minister, Gordon Brown, whose support for an elected chamber was longstanding.

Yet, despite some positive murmurs in 2007, particularly in the *Governance of Britain* (Cm 7170, 2007) Green Paper, there were no significant attempts to reform the second chamber. The expenses crises, however, prompted renewed discussion of Lords reform, which was repeatedly used as an example of how the Labour government had failed to fulfil its commitments on constitutional change and democratic reform, with that failure resulting, at least in part, in the expenses debacle itself. Even the Constitutional Reform and Governance Bill, introduced in July 2009 partly in response to the expenses crisis, promised only to bring in measures that would provide for the eventual removal of the hereditary peers reprieved in the House of Lords Act 1999. In its final days in office, the Labour government committed to plans for a referendum on implementing a predominantly elected second chamber, in part to woo the Liberal Democrats in the event of a hung parliament. The Conservative–Lib Dem coalition government agreement included plans to pursue Lords reform with the goal of a wholly or mainly elected House, overseen by Deputy Prime Minister Nick Clegg, although this matter had low priority for the Conservative party, and the much delayed proposals – finally announced in May 2011 (see Chapter 2) – are far from certain to make it into law.

House of Lords reform is, of course, one area where Westminster has little to learn from the devolved institutions, which are all unicameral, and there is no serious support for a shift to unicameralism at Westminster. A unicameral parliament may work well in a nation of only a few million people, but bicameralism tends to be the norm in nations with populations the size of the United Kingdom (some 65 million) mainly because of the breadth, depth and range of work required of it.

A significant second chamber development in recent years concerns how much more assertive the chamber has become since the hereditary peers were removed, and how much more willing it is to challenge the government on its legislation and subject it to increasingly more rigorous scrutiny (Russell and Sciara 2008). This was forcefully demonstrated in early 2010 as the House of Lords subjected the government's bill on the referendum on the Alternative Vote to extensive scrutiny and amendment, sitting through the night in order to do so, with the bill only securing agreement following extensive 'ping pong' between the two Houses and an attempt by Labour peers to impose a 40 per cent turnout threshold for the May 2011 referendum. This move was vigorously resisted by the government, but the bill only secured royal assent with hours to spare in order to ensure the proposed referendum could actually go ahead as planned. This evidence of the functional value of the second chamber in legislative and scrutiny terms, despite the serious problems it poses in terms of democratic legitimacy in its current manifestation (Kelso 2006), is also a fundamental justification for retaining bicameralism at Westminster.

Conclusion

The expenses crisis which preceded the 2010 election ensured that the political parties entered the 2010 general election with manifestos which explicitly addressed the issue of the functioning of parliamentary democracy and how they intended to make it work better through various kinds of institutional and constitutional change. The hung parliament that resulted from the 2010 general election then moved questions about parliamentary reform outside the realm of constitutional anoraks and firmly into the territory of party political life or death.

Yet, beyond the specifics of that one episode, this chapter has drawn out broader, and more long-lived, trends with respect to parliamentary development. As far as the Westminster parliament is concerned, there is now a very clear shift away from a chamber-based institution – where most things happen on the floor of the House of Commons – and towards a committee-based institution, illustrated by the growing emphasis given to work done in new public bill committees, select committees and committee-based scrutiny of the prime minister.

Debates about how legislation is examined and tested, how government is scrutinised, how the public engages with elected representatives, how those who sit in parliament come to do so, and how they are held to account, are not new. Yet they continue to be of huge significance in British politics, and demonstrate the need for further development of parliamentary infrastructures throughout Britain. Such debates have been made even more interesting in the last decade because of the growing reflexivity between the various parliaments and assemblies which now exist; the increasing extent to which they are willing to look to, and learn from, each other; and the complex institutional reality which now characterises the new parliamentary landscape in Britain. In 2009 these debates were given a new prominence as a result of the MPs' expenses scandal, underlining the mismatch between public expectations of parliament and the reality of the institution as it operated, and bringing front and centre a whole range of debates about the purpose of parliament, how it ought to be reformed, and how each of the parties would start the rhetorical task of rebuilding public trust in parliament if returned to government. In 2010, the hung parliament and coalition government which emerged from the general election provided the opportunity for some key reforms – fixed parliaments, recall of MPs, backbench control of House time, second chamber reform – to be placed at the centre of the governing agreement forged between the Conservative and Liberal Democrat parties. The longevity of that coalition will therefore have clear implications for the progress made on some of these big issues for Westminster.

Chapter 5

Elections and Voting

DAVID DENVER

Elections are central to democratic political systems. It is through elections that citizens participate directly in the political process and ultimately determine the personnel and policies of governments. General elections are major national events accompanied by greatly increased political activity, discussion and interest, and intense media coverage. Such is the importance of general elections that, as David Butler (1998: 454) observed, 'History used to be marked off by the dates of Kings ... Now it is marked by the dates of [general] elections'.

We have, of course, lots of other elections other than those used to choose Members of Parliament. In addition to local government elections, we have had since 1979 European Parliament elections every five years, usually providing an interesting mid-term diversion. A further new set of important elections – to the Scottish Parliament and the Assemblies in Wales and Northern Ireland – was added in the late 1990s following the implementation of devolution. There are now, one might say, elections galore in the UK – and certainly enough to keep the keenest student of elections happy. Even between regular elections there are occasional by-elections to whet the appetite and also regular opinion polls measuring the electorate's voting intentions which have become essential tools of the psephological trade.

It is not just that there is now much more electoral data available than previously. Until fairly recently, Britain was wedded to the single member plurality system (SMPS) of election at all levels, with interest in change being confined to a small band of enthusiasts. Since the late 1990s, however, a variety of other systems has been introduced (as summarised in Table 5.1), and it is clear that the UK has become a veritable laboratory for anyone interested in the operation and impact of different electoral systems, even though using the Alternative Vote for general elections was decisively rejected in the May 2011 referendum.

This chapter focuses on two key electoral questions: why do people vote (or not) and why do they vote for one party rather than another? Political participants, observers and commentators, as well as academics, have sought answers to these questions since elections were invented and they still form the core of modern studies of voting.

Table 5.1   *UK electoral systems (as at 2010)*

System	Elections
Single Member Plurality System (SMSP) (a.k.a. First-past-the-post: FPTP)	House of Commons Some English councils/some wards in Welsh councils
Multi-Member Plurality System (MMPS)	Some English councils/some wards in Welsh councils
Mixed-Member Proportional (MMP) (a.k.a. Additional Member System – AMS)	Scottish Parliament Welsh Assembly London Assembly
Single Transferable Vote (STV)	Northern Ireland Assembly Scottish Councils
Regional Party (Closed) Lists	European Parliament
Supplementary Vote (SV)	Elected mayors in England

Turnout and turning out

Although the two are intimately related, it is useful to distinguish between two distinct analytical approaches to the study of electoral participation. The first focuses on 'turnout' – the aggregate percentage of the eligible electorate voting in an election – whether in different wards, constituencies, regions or countries. This varies according to the type of election and also over time; in any one election it varies across electoral units (such as constituencies). The second approach focuses on individuals – some 'turn out' in an election and some don't – and the key questions to be considered are: who votes, who doesn't and why?

In attempting to answer these questions three key approaches have been developed. The first concentrates on the social locations and circumstances of individual voters. It suggests that the resources that underpin political participation (knowledge, skills and time) are unevenly distributed across different social groups as are levels of involvement in community networks. As a result, some groups vote more than others. The second derives from rational choice theory and directs attention to the costs and benefits of voting, suggesting that turnout will be greater when there are more incentives to vote and costs are kept at a minimum. A third approach focuses on the connections between parties and voters. It is concerned with how parties mobilise voters and the impact of voters' identification with parties. Although these three approaches do not exhaust possible lines of explanation, they provide valuable frameworks within which to discuss variations in turnout and 'turning out' in Britain.

Variations in turnout

It is possible to identify variations in turnout across different types of elections, when comparing over time, and when comparing constituencies. All three variations offer useful insights into the factors driving turnout.

Different types of elections

Table 5.2 shows the turnout at different types of election in Britain between 2005 and 2010. Interpretation is complicated by the fact that different elections are sometimes held on the same day but even so it is apparent that different types of elections do not attract the same level of interest on the part of the electorate. The lowest turnout was for the 2009 European Parliament elections (34.5 per cent). European elections have consistently held the wooden spoon for participation (although the low level of interest in them has been partially disguised by holding them on the same day as local elections in both 2004 and 2009). Turnout in the 2007 Scottish Parliament election was well over 50 per cent but it was significantly lower in the Welsh Assembly elections of the same year. The two general elections at the start and end of the period saw the highest turnouts, even although participation in these was still poor by historical standards.

Clearly, then, the electorate do not view all elections as equally

Table 5.2   *Turnout in British elections, 2005–10 (percentages)*

General election 2005 (GB)	61.3
English locals 2006	36.6
Scottish Parliament 2007	53.9
Welsh Assembly 2007	46.4
English locals 2007	38.3
English/Welsh locals 2008	35.6
London Mayor 2008	45.3
English locals 2009	39.3
European Parliament 2009	34.5
General election 2010 (GB)	65.3

significant or 'salient'. Rather, turnout varies according to the perceived importance of the body being elected. In this case, the second approach mentioned above relating to the costs and benefits of voting provides a useful explanatory framework. The European Parliament is seen as remote (its activities being virtually unreported in the British media) and there is a good deal of antipathy to the European Union in general. Local councils have steadily lost powers to the central government and voters could be forgiven for thinking that it does not make an enormous difference whichever party controls their council. The Scottish Parliament has extensive powers, however, and that is reflected in the relatively good turnout, while the Welsh Assembly, which has lower turnouts, is more restricted (and setting it up was much more controversial). Despite devolution, general elections are still seen by the voters as the most important contests; as suggested above they are major national events.

Although the idea was first developed in relation to European elections, all elections in Britain other than general elections can be described as 'second-order' elections (Reif and Schmitt 1980). Scottish Parliament elections are at least a partial exception but in local elections, for example, not a great deal appears to be at stake, there is much less media coverage and the parties do not campaign very strongly. In general elections, on the other hand, there is saturation media coverage, the parties mount intense national and local campaigns and the electorate usually think it important who wins. These are 'first-order' elections and electors are therefore keener to turn out and vote in them.

General elections over time

Figure 5.1 charts the percentage turnout in general elections since 1950. There were very high turnouts in the first two elections (1950 and 1951) and then a long period with no discernible trend. In 2001, however, turnout slumped dramatically to a record low. There was something of a recovery in 2005 and (more so) in 2010 but, even so, national turnout remained well below the average for the post-war period.

In part, these variations can be explained by the expected closeness of the election concerned, together with the extent to which the parties were perceived as offering significantly different choices (Clarke *et al.* 2004: 261–74). There is clearly more incentive for people to vote if they think that an election is likely to be close, rather than a foregone conclusion, and if they believe that significantly different policies would be pursued by the different parties. In 2010, for example, a much closer election was expected than had been the case in 2001 and 2005 and, as would be expected, turnout did increase. However, this is plainly not the whole story as participation was still left at a relatively low level.

Figure 5.1   *General election turnout in Great Britain, 1950–2010*

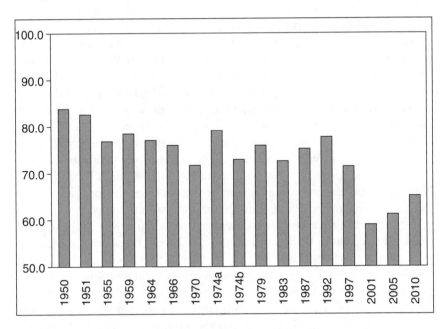

Variations across constituencies

In any general election turnout varies markedly across constituencies. In the 2010 election, for example, excluding Northern Ireland, it ranged from just over 44 per cent (Manchester Central) to almost 78 per cent (East Renfrewshire). Investigations of these variations have drawn attention to two main sorts of explanatory factor: the social composition of constituencies and the safeness or marginality of the seat.

Table 5.3 shows correlation coefficients measuring the strength and direction of the relationship between the social composition of constituencies and turnout levels in 2010. The closer a coefficient is to zero, the weaker the relationship. A positive figure means that as the score on the variable in question increases, so does turnout; a negative coefficient shows that as a variable score increases, turnout decreases. Turnout in the 2010 election, in general, was consistently higher in more prosperous, middle-class constituencies and also in more rural areas; it was consistently lower in large cities and in less affluent areas with higher levels of social housing. The patterns revealed in Table 5.3 are very well established and have changed little over the last 50 years at least. This familiar pattern of turnout variation is one that is also found at local and devolved elections (Rallings and Thrasher 1990; Denver and Hands 2004).

Table 5.3   *Correlations between turnout and constituency characteristics, 2010*

% professional & managerial	0.645	% in agriculture	0.370
% manual workers	−0.669	persons per hectare	−0.390
% owner-occupiers	0.650	% ethnic minority	−0.244
% social renters	−0.691	% with degrees	0.362
% private renters	−0.125	% with no car	−0.788
% aged 18–24	−0.396	% aged 65+	0.287
		Constituency marginality 2005	0.459

Notes: 'Marginality' is 100 minus the winning party's ('notional') percentage majority in the 2005 election. All of the coefficients shown are statistically significant.

Table 5.3 also shows a positive correlation between previous marginality and turnout. In other words, the more marginal the seat, the higher was the turnout. Electors are more inclined to go to the polls in places where the contest is likely to be close than in places that are rock solid for one party or another. It is also the case that parties campaign harder – efforts at mobilisation are greater – in constituencies where the result may be in doubt than in those where they have no chance or expect to cruise to victory.

It is important to emphasise that the coefficients in Table 5.3 tell us nothing about the behaviour of individuals, only about constituencies. Thus we cannot infer from the strong positive correlation between the proportion of owner-occupiers in a constituency and turnout that owner-occupiers as a group vote in greater proportions than others. Just because the proportion of households without a car is negatively related to constituency turnout does not of itself tell us that people without cars are less likely to vote. Both *may* be true but from aggregate data we can only draw conclusions about collectivities (constituencies in this case) and not about the individuals who comprise them. To investigate variations in the propensity of individuals to turn out we have to make use of survey data.

Variations in 'turning out'

Over the past 30 years or so, a wealth of evidence has accumulated enabling us to describe who votes and who doesn't in Britain (see, for example, Clarke *et al.* 2004; Denver 2007). In terms of social characteristics, there is a broad consensus among researchers that propensity to vote varies with age, marital status, housing tenure and residential mobility. Older people turn out more than younger age groups, married people more than those not married, owner-occupiers more than renters and long-term residents of a community more than recent arrivals. No other social characteristics have been consistently found to affect turnout. Unlike in many other countries, for example, there is no significant difference between men and women in this respect and, once other factors are taken into account, the evidence about occupational class is mixed.

Figures showing the turnout of different social groups in the 2010 election are given in Table 5.4. The regular differences remain – turnout was higher among those who are married (or widowed) and owner-occupiers. It also increased very steadily with age (although the turnout of young people was not as bad as in the 2005 election). In line with most recent surveys it is also the case that those who have white-collar occupations, are better educated and better off were more inclined to vote. As noted above, explanations of the social patterns of non-voting frequently refer to the different resources (such as knowledge, skills and time) available to different groups

For many citizens, however, voting is not a matter of bringing resources to bear or calculating costs and benefits but can best be described as 'expressive' or 'normative'. 'Expressive' voters may turn out to express their support for democracy but more commonly they are expressing their long-term commitment to, or support for, a party – their party identification. The more strongly someone identifies with or supports a party, the more likely they are to vote. This is not difficult to understand; people who are strong party supporters are more likely to want to demonstrate their support by voting than those with a less strong commitment or none at all. The figures in Table 5.5 show that this happens consistently. Moreover, there is no marked decline in turnout in the last few elections among 'very strong' identifiers. The problem is that there are now fewer strong identifiers than there used to be. In the 1960s over 40 per cent of voters had a very strong party identification and only about 10 per cent had no attachment. In 2010, according to the British Election Study (BES) internet poll, the respective figures were 18 per cent and 16 per cent. So the group with the highest turnout has been decreasing in size and the one with the lowest turnout increasing. We have here a major source of the recent lower turnouts in Britain.

'Normative' voters go to the polls because they see it as part of a citizen's duty to vote. In 2010, a large majority of BES pre-election respondents agreed that it is every citizen's duty to vote (75 per cent) and most also said that they would feel guilty if they didn't vote (56 per cent).

Table 5.4 *Turnout of social groups in 2010 (percentages)*

Sex		Housing	
Men	65	Owner-occupiers	67
Women	61	Renters	52
Marital status		*Highest education qualification*	
Married/Widowed	70	None	53
Live with partner	53	GCSE (or equivalent)	62
Separated/divorced	59	A-level (or equivalent)	63
Single/never married	56	Technical	63
Occupation		Professional	64
Professional and managerial	71	Degree	67
Other non-manual	61		
Manual	54		
Age		*Income*	
18–24	48	Lowest third	55
25–34	55	Middle third	65
35–44	60	Top third	70
45–54	65		
55–64	69		
65+	77		

Data from: British Election Study (BES) 2010 post-election survey. The original data have been weighted to reflect the actual turnout in the election as well as for demographics

Table 5.5 *Turnout by strength of party identification, 1997–2010 (percentages)*

	Very strong	Fairly strong	Not very strong	No party identification
Voted 1997	82	83	65	57
Voted 2001	83	77	56	27
Voted 2005	79	70	57	33
Voted 2010	82	75	61	36

Data from: Relevant BES surveys

Table 5.6   *Voting as duty by age group, 2010*

	18–24	25–34	35–44	45–54	55–64	65+	All
Agree voting is duty (%)	58	68	74	74	80	88	75
Agree feel guilty if did not vote (%)	31	47	48	60	68	73	56

Data from: BES pre-campaign face-to-face survey 2010

When the figures are broken down by age, however (see Table 5.6) a striking pattern emerges. Younger people are clearly less likely to think of voting as being a duty than older people. It has been suggested (Clarke *et al.* 2004) that the 'Thatcher' and 'Blair' generations are significantly less 'civic minded' than their predecessors. This also helps explain recent poor turnouts – even when a close result is expected as in 2010 – and is likely to continue to have a depressing effect on turnout for some time.

Party support

The sudden slump in turnout in 2001 provoked much hand-wringing among the chattering classes and the continuing poor turnouts since then suggest, worryingly, that a significant portion of the electorate has become disengaged from electoral politics. Nonetheless, in the immediate aftermath of elections commentators generally pay little attention to turnout. What matters most is how the parties do. In analysing party support we can make a distinction analogous to that between turnout and turning out. On the one hand, there is a focus on 'party performance' – the overall shares of votes (and seats) won by the various parties in different elections, at different times and in different places. On the other, the concern is with how and why individual voters decide which party to vote for – their 'party choice' – and hence on why elections are won and lost. As the last point implies, there is, of course, an intimate relationship between the decisions of individuals and the outcomes of elections.

Party performance

Table 5.7 shows the distribution of support among the parties at the general elections in 2005 and 2010. The Conservatives' vote share increased in 2010 and they came out on top for the first time since 1992. Support for Labour slumped while the Liberal Democrats registered a slight improvement. 'Other' parties (especially UKIP and the BNP) also advanced. These changes were not enough, however, to provide the Conservatives with a majority in the House of Commons. Although they obtained a larger vote share than Labour had in 2005 they won just under 50 fewer seats due to the bias of the electoral system against them.

There was a gap of five years between the two elections, of course, and we can use opinion poll data to provide a detailed picture of the course of party popularity over the inter-election period (see Figure 5.2). After the 2005 general election – as is normal for the winning party – Labour received a short-term fillip in the polls, its post-election 'honeymoon'. Within a few months, however, support for the government began to decline and this continued more or less steadily for almost two years. During this period, David Cameron became Conservative leader and soon afterwards, for the first time in many years, the Tories established a clear and sustained lead over Labour in voting intentions. In June 2007, however, things changed dramatically. Gordon Brown became prime minister and Labour's popularity increased sharply. This improvement proved to be short-lived. In the last few months of 2007, as Brown dithered over whether or not to call a general election, support dropped back and things got worse in 2008. Following a poorly received budget in March, support for the government dropped like a stone, leaving David Cameron's Conservatives with a huge lead. In late 2008, however,

Table 5.7   *Share of votes and seats won (Great Britain) 2005 and 2010*

	2005 %	2010 %	2005 N	2010 N
Conservative	33.2	37.0	198	306
Labour	36.1	29.7	355	258
Liberal Democrat	22.6	23.6	62	57
SNP/Plaid Cymru	2.3	2.3	9	9
Other	5.8	7.5	4	2

Notes: The Speaker is treated as an 'other'.

Figure 5.2   *Trends in party support, 2005–March 2010*

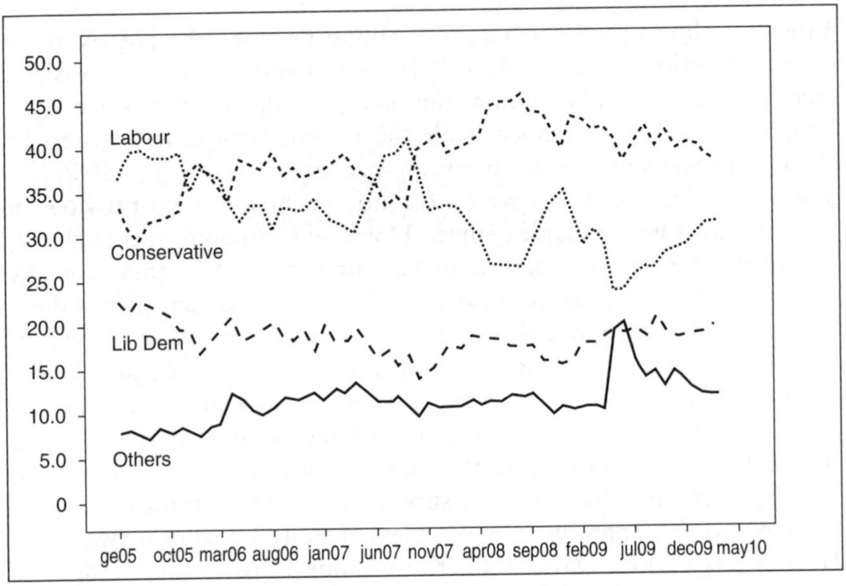

Note: For each month the graph shows the mean percentage intending to vote for each party on the basis of results from five firms which polled consistently throughout the period: Communicate Research, ICM, IpsosMORI, Populus and YouGov.

the prime minister appeared to distinguish himself in handling the financial and economic crisis and Labour narrowed the gap between themselves and the Conservatives. Again this improvement proved to be short-lived and during the first part of 2009 the Conservatives maintained a clear lead over their rivals. As usually happens in the run up to an election, however, the government's standing with the electorate improved steadily, if slowly, from the summer of 2009 and the gap between the two leading parties narrowed.

The popularity of the Liberal Democrats declined quickly after the 2005 election (as it usually does after elections) then wobbled about a bit before declining further during 2007. In December of that year Nick Clegg replaced Menzies Campbell as party leader and the fortunes of the party recovered a little. From early 2009 the party's position slowly improved. For most of the period, 'others' (which includes the SNP, Plaid Cymru, the Green party, UKIP and the BNP) hovered around 10 per cent of voting intentions. This was an unprecedented level of sustained support for 'minor' parties. In May/June 2009, around the time of the European election, support for others shot up (as had happened at the previous European election in 2004) but drifted down as the general election approached.

The level of support for others and the fact that the Conservatives were more popular than Labour most of the time are the two features that stand out most clearly in the graph and both were confirmed in various 'second-order' elections during these years. At local elections, the Conservatives made spectacular progress so that by 2009 they had many more councillors in England and Wales than either Labour or the Liberal Democrats (or, indeed, both combined). In London in 2008 the Conservative Boris Johnson ousted Labour's Ken Livingstone as mayor. In the Scottish Parliament election of 2007, Labour lost its position as the most popular party in Scotland for the first time in almost 50 years (and the SNP formed a minority government). In the European Parliament elections of 2009 Labour came third in share of votes, with only 15.7 per cent, behind the Conservatives (27.7 per cent) and UKIP (16.5 per cent). In this election too, the British National Party (BNP) won two seats.

To a large extent, the ups and downs of party popularity both in the inter-election period (and during the 2010 campaign – as discussed in Box 5.1) are related to voters' reactions to the party leaders. Menzies Campbell was ditched by the Liberal Democrats because the party was languishing in the polls and his replacement by Nick Clegg appeared to bring about a slow improvement. David Cameron's predecessors as Conservative leader – Michael Howard and, before that, Iain Duncan Smith – had been unable to make much of an impression on the electorate. Cameron was more successful and under his leadership the Conservatives achieved much better poll ratings. When Gordon Brown became prime minister in June 2007 the change in Labour's fortunes was immediate. When he became unpopular, Labour support fell. The importance of the leaders to their parties' fortunes during the campaign is obvious.

In general (although the data are not shown here). opinion poll trends in party support are closely related to trends in the electorate's overall satisfaction with the various party leaders, views about which would make the best prime minister and assessments of how well each is doing his job. Since few voters will have a clear idea of what being leader of the opposition entails, far less being Leader of the Liberal Democrats, these sorts of poll questions probably tap vague impressions of the politicians concerned – whether they seem generally likeable and competent – rather than reflecting very well-informed judgements. However, the fact that overall levels of party support and overall reactions to leaders are closely associated is not proof that one (satisfaction or dissatisfaction with Gordon Brown, for example) causes the other (decisions about which party to support). The two matters are obviously connected – by voting for a particular party people are in effect voting for a particular person to be prime minister – but it is possible that both are caused by something else, such as how well the government is managing the NHS, for example.

Box 5.1   The 2010 election campaign

Entering the 2010 election campaign things looked fairly rosy for the Conservatives, bleak for Labour and unexciting for the Liberal Democrats. What happened next, however, was little short of sensational. For the first time in Britain there were televised live debates between the party leaders with the Liberal Democrat leader, Nick Clegg, being accorded the same status as Gordon Brown and David Cameron. Figure 5.3 charts the trend in voting intentions from the day that the election date was announced through to the actual result on polling day.

The first leaders' debate took place in the second week of campaigning. By general consent, Nick Clegg made the best impression and, as the graph shows, the impact on public opinion was electric. Two YouGov polls over the weekend following actually put the Liberal Democrats in the lead. Although they declined from this peak during the next week, the Liberal Democrats largely held on to their new-found eminence and were consistently running second to the Conservatives. The latter's ship steadied somewhat but Labour slipped into third place. There was no clear 'winner', in the second leaders' debate but it was widely thought that David Cameron came off best in the third. Whether as a result of this or not, the Conservatives inched forward in the penultimate and also the last week of campaigning while the other parties remained close together in the high twenties. In the event, Labour performed slightly better than expected and the Liberal Democrats somewhat worse. Indeed, the apparent last-minute evaporation of Liberal Democrat support remains one of the mysteries of the election.

→

In addition, the published poll figures are aggregated responses to the relevant survey questions and tell us nothing about the extent to which individual voters relate their choice of party to their evaluations of leaders – a question considered further below.

Variations in party performance across constituencies

A glance at constituency election results is enough to confirm the rather obvious point that party performances vary from place to place (and the same is true of wards in local elections). Elections would be rather boring if they didn't. As with turnout, an important strand of electoral analysis in Britain focuses on attempting to explain these variations. In the first place, there are important regional differences. Table 5.8 shows voting patterns in different parts of Britain and it is clear that, with the

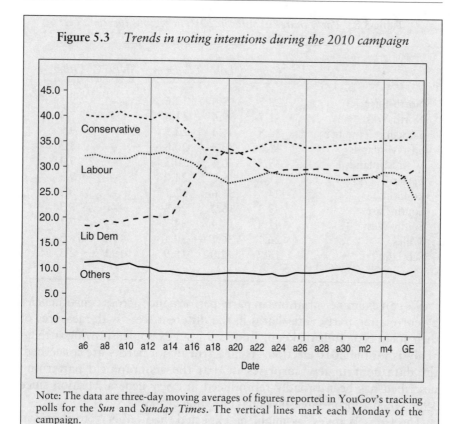

Figure 5.3   *Trends in voting intentions during the 2010 campaign*

Note: The data are three-day moving averages of figures reported in YouGov's tracking polls for the *Sun* and *Sunday Times*. The vertical lines mark each Monday of the campaign.

exception of London, there remains a broad north–south division. Labour's strongest areas outside London are Scotland, Wales and the three northernmost English regions. In each of these it was the largest party. On the other hand, Labour trailed the Conservatives in the Midlands and came a poor third in the south and east of England. Conservative support across regions is a mirror image of that for Labour but the Liberal Democrats had a relatively even spread of support across the country although, as usual, in 2010 they did rather better than average in the south of England and, on this occasion, rather poorly in Scotland. A north–south division is even more apparent in terms of seats won. In Scotland, Wales and northern England, despite making gains, the Conservatives won only 52 seats compared with 171 for Labour and 25 for the Liberal Democrats. In the eastern, south-east and south-west regions, by contrast, the tally was 162 for the Conservatives, 10 for Labour and 23 for the Liberal Democrats.

Table 5.8   *Party shares of votes in 2010 in regions (percentages)*

	Con	Lab	Lib Dem	SNP/PC	Other
North-East	23.7	43.6	23.6	–	9.1
North-West	31.7	39.4	21.6	–	7.3
Yorkshire/Humber	32.8	34.4	22.9	–	9.9
East Midlands	41.2	29.8	20.8	–	8.2
West Midlands	39.5	30.6	20.5	–	9.4
Eastern	47.1	19.6	24.0	–	9.3
London	34.5	36.6	22.1	–	6.8
South-East	49.3	16.2	26.2	–	8.3
South-West	42.8	15.4	34.7	–	7.1
Wales	26.1	36.2	20.1	11.3	6.3
Scotland	16.7	42.0	18.9	19.9	2.5

We can examine variations in party performance across constituencies by correlating party vote shares in the different seats with measures of their socio-economic makeup. Table 5.9 is an example, showing such an analysis for the 2010 election. As far as the major parties are concerned, the data contain few surprises in that the geographical patterning described has been broadly reproduced in every general election since 1966 when appropriate census data became available.

The Conservatives, as might be expected, had larger vote shares in constituencies where there were more professional and managerial workers, owner-occupiers, older voters, people with degrees and in more rural areas. They performed less well where there were more manual workers, social renters, younger people, students, those having no educational qualifications and no car, people belonging to ethnic minorities, and in more urban areas. The pattern of Labour support was almost a mirror image of that for the Conservatives while that for the Liberal Democrats was, broadly, a paler reflection of it. Unlike the Conservatives, however, the Liberal Democrat vote was slightly stronger where there were more young people and students. This may reflect impressionistic accounts during the campaign that younger people were the most impressed by Nick Clegg's performance in the leaders' debates.

The large numbers of UKIP and BNP candidates in 2010 enable us to present a similar analysis of variations in these parties' votes. The coefficients for UKIP are an unusual mixture. For example, the party did better where there were more owner-occupiers but also prospered where there were more manual workers and people lacking educational qualifications. On the other hand, UKIP did worse in areas where there were more

Table 5.9 *Correlations between party shares of vote in 2010 and constituency characteristics*

	Conservative	Labour	LibDem	UKIP	BNP
% professional/ managerial	0.553	−0.532	0.317	−0.152	−0.558
% manual workers	−0.602	0.591	−0.349	0.116	0.573
% owner occupiers	0.603	−0.552	0.088	0.295	−0.123
% social renters	−0.676	0.680	−0.247	−0.227	0.306
% aged 18–24	−0.406	0.313	0.094	−0.304	−0.076*
% aged 65+	0.293	−0.409	0.162	0.343	−0.073*
% in agriculture	0.296	−0.481	0.232	0.186	−0.235
Persons per hectare	−0.315	0.387	−0.031*	−0.291	−0.021*
% with degrees	0.164	−0.238	0.351	−0.378	−0.582
% no qualifications	−0.538	0.582	−0.424	0.139	0.642
% students	−0.344	0.216	0.180	−0.334	−0.175
% with no car	−0.738	0.737	−0.218	−0.319	0.225
% ethnic minority	−0.229	0.343	−0.078	−0.301	0.005*
(N)	(630)	(630)	(630)	(556)	(337)

Note: All coefficients are statistically significant at the 0.01 level except those asterisked.

professionals and people with degrees (characteristic of more middle-class areas) but also where there were more social renters, people with no car and ethnic minorities (characteristic of more working-class areas). The BNP clearly did better in urban working-class areas – there are strong positive correlations with proportion of manual workers, social renters, people with no educational qualifications and having no car – and significantly less well the more professionals and managers, people employed in agriculture, owner-occupiers, students and people with a degree there were in a constituency.

It is important to emphasise again, however, that this sort of analysis relates to *constituencies* and not *people*. The figures tell us how well the parties perform in different sorts of constituencies; we cannot use them to deduce how different sections of the electorate vote. To do that, survey data are required.

Explaining party choice

Early studies of party choice in Britain concentrated heavily on describing 'who votes for whom'. The implicit assumption was that parties represented different groups and membership of the relevant groups was enough to explain why someone voted for the appropriate party. In the 1960s, however, this approach was refined by David Butler and Donald Stokes (Butler and Stokes 1969) who put forward what can now be described as the classic explanation of party choice. In brief, this suggested that the voter's choice of party was largely based on class and party identification. Most working-class people voted Labour and most middle-class people voted Conservative. This basic alignment was supplemented by the fact that most people were brought up to think of themselves as supporters of one party or another (with upwards of 40 per cent of the electorate describing themselves as *very strong* party supporters) and thus developed an enduring loyalty to a party which they would support, for the most part, through thick and thin. The emphasis in this explanation is on stability – class and party identity didn't change much and so most people always voted for the same party – rather than volatility. Electoral change would be slow and gradual.

With the passage of time, however, psephologists have largely discounted the Butler–Stokes explanation. As already mentioned, party identification has declined markedly. Moreover, although the subject sparked some lively academic debate in the 1980s, there is now ample evidence that social class is no longer a very good predictor of party support (Clarke *et al.* 2004, 2009). How, then, are we to explain party choice at the start of the twenty-first century?

Valence voting

The short answer is 'valence voting' (Clarke *et al.* 2004, 2009) although the meaning of this is not immediately apparent and requires some explanation. In their earlier work, Butler and Stokes made a distinction between what they called 'position' issues and 'valence' issues. Position issues are those on which people can take positions (for or against public ownership of industries, for example). Valence issues are issues on which nearly everyone takes the same side. Not many favour increased crime or oppose peace and prosperity, for example. In recent times, politics has come increasingly to be about valence issues – the differences between the parties on position issues have become relatively small as they all crowd into the 'middle ground'. For voters deciding which party to support, then, the question is not which party has the ideological or policy positions that they approve of but which is likely to be most competent at achieving the goals that are widely shared among all voters (such as reduced crime, a healthy economy, a well-run health service). Making judgements like this is not straightforward and some voters at least, therefore, tend to use a convenient short-cut. They make judgements about the party leaders, which is a much simpler task. We don't need to know much about policies or politics to decide whether we like or dislike the party leaders whom we see often enough on TV. We can all have opinions about people without necessarily knowing very much about them.

The key to party choice nowadays, this argument suggests, is how well parties perform or might perform in office and how voters rate the different party leaders. It is worth noting that this last point is the exact opposite of what the Butler–Stokes model implies. It used to be that people's party identification determined what they thought about party leaders. Labour supporters liked Labour leaders and disliked Tory leaders. For Conservatives it was the other way round. Now that party identification has withered, it is evaluations of party leaders that seem to influence strongly the voters' choice of party.

Unlike voting based on class or a party identification largely inherited through the family, evaluations of leaders are subject to rapid change. For a long time in the 1980s, Prime Minister Margaret Thatcher was thought by the voters to be 'resolute' and 'determined'. As she became unpopular she was seen more as 'stubborn' and 'inflexible'. Tony Blair was initially thought of as 'sincere' and 'trustworthy' but by the end of his premiership large majorities of the electorate thought that he had lost touch with ordinary people and could not be trusted. In September 2007, according to IpsosMori, 44 per cent of the public were satisfied with the performance of the Prime Minister, Gordon Brown, and 26 per cent dissatisfied. Less than a year later, in July 2008, 21 per cent were satisfied and 72 per cent dissatisfied.

Opinions about party leaders were strongly related to party choice in 2010. For example, Table 5.10 shows the relationship between voters' preferred prime minister and their party choice and the two are obviously closely connected. Of those who had a clear preference for prime minister the great majority voted for his party (even although quite a lot of Clegg admirers did not). It is theoretically possible, of course, that – as Butler and Stokes would have had it – reactions to leaders are conditioned by a person's choice of party which has been made on other grounds. That is to say that the causal connection still runs from party preference to leader evaluations rather than vice versa. This could be the case for some voters but it is an implausible interpretation of the behaviour of the modern electorate as a whole. More detailed analysis than is possible here demonstrates that leadership evaluations continue to affect party choice even when numerous other variables (including party identification) are taken into account (Evans and Andersen 2005).

Table 5.10   *Preferred prime minister and party choice, 2010 (percentages)*

	Cameron	Brown	Clegg
Conservative	82	1	6
Labour	2	80	13
Liberal Democrat	8	13	74
Other	8	6	7

Data from: BES 2010 post-election internet survey

There is more to valence voting than reactions to the party leaders, however. Evaluating the leaders is only a short cut to making a more general evaluation of the overall relative competence of the parties in relation to achieving goals that are widely shared. The voter is pictured as to some extent weighing up how well the governing party has done and is likely to do in future, compared with how well the other parties might do. Since the latter has to be speculative, voters are likely to rely more on the rather harder evidence of what the government has done. In this explanatory framework, therefore, elections are clearly performing their basic function in that they are being used by the voters to hold the government accountable rather than as an opportunity to express tribal loyalties. In the Scottish Parliament election of 2007, for example, survey respondents were asked to evaluate how well Labour had performed as the Scottish government. Of those who thought the party had done a good or fairly good job 58 per cent voted Labour whereas only 6 per cent

Table 5.11   *Evaluation of government performance and party choice in 2010 (percentages)*

	Economy		NHS		Immigration	
	Well	Badly	Well	Badly	Well	Badly
Conservative	14	67	11	64	14	67
Labour	67	4	58	3	71	15
Liberal Democrat	23	21	25	19	22	21
Other	5	12	6	13	4	12

Data from: BES 2010 post-election internet survey

of those who thought the performance had been bad or fairly bad did so. Again this pattern proved robust when other variables (including underlying partisanship) were taken into account (see Johns *et al.* 2009).

A similar pattern is evident in the 2010 general election. BES respondents were asked how well they thought the incumbent government had done in a number of important issue areas. On managing the economy in general 33 per cent said that they had done fairly or very well and 51 per cent fairly or very badly (the remainder having no clear view). On the National Health Service the respective figures were 37 per cent well and 46 per cent badly while on immigration they were 14 per cent well and 67 per cent badly. All of these can be considered valence issues and when we relate these evaluations of government performance to party choice the results are as in Table 5.11. Plainly, very few people voted Labour if they thought that the government had done badly on each of these issues. On the other hand, majorities – if not overwhelming ones – of those who thought that the government had done well turned out to support Labour. The problem for Labour was that rather more people were critical of government performance than willing to voice approval.

Is that it?

In many ways the 'valence voting' explanation of party choice is relatively straightforward. It also chimes with media coverage and public discussion of elections in a way that some earlier theories did not. What, indeed, could be more obvious than saying that people decide which way to vote on the basis of their estimation of the party leaders and of the performance of the government on important issues? From this perspective there is no mystery about the fact that the Conservatives recovered from three successive general election defeats to emerge as the largest party in both votes and seats in 2010. They found a relatively likeable and competent leader while Gordon Brown lacked his predecessor's popular appeal. The government, moreover, was regarded as less than competent in a number of key areas.

Nonetheless, explaining why people vote the way that they do cannot be too simplistic. The electorate is large and heterogeneous and no one would argue that all of them are valence voters. There remain large numbers who identify with a party and support it no matter what. There are also some voters who have clearly worked out positions on central (or even not so central) policy issues or take a particular ideological position and make their decisions in elections on that basis. There may even be a few voters who still think of politics in class terms. There are also numerous other influences on voting that need to be taken into account

– the mass media, campaigning, regional differences and specific events such as the Iraq war, for example. Valence voting is itself a simplifying device for analysts. Nonetheless, valence concerns have clearly increased in importance among the electorate. This has been encouraged by the rise of television as the primary means of political communication and the intense focus of the media on party leaders. This makes for a tough life for the latter – the fortunes of their parties are largely riding on their shoulders and, these days, the penalty for failure is swift demotion. Another consequence is that, in choosing leaders, parties increasingly have to pay attention to the electoral appeal of likely candidates (rather than ideology, standing in the party or even the ability to govern, for example). Whether this is a welcome development is a matter for debate.

Chapter 6

Political Parties and the British Party System

PHILIP COWLEY

After the 1997 general election the UK was governed by one political party. After the 2010 general election it was governed by ten. The Conservative–Lib Dem government was the first peacetime coalition at Westminster since the 1930s. Following the Scottish and Welsh elections in 2007, both the Scottish National Party and Plaid became parties of government, and in Northern Ireland the executive comprised five separate parties: the Democratic Unionists, Sinn Féin, the Ulster Unionists, the Social Democratic and Labour Party and the Alliance. Moreover, in each of these four cases, the administration was not the majority government usually associated with Westminster-style systems, but instead either a coalition (as in Westminster, Wales, Northern Ireland) or a minority administration (Scotland).

This remarkable shift has in part been the result of the changing nature of government (and governance) in the UK, especially the process of devolution on which Labour embarked after 1997. But it is also a result of the continuing fragmentation of the British party system, a process which began long before, but which picked up pace after 1997. In historical perspective, however, it is nothing new. Prior to the partition of Ireland in 1922, Irish Nationalist MPs frequently formed a sizeable bloc in the Commons, often holding the balance of power, and coalition or minority governments have been far more common than is often realised. Of the 60 years between 1885 and 1945, only ten saw one party govern by commanding a majority in the House of Commons (Searle 1995) and there has long also been extensive experience of coalition in local government (Laver *et al.* 1987; Mellors 1989). But, in terms of the transformation since 1945, it looks as if 2010 was another staging post in the long march away from two-party politics in Britain.

The fragmentation of the party system

At the general election in May 2010, a full third of British voters opted for a party other than Labour or the Conservatives. It was the lowest combined two-party share of the vote since and including 1922, the first election after the partition of Ireland, and the first since Labour overtook the Liberals in the popular vote (Curtice *et al.* 2010). It was not a freak result: the combined two-party share has been dropping steadily for decades, and similarly low figures are also now seen in other British elections (as Table 6.1 shows). In 2009 the combined Conservative and Labour share in the European Parliament elections fell as low as 43 per cent, and was also below 50 per cent in Scotland and a mere 55 per cent in Wales in the devolved elections of 2007. The elections of 2011 saw the Con–Lab share in Wales rise slightly (back up to 67 per cent) but it fell yet further in Scotland (to just 46 per cent). And where one of the major parties has been pushed out of a top two position it is not as if an alternative two-party system has replaced it. The only (partial) exception to this pattern of fragmentation is the London Mayoralty, where in 2008 almost 80 per cent of votes went to either the Conservative or Labour candidates. But the London Mayoralty can hardly be claimed as a bastion for the established parties, since in the first election in 2000, the Conservative and Labour share was a mere 40 per cent, with Ken Livingstone winning as an independent, beating all the parties. The high percentage in 2008 was more a product of the two main parties fielding high profile candidates, in Livingstone and Boris Johnson; in the London Assembly elections, which took place on the same day, the two-party share was noticeably lower, at 65 per cent.

In terms of votes, the most significant cause of the fragmentation of the party system has been the rise of the Liberal Democrats (and their various predecessor parties). In the end, the 2010 result was widely seen as a disappointment for the party; despite 'Cleggmania' and the surge in the opinion polls that the party experienced in the polls during the campaign – discussed in Chapter 5 in this book – the party ended the election losing seats compared to their position in 2005. Yet they did this polling some 24 per cent of the vote. This was the best Liberal Democrat share ever achieved, and the second best by a third party since 1923, only bettered by the Liberal–SDP Alliance in 1983. To focus on the detail of the Lib Dems' performance – and the fact that they failed (yet again) to break through – is to ignore the fact that (yet again) they form a sizeable bloc in the Commons, on a par with that in the 1920s, and that they were the choice of one in four voters.

In the European elections in 2009 a full 40 per cent of the votes went to parties other than the Conservatives, Labour and the Lib Dems. The

Table 6.1   *Two-party shares, 2007–11*

	% share of vote (Con+Lab)	*% share of vote (top two parties)*	*Top two parties, if not Con+Lab*
Scottish Parliament (2011)	46	77	SNP/Lab
Welsh Assembly (2011)	67	67	
Westminster (2010)	67	67	
European Parliament (2009)	43	44	Cons/UKIP
London Assembly (2008)	65	65	
London Mayor (2008)	79	79	

Notes: The figures for Scotland, Wales and the London Assembly are for constituency results; those for the London Mayoralty are first preference votes. Data for Westminster and for the European Parliament exclude Northern Ireland.

vote share being claimed for the 'others' in opinion polls diminished as the general election approached, and collectively they polled just under 10 per cent in 2010. Yet this was up by around two points on 2005, and represented the highest share ever seen in British politics. The three most established of the UK-wide minor parties – the BNP, Greens and UKIP (discussed in Box 6.1) – are now all realistic contenders for seats in at least one parliament or assembly, as well as in local government. They also all matter as a constraint on the activities of the major parties, who are constantly aware of the manoeuvrings on their flanks, aware that the attractions of the minor parties can (and do) cost them votes.

Numerically the least significant splinter from the two-party mould are the nationalist parties in Scotland and Wales (along with Northern Ireland, which is discussed in Chapter 8 of this book). In any UK-wide context, the nationalists are fairly insignificant (it is notable that UKIP alone garnered more votes in 2010 than the Scottish and Welsh nationalists combined), but this comparison obviously understates their importance in the countries themselves. By 2010 both were parties of government. In the 2007 Scottish Parliament elections, the Scottish Nationalist Party polled some 33 per cent of the constituency vote, and managed to push Labour, once so hegemonic in Scotland, into second place. In 2011 they polled better (45 per cent) and achieved a majority of seats. The European elections in 2009 also saw them top the poll in Scotland. Even in the Westminster election – where they tend to do less well – they still polled 20 per cent of the Scottish poll in 2010. In Wales,

Box 6.1   The BNP, the Greens and UKIP

The 2010 election saw a record electoral challenge from the British National Party (BNP), the Greens, and the United Kingdom Independent Party (UKIP). All stood more candidates than they – or any of their precursor parties – had ever stood before, and made serious challenges for a number of seats. The results, themselves, were also record-breaking.

In early 2006 David Cameron had dismissed UKIP as a 'bunch of fruitcakes and loonies and closet racists'. Yet the party would push Labour into third place in the European elections in 2009, and in 2010 they averaged 3.5 per cent of the vote where they stood and 3.2 per cent of the overall British vote, the best performance by a 'minor' party in history. They did not, however, manage to take any seats and within months of the election, the party's leader, Lord Pearson announced he was standing down – saying that he was 'not much good' at party politics – and Nigel Farage was subsequently re-elected as party leader, a position from which he had resigned in 2009.

The BNP secured their first members of the European Parliament in 2009, and in 2010 polled some 1.9 per cent of the British vote, again more than any far far-right party had ever managed. They polled an average of 3.8 per cent in seats they were contesting. Yet they too failed to capture any seats. The party's leader, Nick Griffin, was heavily defeated in Barking, a seat which the party had thought it could take from Labour (but where they eventually came third). And despite the record performance, the BNP share of the vote in seats where it stood was actually lower than in 2005, and the failure to break through, allied with disappointing council election results, was to trigger a post-election split within the party.

In many ways, the Greens had an appalling election. They averaged only 1.8 per cent of the vote where they stood, which was down on their performance in 2005, and just 1.0 per cent overall. They saved a mere handful of deposits. But they managed to capture a seat – when Caroline Lucas became the UK's first Green MP, taking Brighton Pavilion from Labour – and that was enough to compensate for failure elsewhere.

Academics, and other observers, often worry about the share of the vote that parties achieve, sometimes down to decimal places. Parties themselves worry far more about the number of seats. The BNP and UKIP failed to take seats in 2010, hence their various post-election troubles. The Greens managed to take a seat, and celebrated the election as a triumph. In itself, though, this is a sign that these parties are now more established as serious political players than they were a decade ago. They are no longer content simply to pile up protest votes.

the performance of Plaid – as Plaid Cymru became known in 2006 – is less impressive, but they polled 22 per cent of the vote in the National Assembly elections in 2007 and entered government in coalition with Labour. Their performance in 2011 saw them fall back slightly, to 19 per cent, and they returned to Opposition, with Labour governing as a minority administration.

The fragmentation of the British party system often attracts much hand-wringing, especially from those who dislike one or more of the newly established parties – most obviously (though not exclusively) the BNP. Yet an alternative way of reflecting on recent developments would be to note that the party system increasingly reflects the varied views of the British public, and probably does so better than the old two-party system, which tended to submerge and mask divergent attitudes. In a distinctly Eurosceptic country like Britain, it is not that much of a surprise for an anti-European party like UKIP to do well in European elections. Research also shows that the BNP's vote distinctly understates the extent of racist sentiment in Britain (Ford 2010). The new party system demonstrates a plurality of views, a diversification of voices and choices, and one which, like it or not, for the foreseeable future is here to stay.

That said, some of the individual parties are less stable. In 2003, a full 18 seats in the Scottish Parliament – the so-called 'rainbow parliament' – were held by parties outside the top four: the Greens took seven, the Scottish Socialists captured six, along with independents and a MSP from the Scottish Senior Citizens Unity. Four years later, they were all but wiped out: the Greens losing five, and the Senior Citizens Unity party and the Scottish Socialists losing all of their seats, with the latter collapsing into internecine warfare. South of the border, Respect – which had been responsible for one of the most memorable results of the 2005 election, when George Galloway had taken the previously solid Labour seat of Bethnal Green and Bow – also ruptured in 2007 when Galloway split with members of the Socialist Workers Party (SWP). The breakaway SWP became known as Left List (and later Left Alternative). Galloway, fighting a different seat, failed to win re-election in 2010. Some of the new parties are 'flash' parties – which appear on the political stage amid much fanfare but then quickly burn out and vanish, often amid internal recriminations. But others are now serious contenders for election and office, rather than merely a depository for the disgruntled and disaffected (although they do certainly still attract more than their fair share of them).

A sceptical take on the events of 2010 might also note that, given the events leading up to the election, what was remarkable was not the extent to which the party system fragmented, but that it did not fragment even more. Given the impact of the expenses scandal, and the widespread disdain for 'mainstream' politics that it fed, the 2010 election should have been a wonderful opportunity for those claiming to be different from the establishment. In particular, it was striking just how poorly independent candidates – of whom much was made in the run up to the election – fared when the votes were counted. With the exception of Sylvia Hermon in Down North (a former Ulster Unionist MP, standing as an independent, but for the seat which she used to represent), independent candidates did not manage a single victory in 2010. There had been at least one 'independent' candidate on the British mainland between 1997 and 2010 (Cowley and Stuart 2009), but both the incumbents – in Wyre Forest and Blaenau Gwent – lost their seats, and no new independents replaced them. Given the public anger of the preceding year this was a poor return on so much anti-politics sentiment. The share of the vote going to the main parties was certainly in decline but votes seeped away to other political parties, not to independent candidates.

Coalition politics at Westminster

The fragmentation of the party system is one of the key factors making hung parliaments at Westminster increasingly likely: the larger the number of seats held by parties other than the main two, the more seats the main parties need to take from each other in order to gain a majority. Hung parliaments at Westminster are made even more likely by a second factor, less often noticed, which is the decline in the number of marginal seats in the UK (Curtice *et al.* 2010), which also makes it harder for any one of the main parties to win outright.

The 2010 election was the first Westminster election since 1992 to be fought from the beginning with the realistic prospect of a hung parliament looming, and the first since 1974 to produce one. In 1974 attempts to form an agreement between the Conservatives and the Liberals had failed, and Labour, under Harold Wilson, had returned to office, to govern as a minority administration until holding a second election in October, at which Wilson had garnered a small Commons majority. By contrast 2010 produced the first coalition seen at Westminster since the Second World War; the first peace time coalition since that formed in 1931; and the first formed by two parties afresh after a general election since modern British politics began. It resulted in a Conservative–Lib Dem coalition, rather than a Labour–Lib Dem arrangement, the realignment of the left which had been the goal of several previous Lib Dem leaders. The formation of the coalition has already generated a series of books and articles attempting to explain it (see, for example, Boulton and

Jones 2010; Laws 2010; Wilson 2010). These, and other accounts, often place emphasis on the particular behaviour of the participants, and the personal chemistry which existed (or didn't) between them. Was Gordon Brown too rude? Did David Cameron and Nick Clegg – as two English, middle-class, public-school-educated men – just 'click'? Were the Labour negotiators unprepared? Were Conservative MPs lied to? All of these questions, and many others, are interesting, and there is no doubt that many of these factors did make a difference during the five days of negotiations that produced the coalition. But coalition-building has produced a detailed academic literature to explain and predict it (see for an introduction, McLean 1987), and what is striking is that most of these theories would predict exactly the outcome seen in May 2010, even without knowledge of the precise events and personnel involved.

For example, in a minimal winning coalition (von Neumann and Morgenstern, 1947) the winning coalition would consist of the smallest number of parties needed to deliver a majority of the votes in the legislature. A larger coalition would involve sharing the spoils of office between more parties, and so would be unnecessary and undesirable from the parties' point of view. The shorthand figure used throughout the 2010 election campaign as the target for a Commons majority was 326 (that is, half of the 650 seats in the Commons, plus one). But because the five Sinn Féin MPs do not take their seats, the real target was 323. As the figures in Table 6.2 show, there were only two combinations that would deliver this outcome with just two parties: either Lab–Con or Con–Lib Dem. No other grouping of just two parties would deliver the votes needed for a majority.

William Riker (1962) pointed out that minimal winning coalitions took no account of the size of the governing bloc; Riker argued that it was better to share the spoils of government – laws, office, etc. – out among as few MPs as possible, and that the winning coalition would therefore be the minimal winning coalition of the smallest size – a minimum size coalition. In this case, that would be a Con–Lib Dem coalition, since that was smaller than the Lab–Con coalition.

Both of these theories, of course, ignore a party's ideology and beliefs. Every party is assumed to be able to form a coalition with every other party, no matter what their beliefs and policies. Axelrod (1970) argued that parties would only be able to form coalitions with parties adjacent to them on the ideological spectrum. The idea of the minimal connected winning coalition is intuitively attractive, and appears to be supported empirically: most comparative studies find that models that attempt to explain coalition formation without including some measure of ideology perform badly (Laver and Schofield 1990). The problem comes with trying to measure the various parties' ideological positions, not least because parties may be far apart on one dimension but close together on another, and in the case of the 2010 result the minimal connected winning coalition depends on where one situates the Lib Dems. If the Lib Dems are seen as a party of the political centre, located somewhere between Labour and the Conservatives, then the minimal connected winning coalition was clearly Con–Lib Dem, as the only combination of two adjacent parties that would deliver the votes necessary to command a majority of the Commons. The problem comes if instead we see the Lib Dems – as many voters and academics did – as a party somewhere to the left of Labour, which was how they had positioned themselves for much of the Blair and Brown era. In such a case, the only minimal connected winning coalition was one involving a multiplicity of parties on the left, of the sort that Labour tried desperately to convince the Lib Dems could be formed (see Box 6.2).

Either way, this does at least help explain the coalition's formation. Based on the electoral arithmetic alone a Con–Lib Dem agreement was a minimal winning coalition, it was the minimum size coalition, and it is also at least plausible to argue that it was the minimal connected winning coalition. No other arrangement came close to being so persuasive.

Another useful way to examine the process of coalition formation is to look at the voting power that each group brought to the table during the negotiations. The relationship between the size of a political party (in terms of the number of MPs it has) and its power is not linear. For one thing, once any party has more than 50 per cent of the votes in the

---

Box 6.2   A Labour–Lib Dem coalition?

Labour tried hard to persuade Liberal Democrats that there was the potential for a Labour and Lib Dem deal after the 2010 election. Adding in the SDLP (a sister party of Labour), and the one Alliance MP (a sister party of the Liberal Democrats) produced a combined strength of 319 MPs, very close to the figure needed for a majority. Assume the acquiescence of the one Green – who had said that they would not vote for a Conservative government – plus that of the four Plaid MPs (with whom they felt a deal could be reached), and a (small) majority was just about plausible, even before allowing for deals to be reached with the parties in Northern Ireland. There was, Labour claimed, an anti-Conservative majority in the Commons, and since Labour and the Lib Dems combined had more seats than the Conservatives they could outvote them as long as the other parties at least abstained. It was a small majority, and one that would have been permanently vulnerable to defections, either by one of the fringe parties or by backbench rebels within one of the main parties, but it was plausible.

Table 6.2   *Seats and power in the 2010 parliament*

| | Seats | | Power |
	N	%	%
Con	306	47.5	39.0
Lab	258	40.1	23.4
LD	57	8.9	23.4
DUP	8	1.2	5.6
SNP	6	0.9	4.2
PC	3	0.5	1.4
SDLP	3	0.5	1.4
Green	1	0.2	0.5
Alliance	1	0.2	0.5
Other	1	0.2	0.5
Total	644		

Note: Excluded are the five Sinn Féin MPs, who do not take their seats, along with the non-voting Speaker. In reality, the three Deputy Speakers do not vote either but they had not been selected at the point at which the parties were negotiating immediately after the election.

Commons it has 100 per cent of the power (subject, of course, to any backbench rebellions). Even below 50 per cent, the relationship is not straightforward either: the amount of power a group has depends as much on the distribution of seats among the other parties as it does on their own strength. Again, this is an area where there is a voluminous (and complicated) academic literature.

In addition to figures for the number of seats in the Commons, Table 6.2 also shows one of the most common measures of voting power: the Shapley–Shubik power index (Shapley and Shubik 1954), which measures the likelihood that a group's withdrawal from any winning grouping of parties would prove decisive in causing that coalition to lose. It is worth noting that despite having almost 50 per cent of the seats, the Conservatives had less power than these raw numbers might indicate, with just under 40 per cent of the voting power. Labour also had less power than first appeared; despite 40 per cent of the seats, they had just under a quarter of the power. All the other parties had more power than their raw numbers indicate, with the Lib Dems commanding the same amount of voting power as the Labour party.

Given the eventual outcome, perhaps the most important set of figures is the difference between the Conservatives and the Liberal Democrats. In terms of seats, the Conservatives outnumbered the Lib Dems more than 5:1, but in terms of the power those blocs of MPs represented the relationship was less than 2:1. The Liberal Democrats ended up with five out of 24 Cabinet seats, including Nick Clegg as Deputy Prime Minister, and a higher share of the other members of the government than would be expected based on the share of the seats. This is difficult for many Conservative MPs to take, especially those on the right of the party, who fail to understand why a party which they outnumbered so heavily received such preferential treatment during the negotiations. To them, the tail appears to be wagging the dog – but such is the reality of coalition politics.

The process of coalition formation also demonstrated one other important difference between the parties. The Liberal Democrats were bound by a series of internal party rules, known as the 'triple-lock' rules, which limited the extent to which the leadership could agree to any coalitions or similar arrangements without party approval. As a result, the five days of negotiations saw repeated meetings of the Lib Dem parliamentary party and the Federal Executive, culminating in a joint meeting of the two, which discussed the four-page draft coalition agreement for several hours, before voting (almost unanimously) to agree it. There was also a special conference of the party – not formally required under the rules, but used as a way of ensuring the process was considered as legitimate as possible – which also voted overwhelmingly to agree to the coalition. The negotiations were driven by the party elites, but in formal consultation with the other wings of the party. In the other parties, the process was much more top-down. The Conservative negotiating process was driven by a handful of David Cameron's close confidents, and involving the Shadow Cabinet and Conservative parliamentary party only when the leadership needed it. No-one outside the key team was shown the draft coalition document before it was agreed, and there was no vote to agree its adoption. For Labour, the Cabinet met once, but the parliamentary Labour Party did not meet at any point, nor did any of the other organs of the party. At the first meeting between the Conservative and Lib Dem negotiating teams, William Hague summed up the Conservative procedures as 'an absolute monarchy, moderated by regicide' (Laws 2010). Labour's approach to the coalition was not much more democratic or inclusive.

The Conservative party

Despite the change represented by the 2010 election, in one important way it represented a return to a familiar normality of British politics: the Conservatives were in government at Westminster, Labour in opposition.

The extended 13-year period of rule of new Labour which ended in May 2010 was historically atypical. Prior to 1997, Labour had never managed to win even two full successive terms in office (let alone three), and Tony Blair himself was prime minister with a secure working majority for longer than all his Labour predecessors combined. The Conservatives, by contrast, enjoyed multiple periods of extended rule – in the 1930s, the 1950s, and the 1980s, including an 18-year stretch between 1979 and 1997.

Yet if the twentieth century was understandably labelled the Conservative century, the prospects for the Conservative party at the beginning of the twenty-first century had not looked good, with disastrous performances in three consecutive elections. Conservative modernisers were particularly influenced by opinion polls which demonstrated that public support for particular policies dropped noticeably once respondents knew they were Conservative policies. The problem therefore was not the party's policies, but the 'brand' (Ashcroft 2005). A key part of the Cameron project for the Conservatives was therefore what was known as 'detoxification', to change the party's image so that voters would be willing to engage with it, rather than reject it out of hand.

Detoxification was an incomplete process by 2010. Surveys showed that voters were still less willing to support a policy once they knew it was a Conservative policy, and while opinion polls showed some three-quarters of voters thought it was 'time for a change', less than 40 per cent agreed it was time for a change to the Conservatives. Private focus groups for both Labour and the Conservatives found a general uncertainty or lack of optimism about what a future Conservative government would look like (Kavanagh and Cowley 2010). The party made significant advances in the 2010 election, making almost 100 net gains, but their vote share was still the fifth lowest since and including 1922, and the increase in the share of the vote – of just under four percentage points – was lower than the equivalent figure on the three previous occasions when the party had ejected Labour (Curtice *et al.* 2010). The party was also hurt by the electoral system, which continued to work against it. In 2005, Labour's 35 per cent share of the vote and 2.8 per cent lead had given it a comfortable majority. In 2010, the Conservatives' 37 per cent share, and 7 per cent lead, left it well short of a majority. Many Conservative MPs – and Conservative supporting newspapers – believed this to be the result of the parliamentary constituency boundaries, which led to plans to reduce the size of the Commons (thus speeding up a boundary review) as well as to reduce one aspect of the bias by ensuring that constituencies in Scotland and Wales were not smaller than those in England. Yet most of the bias in the system is not due to unfair boundaries, but due to differential turnout (with turnout in Labour seats being noticeably lower than in Conservative seats) and to Labour's vote being more efficiently distributed (Curtice *et al.* 2010). As a result, the boundary changes may reduce the bias against the Conservatives but they will not eliminate it.

The creation of the coalition both provided the additional seats required to create a working majority, but also helped further detoxify the Conservative brand. Ironically, therefore, Cameron (and those Conservatives who share his political outlook) was helped by his failure to win a majority. Prime minister Cameron is in a stronger position as the head of a coalition government with a comfortable majority than he would have been as head of a Conservative government with a narrow majority, attempting to implement cuts but permanently vulnerable to opposition. The coalition enjoys a large Commons majority, of more than 80. It is not quite of landslide proportions, but is larger than the majorities enjoyed by Winston Churchill (after 1951), Anthony Eden, Harold Wilson (1966–70 excepted), Edward Heath, James Callaghan, Margaret Thatcher (in her first term), John Major (after 1992), as well as Tony Blair and Gordon Brown in Labour's third term. As that list indicates, smaller majorities have proved perfectly sufficient to last for full four or five year terms, and (for the most part) to withstand backbench revolt.

Many on the Conservative right, however, are seriously disgruntled, both by Cameron's failure to win the election (they were unimpressed by the party's election campaign), and, as importantly, by the policy compromises that flowed from the coalition agreement. Those Conservatives in government mostly soon reached harmonious working relationships with their Liberal Democrat counterparts; but those MPs outside of Government, as well as many in the wider party, are worried about the Conservatives' direction of travel, fearing that the party's agenda will prioritise what the website ConservativeHome calls 'liberal Conservatism' over 'traditional Conservatism'.

Newly elected governments normally enjoy the benefit of a honeymoon with their backbenchers (Cowley 2009). The prime minister's authority is usually at its highest, the party is implementing its manifesto and many MPs – and especially the new ones – fancy a career as ministers, and believe it awaits them if they behave. And most MPs have a desire not to do anything stupid that is likely to send them back into opposition, thus placing a premium on unity. There has however been no such evidence of a honeymoon in the case of the coalition. Of the first 160 divisions in the Commons up until Christmas 2010, there had been rebellions by Government MPs in some 53 per cent of votes. This would be a high figure compared to any period since 1945, but when compared to the first sessions of parliaments following a change in government the contrast was especially starker. Between 1945 and 1997, the six sessions immediately after a change in government saw rates of rebellion of between zero (1964) and 6 per cent (1979) of divisions (Cowley 2009). The rate of rebellion seen at the start of the 2010 Parliament was therefore almost ten times greater than what had until then been the post-war peak. Although most of the attention focused on the rebellions from the Lib Dems (especially over tuition fees, as discussed below), the figure for the Conservatives was higher (at 38 per cent) than that for the Lib Dems (25 per cent). Many of the rhetorical resources that whips can normally deploy are absent. The claim that backbenchers owe the new prime minister loyalty, for example, does not wash with many Conservative MPs, especially those on the right of the party, who do not credit David Cameron with victory but blame him for failing to deliver an outright majority for the party. And the argument that it is important to implement the manifesto also does not carry much weight, given that MPs are frequently being asked to vote for things which were either not in their manifesto or which were the exact opposite of what had been in the manifesto. Even the mass of new Conservative MPs – usually much less willing to defy their whips (Cowley 2002) – have proved surprisingly willing to rebel. The result is that the parliamentary wing of the government in the Commons is already proving far more troublesome than would normally be expected at this stage of a parliament.

The Conservative right is especially worried about talk of any future deals with the Liberal Democrats. By the end of 2010, the former prime minister John Major had called for the coalition to be made permanent, as had Nick Boles MP, the former Head of the Policy Exchange think tank, and close to Cameron (Boles 2010). Those on the right of the Conservative party, already feel neutered by the coalition, and are extremely sceptical about the possibility of any continuing deal.

The Labour party

Labour returned to Opposition at Westminster in 2010, suffering a net loss of 90 seats and some million votes. There was a widespread feeling in the party that it could have been worse. Particularly after Gordon Brown's encounter with the Rochdale pensioner Gillian Duffy during the election campaign, there were fears among some in Labour's high command that they were about to go into meltdown (Kavanagh and Cowley 2010). Yet it was a sign of how low expectations had become that the performance in 2010 was seen as anything other than disastrous. A share of 29.7 per cent of the vote was the lowest since the 1983 disaster and the second worst since 1918 when the party had first fought elections on a national basis. For the first time in its history the party had lost vote share in three successive general elections.

Labour's vote held up better in some parts of the country than others, but it was all but wiped out in many of the seats Labour captured in 1997 and 2001. Over a quarter of Labour MPs in the new Parliament came from Scotland and Wales. This triggered discussion of Labour's 'Southern Problem', echoing Giles Radice's influential 1992 pamphlet *Southern Discomfort*. Indeed, Radice himself returned to the fray, releasing an updated version (Diamond and Radice 2010), claiming to identify serious problems for Labour in the south of England (by which the authors really meant the south and the Midlands). A minority of southern voters claimed to know what Labour stood for; in so far as they did have a view of the party it was of a party that is closest to benefit claimants and the trade unions; and they had a poor view of Labour's record in government, with only a very small minority believing that the party had managed to improve public services without much waste. Yet while it was true that on many of these criteria southern voters took a more hostile view of Labour than did voters in the north or in Scotland, the true picture to emerge from Radice and Diamond's 2010 study was that after 13 years in power, voters everywhere had an overwhelmingly negative impression of Labour. Voters in every region of Britain, for example, claimed not to know what Labour stood for, and felt it was closest to benefit claimants and the trade unions (the third placed group, also not exactly good news for Labour, was 'immigrants'). Similarly, southern voters thought that Labour wasted money, but so did voters everywhere. Just one in ten voters overall thought that Labour had improved public services without much waste. True, the figure rose to 13 per cent in the north, and was as low as 7 per cent in London and the rest of the south, but to focus on that 6-point difference was to miss the key finding from the survey: which is that voters everywhere thought Labour wasted money on a large scale over their time in government. The essential reason voters in the South didn't think much of the Labour party is because the electorate as a whole didn't think much of it. Labour in 2010 did not have a Southern Problem. It had an Almost Everywhere Problem. It was saved from further collapse only by the success of its incumbent MPs, and by doing better than expected in seats with large ethnic minority populations.

Ed Miliband became Labour leader in September 2010, beating four other contenders for the position. These included his brother, the former Foreign Secretary, David Miliband, who had been the bookies' favourite, and who then announced he was retiring from frontline politics. Table 6.3 shows the voting figures for the various rounds of the contest,

Table 6.3 *The Labour leadership contest 2010 (percentage support)*

Candidate	Round 1	Round 2	Round 3	Round 4
Diane Abbott	7.42	Eliminated	–	–
Ed Balls	11.79	13.23	16.02	Eliminated
Andy Burnham	8.68	10.41	Eliminated	—
David Miliband	37.78	38.89	42.72	49.35
Ed Miliband	34.33	37.47	41.26	50.65

conducted under the Alternative Vote (AV) system. David Miliband led in every round of the contest, until the very last, at which point Ed Miliband pulled narrowly ahead. In itself, an outcome like this is not exceptional. The three main parties all use different mechanisms to elect their leaders but all allow for the possibility that candidates not ahead in the initial rounds of any contest will go on to win. In addition to Miliband, that was also true of David Cameron in 2005, as it had previously been of William Hague in 1997 and Iain Duncan Smith in 2001 (and as it had also been for Harriet Harman when she was elected Labour's Deputy Leader in 2007). It is ironic that the Liberal Democrats, the one party which whole-heartedly believes in the principle of the transferable vote, is the only major party in which the winning candidate in all their leadership elections would have been the same under first-past-the-post.

Ed Miliband's problem was the different support he received from within the various sections of Labour's electoral college. Even after transfers on the final round, he remained behind David Miliband among the first two sections, MPs and MEPs and party members. David Miliband led among both groups throughout every round of voting. Ed Miliband was ahead only among Section 3: affiliated organisations, mostly union members, helped by the support of several of the larger unions. In one sense, there is nothing wrong about this. There is little point in having an electoral college with three elements if those elements are not allowed to disagree, but it led to complaints that he did not fully enjoy the support of either his parliamentary party or the party in the country. Less noticed, however, Miliband's victory also confirmed one other noticeable recent trend in British party politics, the rise of the career politician (see Box 6.3).

Perceptive Labour strategists are well aware that they face major challenges over the next few years, and that sitting back and waiting for the coalition to implode is not a sensible strategy. They are aware of the damage done to Labour's brand by the end of the Brown government, and that the party had lost its reputation for economic competence –

Box 6.3 The continuing rise of the career politician

First elected to the Commons in 2005, Ed Miliband became leader of the Labour Party after just one term in the House of Commons. When he faces David Cameron at Prime Minister's Questions, he takes on someone who was also elected to lead their party after just one term in the Commons. And sat next to David Cameron is the Deputy Prime Minister, Nick Clegg, who was elected to lead his party after a mere two years at Westminster.

When all three of the major parties elect leaders with (at most) just one parliament's experience under their belt, it is a sign of a major development in British politics. Compare that to the generation they replaced. Gordon Brown was first elected in 1983, and did not become leader of his party until 2007. David Cameron replaced Michael Howard, first elected in 1983, becoming leader in 2003. And Nick Clegg replaced Ming Campbell, who became leader in 2006, having been elected in 1987. During the post-war era, and prior to David Cameron, the Commons experience of a Conservative party leader before holding that office, was an average of 22 years, for Labour prior to Miliband the average was 19 years, but none had been elected with as little experience of the Commons as Miliband and Cameron. For the Liberal Democrats, the average was a bit lower, at 16 years, but again none had had so little parliamentary experience as did Clegg.

This represents a speeding up of party political life, as well as a diminution of the role of the Commons as the testing arena for aspirant politicians. In part it is because all of them had significant political experience at a reasonably senior level before they entered the Commons, as special advisers or, in Nick Clegg's case, as an MEP. Criddle (2010) notes that a full two-fifths of Labour's new 2010 intake had experience as ministerial or MPs' aides, with the career politician making advances in the other parties as well. The career politician remains a minority in the Commons as a whole, with plenty of MPs with a broader experience of the world. But for those who want an accelerated route to the top of the political parties being a career politician now looks to be the only game in town. It is not obvious that that is something to be celebrated.

gained at some considerable cost in the early 1990s. This had historically been a strategic weakness of Labour's. Even when the Conservatives were unpopular, they were traditionally always seen as more competent. They are also aware that Labour traditionally does opposition very well but finds winning elections harder, and worry about the possibility that – in an era of widespread spending cuts – Labour taps into opposition to individual cuts, scoring easy political points, but only at a cost of not being seen as responsible with the overall economy. And they worry about the lack of a political narrative to replace that of New Labour. Miliband declared that New Labour was dead, but it was less clear what had replaced it.

The party also faces the tricky issue of how to deal with the Liberal Democrats. After the failure of the Labour–Lib Dem coalition talks in May 2010, the mainstream Labour reaction to the Lib Dems was akin to that of a spurned lover, with much talk of their betrayal, often accompanied by personal attacks on senior Lib Dems. There are those within the Labour party who believe that the party will manage to win an outright majority at the next election. Yet the logic of the fragmentation seen in British party politics over the last few decades is that this may become increasingly less likely, and that another hung parliament after the next election remains a more realistic possibility. If so, then Labour will need the support of the Liberal Democrats. Despite knowing that the chances of an outright victory in 2010 were unlikely, Labour did very little preparation for the negotiations that followed (and most of what they did was done very late in the day). A sensible strategy for 2015 is to understand that what happened in May 2010 was not unusual, and that preparations for the possibility of talks with the Lib Dems should begin sooner rather than later. December 2010 saw Ed Miliband begin that task, with a speech that reached out to disgruntled Lib Dems to work with Labour.

The Liberal Democrats

Of the three main parties, it is the Liberal Democrats that have been most changed by the events of 2010. Entering government in coalition has been a transformative event, but not a painless one. Within six months of entering government, Lib Dem support in opinion polls had fallen from the 24 per cent at the election down to single figures (one poll in December 2010 had them on 8 per cent), and the party was being widely criticised for a series of u-turns and compromises it had carried out, as the government carried out widespread spending cuts. The party had suffered electorally before (it had polled badly following the painful merger between the Liberals and the SDP in 1988 as well as during periods after Charles Kennedy stepped down in January 2006) but then its fate had been to be ignored or ridiculed. The latter half of 2010 saw it actively disliked, a new experience for many Liberal Democrats.

Particularly damaging was the issue of student fees (explained in Box 6.4) which proved the first major policy crisis of the coalition in late 2010. On the face of it, this was a simple case of how politicians will say anything to win votes, and how promises made in opposition can come back to bite a party in government. Yet it also revealed several insights into the functioning of coalition politics in the UK, at least in its early days.

First, it illustrated Nick Clegg's initial approach to the coalition: a belief that, having entered coalition, the Lib Dems had to back the government's programme en masse, and could not cherry-pick the bits that they liked and publically reject those they did not. The aim was to show responsibility, to win the trust of their Conservative partners and to demonstrate to the electorate that the party had matured from a party of opposition into a party of government. It would, for example, have been perfectly possible for the Lib Dems to have denounced the Browne review into university funding, and to have refused to have had any part in formulating the government's response. In such circumstances, the measure might even have been defeated, but the cost to the coalition's internal functioning would have been considerable. Even before the

---

Box 6.4   Student fees

The first major test of the coalition came over the issue of fees for university undergraduates. The outgoing Labour government had set up a review of university funding, under Lord Browne, the former chairman of BP. The Conservative manifesto had agreed to 'consider carefully' the results of the Browne review (Labour's manifesto was even vaguer). The Lib Dem manifesto, however, explicitly promised to work towards the abolition of fees, and in addition all the Lib Dem MPs signed a public statement organised by the National Union of Students, pledging themselves to vote against any raise in tuition fees.

The subsequent coalition agreement merely awaited the response of the Browne review, but – as a measure of the Lib Dem position – allowed them to abstain if they were unhappy with the government's response to the review. It did not, however, allow them to vote against, something which would have risked defeating any measure brought forward.

The eventual policy, which included allowing fees to rise to £9000 (albeit with conditions), triggered mass student demonstrations and when it came before the House of Commons in December 2010 caused the Lib Dems to split three ways. The frontbench, along with a handful of backbenchers, voted for the measure, but the majority of backbenchers refused to back it, some abstaining and 21 voting against, the largest rebellion in the history of the party since its formation in 1988. As a proportion of the parliamentary party that was a rebellion by 37 per cent of their MPs, proportionately higher even than the 2003 Labour revolt over the Iraq war.

damage done to the Lib Dems' standing as a result of the fees vote, however, there were senior Lib Dems wondering about the wisdom of the approach, and whether they needed to do more to talk about their distinctive contribution to the coalition.

And second, the issue of tuition fees also revealed the extent to which it was the Lib Dems who were suffering politically as a result of the unpopular decisions the coalition was making. Increasing student fees was also a policy pursued by the Conservatives – yet the Conservatives were not suffering any obvious electoral penalty. Labour politicians argued that the Lib Dems were functioning as the Conservative party's 'human shield' – a relatively common phenomenon for the junior partners in coalitions – taking the pain, while the Conservatives got on with governing.

The kerfuffle over tuition fees however also demonstrated the growing pains involved in the shift from single-party to multiparty government. The Lib Dems were widely condemned for what was seen as a betrayal, with lots of talk of their broken promises. Yet hung parliaments and coalitions *require* broken promises; they cannot function with them. As soon as parties do not win office outright, the manifesto transforms from a set of pledges into a negotiating position. Parties can certainly insist on red lines – the things that they would refuse to compromise on – but it seems an unlikely proposition to argue that university funding is the only red line the Lib Dems should have had. This was both a failure of the media (and the public) to understand the realities of coalition politics, but it was also a result of the way the parties (and not just the Lib Dems) had campaigned for office – and especially the stupidity of the Lib Dems in agreeing to sign the NUS's pledge on student fees, something which many of them soon realised was a mistake. This raises the possibility of a shift in campaigning in future: whereas the 2010 election was fought as a campaign for single party government; the next election will be fought as a campaign for single *or* multiparty government, with parties being much less willing to tie themselves down in that way. As one Lib Dem MP remarked on the day of the student fees vote, the only pledge they would be making at the next election was not to make any pledges.

As a result, less than six months after entering government, there were plenty in the media writing the Liberal Democrats off, arguing that the damage done to the party as a result of their coalition with the Conservatives was irreversible. Many within the party itself were more sanguine, though hardly carefree. First, they argued that there had not been a pain-free alternative in May 2010. If the party had opted to stay out of government entirely – or merely propped up a minority government in a confidence and supply arrangement – they would have been criticised for ducking the challenge of government. They also feared the consequences of a second 2010 election, for which the party had no funds. A coalition deal with Labour was also hardly a pain-free option: it would have involved keeping a rejected government (and, at least initially, also a rejected prime minister) in power; it would have involved attempting to govern with a patchwork quilt government with a tiny or non-existent majority; and the policy issues tackled by the coalition would still have been present. Painful issues such as university funding and public sector cuts would still have faced them.

Second, party insiders would point to potential upsides. After the 2010 contest, the party carried out a private polling exercise among those who considered voting Lib Dem but did not do so; the most common reason for rejecting the party was that voters did not think it was a serious party of government, a problem that had plagued the party since its formation (Kavanagh and Cowley 2010). By contrast, the Lib Dems will fight the next election as a party of government. Moreover, whatever their poll ratings, they will fight it on much more of an equal footing than ever before; having struggled in the past to get their message heard, they will now be taken seriously, both as a party that has been in government and as one that might re-enter government. They recognise that they will lose some of the voters who used to support them, but hope to gain others by demonstrating that there were able to take difficult decisions. They also hope to have been able to kill the argument – deployed against them repeatedly in recent elections – that hung parliaments necessarily led to instability and bad government. Those Lib Dems with experience in Scotland would also point to the experience there, after 1999; at first, going into coalition with Labour damaged the Lib Dem poll ratings – which dropped to half of their pre-coalition level, but as the 2003 election approached, and as the party was able to demonstrate the results of having the Lib Dems in government, so the poll ratings climbed back again. None of this guarantees success, but it explains why many within the party saw less cause for concern than commentators outside.

The problem is that the electoral cycle in the UK no longer allows parties four or five years slowly to rebuild; British party politics is now a year-on-year set of different electoral contests. Within a year of the coalition being formed the Lib Dems would face both the referendum on the Alternative Vote which they had secured as a result of the coalition negotiations (and which was convincingly defeated), followed by elections in Scotland and Wales (where being in an alliance with the Conservatives at Westminster hurt them badly, their vote more than halving in Scotland).

Conclusion

For all the surprise about the result and the subsequent coalition, the 2010 general election was as much a confirmation of existing trends in British party politics as it was a new development. The hung parliament produced in 2010 was not some fluke, but the result of long-term trends in British politics, of which the most obvious was the increasing fragmentation of the party system, decade on decade. The outcome merely brought Westminster in line with what is happening in other parts of the UK.

The irony was that in the immediate aftermath of the formation of the coalition, and with the Lib Dem share of the vote in apparent freefall in the opinion polls, it looked as if two-party politics might be back on the agenda. Opinion polls in late-2010 had the two major parties combined polling over 80 per cent of the vote, which (if repeated in a general election) would return party politics to something similar to that in the 1960s. A further irony was that, for once, the Lib Dem share of the seats in the Commons had begun to match its share in opinion polls, at a mere 8 or 9 per cent. Nick Clegg appeared to have achieved proportional representation, if not quite in the way that he might have wished. Yet it is too early to predict how the electoral landscape would pan out. Caution is needed. For instance Labour might have moved level with the Conservatives in some polls by September 2010 (and pulled slightly ahead in most polls by the end of the year), but some on the left failed to realize that this was a fairly familiar pattern. After losing in October 1951, Labour had pulled ahead in opinion polls by January 1952, but it did not stop the Conservatives enjoying 13 years in government. In 1970, after a June election, Labour were level by October; that did not stop Ted Heath polling more votes four years later (even if he did not secure enough seats to cling on). And in 1979, following a May election, Labour had pulled ahead in the polls by the following month. In other words, in 1979 Labour led Mrs Thatcher's government within a month of the election and yet were still out of power for the next 18 years. Early opinion poll leads – or impressive by-election performances – should not blind Labour to the challenge that it faces. The English council elections of 2011, in which Labour did well, but not exceptionally, reminded many Labour strategists of the challenges that remained.

The election marked an important transformation point in British party politics. For much of the last three decades the prospect of a realignment between Labour and the Liberal Democrats (or their predecessors) had been a fixture of political debate. A realignment of the political left had been an aim of Blair's New Labour project, scuppered only by the scale of Labour's win in 1997. Yet it was David Cameron's

Conservatives which managed to negotiate the coalition, opening up the possibility of a centre-right realignment instead. By late-2010 there was talk of the possibility of the coalition continuing into and beyond the next general election, of electoral pacts between the Conservatives and the Lib Dems, either in total or partial (such as not standing against candidates against coalition ministers, for example). All this was denied officially, but it was indicative of the extent to which British party politics was in flux.

The electoral geography at the next election requires the Conservatives to be ahead by more than 11 percentage points to govern as a single party. Labour need to be ahead by around three points. That is a range of 14 points, the largest in the post-war era (Curtice *et al.* 2010). Even without the introduction of the Alternative Vote (AV) the chances of future hung parliaments – and future coalition discussions – remain high. The parties that prosper in the next decades will be those who understand this, and plan accordingly.

Chapter 7

Territorial Politics in Post-Devolution Britain

ROGER SCULLY AND RICHARD WYN JONES

Devolution, the establishment of directly elected legislatures and associated governments for Scotland and Wales, represents one of the most momentous developments in the recent political history of the UK. Its significance has been widely recognised by leading political commentators. Anthony King, for instance, has judged devolution to Scotland to be a transfer of powers on 'a scale unprecedented in the history of mainland Britain and possibly without precedent in the history of the democratic world' (2007: 347). Some observers believe that it may even unleash forces that lead to the dissolution of the UK.

Yet, despite its importance, devolution remains remarkably little understood. Senior politicians at Westminster rarely acknowledge how devolution limits their powers. Civil servants, and those working for the BBC, are regularly exhorted to be 'devolution sensitive' – to remember that the UK now comprises four distinct policy and political spaces. That they need to be so reminded is telling. And the London-based print media largely avoid reporting politics at the devolved level, ignoring all but the most momentous of developments. Even in Scotland and Wales, the focus tends to be exclusively on developments in one's own country. In all of this, the 'big picture' of devolution – what it means for the UK as a whole – remains largely unexamined. This is what this chapter aims to draw attention to, while also focusing on recent developments in both Scotland and Wales.

Why devolution matters

How can we explain the disjuncture between importance and interest: between the momentous changes to the UK being brought about by devolution, and the widespread lack of engagement with these developments? One key point is that devolution is *uneven*: it has impacted on different parts of the UK very differently. Scotland and Wales have seen the establishment of new institutions – embodied in striking new buildings in

Edinburgh and Cardiff – that are increasingly recognised as the focus of the civic and political lives of their respective nations. Nonetheless, Scotland and Wales constitute only a relatively small part of the UK as a whole. Scotland has around a quarter of the UK land mass, but its population of around 5 million is only 8.5 per cent of the UK total. Wales is smaller still at around 3 million (5 per cent). Much of the lack of attention to devolution surely follows from its apparent lack of impact on England, which is overwhelmingly the largest part of the UK. But appearances can be deceptive. Although no new specifically English institutions have been created in response to devolution, and while the institutions of the central UK state remain essentially unchanged, devolution has had a profound impact on what those central institutions actually do. For example, the UK government's health minister is now, in practice, the English health minister. S/he has little influence over the devolved territories. The same is true of UK ministers for education, local government, transport and many other fields. Few UK ministerial portfolios remain relatively unaffected by devolution – most obviously defence, foreign affairs and the Treasury. In short, devolution is having a far-reaching effect on how the UK is governed. But there is (as yet) very limited recognition of this, and many still believe that devolution concerns only the margins – the so-called 'Celtic periphery' – of the UK.

Another factor that mitigates against taking devolution seriously is its *asymmetric* nature. There is no common scheme of devolution: rather, Scotland, Wales and, indeed, Northern Ireland (see Chapter 8 in this book) have very different devolution arrangements, reflecting different historical traditions and different constitutional principles. This means that understanding devolution can be challenging. To understand how a particular policy area is dealt with in Scotland will not necessarily offer you much guidance for how things are done in Wales. Even broad 'rules of thumb' can be difficult to establish. Thus, while it is generally true that Scotland is more devolved than Wales, there are instances where devolved Wales has diverged more from England than has Scotland. And there are also instances where, for political reasons, the rhetoric of difference is more marked in Wales even when this is not matched by substance. All of this means that understanding devolution requires no small investment of time and effort.

But for students of politics the rewards for this investment are great. Properly understanding the nature of the current devolution settlements for Scotland and Wales – and, for that matter, the absence of similar arrangements for the regions of England – requires us to engage with the long historical evolution of the UK as a 'State of Unions' (Mitchell 2009). Doing so not only sensitises us to the internal complexities of British history, which are much greater than most popular treatments allow; it may also help us to engage with broader questions about the extent to which contemporary political structures, attitudes and behaviours have deep historical roots (Putnam 1993). The UK's devolved territories also offer fascinating contemporary examples of political systems in development. Here we may observe, at close quarters, the interaction of institutions, individuals and ideas – and before time has encrusted the habits, traditions and accepted wisdoms characteristic of more mature (and typically more stagnant) political systems. Conversely, by exploring the impact of devolution on the UK state, we may observe how a long-established system adapts (or, perhaps, fails to adapt) to such a radical new departure. And for the student of public policy, devolution provides a 'living laboratory' – in which we can see how broadly similar problems are approached from different angles and with different emphases, leading, in turn, to different outcomes. What works, how and why? In short, there is nothing peripheral or parochial about devolution. Rather, it provides a new context in which to explore some fundamental questions about political life.

Parties and elections under devolution

After their creation was endorsed by referendums in 1997, the first elections to the Scottish Parliament and National Assembly for Wales (NAW) were held in May 1999. With each body serving a fixed term of four years there have now been four sets of elections, with the most recent elections held in May 2011. The elections are held under a two-ballot Mixed-Member voting system which elects representatives from both constituencies and regional party lists. Unlike the system used for general elections to Westminster, there is a significant element of proportional representation.

As well as the electoral system used, something else has been distinctive about all of the devolved elections held in Scotland and Wales. Levels of voter participation have been significantly lower than at UK general elections. In 2007, turnout on the constituency ballot was 51.7 per cent in Scotland and 43.6 per cent in Wales, compared with 63.8 per cent and 64.9 per cent respectively at the 2010 UK general election. To a great extent, this indicates that fewer people think that devolved elections matter than general elections – particularly so in Wales, with its more limited form of devolution. But lower turnout does not seem to result from opponents of devolution refusing to vote in elections for institutions they reject: in Wales, those who voted against creating the Assembly in the 1997 referendum were no less likely to take part in its first election, in 1999, than those who had voted in favour (Scully *et al.* 2004).

Table 7.1　*Elections to the Scottish Parliament, 1999–2011*

Party	1999 % vote	MSPs	2003 % vote	MSPs	2007 % vote	MSPs	2011 % vote	MSPs
Labour	36.2	56	32.0	50	30.6	46	29.0	37
Conservative	15.5	18	16.1	18	15.2	17	13.2	15
Lib Dems	13.3	17	13.6	17	13.7	16	6.6	5
SNP	28.0	35	22.3	27	32.0	47	44.8	69
Others	7.0	3	16.1	17	8.5	3	6.6	3

Scotland 1999–2007

In Scotland in 1999, the Labour party was able to repel the challenge of the SNP with some ease. Donald Dewar, who as Scottish Secretary had steered the Scotland Act through Westminster, was duly installed as Scotland's First Minister when the new parliament convened in Edinburgh, at the head of a Labour–Liberal Democrat coalition holding a comfortable majority in the 129-seat parliament. As Table 7.1 shows, Labour lost some ground in the 2003 election, but continued to hold a secure majority in combination with the Liberal Democrats in a coalition that persisted for the whole of the parliament's second term.

The third election in May 2007 saw more dramatic changes to party politics in Scotland. A resurgent SNP narrowly emerged as the largest single party, although well short of a majority. With no other politically viable coalition holding a majority either, the nationalists established a minority government; their party leader, Alex Salmond, became Scotland's First Minister. As we discuss below, minority government meant that some nationalist policies had to be shelved; on other matters, the SNP government needed to negotiate deals with other parties on an issue-by-issue basis. The Scottish experience of minority government has shown that the lack of a secure parliamentary majority certainly makes it harder for a party to implement its policies; but it has also demonstrated, as many other political systems around the world have done, that minority government does not *necessarily* mean chaos (Strom 1990). The dramatic result of the 2011 election produced the first single-party majority in the Scottish Parliament for the SNP: it remains to be seen how the party will use this new strength.

Wales 1999–2007

Party politics in Wales under devolution has proved surprisingly dramatic. The first Assembly election in 1999 saw a surge in support for the Welsh nationalists, Plaid Cymru, depriving the Labour party – long the hegemonic force in Welsh elections – of the overall majority it had been all-but-universally expected to achieve. A period of minority government followed – which in this instance was rather turbulent, and included the resignation of the Labour leader, Alun Michael, before Labour formed a coalition with the Liberal Democrats. A modest Labour recovery in 2003, and a significant Plaid Cymru decline, then allowed Labour to govern on its own. But its majority was thin, and proved transitory. By 2005, Labour was again a minority government. And after losing further ground in the 2007 election, it was forced to seek a coalition again, this time with Plaid Cymru. Although it has remained the largest and strongest party, and improved its position in the 2011 election, Labour has not been able to dominate NAW elections in the same way that it has dominated general elections in Wales for decades. Party politics in the Assembly have thus been much more evenly balanced that could have been envisaged pre-devolution. Party politics have also become more obviously 'Welsh': not only because of the greater support enjoyed by Plaid Cymru in devolved elections, but also because the Welsh branches of the British parties have sought to burnish their Welsh credentials by, rhetorically at least, stressing their autonomy from their respective 'London' leaderships. In this way, the previously 'nationalist' assumption – that Wales is a nation and this sense of nationhood requires political and institutional expression – has become rather more part of the mainstream (Wyn Jones 2001).

Table 7.2   *Elections to the National Assembly for Wales, 1999–2011*

Party	1999 % vote	AMs	2003 % vote	AMs	2007 % vote	AMs	2011 % vote	AMs
Labour	36.5	28	38.3	30	30.9	26	39.6	30
Conservative	16.2	9	19.5	11	21.9	12	23.8	14
Lib Dems	13.0	6	13.4	6	13.3	6	9.3	5
Plaid Cymru	29.5	17	20.5	12	21.9	15	18.6	11
Others	4.9	0	8.3	1	12.2	1	8.8	0

Prior to devolution, Scotland and Wales were both examples of what scholars of political parties have termed 'One Party Dominant' systems (Webb 2000). Labour has won a majority of Scottish and Welsh parliamentary seats in all recent general elections. Westminster elections have changed rather little under devolution. But in the Scottish Parliament and the National Assembly for Wales a much more balanced multiparty politics has emerged. With it, forms of government that were hitherto rather alien to modern British experience – coalition and single-party minority – have come to be the norm, not the exception. In Scotland, this has also led directly to dramatic changes in local government: the Liberal Democrats insisted on the introduction of the Single Transferable Vote system of proportional representation for local elections in 2007. This produced multiparty politics in nearly all Scotland's local authorities, many of which had long been one-party fiefdoms (Bochel and Denver 2007). And within the devolved chambers in both nations, the character of party politics has also altered somewhat. Party politics is no longer exclusively about competition – seeing other parties only as rivals from whom one seeks to win votes and seats. Electoral competition remains very important, but parties must also now pay much more attention to their ongoing relationship with others with whom they will likely need to cooperate, and may even wish to form a formal coalition, between elections.

Institutional and constitutional politics

Developing the institutions

Empowered by a model of devolution that allows it to legislate on all issues not formally reserved to Westminster (or forbidden by the UK's international treaty obligations), the Scottish Parliament has, since its creation, rapidly become the central focus for the country's political, civic and economic life. London still matters, not least because a significant number of Scottish MPs (including Gordon Brown) have held senior positions in the UK government. But the main political business concerning Scotland's national life has increasingly occurred in Edinburgh. The Scottish Parliament itself is a recognisable progeny of Westminster. The design of the new institution included some self-conscious 'modernisation' in relation to working practices, increased transparency and various attempts to make the political process more accessible to the general public at large as well as civil society actors. Nonetheless, there are obvious continuities with the Westminster model (Mitchell 2010). One clear similarity is the power of the executive within the legislature – certainly when the executive commands a parliamentary majority, as it did in Scotland until 2007.

Devolution to Wales was not only much less far-reaching; it was also less well thought out. Changes in the planned structures of Welsh devolution began even as the original legislation was being considered by the UK parliament. At that stage, the planned internal structure of the NAW was altered, from the committee model traditional in UK local government, to a cabinet system more typical of a parliamentary context

(Rawlings 1998). This was the beginning of a process of constitutional revision that remains ongoing, as the limitations of the original model of Welsh devolution have become apparent. The general trends in this process of almost continual change have been away from the original 'executive devolution' model and an experimental, hybrid model of internal organisation, and towards more expansive legislative powers and more orthodox, parliamentary organisation and working practices. There have been several important milestones in this process. In 2000, after the enforced resignation of the original First Secretary, Alun Michael, the scrutiny and legislative functions of the Assembly began to be demarcated more clearly from the executive. The latter was named the 'Welsh Assembly Government', and Michael's successor, Rhodri Morgan, adopted the title of First Minister (thus bringing Wales into line with Scotland and Northern Ireland). In 2004 the independent Richard Commission recommended far-reaching reforms of Welsh devolution to more closely resemble the Scottish model (Richard Commission 2004). The Commission in effect argued that the Welsh model of devolution was deeply flawed. In response to the Richard Commission report, a new Government of Wales Act was passed in 2006. This followed some, though not all, of the Commission's recommendations. The Act formalised the division between the government and legislature, and gave the latter enhanced, though tightly constrained, legislative powers. Also part of the Act was the provision to transfer fuller law-making powers to the NAW in the event of a 'Yes' vote in a future referendum. But even after this occurred, in March 2011, Welsh devolution is still rather less far-reaching than that granted to Scotland or, indeed, Northern Ireland: the asymmetries in the structures of devolution have been reduced but far from eliminated.

Extending devolution after 2007

The declared aim of the SNP government that took office in May 2007 was to hold a referendum on Scottish independence during the four-year term of the parliament. As a prelude to introducing legislation into the parliament to permit this referendum, the SNP government embarked on what it termed a 'National Conversation' about options for Scotland's constitutional future. This attempt to seize and shape the agenda was countered by the three unionist parties (the Conservatives, Labour and the Liberal Democrats). In an unprecedented act of cooperation, they combined to establish a commission to consider options for enhancing the powers of the Scottish Parliament short of independence; the commission's report proposed enhanced financial powers (Commission on Scottish Devolution 2009). Thus, all four main political parties now support strengthening the Scottish Parliament. Indeed, with nationalists stressing that an independent Scotland would maintain a 'social union' with the remainder of the UK, and with unionists now supporting strengthened devolution, there is perhaps greater common ground over Scotland's constitutional future than recent public acrimony has suggested. Nonetheless, there remain fundamental differences between the SNP and the other major parties about whether a referendum should occur, and what would be the desired outcome of any such vote. And this issue is likely to continue to rumble on for some time. The SNP are aware that while the chances of a 'Yes' vote for independence currently appear slim, there is more secure majority support in Scotland for giving people the chance to vote on the issue, as well as for enhancing the powers of the Scottish Parliament to at least some degree. Reflecting this, the SNP government's detailed proposals for a referendum, published in February 2010, advocated a two-question vote in which a 'More Powers' option, as well as 'Independence', were open to voters (Scottish Government 2010).

In Wales, a central part of the 'One Wales' coalition deal between Labour and Plaid Cymru in 2007 was a commitment to hold a referendum on further powers for the NAW by the end of its four-year term. Following on from this commitment, the coalition government established the All Wales Convention. This it charged with investigating the state of public opinion and engaging public interest in the relevant issues. In the event, the Convention could make little progress in generating public interest in the rather arcane subject of alternative models of devolved government; nor was it able substantially to advance knowledge of public attitudes, on which research already suggested that a referendum was 'winnable' but could not be guaranteed to be won. However, the Convention's own investigation of the constitutional alternatives led it to give strong endorsement to holding a referendum and securing a 'Yes' in such a vote (All Wales Convention 2009). And although some in the Labour party – most notably the then Secretary of State for Wales Peter Hain – publicly voiced their qualms about moving ahead, the formal vote requesting the referendum was passed by the Assembly unanimously in February 2010. With the Conservatives in the NAW supporting the referendum, and the new, Conservative-led UK government not 'standing in the way', agreement was reached to hold the referendum, and Welsh voters emphatically backed greater powers for the NAW in March 2011 by 63.5 per cent to 36.5.

Devolution and government policy

Consensus politics?

At the onset of devolution, it appeared likely that the policy agendas pursued in the Scottish Parliament and the NAW would be somewhat farther to the left than those typically followed by UK governments. The Conservative party was deeply unpopular in both Scotland and Wales, which had for many years tended to vote for parties of the centre-left to a greater degree than England. As Ron Davies, the principal architect of Welsh devolution, suggested 'Devolution is not an end in itself but a means to an end...we can create a country that more fully embodies the values of social justice and equality which have long animated the people of Wales' (1999: 15).

In Scotland, while Labour leaders in the coalition government generally avoided trumpeting differences with the UK government, the policy agenda followed up to 2007 was widely perceived as cleaving further to the left. Prominent examples of this were the abolition of upfront university tuition fees, and the free provision of personal care for the elderly. While fundamental disagreements remained with the main opposition party, the SNP, over Scotland's constitutional future, there was considerable common ground between government and opposition on socio-economic policy – what some observers have termed a 'progressive' social democratic consensus in devolved Scottish politics (Keating 2007; Osmond 2008). In Wales, by some contrast, from 2000 onwards Rhodri Morgan actively sought to heighten public awareness of policy differences between Cardiff and London – indicative of what he termed 'Clear Red Water'. Morgan ostentatiously contrasted the 'New Labour' brand of Tony Blair with the 'Classic Labour' approach he was following in Wales (Morgan 2002). Among the policy manifestations of this approach were the abolition of prescription charges for all in 2007, the provision of free local bus travel for all pensioners, and the abolition of national school tests for pupils under 16.

Since 2007, and notwithstanding the suggestions the party had occasionally made in opposition of being farther to the left than Labour, the policy agenda of the SNP government has continued within the broad social democratic consensus. The SNP have not, for instance, made any attempt to use the income tax-varying powers of the Scottish Parliament to raise additional revenue. There was an attempt made to introduce a local income tax in place of the Council Tax – a measure that would have broadly benefitted those on low incomes over the more affluent – but this fell victim to parliamentary arithmetic, as the SNP could not garner sufficient votes to proceed with this policy. But the more controversial SNP policies and government decisions have often been away from the mainstream of socio-economic policy: on constitutional matters (see above), or the decision by the SNP Justice Minister in August 2009 to release the man convicted over the Lockerbie bombing, Abdelbaset Ali al-Megrahi, back to Libya on compassionate grounds.

In Wales, the Labour–Plaid coalition from 2007–11 also continued to follow the broad direction of a social democratic consensus. Here, of course, implementing government policies was made much easier by the substantial Assembly majority enjoyed by the coalition. There was certainly no attempt to reverse previous government policy on the provision of universal benefits such as free prescriptions and bus travel for pensioners. There was, though, a somewhat greater emphasis given to broadly 'cultural' issues by Plaid Cymru ministers holding this portfolio, and also some efforts made to expand the provision of Welsh-medium education in schools and also universities.

Emerging differences?

As well as permitting governments in Edinburgh and Cardiff to follow different policy directions from the UK government in London in some areas, devolution has also enhanced the possibilities for policy learning and the comparison of different experiences. Of course, it has always been possible for governments to look abroad for lessons on what works well and what does not. But with the several governments within the UK sometimes following different paths, the contrasts have been made more obvious; the lessons are perhaps easier to draw. Thus, the UK government was able to observe the Scottish experience of free personal care for the elderly for several years before bringing forward proposals in this area for England in 2009. On policies as diverse as university funding and student fees, the structuring and clinical priorities of the NHS, and the curriculum and testing regime in schools, there are now differing approaches followed across the nations of the UK. And there is at least the potential for governments to draw useful lessons from these.

In general, political differences along the traditional left–right dimension have been rather muted in both Scotland and Wales in recent years. Differences may become starker as diminishing financial resources force harder choices to be made. But in both nations, the Conservative party, while insisting on the need for the long-term development of a smaller public sector and more vibrant enterprise culture, have sought to close the ideological gap that opened between itself and the Scottish and Welsh peoples during the 1980s (e.g. Gove 2010; Melding 2009). Political debates in the two nations have since 2007 increasingly focused on the constitutional issues discussed earlier. Here too the Conservatives have sought to play a more constructive role than their history as die-hard opponents of devolution in the 1997 referendums might suggest, just as they have tried to appear increasingly positive to the culture and language of Wales. All of this has served to moderate the tone of many of the policy differences between the parties. But there is ample scope for this to change in the next few years, with non-Conservative governments in Cardiff and Edinburgh positioning themselves as defenders of their nations' interests against a regime of austerity advanced by a Conservative-dominated government in London.

Public attitudes to devolution

What have the people made of the first decade of devolution? The 1997 referendums suggested that the people of Scotland were strongly supportive of devolution; those of Wales much less so. Substantial research has been conducted into public attitudes in subsequent years, and this research has often been able to ask more subtle questions than simply 'Devolution – yes or no?'

Research has consistently demonstrated that very few people in Scotland want to return to pre-devolution forms of government. However, there have also consistently been a substantial number of people wishing home rule for Scotland to be taken further, with many of those wanting to go as far as independence (Curtice 2008). In Wales, research has shown a very significant change in public attitudes over the first decade of devolution. The number of people fundamentally opposed to devolution has fallen considerably. But there has been no increase in those supporting independence (Wyn Jones and Scully 2010). Rather, the overwhelming majority of people in Wales support devolution within the UK – either on the current model, or with enhanced powers for the National Assembly (see Table 7.3).

How can we best explain public attitudes, and the changes in them, in Scotland and Wales? The referendum campaigns seeking to persuade the Scots and Welsh to support devolution placed great emphasis on how devolution might lead to more effective and responsive government in the two nations. Conversely, there was considerable fear among supporters of devolution that if the new institutions were not identified with clear policy successes, and improvements in the lives of people, then there might be a public backlash against the very principle of devolved government. But in practice, this is not how things have turned out. Detailed research has shown that while few people think that devolution has made daily life, or the quality of public services, in Scotland and Wales worse, there are not very many people who think that it has improved things greatly. Public evaluations of the policy records of the devolved administrations are distinctly moderate (Curtice 2005). Why, then, has public support for devolution remained strong in Scotland, and grown substantially in Wales, if most people do not think that it has substantially improved their lives? At least two factors appear to be in play. One is that people make comparisons between government in Edinburgh and

Table 7.3   *Constitutional preferences, Scotland and Wales 2009 (percentages)*

Q. 'Which of these statements comes closest to your view?'	Scotland	Wales
There should be no devolved government in Scotland/Wales	6.9	9.0
The Scottish Parliament/National Assembly for Wales should have fewer powers	4.0	6.3
We should leave things as they are now	27.6	27.6
The Scottish Parliament/National Assembly for Wales should have more powers	38.9	41.6
Scotland/Wales should become independent, separate from the UK	20.0	13.9
Don't Know/No Answer	2.5	1.6

Data from: Citizens After the Nation State survey, 2009

Cardiff on the one hand, and that in London on the other. Most people have had a limited regard for the competence and achievements of the devolved administrations, but they have had very similar attitudes (at best) about UK governments. Where research indicates that people do make a distinction between the two levels of government is that they trust the devolved administrations to be focused on the problems of Scotland and Wales to a much greater extent (Wyn Jones and Scully 2010).

A second factor underpinning public attitudes to devolution is that in Scotland and Wales, as in most political systems, many people are able to distinguish their specific attitudes to current governments and their policy record from a broader, more diffuse sense of how they believe they should be governed. And even among many of those who have been relatively unimpressed by what devolution has delivered in practical terms, there has come to be acceptance of an important principle: that, at least over a substantial area of government activity, the major decisions for Scotland and Wales should be made by, respectively, Scottish and Welsh political institutions (Wyn Jones and Scully 2008).

What has been the reaction to devolution of the majority nation in the UK? Two points emerge very clearly from the research on public attitudes in England. The first is that relatively few English people appear to object to devolution for Scotland and Wales. If the Scots and Welsh wish to have

Table 7.4 *Constitutional preferences, England 2007 (percentages)*

Q. 'With all the changes going on in the way the different parts of Great Britain are run, which of the following do you think would be best for England?'	
For England to be governed as it is now, with laws made by the UK parliament	57.5
For each region of England to have its own Assembly, which runs services like health	14.4
For England as a whole to have its own new parliament with law-making powers	17.5
None of these	2.0
Don't Know/No Answer	8.6

Data from: British Social Attitudes survey, 2007

partial self-government, the English are generally willing to accept this. The second point is that devolution for Scotland and Wales has not generated any substantial public demand for some English counterpart. Neither of the two most widely touted options, regional government or an English parliament, command substantial public support (see Table 7.4).

Finally, has a decade of devolution produced any identifiable changes in people's basic sense of national identity? Here, as elsewhere, experience has differed from what many anticipated. It was widely believed that devolution might weaken the attachment to Britain within Scotland and Wales, lead people to focus on Scottish/Welsh concerns, and come to feel more strongly and exclusively Scottish or Welsh. In fact, there is little or no evidence of this happening. Levels of reported British identity have remained largely unchanged in both Scotland and Wales (Wyn Jones and Scully 2010). If anything has changed, it is the political *implications* that people link to their identity. More people have come to see Scottish and Welsh self-government as a natural corollary of Scottish and Welsh national identity. The greatest changes to national identities have actually occurred in England. Here, research shows that people have become much more likely to distinguish between Englishness and Britishness, and to affirm an English identity. But this growing English national identity is not (or at least, not yet) seen by most of those who hold it as implying the need for specifically English political institutions (Curtice and Heath 2009).

The future of devolution

Devolution has led to obvious and fundamental changes in political life in some parts of the UK. It is no exaggeration to claim that politics in Scotland, Wales and, for a wider combination of reasons, Northern Ireland, has been transformed. The impact of devolution on other parts of the UK state has been rather less apparent. English regionalism seems to have died a largely unlamented death, while the appetite for a devolved English parliament remains limited. And while the effective reach of the UK government now, on many matters, extends only as far as England, the state often manages to give at least the impression of being remarkably unaffected by devolution. Thus, while the devolved territories now exist in what some have called a 'quasi-federal' relationship with the UK state, the state has developed few of the elaborate institutional structures that normally exist in federal systems to manage relationships between the state and the sub-state level. The relationships between London, on the one hand, and Cardiff, Edinburgh and Belfast, on the other, are almost exclusively bilateral and *ad hoc* in nature (Trench 2007).

An important question to consider, however, is whether the new constitutional status quo can and will persist. Is it not inevitable that, at some point, asymmetry will become unsustainable and that the 'English question' will have to be addressed? Relatedly, is it not also inevitable that the twin roles of Westminster being both the locus of power for the UK state, and the *de facto* parliament and government of England – will eventually come into conflict?

A defining virtue of the UK political system has often been held to be its flexibility and pragmatic ability to absorb, or simply ignore, apparent anachronisms, anomalies and contradictions. And we should not *assume* that the tensions inherent in uneven and asymmetric devolution must lead to major systemic crises. If the UK were going to collapse under the weight of its internal logical contradictions, it probably would have done so by now! But there are reasons to believe that devolution will eventually require further adjustments, affecting both England and the central state institutions. Chief among these reasons is the so-called West Lothian Question (WLQ). The West Lothian prefix originated in the rancorous debates around devolution in the 1970s, but the question itself has been asked in various forms since home rule was first placed on the political agenda. In its starkest form it might be posed as follows: how can one possibly justify a system which allows MPs elected to the Westminster parliament from west Lothian (or west Wales and west Belfast for that matter) to decide on education policy for England, when the existence of devolution means that English MPs do not enjoy corresponding influence on education policy in Scotland, Wales or Northern Ireland?

One response to the WLQ is to argue that English MPs make up such an overwhelming majority of the House of Commons that members representing the devolved territories only rarely have a decisive impact on any parliamentary votes. In other words, while all this might be a problem in theory, it's not really a problem in practice and so we shouldn't worry too much about it. But the result of the 2010 UK general election, where the Conservative party won a clear majority of English seats, yet were left well short of an overall majority thanks to the results in Scotland, Wales and Northern Ireland, suggests that this problem is far more than merely theoretical. And an alternative view is that, left unaddressed, the iniquities exposed by asking the WLQ could well lead to growing resentment among English voters; a credible answer must therefore be found. This, however, is easier said than done. As we have seen, one potential solution, namely to establish regional Assemblies in England, has minimal popular support. The same is currently true of another potential solution, an English parliament. The idea of an English parliament is also treated with deep suspicion by the main UK political parties: most leading politicians fear that a powerful English parliament would inevitably emerge as a rival centre of power and authority to Westminster.

With these possible solutions considered unacceptable or impractical, an alternative answer to the WLQ that has been proposed is to introduce procedural changes at Westminster to stop non-English MPs from voting on those matters that relate only to England. A version of this superficially simple and elegant solution was supported by the Conservative party in their 2010 election manifesto. But it is far from clear how 'English votes for English laws' could work in practice. For one thing, the dividing lines between English and non-English legislation are less clear than they might appear. Under the current budgetary formula, the funding implications of England-focused legislation almost invariably have knock-on financial implications for the devolved territories. Furthermore, under the asymmetric structures of devolution, Westminster legislation very rarely divides neatly into England-only and UK-wide categories. Rather, the vast majority of current legislation represents a mosaic or patchwork quilt: depending on the exact issues being legislated upon, some parts of a given piece of legislation may deal with England-only, others with England and Wales; others with Wales-only; others with England, Scotland and Wales or even, on occasion, England, Wales and Northern Ireland. Deciding when certain MPs ought to be excluded from certain parliamentary votes would not be clear and simple. And even if an acceptable and sustainable dividing line between

English and non-English legislation could be found, the following 'night-mare scenario' remains plausible. Imagine a situation where a UK government was elected without an overall majority in England, but rather relied on MPs from the devolved territories for its majority. How then could England be properly governed? At that point the hybrid nature of the UK's governing institutions would be cruelly exposed and the asymmetries of the current system surely rendered unacceptable. Given the relative size of England, this scenario is only likely to be realised infrequently. But it is one that should concern proponents of apparently straightforward procedural solutions.

When considering all of these, we should also bear in mind that until May 2010, devolution was tested in relatively benign conditions. The same party which had been in government in London held a large major-ity of Welsh and Scottish parliamentary seats, and had been in govern-ment (either alone or in coalition) throughout in Wales, and for the first eight years of devolution in Scotland. Furthermore, this was a time of relatively plentiful financial resources. During the next few years public spending will be squeezed, with increased potential for national rivalries and resentments as to how finance is allocated across the UK. At the same time, the Conservative-led UK government enjoys only fairly limited support outside England. While the latter circumstance might help Labour rebuild its support in Scotland and Wales, it is just as plausible that it might reinforce Scottish and Welsh nationalist resentments against what may be viewed as an essentially 'alien' London government. While conflicts are not inevitable in the next few years, they are increasingly likely.

Conclusion

Devolution, as one of its progenitors once astutely observed, is 'a process, not an event' (Davies 1999). The creation of the Scottish Parliament and the National Assembly for Wales has already led to profound changes in the political life of Scotland and Wales. And many of these changes are still ongoing. Devolution has also posed wider ques-tions about the nature of the UK state and how it adapts to devolution. It is far from clear that satisfactory answers have yet been found to those questions. They are questions which any serious student of UK politics must seek to understand and engage with.

A final question to consider is whether devolution does make the even-tual break-up of the UK more likely. In the 1990s, prior to the creation of the Scottish Parliament and NAW, the Labour party's leader in Scotland suggested that devolution would 'kill nationalism stone dead'. A decade into devolution, with the SNP a majority government in Edinburgh and Plaid Cymru having been coalition partners in Cardiff, this prediction has been proven emphatically false. But support for the SNP or Plaid Cymru is not the same thing as support for independence. Independence continues to have very limited support in Wales, while support has not grown in recent years in Scotland. Devolution has undoubtedly made Scotland and Wales more distinct in their politics and government. Devolution also provides a clearer path towards independence. But it does not necessitate that this path will be taken.

Chapter 8

Power Sharing in Northern Ireland

CATHY GORMLEY-HEENAN

The causes and consequences of the conflict in Northern Ireland are complex. There are no simple answers to questions about when the conflict actually began and whether the conflict is now finally over. There are several explanations (see McGarry and O'Leary 2004), but the most commonly cited manifestation has been the extent of the divisions between the two main communities in Northern Ireland – Protestant–Unionist–Loyalist and Catholic–Nationalist–Republican – and their different constitutional preferences in relation to the status of Northern Ireland. Unionists and Loyalists want Northern Ireland to remain part of the 'Union' – the United Kingdom of Great Britain and Northern Ireland. Nationalists and Republicans want Northern Ireland to become reunited with the rest of the island of Ireland and to have total independence from Britain.

After years of violence, which resulted in the deaths of more than 3,600 people (see McKittrick *et al.* 1999), the Good Friday Agreement (GFA) was signed between the British and Irish governments and endorsed by the majority of the political parties in Northern Ireland. This agreement provided a new, and agreed, constitutional settlement for Northern Ireland based on a devolved government within Northern Ireland, established cross-border relationships between Northern Ireland and the Republic of Ireland and established east–west relationships within the British Isles. The nature of the devolved government was asymmetrical to those agreed for Scotland, Wales and London in 1997.

Particular to devolution in Northern Ireland was a system of consociationalism (a form of power sharing) between the two main community groupings. Consociational theory identifies four key characteristics of such a democracy:

- There should be a grand coalition between the leaders representing the major groupings in society in a power sharing executive;

- those elected as representatives of these groupings have the right to disagree with government decision-making and have a vetoing power to ensure that only decisions with mutual agreement will be passed;
- representation to elected office must be on an entirely proportional basis; and
- there must be room for segmental autonomy where groups have the authority to look after their own internal affairs (Lijphart 1977).

These four characteristics were evidenced in the GFA and have been applauded (McGarry and O'Leary 2004) and criticised (Taylor 2009) in equal measure. Their respective arguments bring us directly to the focus of this chapter, which is whether this system of power sharing in Northern Ireland has actually worked. How would we know? What would it take to show that the process is working and what does 'working' actually mean? Can one consider power-sharing 'success' to mean simply a functioning Assembly and executive? Might success be considered as this *plus* the absence of both violence and the threat of violence in Northern Ireland? Some people would say power sharing was working if it (almost) stopped violence and nothing else. Others still might suggest that the only true measure of success is in terms of improved community relations between the two main communities.

With these questions in mind, the chapter is presented in three parts: First, it examines the operation of the power-sharing arrangements since May 2007, with a focus on any dislocation between theory and practice, and highlights some of the most obvious concerns. For example, do these arrangements actually promote the sharing of power, or rather the splitting of power and/or the snaring of power? Using this question, the chapter then explores the political opportunities and difficulties which have presented themselves. Second, the chapter considers perhaps the biggest institutional difficulty of all: the limited forum for the articulation of criticisms. The design of the power-sharing arrangements in Northern Ireland has meant that there exists no formal opposition to the government since the four largest political parties each have seats in the executive in a mandatory, as opposed to voluntary, coalition. How might protest, opposition and dissent be articulated in such an environment? Third, and finally, the chapter steps back from the mechanics of power sharing to consider how the mix of cooperation and conflict might affect the future political landscape of Northern Ireland, if at all?

It is important to set the most recent power-sharing experience (from 2007 to present) in context by reflecting briefly on the opportunities and difficulties experienced from the initial signing of the GFA.

Power-sharing opportunities and difficulties 1998–2007

The power-sharing institutions established by the GFA were more often in suspension than in operation between 1999 and 2007. Full power was devolved to the Northern Ireland Assembly in December 1999 but, by February 2000 it had suffered its first suspension as a result of tensions over IRA decommissioning and the potential collapse of the institutions should the First Minister (David Trimble of the Ulster Unionist party (UUP)) follow through on his threats to resign (see Figure 8.1). Another two short suspensions followed in 2001 in a bid to break the deadlock over decommissioning. In 2002, after a series of further political crises, devolution in Northern Ireland was suspended for more than four years. This latest suspension was the product of both the IRA's refusal to fully decommission its weapons and of profound divisions within Unionism. The restoration of the Assembly in 2007 was the consequence of the decision by the Democratic Unionist party (DUP), by then the largest unionist party in Northern Ireland, to share power with Sinn Féin, the largest nationalist party.

Figure 8.1   *DUP versus UUP electoral rivalry 1998–2011*

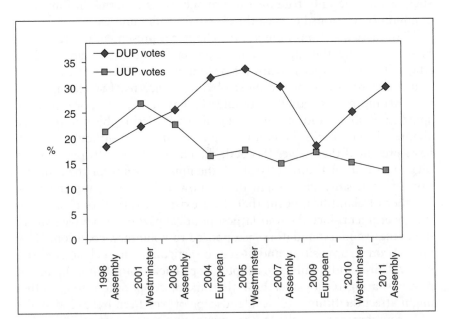

Note: *2010 Westminster. The UUP fought this election jointly with the Conservatives under the banner 'Ulster Conservatives and Unionists: New Force'. Of their 102,631 (15.2 per cent) vote share, 90,910 (13.5 per cent) went to UUP candidates and 11,451 (1.7 per cent) to Conservative candidates.

Figure 8.2   *Sinn Féin versus SDLP electoral rivalry 1998–2011*

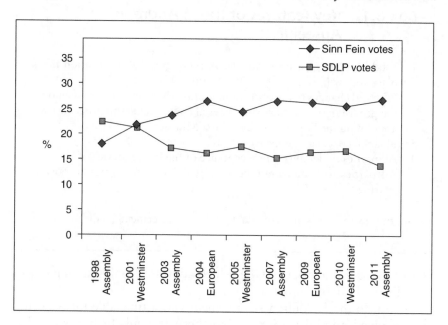

Arriving at this juncture was, however, a complicated and lengthy affair. The DUP had played no part in the negotiations which led to the initial power-sharing agreement, the GFA, in 1998. Their intra-ethnic rival party, the UUP, had been the largest unionist party during the period of negotiations leading up to that Agreement and were broadly supportive of the power-sharing arrangements that had been put in place. However, the initial years after the Agreement were fraught with many difficulties for those parties which had signed up to its implementation but none found it more difficult than the two largest parties at the time, the UUP and the nationalist Social Democratic and Labour party (SDLP). These parties were soon electorally eclipsed by their intra-ethnic and less moderate rival parties, the DUP and Sinn Féin (see Figures 8.2 and 8.3).

This development of an electoral shift away from the more moderate political parties towards the political extremes raised concerns about the viability of the 1998 Agreement. How could the DUP, so inimically opposed to this agreement, agree to its implementation? While the Northern Ireland Assembly remained in suspension, renewed talks began between the British and Irish governments and the main political players in Northern Ireland. By May 2007, two important issues had been resolved. First, the IRA had decommissioned its weaponry and this obstacle was no longer central to politics in Northern Ireland. Second, the St Andrew's Agreement of 2006 articulated additional provisions and

---

Box 8.1   Key features of the St Andrews Agreement

1   Establishment of a transitional Assembly until full restoration takes place following a new Assembly election
2   Practical changes to the operationalisation of the institutions including the provision of a statutory ministerial code, changes to procedure for appointing the First and Deputy First Minister
3   Financial package for newly restored executive
4   All parties to demonstrate acceptance of the Police Service of NI
5   All parties to demonstrate genuine willingness to engage in power-sharing

See full text at: www.nio.gov.uk/st_andrews_agreement-2.pdf

---

clarifications to the original GFA which addressed long-standing objections by the DUP (see Box 8.1).

Central to the St Andrew's Agreement was a timetable for restoring the devolved administration to Northern Ireland. In line with this timetable, devolution was duly restored on 8 May 2007 with Ian Paisley, the leader of the DUP, and Martin McGuinness of Sinn Féin, appointed as first and deputy first ministers respectively.

Restoration of power sharing in 2007: a sign of success?

There are two contrary indications for the restoration of devolution in Northern Ireland. Supporters of consociationalism, including Brendan O'Leary (an academic and policy adviser to Irish, British and American government officials during the peace process), suggested that the DUP-SF agreement represented the outworking of the peace process logic of bringing the extremes to the centre rather than building from the centre to the extremes (see McGarry and O'Leary 2006, 2006a). What favoured this view was mainly the consequence for Unionism. Getting the DUP fully onboard might resolve the distinction in Unionism between 'legalism' and 'existentialism' or, in other words, the distinction between the constitutional status claimed by David Trimble (UUP) and the sense of 'existential' wrong felt by many unionist voters and exploited by the DUP. With Paisley as first minister that gap could be closed significantly. The outcome of this would be moderation through responsibility. In contrast to this is the Paul Bew thesis (an academic and adviser to the UUP leader David Trimble during the peace process) which suggests that the weakening of the UUP–SDLP core undermined the foundations of constructive power sharing in Northern Ireland (see Bew 2007: 111–13). The outcome of this would inevitably be one of frustration through irresponsibility. This thesis was built on the premise that an arrangement based on the principle of sharing was likely to require the empowerment of those genuinely committed to that principle rather than those who were not. It assumed that DUP–SF power sharing was inherently unstable because it was about place (power) rather than content (policy) and the inability to deliver on content would undermine the institutions. The experience of devolution since May 2007 allows us to test these two theses in Northern Ireland in terms of place – the structure of government – and content – the performance of governance.

Power sharing, power splitting and power snaring

Power sharing

The original power-sharing arrangements contained within the 1998 GFA included the following features: The establishment of a Northern Ireland Assembly made up of 108 MLAs (Members of the Legislative Assembly) with cross-community consensus or 'parallel consent' required of any key decisions taken by that Assembly; the establishment of a Northern Ireland executive with a mandatory coalition of the executive members who would be appointed to office; and the use of the d'Hondt system which would allocate the ministerial seats proportionate to the size of the parties therein and the total number of seats allocated to each party within the Northern Ireland Assembly.

This last listed electoral mechanism is based on a mathematical formula which initially uses a dividing figure of one to allocate the first seat and then a dividing figure of the total number of seats gained plus one in subsequent rounds of allocation until all remaining seats have been allocated. For example, in the allocation of ministerial seats in December 1999, the UUP were first to allocate because they held 28 Assembly seats and were the largest Assembly party. For the second round of allocation, UUP dividing figure became 2 (1 seat allocated +1) to give them a revised figure of 14. Because of this, the UUP were no longer the 'largest' party in the second round and the SDLP as the new 'largest' party (with 24 seats) were able to allocate in the second round. Table 8.1 illustrates each of the 10 allocations of ministerial office, highlighting in bold the allocation of the ministerial office to the party with

Table 8.1   *Appointment of Northern Ireland executive ministers using d'Hondt, December 1999*

Allocation number	1	2	3	4	5	6	7	8	9	10
UUP (28 seats)	28	14	14	14	14	$9\,{}^1/_3$	$9\,{}^1/_3$	$9\,{}^1/_3$	7	7	3 nomina-tions
SDLP (24 seats)	24	24	12	12	12	12	8	8	8	8	3 nomina-tions
DUP (20 seats)	20	20	20	10	10	10	10	$6\,{}^2/_3$	$6\,{}^2/_3$	$6\,{}^2/_3$	2 nomina-tions
Sinn Féin (18 seats)	18	18	18	18	9	9	9	9	9	6	2 nomina-tions
Alliance (6 seats)	6	6	6	6	6	6	6	6	6	6	0 nomina-tions

Data from: Northern Ireland Legislative Assembly

the largest number of seats in that particular round using the d'Hondt formula.

The intent was that these structural arrangements would allow for, at best, the emergence of common positions or, at worst, at least a sense of collective responsibility.

Power splitting

Problems with the implementation of these power-sharing arrangements and problems of mistrust between the various protagonists resulted in a series of hitches, delays, setbacks and the eventual suspension of the devolved institutions in 2002. Between 1999 and 2002, there was more evidence of power splitting than power sharing with the development of separate spheres of administrative competence and members of the executive going on 'solo runs' in respect of their respective departments. For example, the two DUP ministers refused to participate in executive meetings because of the presence of Sinn Féin and instructed their departmental officials not to provide the executive with any information unless there was explicit approval from the DUP ministers (BBC, 2000). Martin McGuinness (Sinn Féin), as Minister for Education in 2002, took the unilateral decision to abolish the primary school transfer examination (the 11+) three days before the last suspension of the Northern Ireland Assembly much to the dismay of unionist executive colleagues who had supported the retention of a transfer test.

Negotiations in St Andrew's in 2006 were held to address the various sticking points of the original agreement, not least this development of power splitting in autonomous ministerial 'fiefdoms'. While the majority of the actors involved in these negotiations remained the same as those involved in the GFA, there was one notable difference. The DUP, who had chosen to play no part in the negotiations which led to the GFA, had become central to these negotiations as the largest unionist party in Northern Ireland after electorally eclipsing the UUP in the 2005 elections when the Northern Ireland devolved institutions remained in suspension. The eventual St Andrew's Agreement, signed by the British and Irish governments, though not formally endorsed by the political parties in Northern Ireland, was a three-page and five-annex document which left most of the original GFA architecture in place and dealt instead with a series of practical changes to its operationalisation as well as policing and the law; human rights, equality, victim and other related issues; and a new financial package from Westminster for the newly appointed executive.

Power snaring

These operational changes to the power-sharing arrangements can be viewed in two ways. Critics might argue that the very laudable and constructive approach to power sharing as agreed by the GFA had, to an extent, been 'snared' by the additional provisions made in St Andrews at the behest of the DUP. Power snaring, in the form of a disposition to frustrate the plans of one's ministerial 'colleagues', was now enshrined in an agreement which was supposed to be about sharing. In short, power sharing had been replaced by power snaring. Supporters might argue that the changes simply gave an added element of checks and balances to the system and might even inspire greater collective responsibility within government.

The actual mechanics of the new arrangements demonstrated an element of truth in both though the DUP pronouncements that they had secured a 'triple lock' (described in more detail below) against undesirable Sinn Féin policy indicated that the constructive approach to power sharing as described by O'Leary was faltering. How so? First, this additional agreement made provision for the inclusion of a revised statutory ministerial code which would ensure that 'all sections of the community were protected'. In practical terms, this meant that decisions taken within the executive would have to have the full consent of the executive to prevent the possibility of executive ministers embarking on 'solo policy runs' (Wilford 2008: 83) or the departments becoming 'autonomous party fiefdoms' (Aughey 2005: 88) in a power-splitting as opposed to power-sharing way. If such consent was not forthcoming and an executive vote was required, any three members of the executive could now demand that this vote be taken on a cross-community as well as majoritarian basis.

In effect, executive proposals which were opposed by either the DUP or Sinn Féin would not succeed in getting through the executive, thereby affording both parties a mutual veto and much potential for executive deadlocks. Such a deadlock happened after only twelve months following the restoration of devolution. The second 'locking' or 'checks and balance' mechanism by which unfavourable policy decisions could be averted was through the provision of the 'petition of concern principle' by which 30 MLA signatories on a petition could refer ministerial decisions back to the executive again for a second review. The DUP are the only party who have in excess of 30 seats in the current Assembly and this means that, at least in theory, the DUP could have the ability to frustrate every single non DUP decision. The third and final 'locking' or 'checking and balancing' mechanism required that decisions taken within the Northern Ireland Assembly and executive would also have to be ratified at Westminster.

Coupled with these specific changes, provision was also made to negate the possibility of communal redesignation within the Assembly once an Assembly term had begun (except in an instance where a member changed political party). Community designation (whereby each MLA has to identify themselves as either unionist, nationalist or other/non-aligned) takes place at the beginning of the Assembly term and is deemed necessary to ensure that the conditions of parallel consent are met. The St Andrew's amendment was likely to have been in direct response to the Alliance party's redesignation in 2001 from 'other' to 'unionist' along with the redesignation of one of the two members of the NI Women's Coalition party, to allow for the election of David Trimble and Mark Durkan as first and deputy first minister in 2001 using the parallel consent voting procedure outlined above. Without their redesignation, it was unlikely that there would have been sufficient unionist support in the House to meet the conditions of parallel consent because of the divisions within the UUP at the time and defections to the DUP. In removing the possibility for redesignation, critics argued that communalism within the Assembly would be further embedded while supporters applauded the fact that a minority party could not hold any balance of power over the majority parties. Supporters of the Alliance party's decision to temporarily redesignate in 2001 argued that it had prevented an unnecessary impasse. The additional conditions, in place after St Andrew's, would again allow for such impasses to occur.

It can be argued, then, that while the GFA was intent on delivering power sharing, it resulted in a system of power splitting; while the St Andrew's Agreement was negotiated, in part, to deal with the unintended development of power splitting, it then delivered a system of power snaring. Of course, this is not to suggest that the power-sharing, splitting and snaring approaches and behaviours are wholly and mutually exclusive as the experience of the devolved institutions post 2007 demonstrate.

Power sharing and snaring in practice: policies and problems

The eventual restoration of devolution to Northern Ireland in 2007 began with a Northern Ireland Assembly election in March of that year. The election results further increased the representation of the DUP and Sinn Féin within the Assembly at the expense of their electoral rivals, the UUP and SDLP (see Figure 8.2). On 8 May 2007, devolution was finally restored amid much fanfare from the international media who had arrived in Northern Ireland to witness this latest instalment of the prolonged Northern Ireland peace process. The honeymoon period for the newly elected first and deputy first ministers, Ian Paisley (DUP) and Martin McGuinness (Sinn Féin), was lengthy with the local media referring to the two as the 'chuckle brothers' such was evident, if surprising, friendly rapport between them. That aside, the restoration of devolution meant that those elected could finally get down to the business of governing and policy-making, something which continued when the DUP's Peter Robinson succeeded Paisley as first minister on his retirement in June 2008. While there are many examples, three policy issues will be used to illustrate the dislocation between the constructivist power-sharing intentions of the GFA, the more positive interpretation of the revisions in St Andrews and that practice of power sharing and policy making since 2007.

Education

First, there has been the rather thorny issue of education reform. The education system in Northern Ireland has always used academic selection in the form of a transfer test (known as the 11+ examination) to determine the eventual academic destination of children moving from primary level to secondary level education. As already noted, Martin McGuinness (SF), as the Minister for Education in the first devolved administration from 1999–2002, had taken a decision to scrap the transfer test with the last test scheduled to be undertaken in 2004. This was a controversial move. The unionist parties were, in the main, opposed to such a change and would have preferred that the transfer test procedures remained. They were aggrieved at what was perceived as a policy 'solo run' by McGuinness that did not have broader support. Although devolution was suspended by 2004, the date of the last scheduled transfer test, direct rule ministers from Westminster endorsed the original decision while moving the deadline for the last test to 2008 to allow time for the post 2008 transfer processes and criteria to be fully agreed. Mindful of the looming 2008 deadline, the DUP argued strongly during the St Andrews negotiations that academic selection in the form of the 11+ should be retained in Northern Ireland. The eventual revised power-sharing arrangements under St Andrews ensured that future ministers would not be able to take solo policy decisions such as McGuinness's original decision back in 2002, since any three ministers in the executive could call for such policy decisions or even proposals to be put to a vote requiring both majority and cross community support within the executive.

Therefore, when Catriona Ruane (SF), the newly appointed minister for education in the 2007 devolved administration, took office she was faced with a difficult situation – a looming deadline and a polity sharply divided along communal lines in respect of education reform. Unlike her predecessor she could not take a solo decision on what would replace the transfer test in 2009. She would have to seek consensus within the executive for her proposal or risk a stalemate on the issue. Finding consensus proved impossible. The result has been that the minister, unable to get any primary legislation on education reform past the likely 'veto' within the executive and/or the assembly, has had to resort to issuing 'guidance' to post-primary level schools on the issue of transfers. This guidance has no legal weighting with schools simply having to give 'regard' to the range of alternative criteria that the minister suggests should be used for transfers. The lack of legal weighting has meant that most of the grammar school sector in Northern Ireland have ignored the guidance and the ministerial view and introduced their own academic selection testing in the autumn of 2009. The lack of consensus on education reform in Northern Ireland has left many of the children and their parents anxious, agitated and angry and the new minister, John O'Dowd (SF), in an increasingly unenviable position.

Policing and justice

The second substantive policy issue concerns the devolution of policing and justice to Northern Ireland. Long running disputes between unionists and nationalists over the timing and nature of the proposed devolution of policing and justice ministry resulted in an absolute deadlock of the executive for five full months (June–November 2008). The St

Andrews Agreement had made provision for the devolution of policing and justice by May 2008 but, when this deadline passed, deadlock ensued with Sinn Féin refusing to allow executive meetings to be convened until the issue had been resolved. An eventual DUP–Sinn Féin agreement on the issue was announced in November 2008 and executive meetings resumed with almost immediate effect. Their agreement was founded on, among other things, the principle that neither the DUP nor Sinn Féin would nominate any of their own MLAs for the position of minister for policing and justice and that the minister would be appointed via the Northern Ireland Assembly using the aforementioned 'parallel consent' procedure and *not* the d'Hondt procedure by which all other ministerial posts were appointed. Under the d'Hondt mechanism, the position would have had to be offered to the SDLP. As such, the SDLP accused the DUP and Sinn Féin of executive 'gerrymandering' (Durkan 2008) and said that they would vigorously contest any process for a seat which was rightfully theirs. Given that this ministerial office is so sensitive, it was always unlikely that any unionist or nationalist candidate would be able to get enough votes within the Assembly to ensure parallel consent. In the end, neither the SDLP nor the Ulster Unionist candidates could attract enough cross party support from the floor of the Assembly and so David Ford, leader of the Alliance Party for Northern Ireland (APNI) – the centrist party which draws its support base from a mixture of Catholic and Protestant voters and particularly within the more middle classes, was elected as the Minister for Policing and Justice in April 2010. With Ford as the newest minister, the Alliance party's role as informal opposition becomes somewhat defunct.

Victims and survivors

The lack of agreement on some policy issues has, on occasion, led to more 'creative' approaches by the two main parties than simply using their mutual vetoes and power snaring each other's proposals. A clear example of this has been in relation to the establishment of a Victims Commissioner for Northern Ireland. The original intention was to appoint a single commissioner who would represent the views of those affected by the conflict in Northern Ireland. A decision was taken by the first and deputy first minister to change the selection process to allow them to appoint four commissioners as opposed to just one (and it should be noted that each were entitled to a full salary as opposed to a pro rata salary based on their increased number of commissioners), a decision widely believed to have been influenced by their inability to agree on a single candidate for the post.

Increasing inertia?

While space here does not permit a fuller examination of the range of policy blockages, some general observations can be made when contrasting the practice of power sharing within the 2007–11 executive and assembly with that of the first devolved administration until 2002. First, less legislation has been introduced during this assembly period than the last and there exists only a 'thin legislative timetable' (Wilford and Wilson 2009: 24). Of the Bills passed, thus far, by the Assembly not one has been contentious or 'key' (for example, the Pensions Bill, the Health Miscellaneous Bill and the Taxis Bill). Second, only one three-year programme for government has been produced by this Assembly in comparison to the three year programme for government which had to be agreed annually by the last Assembly – in other words there has been no change to the original programme for government which put the economy and economic development at the heart of its business despite the worldwide economic downturn which began soon after this programme for government had been agreed. Third, there were more than double the amount of North–South ministerial meetings (plenary, institutional and sector) held in the previous assembly. These comparisons could suggest something fundamentally wrong with the new arrangements, in so far as they have been used to inhibit rather than facilitate good government in Northern Ireland. In short, there has been less action by this administration than by their predecessors. Birrell's (2009) argument goes one step further to suggest that devolution has made little difference to many aspects of how Northern Ireland is governed, particularly in relation to the role and scope of the powers of quangos or public bodies in Northern Ireland. It would seem that Bew's thesis of frustration through irresponsibility (or in this case increasing inertia) may become increasingly significant.

Opposition, protest and dissent

Political opposition

As noted, the terms of the GFA and the St Andrews Agreement, with its mandatory power-sharing coalition, leaves no room for a formal opposition within its composition. Between 2008 and 2010, only the four main parties (DUP, SF, UUP and SDLP) had seats in the executive. The remaining parties elected to the Assembly (the Alliance party with seven seats, the Green party with a single seat, the Progressive Unionist party (PUP) with a single seat and one independent) were assumed to be the Assembly's informal opposition, although the appointment of the

Figure 8.3   *Composition of Northern Ireland Assembly in January 2011 (with 108 seats)*

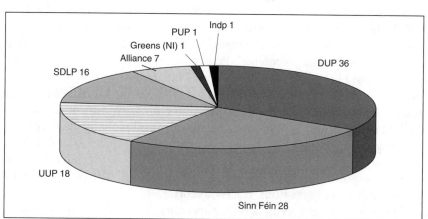

Alliance party's David Ford as minister of policing and justice in April 2010 has already reduced the informal opposition numbers significantly.

However, an informal opposition holds no weight in terms of the mechanics of the power-sharing arrangements since all, with the exception of the PUP which is a unionist based party, would be designated as neither unionist or nationalist in the Assembly communal designation records. This designation of unionism or nationalism is critical to the working of the principles of parallel consent and, in effect, renders the position of those without such designation as ineffectual. While supporters of the consociational arrangements would point to a clear majority united being much more preferable and more democratic than a simple majoritarian method of election, others would argue that there is a need for a voluntary as opposed to mandatory collation, to allow for the establishment of a bona fide formal opposition. The counter argument to this, of course, is that formal structures for 'opposition' are clearly marked out within the executive and assembly through the 'locking' mechanisms. This, however, only explains the opposition from those bound into the current devolved arrangements. Protest and dissent against these arrangements has taken many forms.

Civic protest

The lack of a formal opposition under the terms of the power-sharing arrangement has led to the local media playing an increasingly important critiquing role, often with bizarre consequences. A letter sent from the Office of the First Minister and Deputy First Minister (OFMDFM) to the proprietor of the *Belfast Telegraph* in March 2009, the largest-selling newspaper in Northern Ireland, voiced disquiet over the paper's coverage of the work of the Assembly and the executive, claimed that 'the relentless negativity of recent editions has disappointed us' (*Sunday Times*, 19 April 2009). Questions by journalists and reporters during government briefings have become increasingly fraught. In one incident, quickly dubbed the 'Purdy Robinson Exchange', Peter Robinson, the first minister, very publicly lost his temper on camera with Martina Purdy, one of the BBC's political correspondents, when she asked whether the OFMDFM should revisit the terms of its three-year Programme for Government (2008–11) in light of the growing economic crisis locally and globally. In a separate exchange with another BBC political correspondent, Gerry Adams of Sinn Féin also appeared to lose his cool claiming that 'journalists have the right and the responsibility and the duty to ask questions. You don't have the right to ask stupid questions' (O'Toole 2007).

The increasing degree of scrutiny and criticism by the media to which the main parties have been exposed may, of course, modify behaviours or change outcomes in the future. The accusations of clientelism levied against the DUP resulted in the resignation of junior minister, Ian Paisley Jr, and was swiftly followed by the departure of Ian Paisley senior as both leader of the DUP and as first minister for Northern Ireland. Iris Robinson MP and MLA, wife of Peter Robinson, resigned all her offices in January 2010 after a damning BBC investigative journalism programme raised, among other things, questions about possible financial impropriety on her part while holding public office. Increasing media speculation on Peter Robinson's own involvement in a land deal with property developers cast a shadow over Robinson which is said to have contributed to the shock loss of his seat as an MP for East Belfast in the May 2010 general election, a seat he had held for 31 years. He remained, however, at the time of writing, first minister (and Ian Paisley Jr, succeeding his father, was elected to Westminster in the same election).

Despite critical media reportage and commentary from the intelligentsia (through online blogs and discussions groups such as 'Slugger O Toole' and 'Agenda for Change'), electoral unaccountability with the current arrangements remains. The degree of party loyalty with Northern Ireland is such that there is no risk of any backbench revolts or 'rebellions' on the scale of Westminster. Opposition from within the political parties is almost negligible. There was the strange exception, however, of the rather bizarre scenario whereby the SDLP voted against the executive's first Programme for Government even though this meant actually voting against their own government minister who had already endorsed the programme at executive level. The role of the statutory, standing and ad hoc committees within the Assembly could be compromised by such party loyalties where party members feel duty bound to defend the actions of the ministers from their own parties as opposed to interrogating their value. One encouraging development here stands out. In March 2009, the Assembly committee rejected a suggestion by OFMDFM to cut their Assembly question time from twice a month to once a month in line with other departments within Stormont. In rejecting their suggestion completely, the Committee pointed out that the Scottish and Welsh first ministers were required to answer questions on a weekly basis.

Militant dissidents

At the most extreme level, there has been the increase in violent activities by dissident republicans who remain opposed to power sharing in Northern Ireland. Such violence resulted in three deaths in 2009. Two British soldiers were killed by the Real IRA in March 2009 and a Police Service of Northern Ireland (PSNI) police officer was killed by the Continuity IRA, also in March 2009. The UK's security services raised the threat level of dissidents in Northern Ireland from 'substantial' to 'severe' in the days prior to the killings and confirmed that it was spending around 15 per cent of its overall resources on 'Irish-related terrorism' (Evans *et al.* 2009). In 2010, PSNI Constable Peadar Heffron was seriously injured when a car bomb exploded as he drove to work and Ronan Kerr was killed in a similar attack in April 2011. Car bombs have also been planted at police stations and courthouses across Northern Ireland; some have exploded, but others have been defused in time. The spawning of new dissident groups from within the original dissident groups illustrates further the seriousness of the issue (Bew 2009). According to the PSNI (2010), the number of shooting incidents increased from 42 in 2007–8, to 54 in 2008–9 and to 79 in 2009–10. The number of bombing incidents doubled from 23 in 2007–8, to 46 in 2008–9, and increased again to 50 in 2009–10. The introduction of 'Operation Descent' by the PSNI in September 2009 resulted in the reestablishment of highly visible police checkpoints and patrols around Northern Ireland, much like those in operation during the 'troubles' and before the unfolding of the peace process.

Has power sharing worked?

On reflection, then, has power sharing, as a process for conflict management, actually worked? The increase in violence and the return of the threat of violence on the streets of Northern Ireland is, obviously, cause for concern. Paul Bew's (2009) articulation of the authorities view on this

– 'that no-one ever believed that the Belfast Agreement meant the absolute end of republican terrorism in Ireland' – does little to diminish the overall impact of his headline article 'Terrorism is back in Northern Ireland'. Ironically enough, it might be *because* some aspects of the power-sharing arrangements seem to be working that the dissidents have upped their game. It begs the question: has Northern Ireland achieved a measure of power-sharing 'success' through a fully functioning Assembly and executive? Has the outworking of the current power-sharing arrangements show the *moderation through responsibility* as articulated by Brendan O'Leary? Or have the foundations of constructive power sharing been undermined through the electoral eclipse of the UUP/SDLP core resulting in an outcome of *frustration through irresponsibility* as articulated by Bew? Thus far, we have seen evidence of both responsibility and of irresponsibility. The parties have been responsible enough to ensure that some 'crises' have been averted. That the *initial* negotiations over the devolution of policing and justice were conducted 'in-house' between the two main political parties without the need for a mediator or brokers in the form of the British and/or Irish governments, counts as remarkable progress. The irresponsibility of reductionist zero-sum politics being rehashed for the purposes of local and national elections do little more than confuse the electorate as to their party's true intentions and undermine any shred of confidence as to the sincerity of their partners in government.

Elections, of course, have unveiled the fairly schizophrenic nature of power-sharing arrangements, with parties aggressively contesting elections *against* one other while sitting in government *with* one other simultaneously, though this is not different from any other PR systems, or from the circumstances which the Conservative–Lib Dem coalition currently find themselves in at Westminster. The 2009 European elections were a classic example of zero-sum politics at work. European issues did not dominate the agendas of the two main parties. Instead, the DUP talked of 'defeating republicanism', 'rolling back the nationalist agenda' and preventing any Sinn Féin victory. Although the DUP had topped the poll in Northern Ireland since the first European election was held in 1979, they went on to suffer considerable losses in this latest European election to the newly established Traditional Unionist Voice (TUV), headed up by ex DUP member Jim Allister. The DUP proportion of the total votes cast dropped from 32 per cent in 2004 to 18.2 per cent in 2009. The overall result was that in a three seat contest, the DUP dropped to third place, with Sinn Féin topping the poll for the first time in Northern Ireland being the only party to have reached the quota with first preference votes of 126,184 even if this was marginally down on 2004. The DUP's third seat was won without actually reaching the quota. In the 2010

Westminster election, the DUP were campaigning for a voluntary coalition government in Northern Ireland in the longer term and the abolishment of community designations within the Assembly voting system to be replaced by a weighted majority vote of 65 per cent. In contrast to the European election manifesto which had almost 30 references to Sinn Finn, there was only one mention of Sinn Féin specifically in their general election materials.

The future political landscape in Northern Ireland

In terms of Northern Ireland policy, the broader effects of the economic crisis should not be underestimated. The economy has been the primary issue within the 2008–11 Programme for Government and both the executive and the Assembly operates in the context of the wider global economic meltdown. The relationship and proximity to the Republic of Ireland has meant that Ireland's problems hold particular concern for Northern Ireland. The establishment in Ireland of a National Asset Management Agency (NAMA) which has been designed to offset the nationalised bank losses of loans given to property developers before the property market collapsed is one such concern. Through this agency, properties and developments will be sold off in an attempt to reclaim the debts accrued. Many of these, however, are located in Northern Ireland. The impact of a flood of properties being sold off in Northern Ireland could have a pronounced effect on the overall property prices in the area which have already suffered great losses since the onset of the economic downturn.

And, although the issue of policing and justice has been resolved in the short term (due to the sunset clause on this agreement lapsing by May 2012), there are a plethora of issues which have either been stubbornly ignored or routinely deferred. The lack of progress on proposals for an Irish Language Act has particularly frustrated Sinn Féin. The effective shelving of the community relations policy, A Shared Future, brings into focus just how divisive the issue of 'sharing' actually is. The lack of agreement on a Bill of Rights for Northern Ireland and how best to deal with the past have once again illustrated the sectarian lines along which agreement and disagreement has gathered.

In addition, prior to the 2010 general election, there was speculation that anti-agreement unionism would again be significant within the future of Northern Ireland. While anti-agreement republicanism had no political mandate in Northern Ireland, anti-agreement unionism did. The TUV, founded in December 2007, won the Dromore by-election in February 2008. Although losing out on the opportunity of a European seat the party did manage to take approximately 40 per cent of the DUP vote share as calculated from the 2004 results. The strength of first preference votes for the TUV (66,197) indicated that the party could, potentially, win six Assembly seats if the party's supporters voted in the same way in a future Assembly election. Buoyed by this possibility, the TUV leader, Jim Allister, stood against Ian Paisley Jr in the 2010 Westminster election. The election results saw the TUV's potential diminish with Paisley securing approximately 46 per cent of the votes in comparison to Allister's 17 per cent . Undaunted, the TUV fought on and secured a seat in the 2011 Assembly elections with 2.5 per cent of the vote.

Coupled with the possibility of a new party within the Assembly is the possibility of the realignment of existing parties. While the expectations that greater cooperation between the UUP, SDLP and Alliance would lead to a formidable opposition and their realignment as a 'formal' opposition, this did not materialise. The attempted realignment between the UUP and the UK's Conservative party through the establishment of the Ulster Conservatives and Unionists – New Force (UCUNF) for the European election and Westminster elections was a failure for the UUP with the party failing to secure a single seat in the Westminster elections. Their only MP in the 2005–10 parliament, Sylvia Hermon, resigned from the UUP in protest at the UUP–Conservative party pact and, standing as an independent candidate, retained her seat at the 2010 general election, leaving the UUP to ponder on the virtues of aligning themselves with the Conservatives to no avail.

Changes in party fortunes within Northern Ireland may be made even more pronounced if there is to be a revision of the current number of MLAs and ministerial departments within the power-sharing arrangement at Stormont. With a review of the size and structure of the government ongoing through the Assembly and Executive Review Committee, we might reasonably expect to see a reduction in the number of ministerial departments and in the total number of MLAs prior to the next Assembly elections, with implications for both d'Hondt and parallel consent processes. In a situations such as this, the d'Hondt system could have its power-sharing capabilities diminished further with the main political parties effectively playing a game of chess, moving to take certain ministerial posts in the hope that their rivals won't get them or will be forced to take other posts that they are less interested in, though many would suggest that this happens already. With the potential downsizing of personnel, we can safely expect to lose some of the familiar faces, not least as a consequence of the expenses furore at Westminster, which, among other things, exposed the degree of double jobbing that existed and 'Swish Family Robinson' finances of the first minister Peter Robinson and his wife, Iris, both of whom drew two salaries as the

Westminster MPs and Stormont MLAs (and with Robinson being additionally remunerated by being first minister) (BBC 2009). While the dual and triple mandates had already been highlighted as potentially problematic (Wilford 2007), the media onslaught crystallised the issue for the parties and has already led to a change in the law which prohibited double jobbers from getting extra money for their dual mandates in the Assembly and Westminster.

But the most potent potential change may be in terms of the largest party grouping in the Assembly, and by extension, the designation of First Minister of Northern Ireland. The 2010 general election results revealed Sinn Féin as the largest party in Northern Ireland with 25.5 per cent of the votes. The DUP received 25 per cent. Should a repeat performance occur in the next Assembly election and Sinn Féin remain as the largest political party, this would mean Sinn Féin would have the mandate to elect the First Minister and Martin McGuinness would become the first minister of Northern Ireland. Such speculation has resulted in renewed debates on possible reactions to a Sinn Féin first minister, and the by extension, the state of the union, the future of unionist politics in Northern Ireland, the idea of unionist unity at best and/or the prospects of unionist electoral pacts for future elections in Northern Ireland (Belfast Newsletter July 2010). In 2010 Gerry Adams resigned his Westminster and Assembly seats in West Belfast to fight and win the constituency of Louth in the 2011 general election in the Irish Republic. Adams's decision to join the 14-strong Sinn Féin contingent in the Irish parliament (the party having won some 10 percent of the vote), indicates Sinn Féin's ongoing pursuit of an all-Ireland political strategy.

Of course, the ultimate indicator of the success or otherwise of the power-sharing arrangements resides with public opinion. The Northern Ireland Life and Times Survey 2009 (NILT; see Table 8.2) asked: 'Overall, do you think that the Northern Ireland Assembly has achieved …'. Almost two-thirds of the survey respondents thought that the Assembly had achieved something – a lot (10 per cent) or a little (54 per cent). This was a positive response in spite of all of the delays and setbacks during the Assembly's implementation and was, perhaps, conditioned by the honeymoon period of the re-established institutions in 2007. Around one in five respondents thought that it was too early to tell.

Some commentators suggest that the real measure of success in Northern Ireland is in terms of improved community relations between the two main communities, as opposed to just progress in government. The ultimate question, then, is whether the consociational arrangements introduced have bridged the gap between the two communities, or if, by entrenching the differences between them, they have helped widen the

Table 8.2   *Northern Ireland Life and Times Survey, 2009*

'Overall, do you think that the Northern Ireland Assembly has achieved ...'.	%
a lot,	10
a little,	54
or, nothing at all?	17
too early to tell	18
Don't know	1

gap at the very same time as having brought peace to Northern Ireland. This is a difficult question to answer. In truth, the simple answer is that 'it depends'. It depends on exactly *how* one chooses to measure community relations in Northern Ireland and/or the gap between the two main communities. For example, it is true that the most people in Northern Ireland continue to live in segregated communities with over 90 per cent of public housing segregated on religious grounds. It is also true, however, that 80 per cent of people would prefer to live in a mixed religion neighbourhood (NILT 2008). Equally, it is true that only 5 per cent of schoolchildren are educated in the integrated schooling sector with the remainder educated in schools with a specifically Catholic or Protestant ethos. Despite this it is also true that 43 per cent of respondents to a 2008 survey commissioned by the Northern Ireland Commission for Integrated Educations would prefer their children or grandchildren to attend an integrated school. Such statistics point to an uneasy coexistence and a real dislocation between what the public say and what they actually do in Northern Ireland. In psychological terms, the gap might be narrowing but in practical terms it is still not. Optimists might point to the latest public policy agenda in the shape of the draft *Cohesion, Sharing and Integration Strategy* produced by the Office of the First Minister and Deputy First Minister and suggest that a real 'sharing over separation' public policy initiative will assist further in narrowing the gap. Cynics would point to the painfully slow political progress on the *Cohesion, Sharing and Integration Strategy* and the effective shelving of its predecessor, *A Shared Future*, as evidence of a lack of political will in providing citizens with the facilities and means to actualise their intent. The narrowing of the gap, whether in real or psychological terms, will, of course, be profoundly affected by any further upscaling of the dissident threat and the fear that this inevitably instils within communities. Violence on the streets of Belfast in July 2010 resulting in injuries to the police and public, as well as a landmine explosion in South Armagh and the arrest of five men in County Louth on suspicion of dissident activity, as well as the murder of PC Ronan Kerr in April 2011, are an illustration of recent attempts to derail the process and the power-sharing arrangements.

So, while those looking in from outside Northern Ireland might applaud the progress that has been made since the GFA in 1998, those on the inside, looking out to their devolved brethren in Scotland and Wales, might well conclude that, apart from the absence of sustained political violence, the situation remains less than ideal. Both the peace process and the power-sharing settlement it has produced remains very much works in progress.

Chapter 9

Anti-Politics in Britain

GERRY STOKER

A key feature of British politics is that large numbers of citizens are alienated from its mainstream practices. The phenomenon of anti-politics finds expression through a strong negative outlook towards politics and disengagement from the formal institutions and practices of politics. Focus group studies have found 'a negative attitude of participants to the term "politics", which was seen as something they did not feel part of or involved in. Instead politics is viewed as the pursuit of an exclusive and disputable elite of hypocrites and liars' (Ram 2006: 190). Turnout in the 2010 general election was slightly up from 2005 but, at an estimated 65 per cent, it is far lower than the turnouts achieved in the 1950s. Typically, a fifth of citizens failed to vote in the 1950s (Stoker 2010: 53, Table 2.1), but in 2010 over a third failed to vote in a tightly contested and high-profile election given an additional boost in public attention by the first ever televised leadership debates.

The need for political reforms to respond to the 'crisis' in our politics and political culture was a strong theme in the televised debates in the 2010 election campaign. All the main parties offered substantial programmes of reform, each framed at least in part in terms of the context set by damaging revelations about MPs' expenses in the spring of 2009. The new coalition government has placed the issue of anti-politics firmly on its agenda with Nick Clegg, as Deputy Prime Minster, choosing political reform for his first solo speech. In this he declared that the new government 'is going to persuade you to put your faith in politics once again' (Clegg 2010). But have citizens lost faith in politics? Did they have faith in the first place? Understanding the factors behind anti-politics is plainly important in designing any reform package. You cannot design a good solution until you understand the problem correctly.

Identifying the problem occupies the first section of this chapter. What are the symptoms of the illness afflicting the British political system? This concern breaks down into several related questions. Do we have an anti-politics culture and, if so, is it a response to recent events or is it more deeply ingrained? Which citizens are disengaging and which are still participating? Do UK citizens have a more negative orientation to the practice of formal politics than that seen in other democracies?

Having explored the boundaries and parameters of the issue, the second section of the chapter looks at some of the core underlying explanations of the perceived problems with our politics. One explanation is that anti-politics emerges in a setting where citizens see themselves as powerless. But there may well be other factors at play too. Do citizens really want to be that involved in politics? What is it about the practice of politics that they find distasteful? Are they turned off by the underperformance of politics and by its failure to deliver desired outcomes? Do citizens really have the opportunity to understand politics?

A third section of the chapter asks how much of a challenge anti-politics poses. Some argue that we should 'do nothing'. Over recent decades, they suggest, citizens have simply become more demanding and more critical; but the political system delivers in much the same way that it always did. What is clear is that the new coalition government is definitely in the 'do something' camp and has put forward a major programme of reform. But will that programme work? We tackle this issue in the concluding section.

Exploring the rise of anti-politics

This section of the chapter looks at evidence about attitudes towards politics and the practice of politics in Britain over time. It shows that some groups, especially those who are socially and economically disadvantaged, may have particular problems in engaging with politics. It also places the British experience of politics in a wider comparative context.

Long-run evidence of negativity

Here are some key findings from a survey about British attitudes to politics:

- 3 in 10 claim 'to never follow' accounts of political and governmental affairs;
- 2 in 10 can name no party leader or any government ministry;
- 3 in 10 'never' talk about politics with friends and acquaintances;
- only 2 in 100 would regard involvement in politics as a preferred non-work activity; and
- 8 in 10 are doubtful of the promises made by candidates in elections.

These figures may not surprise you, until it is noted that the survey from which they come was conducted, not today, but in 1959. Indeed, it was the first major academic study that looked in depth at public attitudes to politics. Its findings were published in 1963 in *The Civic Culture* a comparative study of democracies by two American academics, Gabriel Almond and Sidney Verba (Almond and Verba 1963: 89, 96, 116, 263). In fact the final finding was not included in the book itself but was reported later in Kavanagh (1980: 145, fn. 58). As Almond and Verba suggest, disengagement from formal politics and cynicism about politicians are not recent phenomena.

Despite substantial advances in educational attainment, knowledge of, and interest in, politics of British citizens appears to have advanced by only a modest degree between the 1950s and the end of the first decade of the twenty-first century. The 2010 *Audit of Political Engagement* (Hansard Society 2010: 119) found about half of the population claiming an interest in politics but with 2 in 10 claiming no interest at all. The findings on these issues have remained relatively consistent since the first audit published in 2004. Moreover, 1 in 10 of respondents in the 2010 audit claimed that they knew nothing at all about politics. Here too the findings are fairly consistent with those reported in 2004 (Hansard Society 2010: 121). Only 4 in 10 of citizens can correctly name their local Member of Parliament (Hansard Society 2010: 122).

Cynicism about politics and politicians already evident in the 1950s appears to have become more deeply ingrained. The unreported finding from *The Civic Culture* expressing citizens' doubts about the promises of politicians indicates a level of scepticism, if not cynicism about politicians in the 1950s that was lost in Almond and Verba's general argument. This famously presented Britain as having a successful democratic culture. By the late 1970s, Kavanagh (1980: 145–7) was able to offer findings that hinted further at lack of trust in politicians. For example, in one survey 58 per cent agreed with the view that 'people become MPs for their own gain and ambition' and in another survey 60 per cent held the view that people involved in politics tell the truth only some of the time. Table 9.1 summarises opinions held about MPs from the 1980s onwards. It is plain that, for a long time, substantial numbers of citizens have viewed MPs as self-seeking money-grabbers and as lacking a high moral code. The expenses row in 2009 may well have reinforced such opinions, but it can hardly be seen as the origin of such views.

The audits undertaken annually by the Hansard Society since 2004 have uncovered further expressions of an anti-politics culture in the UK. The picture is more nuanced than we typically acknowledge, but the problems appear deep-seated. Not everyone 'hates' politics and not everyone is disengaged from it, but there is undoubtedly substantial anti-political sentiment in British society. According to survey analysis from the 2010 *Audit of Political Engagement*, roughly two-thirds of citizen respondents could be categorised as falling into the anti-politics camp in

Table 9.1 *Support for negative views about MPs from the 1980s onwards (percentages)*

Statement: 'Most MPs make a lot of money by using public office improperly'

Year	Agree	Disagree	Don't know
1985	46	31	23
1994	64	22	14
2009	68	28	4

Statement: 'Most MPs have a high moral code'

Year	Agree	Disagree	Don't know
1985	42	35	23
1994	28	59	15
2009	37	58	4

Data from: IPSOS/MORI (2009)

that they were found to be disengaged from or to be expressing consistently negative views about the formal political processes and governing arrangements of our society (Hansard Society 2010: 51). Specific clusters include: just under 1 in 10 'detached cynics', nearly 1 in 10 'bored and apathetic', a further 1 in 10 'alienated and hostile' and nearly a quarter 'disengaged and distrustful'.

As we have seen, though they have hardly helped, today's negative views about politics are not simply a product of the row over MPs' expenses that dominated news during May 2009. We can be confident about making this claim in part because the *Audit of Political Engagement* has asked many of the same questions on an annual basis since its launch in 2004. The 2010 *Audit* (Hansard Society: 126, 124, 128) confirms that only a quarter of the population trust politicians generally, less than a third are satisfied with the job done by MPs and only 2 in 10 of citizens would be proud if a family member were to be or become a local or national politician. But these appear to be settled views, with no significant shift of opinion recorded between 2004 and 2010. Anti-politics plainly is an embedded feature of British political culture.

Yet it may well be that there is an increased sense of disempowerment when it comes to influencing the political system. According to Almond and Verba (1963) in the late 1950s, 8 out of 10 British citizens felt they could influence local decisions and 6 out of 10 felt that national decisions were in their span of influence. Regular surveys by the Hansard Society at the beginning of the twenty first century show that only 3 in 10 now feel that local decisions are in their grasp and that only 1 in 10 feel that they can influence national decisions.

Of course, there are big difficulties with some elements of how Almond and Verba conducted their survey in the light of modern techniques and the questions asked do not exactly match those posed today. But it nonetheless credible to suggest a significant drop in the sense of political efficacy (see Stoker 2010, for a fuller analysis).

There is also evidence of disengagement from active involvement in formal politics (Stoker 2006: ch. 6). Membership of political parties has shifted from over three million to less than one million in the first decade of the twenty-first century (while the population has grown significantly) and there is evidence that much of that membership is relatively inactive, handing over dues and doing little else to engage. Similarly, although there are a plethora of interest, campaign and protest organisations, many of those have a 'cheque book membership' that hands over funding but engages little in the direct activity of politics itself. In the world of parties, interest groups and even protesting, a professionalised class of specialists has taken to running the show, relying on citizen activists as campaign fodder rather than as seeing them as active participants in a process of political reflection and debate.

Yet this notwithstanding, there does seem to be an increased appetite for political reform. Survey findings going back to the 1970s show only half the population regarding our system of governing as in need of reform. In 2004 the first Audit revealed that 60 per cent of the population viewed the system of government in Britain as needing 'quite a lot' or 'a great deal' of improvement. But by May 2009, at the height of the expenses scandal, this figure had jumped to 75 per cent, falling back to 69 per cent when the 2010 audit survey was conducted in November 2009 (Hansard Society 2010: 120). We are not, it seems, facing a group of citizens that have become so alienated and disengaged from politics that any reforms are dismissed and discounted as a pointless exercise. Some two thirds of those surveyed for the 2010 audit disagreed with the statement that politics is a waste of time (Hansard Society 2010: 125) and over a third of the population, according to the 2010 audit, continue to believe that if they were to get involved in politics they could change the way the UK is run – exactly the same proportion as in 2004 (Hansard Society 2010: 125).

There are some other shafts of light in the dark picture painted so far (see Tables 9.2 and 9.3). An IPSOS/MORI (2009) opinion poll taken at

Table 9.2   *Percentage agreeing that that they do trust their local MP to tell the truth compared to MPs in general*

Year	Local MP	MPs in General
2004	47	27
2006	48	30
2009	40	20

Data from: IPSOS/MORI (2009)

the height of the MPs' expenses scandal still showed positive attitudes to the Scottish Parliament and Welsh Assembly and more positive attitudes to local MPs than MPs in general. These finding suggest that perhaps a different style of politics and a more connected political practice could be seen as an antidote to the culture of anti-politics. We will return to these options when discussing reforms later. For now, we can conclude that anti-politics appears to be a core and long running part of British political culture but that citizens have not entirely lost their faith in more decentralised forms of politics or in politicians to whom they feel some connection.

Table 9.3   *Extent of dissatisfaction with the way various political institutions are doing their job*

Year	% Satisfied	% Dissatisfied
Westminster Parliament		
2001	45	30
2009	20	63
Scottish Parliament		
2001	54	21
2009	49	35
National Assembly for Wales		
2001	39	29
2009	70	26

Data from: IPSOS/MORI (2009)

A social divide in British politics?

An important part of understanding Britain's anti-politics culture is to recognise the importance of education and employment type in influencing levels of political involvement. Teachers, media and business professionals participate more than the unskilled and unemployed. The evidence presented in Table 9.4 from the 2008 *Audit of Political Engagement* in Britain suggests that citizens from professional and managerial social groups are twice as likely as those from unskilled groups to vote, donate to a party or campaign and they are four times more likely to have engaged in three or more political activities in the previous year. The material presented in Table 9.5 investigates whether divisions of social class feed into different attitudes towards the political system. The differences are not stark, but those less engaged tend to have more negative attitudes towards formal politics.

There are also other differences to be observed among different social groups in terms of their political engagement and attitudes. Young citizens are generally less involved in formal politics and there are some subtle gender and ethnic differences (see Stoker 2010 for a fuller discussion). But it is the divide based on social class and occupation that is the starkest. Keaney and Rogers (2006: 9) argue that evidence of a major social class divide between those who engage politically and those that do not is deeply troubling because it suggests 'that, for whatever reason, certain parts of the electorate do not feel that they have a stake in their democracy – a good indication that society is not treating those groups

Table 9.4   *Political activism in 2007: social grades compared*

Activity	% A–B social class	% D–E social class
Propensity to vote	66	34
Contacted elected representative in last two or three years	16	10
Donated to a political party	7	2
Donated to a charity or campaigning organisation	52	24
Engaged in three or more political activities in last two or three years	21	5

Data from: Hansard Society (2008)
Note: The social grade definitions are as used by the Institute of Practitioners in Advertising. A and B social grades includes those with professional and managerial jobs. D and E include semi-skilled and unskilled manual workers and those living at the lowest levels of subsistence.

Table 9.5   *Political attitudes in 2009: social grades compared*

Attitude to our governing system	A–B	D–E
% thinks it works well	30	21
% thinks it needs improvement	69	77
% agree that MPs make a lot of money using public office improperly	55	78
% disagree that most MPs have a high moral code	60	59

Data from: Hansard Society (2008)

fairly. Worse still, it threatens to give those who do vote unfair influence over the political system'. There are also reasons to think that an alienated section of the electorate may turn to simple forms of populist politics to express their frustration with mainstream politics. At the very least, a democracy should concern itself with being legitimate in the eyes of all citizens.

Anti-politics in comparative perspective

The crisis in politics appears to be deeper in some countries rather than others. Taking the European region illustrates the point. Norris (2008) divides its countries into four groups: Nordic, Northern, Mediterranean and Central (composed largely of the former communist countries). Table 9.6 presents data from a country from each of these divisions and compares that with data on political activism in the UK (which Norris includes as part of the Northern group). The picture that emerges is of a Nordic group, represented here by Denmark, that is top in terms of most forms of activism and a central Europe group, illustrated here by Poland, that has relatively low activism. The UK emerges overall with a lower to middle ranking in European activism. We are not as good political joiners – of parties, groups and organisations – as the Nordics, other members of the Northern group and even the Mediterraneans. But when it comes to individual political acts, with the exception of voting, we do seem as prepared to sign petitions, wear campaign badges, and boycott goods and services as many of our fellow Europeans.

Britain's anti-political culture

It would seem fair, judging from the evidence considered above, to argue that British culture has a strongly anti-politics trait. British citizens it

Table 9.6 *Political activism compared, 2002–6 (percentages)*

Country	Voted in last general election	Contacted official	Worked in party or action group	Member of party	Worked in another organisation	Signed petition	Demonstrated lawfully	Boycotted goods	Worn campaign badge or sticker
Nordic:									
Denmark	87	19	4	6	22	31	7	25	7
Northern:									
Germany	74	12	4	4	20	30	9	24	5
Mediterranean:									
Spain	73	12	6	3	16	24	23	11	10
Central:									
Poland	61	8	2	1	5	7	1	4	3
UK	65	17	3	2	9	39	4	23	9

Data from: Norris (2008) from European Social Survey Cumulative file 2002–6

appears were never that enthusiastic about trusting politicians but disenchantment and even alienation from the political system appears widespread at the beginning of the twenty-first century. Combining attitudes and activism from the Hansard Society (2010:51) data it is possible to put nearly two-thirds of the population in the anti-politics camp. In comparison with other Europeans, the British are relative non-joiners when it comes to formal political organisations. Moreover, the propensity of British citizens to vote and to join in political campaigning appears to have developed a strong class bias. The socially and economically disadvantaged also appear the most alienated from politics and political activism; managerial and professional elites dominate the political scene but even they seem to have acquired a preference for individualistic or non-traditional forms of engagement. Large majorities of all social groups are clear that the political system needs improving to a substantial extent.

Explaining disengagement

We are increasingly clear and certain about what citizens think about our political system and governing processes. What we are far less clear about is how and why they have come to this judgement. There are hints in the evidence suggesting that perhaps many citizens feel powerless, others appear alienated by the practitioners and the dark arts of politics, and the performance of politicians appears to satisfy only a minority, others appear to struggle to accept or comprehend the nature of modern democratic politics. These hints lead us to more general theories of anti-politics. It is helpful to think about the possible broad causes of anti-politics under five headings: power, process, partisanship, performance and proficiency.

Power

One common explanation of alienation is that citizens have been made to feel *powerless*. This perspective was a strong theme in the Power Commission (2006), an independent inquiry into Britain's democracy chaired by Helena Kennedy. In the foreword to the Inquiry's report she makes it plain that powerlessness is the key issue:

The disquiet is really about having no say. It is about feeling disconnected because voting once every four or five years does not feel like real engagement...Politics and government are increasingly slipping back into the hands of privileged elites as if democracy has run out of steam...Too often citizens are being evicted from the processes. Ways have to be found to engage people. (Power Commission 2006: 10–11)

In his speech on the political reform agenda the Deputy Prime Minister Nick Clegg appears to endorse this understanding stating: 'When people have power they use it. And when they are denied it, there is anger and disappointment' (Clegg 2010).

There are a number of different versions of the empowerment argument (for a further discussion, see Smith 2009). There are liberal and more collectivist variations of the argument, with the former placing greater emphasis on individual empowerment and freeing the individual from unnecessary state interference and the latter concentrating more on greater opportunities for collective engagement in decision-making. Some favour more popular or direct forms of citizen engagement, such as petitions or referenda, while others prefer forums in which citizens are encouraged to become better informed and to debate, deliberate and judge what is in the common good. It is, of course, possible to hold the view that there is value in all of these positions. From such a view, the problem confronting our politics is that a felt sense of powerlessness is widely present among citizens and that their impulses to make individual or collective contributions to society are, as a result, consistently thwarted.

The implication in the analysis of the Power Commission (2006) is that power has been taken away from citizens by political elites. But does this stack up? Was government more open, engaging and participatory in the 1950s compared to now? That would be a difficult claim to establish as arguably the arrival of 24-hour news media and the internet have put more information in the public domain than ever before, politicians are generally more accessible to their constituents, and we are almost overloaded with opportunities for consultation. So maybe it is citizens that have changed; we have become more educated, informed and demanding. Perhaps in the 1950s, British citizens were more deferential to authority and more willing graciously to accept what their political masters offered. As Norris (2009) argues, 'critical citizens who are mistrustful of institutions may become more motivated to become active, in order to reform the state, not less'. Politicians need to accept that citizens are more demanding and more capable of challenging them and their slowness in accepting this reality is the main cause of anti-politics. The Deputy Prime Minster (Clegg 2010) plainly thinks that is the main message:

This government is going to transform our politics so the state has far less control over you, and you have far more control over the state.

This government is going to break up concentrations of power and hand power back to people, because that is quite simply how we can build a society that is fair...I'm not talking about a few new rules for MPs; Not the odd gesture or gimmick here or there to make you feel a bit more involved. I'm talking about the most significant programme of empowerment by a British government since the great reforms of the 19th Century.

The solution to anti-politics, on this analysis, is giving people more power.

Process

But is it the case that citizens want more power? Maybe they just want politicians to do their job properly and get on and govern in the general interest. In a critical commentary on Nick Clegg's political reform speech David Aaronovitch (2010), the *Times* columnist, queried how much empowerment to run public services and make decisions citizens really want. He concluded:

I am under no illusion that most people actually want it. They don't. They don't want to run hospitals or (save a very few usually admirable folk) schools. They want to make individual decisions for themselves and that's about it. And this needs to be faced, not rhetoricised away.

There are real limits to the amount of direct power that citizens want and their alienation is more a concern with the way that politics is conducted by others. Indeed, greater engagement and involvement by citizens in decision-making can often lead to enhanced frustration and anger as people are exposed to the conflicts and complexities of shared decision-making (for a review of the evidence, see Theiss-Morse and Hibbing 2005). Perhaps the key challenge is not empowering citizens but sustaining their faith in the processes of politics undertaken by their representatives.

This view is supported by many academic observers of politics. Central authors here are John Hibbing and Elizabeth Theiss-Morse (2001, 2002, 2005) and although their evidence relates to the United States it could be seen as applicable to Britain. As they argue:

The key to creating a process that makes people feel good about government is not finding ways to get people more involved in politics ... Many ordinary Americans are surprisingly eager to have someone else make political decisions ... But here is the kicker ...They...want to be secure in the belief that whatever decisions that have been made were taken in the interest of the people and not in the self-interest of the decision-makers. (Hibbing and Theiss-Morse 2001: 248)

Evidence from the Hansard Society audits since 2004, as noted earlier, reveals plenty of concern about whether politicians are acting out of selfish motives rather than driven by the public interest.

What is it about the processes of politics that alienates citizens? There are several possible elements. Some might have a concern about the procedural fairness of political decisions and the justice of decisions taken (were all the right stakeholders and bits of evidence brought into play?). Some may have a negative reaction to the rhetoric of conflict that often surrounds politics. Interestingly, research by Birch and Allen (2009) suggests that the public believe MPs should be more ethical than the general public, with nearly two in three citizens arguing that politicians should be held to higher standards than ordinary members of the public. As this suggests, anti-politics may in part be a result of the (perhaps unrealistic) expectations about fairness, ethical veracity and support for the common good that are loaded onto politicians by citizens. The solution would appear to be to maximise transparency and accountability, so that both the impression of wrongdoing and its practice can be stamped out of the political system.

Partisanship

A further theory starts its argument with a concern about the decline in *partisanship*. This is seen as undermining the institutional mechanisms that engaged citizens in politics in the past. Citizens were brought into politics, so the argument runs, by formal and informal institutions that used the hook of partisanship to get citizens engaged. Churches, voluntary organisations and, above all, political parties were structured around their capacity to mobilise voters in big blocks (Dalton and Wattenberg 2002). Citizens defined their involvement in politics through their membership of, and loyalty to, social groups around class, ethnicity or religion. But social and economic changes have brought in their wake a decline in such 'cleavage politics' (Eijk and Franklin 2009). This has in some ways liberated voters and meant that their loyalty cannot be taken for granted but has instead to be earned. But it may also have rendered invalid many of the traditional ways in which citizens were brought into politics.

At the time of Almond and Verba's study of politics in Britain over 9 in 10 of all voters either supported the Labour or Conservative parties with a percentage turnout in the high seventies or low eighties. These parties reflected, in a broad sense, major social cleavages between the working classes and middle and business classes and those that identified with them. In the 2010 election only around 65 per cent voted for either of these 'big' parties and turnout was in the mid sixties. The linked processes of partisan dealignment and falling electoral participation have meant that large swathes of the population have no direct connection to formal politics and are not socialised in the norms of engagement. They may participate in single issue campaigns but have lost their loyalty to the main formal institutions of political parties that mobilised citizens in the past. It is difficult to see what the solution is to the loss of the role partisan institutions played in bringing citizens into politics in a world where social cleavages are less stark. Perhaps new forms of mobilisation through the internet will support a different, but still effective, form of mobilisation?

Performance

A fourth line of argument about what drives anti-politics is that it reflects the failure of politics to deliver outputs or societal outcomes that citizens value. In short, it is the *performance* of politics that is the cause of dissatisfaction. An early version of this argument made in the 1970s was that government was overloaded with demands from the public and, because elected politicians could not afford to disappoint us, so a cycle of rising spending and subsequent fiscal crisis would occur (for a discussion of this work see Held 2006: 190–201). Given the events of the last few years, this argument might be seen as still having some substance to it (Flinders: 2009). A further version of a performance failure argument emerged strongly in the 1980s and 1990s around the impact of globalisation, which was seen as taking power away from national democracies and so undermining the capacity of politics to deliver (for critical commentaries, see Gamble 2000; Hay 2007a).

A more recent variation runs with the argument that we have shifted the balance in our politics from a partisan to a valence political world where societal ends are agreed and the core political issue has become how to judge the relative competence of the parties and politicians to achieve the desired ends (Clarke *et al.* 2009). Politics then becomes focused on the performance of the government and leaders or what prospective opponents offer. But this focus on performance in turn has created a rather shallow form of political exchange in which the allocation of credit or blame for performance lies at the heart of our contemporary democracy. Given the high stakes and uncertainty involved, voters rely heavily on campaign cues and party leader images as guides to electoral choice. In the context of the contingencies of politics, citizens are invited to be spectators in a game of credit taking and blame avoidance that almost inevitably creates the cycles of short-term hope and long-term disappointment that characterise Britain's current political culture.

A response to the concern about performance might be phrased as trying to persuade citizens that politics is to some extent bound to disappoint (Stoker 2006: ch. 4). People can assume that most other people agree with them (or would do if only the issue were explained to them properly) and that the ideal outcome is one that suits them in every detail. If you don't like something you see in a shop you can go elsewhere. But in politics the only way to get something is to use voice – by expressing your concerns in concert with others. This carries far more costs than the exit mechanism available to us in market transactions. People generally don't like making a lot of effort for little reward. Accordingly, offloading responsibility onto others is a very common coping mechanism in political exchanges. But expressing your interest or opinion is only the start of a more general challenge in politics. You have not only to make your views known, you also have to listen. Politics is not about individual choice; it is about collective decisions. Politics often involves a stumbling search to find a collective response to a particular problem. It is not the most edifying of human experiences. It is rarely an experience of self-actualisation and more often an experience of accepting second best. The results tend to be messy and contingent – and they invariably create a mix of winners and losers. Our collective will – which is what politics is supposed to express – is not easy to fathom or always comfortable to accept once it is decided upon.

Proficiency

A final line of argument holds that large swathes of British citizens lack the *proficiency* to understand about how politics works (and could ever function) and, as a result, hold negative views of politics. We citizens lack the competence and comprehension to be good citizens. This line of argument is rarely heard from politicians for the obvious reason that appearing to insult the voter is not widely viewed as a winning strategy. However, the argument has been made by academics from time to time. But their focus is not simply on the ignorance on the public but more the lack of an environment in which civic understanding and comprehension could reasonably be expected to develop. Bernard Crick's famous *In Defence of Politics* (2000) powerfully advocated not just citizenship education but a wider drive to create the conditions for civic understanding and exchange. Stoker's *Why Politics Matters* (2006) presents a modernised version and development of some of the same arguments. And Matt Flinders's (2010) inaugural lecture at the University of Sheffield is couched in a similar vein. He pulls no punches in suggesting that:

the public have become politically decadent in their expectations about what politics should deliver... I want to suggest that people 'hate politics' because they simply do not understand it; and they are generally not helped to understand it by the media (or university professors of politics for that matter). There may also be a demographic factor at play: this contemporary climate of anti-politics is arguably rooted in a generation that has become complacent and parochial, and in doing so have forgotten the alternatives to democratic politics.

For anti-politics to be addressed, then, the naivety about politics would need to challenged and replaced by a broader civic orientation and practice. There are several links here to other explanations of anti-politics. Maybe citizens have expectations about the fairness, ethical performance capacity of politics that just cannot be delivered. As Theiss-Morse and Hibbing (2005: 227) put it, 'good citizens need to learn that democracy is messy, inefficient and conflict-ridden'.

Perhaps if anti-politics is going to be addressed it is these fundamental understandings of politics that need to more widely disseminated. If citizens are becoming less deferential and more critical, then a stronger civic culture needs to be built to enable citizens to take on that more active engagement with a realistic understanding of what politics can deliver. Unfortunately the track record of citizenship education aimed at young people indicates that it is not easy to engage citizens with a deeper understanding of politics, especially in the context of a wider media coverage of politics that tends to emphasise its more negative aspects (Stoker 2006; Kisby and Sloam 2009).

Some proposed solutions

In this section we examine two possible responses to the uncertainty that surrounds our understanding of anti-politics in Britain. The first argument is that the political system will adapt to deal with anti-politics. The second is we need to actively restore citizens' faith in the formal political institutions.

Do nothing: we are adapting

It is perhaps a little unfair to describe this strategy as 'do nothing'. The argument is more subtle than that and rests on two broad propositions that find much support. First, there is a limit to the amount of real engagement that citizens actually want – despite what they may actually say in survey responses, a point made earlier. Second, there are signs that the political system is adapting. There are parts of it – especially the local and devolved elements – that are working and all that might be required is an extension of the evolution in British politics that is already under way.

The starting insight here is that there is no clear level of engagement or participation that makes for a healthy democracy. So evidence of voter decline or limited participation in political activities is not necessarily a bad thing for a democratic country. As Norris (2008: 14) argues:

> [T]he underlying normative judgments about what level of citizen participation is intrinsically valuable, which often colour evaluations of the empirical evidence, remain open to debate. It is commonly assumed that the democratic state which flourishes best is one which encourages moderate participation but the systematic linkages between mass political behaviour and the stability of democratic states involves a long and complex chain, and a more cautious interpretation of the broader implications would be wise.

What makes for a stable democracy is more than voter turnout as the cases of the United and Switzerland show it is possible to sustain a democratic system with consistent low voting turn out. Again, as Norris (2008: 14) suggests 'a glance at some of the persistent outliers quickly reveals that there is no optimal level of participation which ensures stable and effective democratic states...There are multiple drivers of the democratisation process'. A strong commitment to power-sharing and wider features of the political culture in a country may play a more important role in sustaining democracy than the levels of voter turnout.

Nor should we necessarily be worried by evidence that citizens are getting less trustful of political institutions. First, that evidence should be treated with caution in that what we may well be witnessing is 'trendless fluctuation over time' (Norris, 2008: 14). Although there is evidence to argue that national politics in the UK has seen some decline in trust and engagement there are other countries where that trend is not so observable. So there may be something particular about recent British experience which has turned citizens off to a greater degree. But even within the UK, as noted earlier and as shown in Table 9.3, citizens appear to be willing to give more credence to their local MP and devolved institutions such as the Scottish Parliament or the Welsh Assembly. So we may be witnessing not so much a rejection of politics but rather a rejection of a particular form of politics that has developed around the 'Westminster Village'. The implication of this is that devolving power to more local and regional institutions, for example, might create a politics with which citizens would be more comfortable which they might see as more legitimate.

The message is: let us not panic. Yes, citizens are becoming less trusting and more challenging but the political system will adapt (Norris 1999a), and will change in a more humdrum and piecemeal way. Political parties and interest organisation will learn to campaign in new ways. Voting levels may stay low and active engagement in politics will remain a minority pursuit, but the nature of British democracy will remain fundamentally the same. In front of a largely passive citizenry it will still have the capacity to respond to critical issues and public concerns effectively enough to sustain the legitimacy of the system and assure a sufficient degree of democratic accountability.

Do something: a radical reform of formal politics

Perhaps in the past, most of Britain's political elite were in the steady evolution camp. But the 2009 row about MPs' expenses seems to have tipped the balance of calculation in all parties towards some mix of radical reforms. The first signs of real movement in response to concern over the issue came in the Brown premiership, although many of its initial proposals were relatively tame (Hay and Stoker 2009; PSA 2007). The mantra has now been taken up by the coalition government, which claims that it is committed to a major programme of political reform. It is possible to review their proposals for political reform (HM Government 2010) and line them up against the various factors driving anti-politics identified in the previous section.

It appears that the coalition buys the argument the citizens need to be empowered. The programme of the coalition government contains measures aimed at directly empowering citizens. These include:

- Funding 200 all-postal primaries over this parliament, targeted at seats which have not changed hands for many years.
- Ensuring that any petition that secures 100,000 signatures will be eligible for formal debate in parliament. The petition with the most signatures will enable members of the public to table a bill eligible to be voted on in parliament.
- Introducing a new 'public reading stage' for bills to give the public an opportunity to comment on proposed legislation online, and a dedicated 'public reading day' within a bill's committee stage where those comments will be debated by the committee scrutinising the bill.
- Giving residents the power to instigate local referendums on any local issue.

There are also measures that appear to be about reassuring citizens about the ethical standards and general interest commitment of politicians. These include:

- Cutting the perks and bureaucracy associated with parliament.
- Consulting with the Independent Parliamentary Standards Authority on how to move away from the generous final-salary pension system for MPs.
- Introducing a power of recall, allowing voters to force a by-election where an MP is found to have engaged in serious wrongdoing
- Preventing the possible misuse of parliamentary privilege by MPs accused of serious wrongdoing.

As this suggests, the focus of the reform agenda fits most easily within the framing offered by the first two explanations of anti-politics considered above. Yet there are other proposed changes that are less easy to see as a response to anti-politics directly, but which could be seen as fitting in with the general view presented in both the empowerment and process positions: namely the need to create greater openness and accountability in the political system. Among these are the following:

- Proposals on electoral reform, which includes provision for the introduction of the Alternative Vote in the event of a positive result in a referendum.
- Creating fewer and more equal-sized constituencies.
- Bring forward proposals for a wholly or mainly elected upper chamber on the basis of proportional representation.
- Establishing five-year fixed-term parliaments.
- Reforming House of Common procedures to give more power to backbench MPs.

This programme of reform is substantial and will be time-consuming and difficult to put in place. But will it work? The answer partly depends on whether the identification of the problem is correct. Here we are back to the heart of the chapter: are the power and process explanations of anti-politics implied by the chosen solution the crucial factors in explaining the rise of anti-politics?

What to do? Are reforms possible?

Having specified the nature of anti-politics and reviewed the explanations we are left in something of quandary about what to do. That is, in part, because the messages that we are getting from existing research are not crystal clear. What is clear is that there was no golden age of politics in Britain that somehow has been lost. There does appear to be a widespread sense of anti-politics, but its causes are not straightforward or simple. There are good arguments for suggesting that citizens need to feel more empowered. But equally there is a lot of evidence to suggest that many citizens do not want to take on the responsibility and effort of running public services or making large numbers of public decisions. In that sense it is difficult not to welcome the coalition's 'do something' attitude to political reform and tackling anti-politics. But it appears equally appropriate to fear that the reforms will not restore our faith in politics in quite the manner the government hopes.

There have to be doubts about the reform strategy in part because some evidence points to the complexities of the issues at stake and how reforms could exacerbate rather than rectify the problem of anti-politics. Given what we know about the social class gradient that steers participation and engagement towards the professional and managerial classes, more empowerment might do nothing more than widen the gap between the political haves and have-nots. In any case it may well be that a majority of citizens are not really looking for more participation but rather a better politics – by which they mean a (more) representative politics with representatives that act as sound judges of the common interest. But in conceding demands to create a political class above reproach – with appropriate ethical and moral virtues – there is a danger of raising unrealistic expectations. We cannot wish away old political realities. Always doing the ethical thing in politics is a near impossible ask. Wrapping your actions in claims about looking to the public interest can prove difficult to sustain. How can we expect politicians that have to fight for votes and retain support not to consider the expediency and short-term impact of their decisions? Especially as citizens increasingly measuring them accordingly on their performance in office, may be ready to shift their vote accordingly. Does not the logic of the system encourage politicians to focus on appeasing those that are more likely to vote than any broader ethical or general interest consideration?

There have to be further doubts about the reform package in part because of the compromises that are implicit in its construction after the 2010 election. A fully proportional election system might be seen as a partial solution to anti-politics (Stoker 2006: 170–2) because it might stimulate competitive elections and encourage parties to mobilise in every seat to attract voters. But the proposed alternative vote system seems like a lowest common denominator agreement rather than a genuine part of this kind of solution.

Finally there is an argument that emerges from this chapter that the solution to anti-politics will require a response to each of its underlying causes. The reform package of the coalition government appears to concentrate on only two out of five underlying causes. This situation suggests that a wider programme of reform in civil society will need to accompany the reforms proposed.

Some see deliverance through a new politics of the internet. Formal politics with its hierarchies, strong leadership and organised groups reinforced elitism in politics but it is giving way to a more open and fluid even democratic approach (Gibson 2009). The narrow agenda setting of the media is being challenged by the rise of the internet. The control and manipulation of information, statistics and analysis by governments and their experts is giving way to world of multiple gatekeepers in which informed citizens can increasingly and effectively hold government agencies to account. So people are more informed, better educated, and with the arrival of interactive internet exchanges, on the cusp of a new politics. The old politics with its technologies of formal organisation and mass media are giving way to a new politics of blogs, social networking and video-sharing sites that lower the costs of campaigning and radically pluralises the political process by providing multiple options for the expression of interests and ideas. The decline in formal politics, and the sense of disempowerment associated with that, reflects the failings of the old politics and its darkest hour before the dawn, which will see the rise of new age of internet-based politics.

There are grounds for caution even among those who see the potential of the internet to heal our anti-politics culture. Context matters, as Gibson (2009) notes, and technology without better political content perhaps would make no difference. Second, the internet and these new forms of campaigning do appear to be attracting a wider range of participants – especially younger people – but there is still concern about a digital divide. The internet may not be an attractive tool for all. Sunstein (2009) argues against the too personalised approach to information and politics that the internet can encourage. An effective democracy, he argues, requires that people encounter some new information or experience without preselection or choice on their part. These haphazard encounters are vital to break citizens from simply talking to like-minded people who reinforce each other's views, creating more fragmentation and extremism. Careful research does indeed suggest that that construction of online deliberation is challenging and difficult (Smith 2010). Furthermore, all democracies require some shared common experiences and, although the internet can deliver on that to some degree, it runs the risk of creating a series of specialised ghettos where citizens live in separate worlds divorced from each other. Politics is an act of collective decision-making and there is no escaping that.

So the internet is no magic solution, although it may have a part to play in lowering the barriers of entry for ordinary citizens into politics. We need citizens to be more realistic about the performance of politics and what it can deliver. We need them to find ways to mobilise that does not rely on fading partisan identities. We need to develop their skills as citizens and grow a stronger civic infrastructure to support politics and we need to do all of these activities recognising the current social inequalities in the attitudes towards and engagement with politics among citizens.

Conclusion

The discussion in this chapter is designed to get us all to realise the complexity of anti-politics as an issue. Too often when we tackle societal issues we go for a solution without really understanding how and if it addresses the underlying problem. Here we get to the heart of a challenge that political science needs to address (Stoker 2010). We need: research to explore in more depth the nature of anti-politics and its drivers for different social groups. We then need to move into a terrain that is generally uncomfortable for political scientists and consider reform options that might work. If the answer is to get citizens to be more realistic about what politics can do, then the question becomes 'what is the burden of responsibility and what practically could political scientists and other social scientists do to be part of the solution'? If the issue is to improve the processes of politics, so they are judged to be fair, do we understand enough about what citizens see as examples of fair politics to make recommendations for change?

Given anti-politics and its negative implications for the practice of democracy, those who study politics have a pressing need not only to understand its causes, but also help to design solutions. Of course we will not be alone in this debate nor will political scientists always be in agreement but we should be in the forefront of the discussion. A good starting point for engagement, of course, is to understand where the discussion currently stands. This chapter has sought to tell us where we are, not tell us how to get to where we want to be. Designing better politics is a challenge that political scientists need to seriously turn their minds to, not as narrow technocratic advisers, but as facilitators of democratic debate.

Chapter 10

Pressure Group Politics

RICHARD HEFFERNAN

Interests, businesses, corporations, trade associations, charities and public sector organisations vie with one another, publicly and privately, to present their case to policy makers and the public. Protest and pressure group politics increasingly forms a backdrop to our political life as groups, for good and ill, either support or challenge some aspect of government policy or call for a change in the status quo. For instance, the Countryside Alliance mobilised 400,000 people to protest attempts to ban foxhunting in September 2002 and some 1.5 million people marched in London against the imminent intervention in Iraq in February 2003. In 2007 the high-profile Make Poverty History campaign brought together some 540 British member organisations, including many charities and developmental non-governmental organisations, to press Western leaders meeting at Gleneagles to make a more substantive, coordinated response to global poverty. Such high-profile public events are often, however, the tip of the pressure group iceberg. Groups range from the powerfully resourced with an international focus, such as those concerned with climate change and the environment, to small scale local campaigners lobbying about planning issues in their town or village. In July 2010, a BBC news item about the possible discontinuation of speed cameras in Oxfordshire reported the comments of spokespersons for Thames Valley Safer Roads and road safety group Brake as well as those of the relevant minister and his opposition shadow (BBC 25 July 2010). This is not unusual. Groups expressing opinions about politics are, it seems, increasingly widespread.

British politics, the space within which ideas and interests compete for power and influence, naturally draws the attention of interest and pressure groups. Representative democracy cannot itself ensure the state operates in the interest of society. The public may elect – and, crucially, can replace – elected politicians, but interest and pressure groups, along-side public opinion and the critical reportage of the news media, help check and balance government. Such groups, be they large or small, professional or amateur, contribute to Britain's 'national conversations'. They operate at the local, the national and the international level and make all sorts of representative claims in all manner of policy areas. They organise opinion, mobilise elements of the public and, from time to time, have government account for its actions and sometimes even change its behaviour.

If opinion matters, then organised opinion, communicated effectively, matters more. Campaigns and causes seek attention in many ways, from low-profile, discreet personalised lobbying of ministers by profession-alised organisation to large-scale, mass protests. Supporters variously write letters, sign petitions and/or else attend demonstrations; often they merely express their opinion to friends and workmates, or make a dona-tion. Celebrities, some of whom confuse self-promotion with civic engagement, front campaigns and make appeals. Some traverse the world, hopping from private house to luxury hotel, to 'warn' of a coming environmental catastrophe. Others, like Joanna Lumley, who fronted efforts by the Ghurkha Justice Campaign to prevent Labour from deny-ing former Ghurkhas the right to settle in the country they served in uniform, use their voice more selflessly for less fashionable, smaller causes.

Groups of various types now penetrate 'the corridors of government and occupy the nooks and crannies of civil society...they greatly compli-cate, and sometimes wrong-foot, the lives of politicians, parties, legisla-tures and governments' (Keane 2009: xxvii). Few lobby government because they are happy with its record or wish to congratulate ministers and officials on their achievements. Groups often loudly and continually complain to – and about – government because their members – or the professionals they employ – are angry with it and want it to 'do some-thing' or to 'stop doing something'. This, for Keane, contributes to some-thing he describes as 'monitory democracy' where pressure groups – alongside other forms of social organisations – are involved in 'the continuous chastening of those who exercise power' (ibid.). Interest and (especially) pressure groups thereby contribute to the 'power monitoring and power controlling devices' (ibid.) enabling civil society to check and balance, sometimes to qualify (even perhaps erode), the power of govern-ment. In contrast to the classic concept of pressure groups as lobbyists of the state, such groups now increasingly lobby the public, so embarrass-ing the state into action as a secondary effect.

Group form and function: associational and promotional groups

Interest or pressure group activity has to be carefully defined. Such groups have, at the outset, to accept (even if they question) the legitimacy of the state (even when challenging its specific proposals). They have to confine their activity to peaceful, non-violent and (mostly) lawful means. Even the small protest groups most influenced by the far left which seek to subvert the status quo invariably pursue reformist, not revolutionary objectives; they might work outside and around the state, but they are not consciously trying to overthrow it. A terrorist group, whatever its objectives, is a terrorist group; it is not an interest or pressure group. Groups engaged in violent, extremist activity such as the loose, often incoherent groups which associate themselves with Islamist extremism, need to be studied under different, narrower criteria.

The political science literature identifies several overlapping definitions of 'interest' and 'pressure' groups. The two, however, should not be confused and the following four operational definitions are therefore offered:

- Organised 'interest' groups and 'professional' associations. These include, classically, trade unions, but also professional bodies such as the British Medical Association or the Law Society.
- Organised 'pressure' or 'cause' groups. Examples are numerous but would include civil rights groups such as Liberty, Amnesty International and other such campaigners for civil liberties; The Muslim Council of Britain operates as a pressure group as does the League Against Cruel Sports (which campaigns against blood sports) and the Countryside Alliance (which opposes the ban on fox hunting) and, most obviously, environmental groups such as Greenpeace and Friends of the Earth.
- Organised 'advocacy' and 'charitable' groups. These would include policy 'think-tanks' such as the Institute for Fiscal Studies, the Institute for Public Policy Research or Policy Exchange. It would also include charitable organizations such as Oxfam or Save the Children and, some suggest, organised, hierarchical religions such as the Church of England or the Catholic Church. They are invariably and explicitly non-party political.
- Organised and unorganised 'social movements'. These, while being harder to pin down, would include groups which campaign for gender, racial and sexual equality and for the civil, political and social rights of those deemed to be discriminated against or unfairly placed outside the mainstream (Grant 2000; Crowson *et al.* 2009; Jordan and Maloney 2007).

Being organised is the essential part of being an interest group. Each of these four groups, even if there is considerable overlap between them, is very different, both in terms of form and mode of operation. This is especially so when it is increasingly difficult to distinguish between, say, the second and the third categories in terms of their configuration and modus operandi. Groups in these two categories may be described as non-governmental organisations (NGOs) because they work – often alongside government – in a specific public policy field. The four types of groups may be usefully explored, however, by applying two broader (and therefore blunter) definitions of group type. These are:

- associational; and
- promotional groups.

Associational groups include organised interest groups and professional associations; promotional groups embrace organised pressure groups, political advocacy and charitable NGOs as well as social movements. Associational groups, 'interest' groups', have members who share something in common. These are groups 'of something' be it members of a trade union, a professional association or a trade organization. Promotional groups, by contrast, can be considered to be 'for something'. Their members often have only a commitment to, not necessarily a direct, personal interest in the 'cause' with which they and the group identify. Either group type exists to secure the advantage of their members or its cause. Both either *directly lobby* or *externally pressure* politicians to either 'do something' or to 'stop doing something'. The means by which they go about this, their chosen modus operandi, is invariably influenced by the status they have been granted by – or have been able to demand from – government. Here the following distinction between different types of associational or promotional groups is useful:

- insider; and
- outsider groups (Grant 2000; Maloney *et al.* 1994).

An insider group is one that operates 'inside' the state and which has its views sought out by government. They are included within policy-making networks and communities and are frequently consulted by government ministers and agency heads. Such insider groups, increasingly identified as 'stakeholders', include, say, the British Medical Association and the National Farmers Union, who make their representations known directly by bargaining and negotiating with policy makers, necessarily engaging in concessions and compromises. Outsider groups are not routinely consulted by ministers and agency heads. Instead they make representations, should they choose to do so, indirectly and usually by mobilising public support for their cause. Outsider groups, such as Greenpeace and Friends of the Earth, jealously guard their independence. They are not prepared to make concessions nor compromise on their policy demands. Promotional groups, broadly speaking, tend to be outsiders and associational groups more likely to be insiders. Promotional groups have to be 'popular', but associational groups need not necessarily reflect a 'climate of opinion'; they need only be powerful or else relevant to the governmental policy community.

Whatever the form of group, its configuration plays an important part in their ability to raise their issue and have it resolved in the way they advocate. Such configuration usually has four principal characteristics:

- Visibility: Is the group well known? Does it have a high public profile?
- Resource level: How well financed is the group? What is its income and sources of funding? How many staff does it employ and with what quality? How professional is its operation? What degree of in-house expertise can it draw on?
- Size of membership: The larger its membership base, the more legitimate (normally) is the group's claim is to speak for people. Members are one source which provides money and money is the principal resource enabling groups to professionalise themselves. The bigger the group, the more chance it will have clout.
- Legitimacy: How relevant is the group? What importance is placed on the cause with which it is associated? How 'salient' is its issue? (for general discussion of group characteristics, see Grant 2000; Crowson *et al.* 2009; Jordan and Maloney 2007).

The first three group characteristics are self-explanatory. Certain groups speak for a more 'salient' issue or cause and are better resourced than others having a greater level of public support, professional expertise or organisational reach. Of course, issue salience, so often the key feature of group politics, is often of central importance to understanding group impact.

The changing nature of groups: social movements and their impacts

Associational group activity in Britain was once largely 'organized around one of the great "estates" that represented the pillars of society: business, labour, agriculture and the professions' (Grant 2000: 33). Professional associations such as the British Medical Association or the Law Society, charged with regulating members of their profession on behalf of the state, still remain ready and able to successfully make representations to policy makers. Business organisations continue to exert a significant influence on decision-makers and agricultural interests, not least the National Farmers Union, are still influential in their smaller policy sector. The trade union movement, however, is today a lesser 'estate' than it once was. Such was its power in the 1960s and 1970s that unions sought – and received – protection and privilege from the state as governments worked with them – and through them – to manage and plan the economy. Where British governments once brought together representatives of capital and labour to manage and plan economic inputs and outputs in a corporatist framework, Labour and Conservative governments have, since the late 1970s, abandoned corporatism in favour of having economic outputs more lightly regulated by the state. This explains the downgrading of the status of unions and their counterpart, the employers' organisations. As a result trade unions are at present a shadow of their former selves in terms of political influence. In terms of their membership only 29 per cent of employees are now a member of a union. In 1979 it was 55 per cent. Union membership is now heavily concentrated in the public sector where density is 56 per cent compared to 15 per cent in the private sector. Routinely denied the opportunity to advise ministers, downsized because of falling membership owing to structural changes in the economy, and tightly shackled by legal restrictions placed upon their activity, unions lack the political and industrial clout they previously enjoyed. The TUC head, Brendan Barber, is hardly a household name. With fiscal pressures likely to lead to a downsizing of the British state in the coming years, trade union membership may fall further, faster under the Conservative–Liberal Democrat coalition. Of course there is always the chance that levels of public sector industrial action will increase as the cuts introduced by the Conservative–Liberal Democrat coalition begin to bite.

British politics is less party-oriented than before and political activism more extra-institutional in character. Some say, as a result, politics is becoming more issue-led (Hay and Stoker 2009). Such issues are increasingly post-materialist, focusing on things such as quality of life, human rights, environmental protection, global justice, racial equality and lesbian and gay rights (Inglehart 1990; Abramson and Inglehart 1995). The advocates of these issues are more likely to be young, economically secure and well educated (Norris 2002; Dalton 2007). Special, sectional 'old school' interests have long been supplemented by 'cause groups supported by reformist members of the middle class' (Grant 2000: 33) which campaigned on issues such as religious toleration, women's suffrage, temperance and animal welfare. Causes, however, increasingly lie at the heart of group activity. Vested interests representing business continue, naturally, to exert a considerable influence because of business's indispensible economic role, but promotional groups have come dramatically to the fore in the past 30 or so years. Cause groups, described above as promotional, pressure groups, have increased in number since the 1960s; supplementing older-style associational groups, but also increasingly supplanting them.

The growth of cause groups owes much to the successful work of emergent 'social movements' based upon 'identity' politics. Social movements are 'formed around the politics of six key issues and/ or social groups: gender and women, sexuality and homosexuals, disability and the disabled, race and the ethnic communities, the pursuit of peace, and the defence of the environment' (Lent 2001: 3). They are, largely, radical movements which argue against the status quo and protest to change it. Such movements are socially liberal and tend to be, if not of the left, then strongly influenced by the left. Having emerged (or, in the case of women's rights, re-emerged) in the 1960s in pursuit of a cultural politics beyond labour rights and economic questions they have become an entrenched and vital part of civic and political life (Drache 2008; McKay and Hilton 2009). The social and civil rights such movements sought have won widespread support. Social movements have therefore become an established, some say pervasive, feature of contemporary political life. The 'personal', as feminists claimed, is 'political'. These social movements, while innovative, should no longer be carelessly described as 'new'. Feminist politics, for instance, in different forms, have long been an established feature of the political scene (Lovenduski 2005; Squires 2007) and arguments for gay equality have featured in public discourses for at least the past 40 or so years.

Over time social movements have exerted an indirect, exhortatory influence over policy makers. They explicitly rejected the hierarchical, professionalised forms of pressure group activity focused on elite-based, discrete petitioning. Instead they embraced radical forms of 'in your face campaigning' which, through public campaigning, subverted the prevailing climate of opinion. Social movements, by challenging the status quo, have often been more concerned with consciousness raising and only then securing changes in public policy. Such tactics, largely reflecting the anti-statist political radicalism of the 1960s, were intended to raise the consciousness of the 'oppressed' while rallying public opinion at large. They were designed to challenge the elite, not merely speak to them. Rights were not to be negotiated about or lobbied for, but to be loudly and aggressively asserted. And, when won, they had to be defended.

One example of a social movement entering the mainstream is the campaign for gay equality. This campaign prompted – but was also the beneficiary of – profound changes in public attitudes toward different sexualities from the 'norm'. The case for equality 'sprang' it is said 'not from argument but from attitude. Pleading had turned into demand' (Parris 2009). Matthew Parris rightly argues that the securing of gay rights reflected 'a very, very gradual shift in informal and formal public attitudes in the west that had been completely unanswered by any formal or legal change' (ibid.). These shifts in public opinion, brought about by the individual and collective actions of lesbians and gays, as well as their straight supporters, reflected the fact that public, organised campaigns for gay equality were both cause and effect; 'sails', as Parris colourfully suggests, 'were put up to a gathering wind: they caught energy; they got motion; and the momentum became unstoppable' (ibid.). In entering the mainstream some social movements, as they have helped change the climate of opinion in their favour, have professionalised themselves. If, in the arena of gay and lesbian rights, we compare how one group, Outrage, and another, Stonewall, operates we can see two clear distinctions. In its heyday Outrage used very public shock tactics to *coerce* policy makers to accept their demands; Stonewall, equally committed to its cause, uses moderate, often discreet forms of lobbying in an effort to *persuade* policy makers to support its case. For Stonewall its advocacy of gay rights requires it to be a professional organisation operating in the mainstream. It addition to lobbying for legal change it challenges the continuing cultural and attitudinal values that allow discrimination to flourish by advising 'the employers of five million people, from IBM and Barclays to the Royal Navy' on gay issues (Summerskill, 2009).

Social movements increasingly seek a voice through professionalised organisations, largely by forming (often self-styled) voluntary and community organisations. Those presently working on black and ethnic minority issues include the 1990 Trust (Blink), Black Londoners Forum, Operation Black Vote, National Assembly Against Racism, Black Police Association and BMEAction.net. There are more explicitly political groups such as Unite Against Fascism. Some Muslims have banded together to form similar organisations such as the Muslim Council of Britain, the UK Islamic Council or the Federation of Student's Islamic Societies; others participate in Islamist organisations explicitly affiliated with a brand of radical, political Islam like the Muslim Association of Britain, the British Muslim Initiative and the Islamic Forum of Europe. In addition the Equality and Human Rights Commission, a state agency, takes up the issues such groups campaign on and there are numerous local campaigns and individuals working on the same issues.

The relative success of social movements, boosted by shifts away from older forms of political activity such as political party membership or trade union participation, have had an enormous impact on the way groups now operate in Britain. To some extent associational and promotional groups now aspire to play an increasingly political role. In 2007 there were some '190,000 charities...registered with the UK Charity Commission, with a combined annual income of £38 billion – equivalent to 3.4 per cent of total GDP. The UK charity sector employs around 600,000 paid staff' (Hansard Society 2007). All, to some extent, lobby and campaign for their cause: indeed, such is the perceived purchase of politicised groups, charitable organisations, particularly those involved in international development, now publicly advocate their cause. British-based charities such as Oxfam, Save the Children and ActionAid no longer limit their work to the physical alleviation of poverty. Instead they engage in advocacy to publicise their issue (and their work) with government and the public, seeking influence within the globalised world at both the national and the international level. Civil and human rights organisations, in aping the demands of social movements, raise their issue by making publicly plain the rights citizens have – or should have – and demanding that the state respects – or provides – such rights.

Making use of the 'public square'

Groups operate within the 'public square'; within the civil society wherein people operate. They address the public largely by means of the media, something which has been greatly assisted by the revolution in communication brought about by the rise of the 24/7 news agenda, the internet-driven explosion in news and communication outlets and the availability of citizen media (Dahlgren 2009; Chadwick 2006). Increasingly, by means of modern media, groups are able to build themselves up through their internet presence and organise their activity by making increasing use of social interactive media such as Facebook and Twitter. Through news reportage, both that provided by the mainstream media and that which they provide themselves, groups try to raise the visibility of their issue. They communicate their demands, both directly and indirectly, by way of the general public, to policy makers. Group leaders, thus, may continue to lobby ministers and governmental officials to support their cause, but more and more they court public opinion as the means to that end. As groups become more organised, professionalised and specialised their public activity becomes ever more central to the work that they do.

The representative claim and its limits

A group may claim to speak for (or represent) citizens (or rather groups of citizens), but often they speak more for themselves. Take the Muslim Council of Britain (the MCB) which boasts '500 affiliated national, regional and local organisations, mosques, charities and schools' (Muslim Council of Britain 2010). It, alongside the 24 national organisations affiliated to it, claims to 'speak for Muslims'. But, as critics maintain, it cannot speak on behalf of each individual Muslim in Britain – and for some there is no such thing as a singular Muslim community. Nonetheless the size of the MCB (and the claims it makes) means it is considered by many, including (at times) the past Labour government, to be the principal representative of Muslim opinion and therefore the means by which the state can work with the Muslim 'community'. Recognition, inevitably, empowers the organisation as much as – and perhaps even more than – its cause. Because it grants both legitimacy and influence it is increasingly useful for causes to become organised and necessary for groups to represent them.

Participation rates in group activities are also not always as inclusive or as representative as they might seem. Participation, obviously, is often confined to the bright, the well educated and the economically comfortable; not the lesser educated and the poor. Groups are, some suggest, increasingly organised 'for' citizens, but are not 'of' citizens' (Stoker 2007: 105; 2006). The increasing professionalization of associational and promotional groups means political activity is more likely to be the preserve of professional radical activists, not interested or concerned citizens. Another danger, if old-style politics are increasingly supplanted by newer style group generated politics, is that this might further encourage what Gerry Stoker identifies as 'individual choice, self-expression and market-based fulfilment of needs and wants' (Stoker 2006: 42). If so, then groups might encourage the prioritisation of ego-tropic considerations (this suits me; it is what I want or need) not build support for socio-tropic considerations (this benefits society; it is in our interest).

Groups, because they provide a means of citizen involvement beyond voting and act as an intermediary between citizens and their government, play an important key role in the democratic process. Because they are considered to make a positive civic contribution to the political process, many activists think they provide a better, more specialised alternative to political parties. Indeed, a growing association with promotional groups may reflect the fact that citizens increasingly see traditional forms of politics as 'synonymous with sleaze, corruption, and duplicity, greed, self-interest and self-importance, interference, inefficiency and intransigence' (Hay 2007: 153). They may also consider that traditional party politics, exemplified by voting, party membership and party identification, is 'sullied' by the compromises and necessary tradeoffs politicians and parties make between office and policy seeking, something demonstrated in phenomena such as declining electoral turnout (Franklin 2004) and the collapse of political parties as membership organizations (Dalton 1996). Many citizens as a result, particularly the young, may thus consider politics is better pursued by associational and promotional 'single issue' group activity.

Traditional politics might be redeemed should parties and politicians, especially those in government, respond to public concerns and deliver on their promises. If so, it would still probably fall, inevitably, to the public to demand them and for parties and politicians to then supply (or claim to supply) them. Of course, the ordinary elector only speaks by casting a vote, usually, in Westminster elections, each five years or so. Their voice is also made present when the public is polled and its opinion aggregated by a pollster or focus group convener. Increasingly, however, associational and promotional groups seek day by day to organise, mobilise and express public demands. These can further divert citizens' attention from traditional to newer forms of politics. If politics, then, has become little more than what our politicians do, then pressure and interest groups can entrench the notion that politics is increasingly about what 'we' ask 'them' to do, not what 'we' seek to do ourselves. The worry is that, whenever the public are consulted, it might be the opinion of the professional activist, not necessarily that of the public, which is communicated to the policy maker (Stoker 2006). Those who join groups can often be 'cash-cow supporters' (Jordan and Maloney 2007: 88), willing to declare their support for the group, but not actively participate it its work.

There is, then, the natural worry that a public debate can be skewed or be unbalanced. Any representative claim has to be carefully evaluated. When some 40,000 people register their support for the murderer (and fugitive) Raoul Moat on a Facebook tribute site, we should note that the claims some people make online should be carefully evaluated. Obviously, no sensible person would take seriously supporters of a murderer and attempted murderer, but other, more mainstream demands might have to be equally taken with the proverbial pinch of salt. It is possible, in a world built around personal expression and 'popular' opinion, for an outraged mob to be easily mobilised (especially in the internet age). The nature of any representative claim is that policy makers have to choose whether they want to (or have to) listen to such claims. Government need not listen. Some 1.5 million people had every right to protest against the intervention in Iraq, but it was the House of Commons (even by means of the government's partisan majority) which had to take such a decision in a representative democracy.

Promotional cause groups and left–liberal criticism of the status quo

Groups are more likely to attract those unhappy with the status quo; their officials and activists are usually eager to challenge or question the government of the day. Take, for example, the ways in which British promotional groups raise their voice on the question of civil liberties. The government has had, since September 11th, to take various steps to protect its citizens from the very real threat posed by Islamic extremists. It has had to balance the security of the citizen with their civil liberty. Some see the state's legislative and legal responses as a natural and acceptable consequence of a manifest terrorist threat (Ormand 2010; Philips 2006), but civil rights campaigners interpret them as unacceptable infringements on established civil and human rights that ought be embedded in British society (Gearty 2007; Ewing 2010). Liberty, formerly the National Council on Civil Liberties, has been at the forefront of this issue. It (and other such groups) have challenged the government's right to seek to detain terrorist suspects for 28 days without charge; questioned the handful of control orders imposed on suspected terrorists who cannot be charged or deported, for fear of torture, to their home countries; opposed extraordinary rendition and the use of detention camps such as Guantánamo Bay; and criticised the police's use of stop-and-search powers to prevent terrorist plots. There are, in addition to Liberty, other radical campaigning organisations such as Human Rights Watch and Reprieve, led by Clive Stafford Smith, which claims to use 'the law to enforce the human rights of prisoners, from death row to Guantánamo Bay' (Reprieve 2010).

A similar lobby operates on migration and asylum, a complex, often vexed public policy issue. A cursory online search online throws up the following British organisations campaigning in favour of immigration and migrants:

> the Immigration Advisory Service; Joint Council for the Welfare of Immigrants; the Refugee Council; No One Is Illegal; Asylum Aid; Medical Foundation for the Care of Victims of Torture; Medical Justice Network; Refugees and Migrant Justice; Immigration Law Practitioners; the Asylum Appeals Project; Migrants Rights Network; Refugee Action; the Independent Asylum Commission; and Red Cross Refugee Services.

To these can be added the many 'politicised' law firms working in this field, for example Birnberg Peirce and Partners or Christian Khan which, while providing their legal service, publicly advocate the liberalisation of immigration law. On the other side of the argument advocating immigration controls, racist far-right political groups aside, is found only Migration Watch, its parliamentary affiliate Balanced Migration and one or two right-of-centre think-tanks.

British campaigning groups often tend to the liberal. In any trade-off between security and liberty, they necessarily, reflexively favour liberty.

They invariably oppose, say, the use of control measures to deal with suspected terrorists or the use of CCTV or the DNA database to deal with crime. They reject any criminal justice measure deemed punitive or harsh. Few, if any, groups campaign in favour of the sensible use of CCTV or, a handful of right-leaning think-tanks and policing organisations aside, make the case for the DNA database. Some 54 per cent of those surveyed might have supported capital punishment in 2009 (with only 30 per cent opposed) (*Metro*, 4 October 2009), but there are almost no, if any, significant groups that campaign for the restoration of the death penalty. There are a number of prisoners' rights advocates, among them the Howard League for Penal Reform, the National Association for the Care and Resettlement of Offenders and the Prison Reform Trust. Their mindset is that prison has, ideally, to be focused on prisoner rehabilitation rather than be 'merely' retributive; punishment has to focus on reforming the 'offender', not merely protecting the public. There are far fewer organised groups calling for the size of the prison population to be increased and fewer still calling for sentences to be made longer and harsher.

Such is the imbalance of voices raised on the subject of prison policy that the former Labour Justice Secretary, Jack Straw, accused many prison reformers, whom he described as the 'criminal justice lobby', of being more concerned about the 'needs' of offenders than those of the victim (*Guardian*, 27 October 2008). A great many citizens, when discussing criminal justice policy, probably believe the state should lock serious offenders up and 'throw away the key'; that a life sentence 'should mean life'. Such opinions, the old mainstay of the saloon bar (less so, perhaps, the Conservative frontbench), are less heard amid the cacophony of organised voices petitioning government about the state of Britain's prisons. Largely speaking victims' rights groups (other than counselling support services) tend to be found at the less professional, more vocational end of the debate spectrum and usually focus on the prevention of specific crimes as opposed to lobbying for some form or mode of punishment. That the public debate on civil liberties is, thanks to the work of liberal cause groups, heavily skewed to the liberal side of the argument could well mean that other voices are not necessarily heard. The absence of a countervailing force able to counter – and at least try to balance – the criminal justice reform lobby means that reform agenda is better placed, when advantaged by media reportage, to provide the voices which the government will hear.

Much promotional group politics, usually pursued by the tireless and the committed (not, usually, the apathetic), as well as the alienated and the angry, are all too often the preserve of the left inclined radical. The radical, non-parliamentary left, unable to make any constructive, realistic contribution on economic questions relating to what the state 'gets' and 'spend', have for some time retreated into identity politics and criticism of Britain's (and the US's) foreign policies. All antiwar, peace campaigners hail from the political left. The more moderate, middle-of-the road critics of Tony Blair and George Bush's 'war on terror' sometimes marched in protest, but such marches were organised by anti-Western far-left fronts such as the Stop the War Coalition. The same may be said of self-styled anti-fascist campaigns such as Anti-Fascist Action. Parliament Square is periodically squatted by 'peace' campaigners, not those in favour of making use of the 'hard' and 'soft' power of the West for humanitarian purposes. This means the promotional group universe is often skewed toward the radical and the left. Self-interested associational groups, such as energy producers and heavy users, or airlines, often challenge the notion of climate change, but there are far more promotional groups campaigning against it than they are groups that challenge the idea of it.

A skewed promotional group universe may unbalance public debate: particularly should a vocal leftist minority seek public attention while the opinion of the silent, moderate majority is found only by opinion research or is expressed at an election. In the US well-resourced conservative and liberal promotional groups have long fought it out among themselves. The political right in Britain has previously sought to rebalance the climate of ideas in its favour through the work of think tanks such as the Institute of Economic Affairs, the Centre for Policy Studies and the Adam Smith Institute (most recently that of the Centre for Social Cohesion and Policy Exchange). Efforts by rightists to set up cause groups such as the Taxpayers' Alliance perhaps then indicates their belated recognition of the potential political purchase that a promotional group can have.

How Britain's political system structures the way associational and promotional groups operate

Britain, in spite of its Conservative–Liberal Democrat coalition government, still sits at the end of Lijphart's scale distinguishing the ideal type majoritarian democratic system from its consensus counterpart. British politics are enacted within a majoritarian, power-hoarding democracy (Lijphart 2001; Flinders 2010). Majoritarian democracies, Lijphart argues, has a pluralist interest group system which features 'a competitive and uncoordinated pluralism of independent groups in contrast with the coordinated and compromise-oriented system of corporatism that is typical of the consensus model' (1999: 171). This, Flinders finds, was not changed by the recent Labour governments which only modified the majoritarianism of the executive-minded Westminster model (2010). To explore how Britain's political system structures the ways in which both associational and promotional groups operate a brief comparison between the opportunities afforded such groups in the very different political systems of Britain and the United States might be useful.

The US has a federal and Britain a unitary political system

The US, being a federal, presidential polity, offers a great many opportunities for interest groups to access the system. The US divides governmental power two ways: first, vertically between all 50 states of the union and the federal government which represents all 50 states; second, horizontally within the federal government (and each of the state governments) by separating the powers of the presidency, the Congress and the Supreme Court (the executive, the legislature and the judiciary), so enabling each branch of government to check and balance each other. Interest groups can thus seek to influence each or all of the three branches of the federal government (and those of the 50 states). From the local to the national, the state level to the federal, there are numerous points by which groups can access the system. A Californian interest group, say, can lobby the governor and representatives at the state level; two US senators and 53 US congressmen at the federal level. The group can then lobby the president and the executive branch. In contrast, within Britain's unitary, parliamentary system there are far fewer access points for interest groups. If Scottish, Welsh and Northern Irish devolution has created new forums within which groups can operate (Flinders 2010) the reach of these fora only encompass some 15 per cent of the British population. Whitehall and Westminster (alongside the European Union where it is granted competence by its member states (Grant 2000; Coen and Richardson 2009) remains the focus of attention for those groups seeking to speak for the remaining 85 per cent of Britons. Local government, beyond lesser, local issues, does not count.

The US Congress is independent of the government, but the British parliament is much more subservient to the government

The presidential system restricts the power of the US president by empowering an independent and powerful Congress. Groups can lobby both the proactive House of Representatives and the Senate, which are, unlike in Britain, separate from and independent of the government. They can lobby both congressmen and senators alike, secure in the knowledge that they can respond to their concern and, if supportive and sufficiently senior, take up their case. With the House of Commons being a more important lawmaker than the Lords, there is in Britain essentially only one really effective legislative chamber for interest groups to lobby; the Lords is a less important revising chamber. However, because the British government, unlike the US presidency, makes use of its parliamentary majority to pursue its legislative programme according to its chosen timetable, the Commons is a reactive, not a proactive legislature. Government, by means of its Commons majority, is in charge of lawmaking. This means that MPs, being divided into frontbencher and backbencher, opposition and government, are less best placed than the more autonomous, independent US senator or congressman to help a group advance their cause by making law. Unlike the US minority legislator, whose support is often be needed to make law in the US congress, the opposition backbench Westminster MP can at best only raise or state the interest group case, not pass laws on its behalf.

US elections are much more expensive to fight than British elections

The US and Britain differ considerably in the way groups use money to highlight their interest or cause by influencing electoral politics. Interests and causes have less opportunity to enter the electoral arena in Britain in comparison with the US. Campaign finance is the lifeblood of the US election campaign; candidates and campaigns have to raise a great deal of money to be elected. In 2008 the average House race cost the winning candidate some $1.1 million and a Senate race $6.5 million. Candidates for all parties collectively raised and spent $1.6 billion. In their race for the presidency Barack Obama raised and spent $533 million and John McCain $379 million. At the 2005 British election, in stark contrast, £41million was spent by the political parties, £1.7 million by third parties such as campaign groups and £14 million by individual candidates. The average parliamentary candidate locally spent just under £4,000 (Electoral Commission 2006). Interests in the US are able, legally, to funnel money to US parties and candidates in large measure. They need not necessarily 'buy' a candidate, merely reward those who agree with their cause (opposing those candidates who do not) and ensure their cause is promoted by their favoured candidate. At the 2010 congressional elections the National Rifle Association intended to spend as much as $20 million, the conservative group, Americans for Prosperity over $45 million and the liberal Service Employees International Union (SEIU) some $44 million (CBS News, 2 June 2010). Spending such vast sums of money is not possible in Britain. Party finance is tightly regulated by law and parties, prevented from buying paid television advertisements, need not seek such funds to expend.

Paid, professional lobbyists can wield considerable power in the
US Congress, but their British counterparts are far less influential

In the US professional lobbyists, guns for hire for special interests, boast-
ing an unrivalled insider knowledge of the political system, identify – and
help exploit – entry into that system by facilitating exchanges between
companies, interests and politicians. They themselves form a multimil-
lion dollar industry. In 2009 health care industry groups were estimated
to spend $1.4 million per day to lobby members of Congress on health
care reform (Common Cause 2009); some $3.5 billion in total was spent
in total by US lobbyists in 2009. In Britain, however, the number of
professional lobbyists has increased recently, employing some 14,000
people (compared to the 90,000 or so people who are paid to influence
the US federal government), but lobbyists do not spend such sums of
money; they do not exert anything remotely like the clout of their more
powerful US counterparts. They perhaps target the national media rather
more than policy makers directly. British lobbyists usually take the form
of public relations firms or public affairs consultants, such as Weber
Shadwick, Portland or Bell Pottinger. Most large-scale corporate
concerns, while prepared to seek advice from public relations professionals, usually have their own in-house lobbying arm. Cause groups
rarely, if ever, use professional lobbyists only because funds are tight and
they also prefer to lobby themselves. British political lobbyists, while
growing in influence, remain relatively small beer compared to these in
the US.

Lobbying in Britain, prime minister Cameron suggested in opposition,
is 'the next big scandal waiting to happen. It's an issue that crosses party
lines and has tainted our politics for too long, an issue that exposes the far-
too-cosy relationship between politics, government, business and money'
(BBC News 2010). Lobbying scandals in Britain usually involve former
MPs seeking to make money on their past connections. In 2010 three
former Labour ministers, Patricia Hewitt, Stephen Byers and Geoff Hoon,
were caught on film attempting to parley their cabinet experience into
consultancy cash. Of course no real consultancy, only a bogus one set up
for a television sting, would wish to make use of ex-Labour MPs when a
Conservative government was likely to be elected. It is also hard to see
what pay off an interest or cause could get by hiring a lobbyist to lobby
sitting MPs (as opposed to lobbying ministers and officials). Their issue
would be raised, sure, but parliament, because it processes the legislative
agenda set by the government (even by a coalition government), is reactive, not proactive. By themselves, shackled by the pro- or anti-
government partisanship which pervades all aspects of the work of the
Commons, MPs cannot make law in the way their US counterparts can.

Concern has been expressed by the number of former ministers, MPs and special advisers who subsequently work for public affairs consultancies, but while greater regulation and transparency is needed, there are few concrete examples of access leading to influence. It is, naturally, difficult to offer a definitive judgement when lobbying takes place privately, discreetly. The attempt in 1997 to exempt Formula 1 from the initial ban on tobacco advertising owed more to Labour rewarding a financial donor than to lobbying on behalf of Bernie Ecclestone. In contrast US political watchers can cite numerous examples of political scandal arising from the interface of lobbyists, interests and members of Congress. The biggest, most significant ethical scandal affecting the House of Commons, the 2009 furore over MPs expenses aside, was that two Tory MPs were paid money to ask parliamentary questions in 1994. Paid to ask questions, note, not to provide the preferred answer to a question. This, it is safe to say, is a state of affairs US ethics advocates can only dream about and something which would make most US lobbyists and their clients (and some past and present members of Congress) laugh.

The US has a 'fixed' constitution stopping government from doing things, whereas Britain has a 'flexible' constitution enabling government to do things

Finally the US system is engineered to limit the power of government. Government is prevented by the US constitution from abridging certain legal rights, so interest and pressure groups can enforce citizens' rights by federal and state courts. Congress and the president might, conceivably, say, enact law to ban the private ownership of guns, but lawyers instructed by the National Rifle Association would successfully have the Supreme Court uphold the second amendment of the US constitution by overturning the law. In Britain, the requirements of EU membership aside, it is parliament, being unable to bind its successor, which makes and unmakes the law. Courts can only interpret parliamentary intent where it is unclear or contradictory, so interest groups, because parliament, led by the government, has made policy by law, have much less opportunity to use the courts to insist upon their rights. This has changed significantly, however, in recent years thanks largely to the Human Rights Act of 1999 (the HRA). British advocacy groups campaigning for civil liberties and human rights now use the rights set out in the HRA to have the courts overturn government policy. Lawyers working with human rights groups have been able to challenge the use of control orders to deal with suspected terrorists and successfully oppose the government's right to deport terrorists to places where they could be in danger of mistreatment. In July 2010 Medical Justice, which provides medical and legal advice to people facing removal, persuaded the high court to declare unlawful the fast-track deportation of certain foreign nationals refused permission to remain in Britain. This is because the HRA asserts the human rights set out in the act, which are interpreted equally to apply to citizens, residents and aliens, and so establishes the higher standard to which the courts can hold all other statute law and any governmental decisions.

Groups therefore have less access to government in Britain, but can, if they obtain access or successfully shape the media agenda, have more impact

British government now, especially in regard to routine policy making and implementation, works within and through a series of networks in Whitehall and Westminster, supplemented by networks in Edinburgh, Cardiff, Belfast and Brussels. British interest groups, because they operate in an unstructured, uncoordinated environment, have to try to enter – or at the very least influence – these networks by seeking out – and making use of – the entry points that enable access to the political system. Thus the opportunity for group influence and effect, while heavily influenced by the salience of the group's issue, is largely structured by the political system. There are more entry points enabling US groups to access the US political system. The drawback is that all sorts of interests, each of which can counterbalance the other, are able to enter the political system. Interests can, with so many actors involved in the legislative process at some many levels of government, block each other from the pursuit of their interest. For instance, for every US pro-choice lobby there is a pro-life lobby and those who advocate for the right to own a gun face off against supporters of gun control; each has their cheerleaders in the Congress. It may, then, be harder to get into the closed system in Britain, but if an interest group successfully persuades ministers or officials to support its cause, redress of some form might then be forthcoming. British interest groups, more likely to be outsider than insider, have often to strive to capture the attention of policy makers; to try to 'push' them in their preferred direction from outside of Whitehall and Westminster, not 'pull' them in it from inside. Of course, because such groups are better resourced than before in terms of their work, they increasingly push loudly and more and more vociferously.

Groups and government

Business interests, given the role the marketplace plays in the generation of national wealth, necessarily have powers and privileges denied others

(Crouch 2004; Coen *et al.* 2010). Groups of various types, speaking on a vast range of issues, have long been a fact of political life, but today, being better resourced, increasingly professionalised and in possession of the modern means of communications afforded by the internet, they can now more than ever 'make present' their demands. Those who work for high-profile associational or promotional groups can often themselves claim a high-public profile. In June 2010, a former senior Downing Street political adviser, Justin Forsyth, beat the ex-Labour cabinet minister, James Purnell to the post of chief executive of Save the Children. Such is the public platform groups are granted (and often demand), someone like the ubiquitous Shami Chakrabarti, who heads up Liberty, has become a public figure of some significance. By leading a cause group she has considerable clout, better access to ministers and officials and a higher media profile (being, for example, a perennial panellist on BBC's flagship politics programme, Question Time) than most backbench MPs (and many frontbenchers).

People who have worked for some or other group increasingly form part of Britain's growing 'political class'; a class composed of individuals who work exclusively in and around politics before entering the House of Commons. Some 12 per cent of MPs first elected in 2010 had a public relations or a public affairs consultancy background, with 19 newly elected Conservative and 11 Labour MPs having worked for a lobbyist before entering the Commons. Nick Clegg, the coalition's deputy prime minister, first elected in 2005, was a lobbyist of the European Union between being an MEP and becoming an MP (something he tries to gloss over). Some 6 per cent of new MPs have an NGO or charity background, but such, however, is the decline in the standing of the trade unions in the Labour party, only some 3 per cent came from a union background (Madano Partnership 2010).

Government, charged with steering the state by making use of its fiscal reach and legal powers, governs hierarchically, but has always to anticipate the likely reaction of the electorate and of powerful interests. With occasional exceptions, however, the relationship between groups and government is entirely asymmetrical. This is because:

- Government possesses power and authority even if, under multilevel governance, it possesses less power than before. Citizens still consider the government as the mechanism to deal with issues and to resolve problems.
- Groups have thus to try to influence (or at the very least to shout loudly at) government.
- Government, however, often decides which groups it wishes to listen to or work with (or has to acknowledge).

- In terms of policy making, then, it is, in the final analysis, government that *decides* because groups merely *advise* (or, in the case of some, *despise* what government has done or intends to do).

Groups inevitably engage with traditional politics. The state – not least the government charged with its affairs – remains – alongside national and international economic and social processes – the ultimate arbiter of what happens in Britain. Groups cannot ignore or bypass the state, but have instead to try to persuade it, plead with it or challenge it to respond to their issue or cause; all too often they use the media to publically make their case. The footprint of the British state, in spite of the neo-liberal re-regulation of the past 30 or so years, has considerably widened in recent years: the state provide services and regulates conduct in the realms of the economy, national security, law and order, health, education and welfare, but additional activities

> that governments seek to encourage, discourage, regulate, monitor, prohibit or offer advice on has grown. Obesity, species extinction, water conservation, smoking, carbon emissions, anti-social behaviour, the use of mobile phones while driving, busking, hate speech, cloning, the number of senior female executives, the transfer of personal data between organisations, doping in sport, road pricing, the transmission of major sporting events on terrestrial rather than satellite television, stalking, binge drinking, the number of medals won at an Olympics – all have become the subject of political debate and government actions. (Bell and Hindmoor: 2009: 93)

Because the state seeks to do more (and is held responsible for more) there are greater opportunities for groups to press their case; so now, more than ever, groups interested in whatever subject area are more likely to have to engage with the government which enacts such policy responsibilities.

Conclusion

One cannot easily lobby 'global processes' or approach 'international capital': if to think 'globally' requires one to act 'locally', one has to lobby the local state in the form of its office holders and functionaries. International organisations can target states to secure international agreements. In Britain, because citizens and organisations, in short, still expect the state to respond to – and hopefully resolve – problems, government remains the first – and often the only – port of call wherein groups raise their complaint(s) and seek redress. Groups now have, thanks to the internet and its related forms of social media, more power than ever before to access and address the public, both nationally and internationally. At the heart of all associational and promotional group activity is lobbying both the state and the public; the state, directly, to get something either done or stopped; the public, in order to raise awareness of an issue and bring additional, indirect pressure on the state to act.

Groups contribute, according to John Keane, to the monitory mechanisms which 'call into question the abuse of state and corporate power across borders. The global uproars that accompanied the American invasion of Iraq, and the devastation of the Gulf of Mexico cause by the criminal negligence of BP, are pertinent examples of monetary democracy in action' (Keane 2010: 6). One might ponder whether, as the left suggest, it is only 'state and corporate power' which merits monitoring, but the monitoring of government by groups clearly has the considerable potential to impact the ways in which we do politics. Such groups tend, however, to be self-selecting and they can often lean, in Britain (if not, say, in the US), toward the liberal end of the spectrum; their causes are invariably selective. Groups can, by usefully giving some citizens the means to speak to policy makers, advantage representative democracy, but they can also help further reduce the trust other citizens have in the representative democracy, particularly in regard to government's capacity to deal with the causes they care about and deliver the goods they need.

The great worry, then, is that associational and (especially) promotional groups will increase 'the demands made on the political system to deliver without aiding any understanding of the need to balance competing demands' (Peters *et al.* 2009: 331). They can, therefore, raise expectations which might not be met. If so, then disappointment can lead to disillusionment when groups generate public complaint that government is incompetent, indifferent, non-responsive or uncaring (and perhaps downright venal). If government cannot – for whatever reason – respond constructively and positively to the groups' demands or needs, then interest and pressure group activity may, conversely, further encourage political disengagement.

Chapter 11

The Politics of Diversity

ROSIE CAMPBELL

Politics in Britain in the twentieth century was always about group differences, with, for most of the century, the accepted division being that of social class. However, the social movements of the late 1960s and 1970s saw the development of additional political fault lines as feminist, ethnic minority and lesbian and gay citizens demanded equality. These claims for recognition of discrimination on the grounds of sex, sexuality and race/ethnicity were soon accompanied by the concerns of other groups such as the disabled and more recently the elderly.

To some extent the demands of these groups were taken up by the British state. Discrimination in the workplace on the grounds of sex or race/ethnicity has long been illegal, and recent legislation protects disabled, lesbian, gay, bisexual and transgender (LGBT) and older workers, as well as allowing same-sex couples to join together in civil partnerships. But managing diversity is not straightforward. British society is seemingly less homogeneous than it was immediately after the Second World War; progressive waves of immigration, the diversification of lifestyles and family structures alongside women's entry into education and employment have made managing diversity ever more difficult. Britain is an increasingly secular society, where since the 1970s the rights of individuals to pursue their preferred way of life have outrun many of the pressures to conform. These demands for individual freedom have often come into conflict with demands for group recognition made by those who identify themselves primarily as belonging to a religion. This problem has become more politically salient after 9/11 and the 7/7 bombings, which had a massive effect on elite and popular discourse about ethnicity, religion and citizenship. This chapter discusses three dimensions of modern diversity – gay rights, gender equality and ethnicity – in each case examining both mass and elite views, before considering the changing way in which the British state attempts to manage diversity.

Gay rights

In the last two decades there have been seismic shifts in the British political elite's attitudes to gay rights. After Labour came to power in 1997 most of the core policy demands of the LGBT community were enacted. Sexual relationships between same-sex couples were completely decriminalised, with the age of consent equalised at 16 in the Sexual Offences (Amendment) Act 2000. In addition, in 2003 the government repealed section 28 of the Local Government Act 1986, which prohibited local authorities from 'promoting' homosexuality. Section 28 had been a highly symbolic galvanising force for the gay rights movement in Britain; Stonewall, now the most visible gay rights organisation in Britain, had been established by a group of activists in response to the legislation. The Labour government first tried to repeal section 28 in 2000, but the attempt was overturned in the Lords. The Scottish Parliament repealed it in 2000 and this was followed by a successful repeal in England and Wales in 2003.

As well as removing discrimination on the basis of sexual orientation from criminal law, Labour between 1997 and 2010 also made significant changes to the legal aspects of same-sex couples' family lives. Perhaps the most significant of these initiatives was the Civil Partnership Act 2004, which allowed same-sex couples to enter a union with all of the rights and responsibilities of civil marriage; in other words, marriage in all but name. Civil partnerships have completely recast the legal protections and status of same-sex couples in Britain; before their creation same-sex couples, who had perhaps spent a lifetime together, were not considered next of kin by hospitals and could be denied visiting rights, they were not the immediate beneficiaries of life insurances or inheritance and were not the legal guardians of any children looked after within the relationship. The law has also been amended so that same-sex couples can adopt; the Adoption and Children Act 2002 dropped the stipulation that adoptive parents must be married, thus allowing same-sex couples (and single people) to apply. Discrimination in the workplace on the grounds of sexual orientation was outlawed in the Employment Equality (Sexual Orientation) Regulations 2003 and the Sexual Orientation Regulations 2007 prohibited discrimination in the provision of goods and services. Most recently the Human Fertilisation and Embryology Act 2008 granted lesbians and their partners equal parental status after successful *in vitro* fertilisation (IVF) treatment.

Section 28 was brought in by a Conservative government and the attempts to maintain it were mostly undertaken by Conservative politicians, many of whom voted against most of Labour's reforms. David Cameron himself voted against the repeal of section 28 in 2003, but in

2009 he made a public apology on behalf of the Conservative party for the legislation, acknowledging that it had been 'offensive to gay people'. Under Cameron the Conservative party modernised its attitudes to gay rights, although there are still tensions within the party, which surfaced during the 2010 general election campaign when Chris Grayling, the then Shadow Home Secretary, was recorded as saying that he had no objection to owners of bed and breakfast businesses from refusing guests on the basis of sexuality, and the Conservative candidate for Sutton and Cheam, Philippa Stroud, was alleged to have led prayer sessions to 'cure' gay people. However, at the level of the party leadership, Cameron has recently promised to allow civil partnerships between same-sex couples to be held in churches and pledged any future marriage tax break will include civil partnerships.

To a large extent the policy demands of the gay rights movement have now been met and organisations such as Stonewall are instead focusing more on altering the attitudes of the general public, where the huge turn-around in the attitudes of the political elite to gay rights has been mirrored by changes in public opinion. The British Social Attitudes (BSA) Survey of 1989 found that 69 per cent of the British public believed that sexual relations between two adults of the same sex were always or mostly wrong; by 2007 the figure had dropped to 36 per cent. The change in attitudes to gay rights is most evident among younger Britons (see Figure 11.1). In fact the percentage of the British public who believe gay sex to be always or mostly wrong among the over-75s (69 per cent) remains at 1989 levels. The same trend is evident when we look at attitudes to gay adoption. The youngest respondents to the BSA were four times more likely than the oldest to support the rights of female same-sex couples to adopt; 60 per cent of the age group 18 to 24 years old were in support of lesbians' rights to adopt compared with just 15 per cent of people aged over 75. Support for male same-sex couples' right to adopt is slightly weaker than that for lesbians, but shows the same clear correlation between age and attitudes.

There are also clear differences by sex, with women being more positive towards gay rights (48 per cent of men in 2007 said that they thought sex between same-sex couples was always or mostly wrong, compared to 31 per cent of women) and by religiosity (72 per cent of people who describe themselves as very religious feel that gay sex is always or mostly wrong compared with 27 per cent of people who are not at all religious). Educational achievement is also important, with 19 per cent of degree holders stating that sex between same-sex couples is always or mostly wrong compared to 58 per cent of people with no qualifications. Thus, attitudes to gay rights are clearly delineated by age and sex, education and religiosity. We will see the significant impact of age and sex again

Figure 11.1 *Attitudes to sexual relations between same-sex couples by age group*

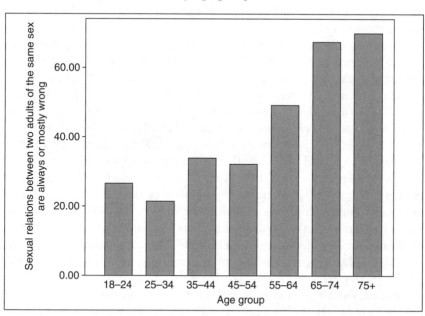

Data from: BSA 2007

when we come to look at racial prejudice, where younger people and women are again the most progressive.

Gender politics

In many respects, recent decades have seen the Labour party reinvent itself as the party that takes gender equality seriously. The election in 1997 of 120 women MPs, 101 of whom were Labour members, raised the bar for the other political parties. The Labour party achieved this historic increase in the proportion of women MPs by using all-women shortlists (AWS) to guarantee the better representation of women in 1997. Following a legal ruling that AWS contravened equality legislation, AWSs were not employed in the run-up to the 2001 general election and the number of Labour women MPs declined slightly. In order to reintroduce AWS the Labour government passed the Sex Discrimination (Selection Candidates) Act 2002 which allowed for equality guarantees for the selection of candidates, along with a sunset clause when their use would no longer be legal. AWS was employed in advance of the 2005 election and the number of Labour women MPs went up from 95 in 2001 to 98 in 2005. The Equality Act 2010 was one of the last pieces of legislation passed by the Labour government; it extends the legislation's sunset clause to 2030.

Alongside addressing the representation of women in politics the party also developed a policy platform focusing on health and education (priority areas for women voters) together with a raft of measures designed to help women achieve something of a work–life balance. Labour introduced legislation to extend paid and unpaid maternity leave, implemented childcare vouchers and child tax credits and invested in the Sure Start scheme, which provided childcare, health and social support in deprived areas. With the exception of maternity leave, in theory these policies should be of equal value to men and women but because women still undertake the majority of the caring work associated with young children, in reality the impact was highly gendered. Thus, Labour were able to present itself as the party most representative of women and women's issues; their 2010 manifesto included pledges to extend childcare provision and to retain the current child tax credit system (Campbell and Childs 2010).

Overall, women are better represented in the House of Commons than ever before; in 2010, 22 per cent of MPs were women compared to just 4 per cent in 1983 (Table 11.1). But the proportion of women legislators is still relatively low. The House of Commons was ranked joint fiftieth in the Inter-Parliamentary Union's league table of women's representation in 2010, lagging behind Rwanda, Sweden, South Africa, Cuba, Iceland, the Netherlands and Finland whose lower Houses or main parliamentary chambers were made up of 40 per cent or more women. Labour remains the most representative of women at Westminster by a wide margin (32 per cent of the parliamentary Labour party are women compared with 16 per cent and 12 per cent for the Conservative and Liberal Democrats respectively), although the Conservatives have begun to close the gap somewhat.

The Conservatives made no real attempt to tackle New Labour on gender equality until David Cameron was elected leader in December 2005. In his acceptance speech, he drew attention to the under-representation of women in the party: 'We will change the way we look. Nine out of ten Conservative MPs are white men. We need to change the scandalous under-representation of women in the Conservative party and we will do that'. In a subsequent speech to the now defunct Equal Opportunities Commission he declared that it was the Conservatives' goal to make 'gender inequality history' by increasing the number of Conservative women MPs, tackling the gender pay gap and addressing childcare issues. The immediate reforms put in place by Cameron

Table 11.1   *Women MPs elected to the House of Commons,*
1983–2010, by party

Party	1983	1987	1992	1997	2001	2005	2010
Labour	10	21	37	101	95	98	81
As % of Lab. MPs	5	9	14	24	23	28	32
Conservative	13	17	20	13	14	17	48
As % of Con. MPs	3	5	6	8	8	9	16
Liberal Democrat	0	1	2	3	6	10	7
As % of LD MPs	0	5	10	7	11	16	12
Total	23	41	60	120	118	128	143
As % of Commons	4	6	9	18	18	20	22

Note: The figure for the Liberal Democrats before 1992 is for the Liberal–SDP Alliance.

included the creation of a priority list of potential candidates, which would be made up of 50 per cent women and from which the top 100 target seats would have to choose their candidates. These initiatives appeared radical as they amounted to equality guarantees that were not substantively much weaker than Labour's AWS. However, the requirement that associations select from the priority list did not last beyond the review stage and the policy was soon watered down considerably. Cameron's focus on gender politics was part of an attempt to reinvent the party, recasting it away from its reputation as 'the nasty party'. In the end the party increased the number of Conservative women MPs from 17 (9 per cent of Conservative MPs elected in 2005 were women) to 48 (16 per cent) Conservative MPs elected in 2010. Alongside efforts to tackle the representation of women in parliament the Conservative party also produced a range of policies clearly targeted at women.

The most progressive of these policies included allowing mothers and fathers to exchange maternity leave from 14 weeks after birth. The transfer of maternity leave rights to fathers is seen as a key demand for women's equality. Many feminists argue that only when employers recognise that men and women may both have caring responsibilities will sex discrimination in the workplace be seriously disrupted (Rake 2009). Labour also supported allowing parents to transfer maternity leave provision but only from six months after birth. That said, many commentators feel that the Conservatives' proposed marriage tax break ran counter to the generally progressive direction of current Conservative policy on gender equality (Campbell and Childs 2010).

In recent years the Liberal Democrats have produced manifestos that aimed to promote gender equality; like the other main parties in 2010 they included policies on domestic violence and women in development. In 2010 they also advocated allowing parents to exchange maternity leave; of the three main parties their policy was perhaps the most radical as it allowed parents to transfer maternity leave/pay from birth. However, the Liberal Democrats are now the weakest of the three main parties when it comes to the representation of women. In 1989 the newly formed Liberal Democrats were the first British party to apply a quota rule (where each shortlist had to contain at least one woman) to selection procedures for general elections, but the party has always rejected measures such as AWS. In 2001 a motion to introduce AWS was put to the party conference: supported by the older women feminists within the party, it was defeated largely by a cohort of younger women who saw the proposal as demeaning (Evans 2011). The tension between women in the Liberal Democrats remains, hindering attempts to improve the parliamentary representation of women. In place of equality guarantees the party relies on rhetoric, encouraging women to seek selection, and equality promotion measures, such as training, equal opportunities selection procedures and financial support (Childs 2008). This approach is not generally successful in improving the representation of women and in 2010 the party returned just seven women MPs (12 per cent of the total). To some extent, the failure to improve on its representation was a result of its poor performance in the election: in seats where the winning party was just 5 per cent or less ahead of the Liberal Democrats (and where the Lib Dems came in second place) the Liberal Democrats had placed seven women out of 16 candidates (44 per cent); had they taken those seats, there would have been a noticeable increase in the number of Lib Dem women MPs.

Although the three main parties are now clearly competing on women's issues at election time they have all been accused of sidelining women politicians. Gordon Brown's final reshuffle resulted in a cabinet that was less representative of women, with one minister, Caroline Flint, describing the prime minister as operating a two-tier government with women excluded from the real decision-making and used instead as mere window-dressing. After the election Harriet Harman took over as the temporary leader of the Labour party, but just one woman put herself forward for the leadership contest (Diane Abbott) and her nomination was only possible because one of the male candidates agreed to nominate her. The newly formed Conservative–Liberal Democrat coalition government was criticised for including just four women in its first cabinet, with only one (Home Secretary Theresa May) in a senior post. Following the coalition's emergency budget the Fawcett Society filed a legal challenge claiming that the government had failed in its legal duty to safeguard gender equality and had not taken sufficient account of how spending cuts would disproportionately affect women (the challenge was dismissed by the judge who described it as 'unarguable – or academic'). After the excitement of 1997, when it seemed that women were making a breakthrough into the political elite, they still remain under-represented as MPs and in the upper echelons of government; only very incremental improvements, if any at all, have been made since 1997.

Part of Labour's rationale for using AWS was to challenge the historic advantage that the Conservative party had among women voters – what is known as the 'traditional gender gap' – with women's votes for the Conservative party helping to explain the party's dominance after the Second World War. The tendency for women to vote to the right of men is an international phenomenon, usually ascribed to women's greater religiosity and their historic lack of exposure to social institutions, such as trade unions, that tend to push people towards the left. In recent years, however, women in many countries have moved slightly to the left of men, a trend known as the 'modern gender gap' (Inglehart and Norris 2000, 2003). In the United States more women than men have voted for the Democratic candidate at every presidential election since 1980. In contemporary Britain there is now generally little relationship between sex/gender and party of vote. There is usually a small gender gap, with women voting for the Conservative party in slightly larger numbers than men, but this relationship is largely accounted for by the fact that women tend to live longer than men and older people tend to be more conservative in their politics than younger people (and the difference is anyway not statistically significant). Nor has there been any evidence of a modern gender gap opening up to replace it, at least overall. However, in 1997, 2001 and 2005 younger women were slightly more likely to vote for the Labour party than younger men. Pippa Norris has termed this the 'gender generation gap' and she suggests that as these women replace older women in the population a modern gender gap is likely to emerge in the UK (Norris 1999b). Evidence from the 2010 election is mixed (as discussed in Box 11.1).

There are however clear sex/gender differences when it comes to attitudes towards gender equality. Women are generally more likely than men to think that efforts to deliver equal opportunities for women have not gone far enough. These findings are replicated in a survey of mass political attitudes where women parliamentary candidates and MPs were found to be more in favour of gender equality and measures to improve it then men (Campbell *et al.* 2010). The authors of the research conclude that in regards to attitudes to gender equality 'women representatives are more like women voters and male representatives are more like male voters...hence [male representatives] may, on average, be less likely than

Box 11.1   The gender gap and the 2010 election

Opinion polls conducted by the survey company IPSOS–MORI show a fairly sizable modern gender generation gap (Table 11.2): younger women (aged between 18 and 24) were 13 per cent more likely to vote for the Liberal Democrats than younger men, while younger men were 10 per cent more likely to have voted Conservative and 3 per cent more likely to have voted Labour. The MORI data show a particular large modern gender gap among respondents aged between 25 and 34, with 40 per cent of men saying they voted Conservative, compared to just 27 per cent of women, although there is little difference over the age of 35.

All such poll results should be treated with caution, because they do not contain a validated vote measure, in which the survey team cross-check the self-reported turnout of respondents against the electoral register, removing memory bias and acquiescence effects from participation, if not actual party of vote. There is reason to believe that using self-reported vote intention or perhaps even self-reported vote without the validated vote measure might be inappropriate for the study of gender differences. And early data from the British Election study showed no evidence of a modern gender gap; if anything, men were consistently more likely to say that they intended to vote for the Labour party than women. These findings would suggest that the modern gender gap that benefited the Labour party among younger voters from 1997 disappeared at the 2010 election (perhaps because the Conservative party has modernised its attitudes to gender equality and women's issues?), although until we have validated data we will not be able to be certain.

women representatives to act for, or otherwise represent, women voters on the many issues affected by [these attitudes]' (Campbell *et al.* 2010: 194).

Race, immigration and Islam

For many years the British political elite spoke of 'multicultural Britain', encouraging the celebration of different cultures and rejecting the forced assimilation of minority groups into the mainstream. However, during Tony Blair's premiership official reports into the causes of riots in Bradford, Burnley and Oldham highlighted the danger of communities living parallel lives. This unease grew in the aftermath of the 7/7 London bombings and there has been a movement away from multiculturalism towards a more integrationist approach that promotes and even 'tests' Britishness.

Table 11.2   *Party of vote 2010 by age and sex*

Sex	Age	Party of vote			
		Conservative	Labour	Liberal Democrat	Other
Men	18–24	29	34	27	10
	25–34	42	23	30	6
	35–54	36	28	23	13
	55+	41	29	16	14
	All	38	28	22	12
Women	18–24	30	28	34	9
	25–34	27	38	27	8
	35–54	33	31	29	8
	55+	42	30	21	7
	All	36	31	26	8

Data from: IPSOS–Mori. N=10211 electors interviewed between 6 April to 6 May 2010, weighted to final result of 2010 general election

Gordon Brown's premiership was particularly associated with the rejection of multiculturalism and the advancement of Britishness. Just before and after he become leader of the Labour party, he made a number of high-profile speeches about the importance of Britishness (Gamble 2008). Cynics might speculate about Brown's motivations for focusing on Britishness. The creation of the Scottish Parliament and Welsh Assembly had brought the 'West Lothian Question' firmly onto the political agenda and sections of the media carried regular stories about the 'Scottish Mafia' highlighting the large number of Scottish Labour MPs legislating on purely English matters. Brown therefore had good political reasons to present himself as a British prime minister rather than a 'Scottish' one.

However, Brown was not the only high-profile figure to question the politics of multiculturalism. There has, for example, been an ongoing debate within the political elite about the potential impact of immigration on attitudes to the welfare state (Ford 2006). Fears concerning the impact of increasing diversity on the British way of life have traditionally been expressed by right-leaning thinkers. But in recent years, the debate has moved to the centre-left with growing concern that the welfare state may become unsustainable in a less homogeneous society (Goodhart 2004). It is theorised that hostility to the welfare state can be explained by racism. Goodhart contrasts America with Sweden and suggests that in a relatively homogenous society, such as Sweden, people tend to be willing to pay higher taxes in return for an effective welfare state because they believe the recipients of the benefits to be 'people like themselves'. Conversely, citizens of a more diverse country, such as the United States, will be hostile to paying for welfare because they suspect that the recipients will be 'doing things they wouldn't do'. Research by Robert Ford has tested whether this thesis holds in the British case, with mixed results. Although individuals who admit to being racist are less supportive of welfare policies, people who live in more diverse local authorities are only very marginally less supportive of welfare than those who live in more homogenous areas (Ford 2006).

Much of the political debate about how to accommodate religious and cultural diversity centres on whether Islamic religious and cultural practices are compatible with British values. Critiques of the burqa and the niqab (full-face veil), for example, argue that they pose a security risk (as individuals are not identifiable), undermine face-to-face communication and are a means of oppressing women. Others argue that in a democratic country women are free to choose what to wear and how to cover themselves and that forbidding the niqab or the burqa interferes with individual liberty. After the July 2010 French vote to ban the wearing of the niqab in public, the Conservative MP, Philip Hollobone, stated that he would not meet with constituents wearing a full-face veil unless they were prepared to lift it to facilitate a productive meeting, but the Kettering MP's position was not supported by the government. Damian Green, the minister of state for Borders and Immigration, said that the coalition had no plans to ban the burqa and that 'telling people what they can and can't wear, if they're just walking down the street, is a rather un-British thing to do'. Another example of the contemporary tensions arising from religious and cultural diversity, also centred on Islam, is whether the call to prayer should be amplified from a new Mosque in Oxford. Proponents of multiculturalism argue that the sound will add to Oxford's cultural diversity and should be celebrated, whereas opponents think it is unreasonable for non-Muslims to be subject to what they believe is a divisive nuisance. As just these two examples illustrate, the political elite are vacillating between supporting a multicultural position that values and even promotes diversity and a more integrationalist approach that seeks to protect and promote traditional British values and culture.

The mass politics of race, ethnicity and immigration have taken on a new flavour in Britain in recent years. Public attitudes to race have altered radically; racial prejudice is declining fast, with each new generation exhibiting lower levels of colour prejudice from the last and with women less colour prejudiced than men (Ford 2008). However, at the same time as colour prejudice is declining, there has been a huge surge in popular concern about immigration. In 2001 36 per cent of respondents to the British Election Study said that the NHS was the most important election issue and just 2 per cent named immigration and/or asylum seekers (terms which are often elided in popular discourse); by 2005 18 per cent of respondents said that the NHS was the most important issue facing Britain, the same proportion as named immigration and/or asylum as most important; and in the 2010 British Election Study 14 per cent of respondents said that immigration was the most important issue, putting the issue joint second behind the economy. Between 2001 and 2010 immigration and asylum therefore went from being a minority concern to being one of the most important issues for the British public. According to the BSA survey of 2008, 65 per cent of the British public agreed or agreed strongly that immigration was a threat to Britain's national identity.

More broadly attitudes to immigration are influenced by attitudes to religious diversity and particularly attitudes towards Islam. According to the 2008 British Social Attitudes Survey there is a division among the British public as to whether increased religious diversity has been good for Britain: 53 per cent of respondents agreed that religious diversity had been a good for thing compared with 46 per cent who disagreed. White Britons exhibit more negative feelings about Muslims than other religious or ethnic groups: according to the 2008 BSA white Britons felt generally positive about white, black, Asian, Jewish, Buddhist, Catholic and protestant people but had more negative feelings about Muslims. In total 38 per cent of respondents agreed that 'nearly all Muslims living in Britain want to fit in' compared with 40 per cent who disagreed. Thus, there is clearly a large section of the public who are hostile to Britain's increasing diversity and have particular concerns about Islam, although there is a counterweight of individuals who feel more positively about changes in the structure of British society.

In Britain the rise of fundamentalist Islamic terrorism has often been attributed to the disaffection of Muslim youth from mainstream society. Yet Maria Sobolewska argues that the debate around Islamic extremism in Britain tends to overlook its political rather than religious origins. She argues that there is an assumption that British Muslims tend to feel alienated from mainstream society and this can be a stepping stone toward extremism. Instead she finds that British Muslims have the highest rates of generalised trust of any ethnic group and that they are least likely to say that they feel they can have no influence over decisions affecting Britain. Yet participation in politics, beyond voting, is low among Muslim Britons. She concludes that the evidence that British Muslims are 'politically alienated and disengaged are mixed' (Sobolewska 2010: 38) but significantly religious Muslims are not more alienated than non-religious Muslims.

Rising rates of net migration combined with fears raised by the spectre of fundamentalist terrorism have brought concerns about immigration and ethnic and cultural diversity to the forefront of political debate. Traditional working-class Labour voters in deprived areas, in particular, have been expressing growing concern about immigration perceiving a threat to employment and access to social services such as housing. Throughout the course of the 2005 parliament the issue of immigration continued to frame public debate, with both the United Kingdom Independence party (UKIP) and the British National party (BNP) enjoying increasing electoral success.

UKIP's main focus is the withdrawal of the UK from the European Union but they are also opposed to immigration, proposing a five-year ban on all immigration to be followed by a points entry system that would require that all immigrants are fluent in English and are 'loyal to the UK, its laws and values'. It is of course not obvious how 'loyalty' would be measured and such a system is likely to discriminate against people from particular religions and cultures. UKIP would also not allow asylum claims from individuals who have travelled through another country viewed as safe. UKIP polled ahead of the Labour party in the 2009 European elections, achieving second place and gaining 16.5 per cent of the vote and 13 MEPs. However, it did less well at the 2010 general election, failed to win a Westminster seat and only increased its vote marginally (although this still constituted the largest vote by a fourth party in British political history).

UKIP may be to the right of the Labour party and the Conservative party on immigration but it is still rather liberal when compared to the BNP. The BNP's election poster 'immigration isn't working' portrayed an imaginary queue of people trying to gain entry into the UK; the first visible applicant was carrying a rocket launcher. Of the 25-plus people visible in the poster none appeared to be white. Given that the largest group of immigrants entering Britain at the time were from EU countries, it was a deliberately inaccurate portrayal of immigration, designed to tap into racial prejudice. The BNP's policies on immigration and asylum include immediately deporting all illegal immigrants, reviewing all recent grants of residence and citizenship, providing grants for people of foreign descent to leave the country, stopping all immigration except in exceptional cases and rejecting all asylum seekers who have passed through a safe country. The BNP also had increasing electoral success prior to the 2010 general election; it gained a London Assembly member in the 2008 elections and in 2009 the party received 6.2 per cent of the national vote in the European Parliament elections, winning two seats: the party leader, Nick Griffin, was elected MEP for the north-west region with Andrew Brons elected in Yorkshire and Humber. As a result of these gains Griffin was invited to be a guest on the BBC's Question Time. The programme sparked a huge public debate as to whether the BBC was right to give the party a platform.

Academic interest in the BNP grew alongside its electoral success. Margetts *et al.* argued that underlying support for the party is suppressed by the single member plurality electoral system (Margetts *et al.* 2004). They claimed that contrary to the belief that British voters are too tolerant to provide any real support for parties of the far right, approximately 20 per cent of the electorate would consider voting for the BNP. This figure has been corroborated by more recent research, which found evidence that many Britons are in favour of the BNP's most radical policies such as the complete cessation of migration and the repatriation of settled migrants; and that as many as 15 to 20 per cent of the British electorate might be persuaded to vote BNP (Eatwell and Goodwin 2010; Ford 2009, 2010). A 2009 YouGov survey of 32,000 people found that the average BNP voter was a working-class man. Some 61 per cent of BNP voters were men, who were disproportionately employed in manual occupations and earned just below the national median income.

Despite predictions of possible success, the BNP did poorly in 2010: although it won more votes than any far-right party in British history (albeit partly as a result of standing more candidates), its targeted campaign failed to win any seats in parliament. Griffin came in third place in Barking – where he had been viewed as a serious challenge by the incumbent Labour MP, Margaret Hodge – and Griffin himself admitted that the result was below expectations. Furthermore, the party was wiped out at the local level in Barking and Dagenham where it lost its entire slate of 12 council seats.

Why did UKIP and the BNP fail to make a breakthrough at the 2010 election despite increased public concern about immigration? There are a number of possible explanations. First, both the Labour and the Conservative parties toughened their policies on immigration, diminishing the attractiveness of the BNP and UKIP. Second, the economy had become seen as the most important election issue, by a wide margin. Third, the European and local elections are viewed as second-order elections where the British public might feel that a protest vote is less risky than at a general election.

In terms of the representation of black and minority ethnic (BME) communities in Britain, Operation Black Vote heralded 6 May 2010 as an 'historic night for Black Britain', as the number of BME MPs went up from 14 to 26. Historically the Labour party has had the most diverse

Table 11.3   *Vote intention by ethnicity (major ethnic groups)*

Ethnicity	Conservative	Labour	Liberal Democrat
White British	33.8%	20.7%	14.1%
White Other	24.4%	19.3%	17.3%
Indian	27.1%	31.8%	12.0%
Pakistani	8.6%	33.3%	18.3%
Bangladeshi	8.3%	37.5%	20.8%
Black Caribbean	19.4%	33.0%	9.7%
Black African	10.8%	62.4%	4.3%
Chinese	40.8%	23.9%	2.8%

Data from: British Election Survey, CMS (N=23,100)

range of MPs and in 2010 it increased the number of Labour BME MPs by two, from 13 to 15. The Conservative party made significant improvements in the number of Conservative BME MPs, up from just two to 11. The Liberal Democrats (and the other parties) do not have any BME MPs at Westminster. After the 2010 election, BME MPs now make up 4 per cent of the British House of Commons; according to the 2001 census 7.9 per cent of the British population is drawn from BME communities. Despite the considerable improvement therefore BME groups are still under-represented in the British parliament, by roughly the same proportion as women.

It has long been established that BME voters are more likely to vote for the Labour party than the rest of the population (Saggar 1998), Although there is not a simple pattern of white support for the Conservative party and non-white support for Labour, as Table 11.3 shows, white Britons (20.7 per cent) and other white groups (19.3 per cent) were the least likely of all major ethnic groups to vote Labour. Of the other major ethnic groups Chinese voters were most likely to say they would vote Conservative (40.8 per cent), followed by white Britons (33.8 per cent) and Indian's (27.1 per cent). Support for the Labour party was highest among black Africans (62.4 per cent) followed by Pakistani voters (33.3 per cent) and people of black Caribbean origin (33 per cent).

Governing diversity

In its attempts to govern and manage diversity, the state faces conflicting demands. The groups that made up the social movements of the 1960s and 1970s made calls for progress that were largely individualistic. The demands for equality made by religious groups instead often focus on being excluded from legislation that is designed to protect the autonomy of the individual. The state must negotiate between, for example, the rights of same-sex couples to adopt and the rights of Catholic adoption agencies (that do not recognise same-sex relationships as a legitimate basis for family life) to their religious beliefs.

To some extent the state has outsourced managing diversity. Initially, it did so to agencies that reflected the demands of the social movements: the Equal Opportunities Commission ((EOC) responsible for gender equality and set up under the Sex Discrimination Act 1975); the Commission for Racial Equality ((CRE) set up under the Race Relations Act 1976); and later the Disability Rights Commission ((DRC) set up under the Disability Rights Commission Act of 1999) were intended to create a more equal society by supporting individuals' discrimination claims. The three separate equality 'strands' (gender, race and disability) were thus represented by different bodies and protection from discrimination was secured through multiple sets of legislation.

Yet equality practitioners, academics and activists become increasingly aware of the gaps in representation, especially that experienced by individuals located where the different approaches to equality fail to meet. For example feminists have been widely criticised for marginalising the experiences of black women (hooks 1982). From this perspective the amalgamation of the old equalities bodies into one single institution, with a remit to cover other equality strands, seemed the most sensible way to tackle the multifaceted nature of inequality. This argument was used by the government to justify its intention to merge the three existing equalities bodies in 2003. The government also cited the EU equalities directives of 2000 (to be implemented by 2003 and 2006) as necessitating a more streamlined and coherent approach to managing equality (Bell 2008; Lovenduski 2008). The new single body, the Equalities and Human Rights Commission (EHRC) came into existence in October 2007; the EHRC's sphere of activity encompassed gender, race and disability alongside age, religion/belief and sexuality as well as human rights.

The effectiveness (or not) of the EHRC and the appropriateness of combining all of the equality strands together has, however, since been subject to fierce debate. The case for a single body as a response to intersectionality has to be balanced against the attendant danger that particular strands will be sidelined in an institutional fight for attention. Moreover, although the equalities bodies have been brought together under one roof, the government departments and ministers responsible for them remain dispersed; under Labour gender equality was covered by the Leader of the House of Commons, disability was covered by the Department of Work and Pensions and race and faith by the Secretary of State for Communities and Local Government (O'Brien 2008). This arrangement was hardly likely to aid the smooth functioning of the new institution.

One of the EHRC's roles is to promote understanding of equality and diversity and it is required to promote good relations between groups (Niven 2008). The legislation underpinning this function turns traditional legal thinking on its head: it sets a desired outcome but does not prescribe how the EHRC should achieve its goals; Deborah Mabbett compares this to asking an institution to promote road safety rather than passing a law enforcing the use of seatbelts (Mabbett 2008). Instead of focusing on legal cases of direct discrimination experienced by individuals, which was the old institutional framework, the new institution tries to monitor the equality practices of public bodies through a 'positive duty' to pre-empt unlawful discrimination before it occurs. A positive equality duty was first applied to public bodies in the Race Relations Amendment Act 2000 which responded to the indirect discrimination found at the heart of the Metropolitan Police during the Stephen Lawrence inquiry. The duty was extended to cover disability in 2006 and gender in 2007. The legislation shifts the emphasis 'from retrospective individual remedy towards prospective prevention of a more systematic sort' (O'Brien 2008: 28).

The focus on prevention gives the EHRC considerable flexibility as to how it might pursue its goals, but this flexibility is likely to prove to be both a strength and a weakness. For example, although the lack of a restrictive set of legal tools may allow for a more bespoke approach to specific problems, it might also lead to vague demands that produce mere box-ticking exercises rather than real change (Mabbett 2008: 46). Furthermore the movement away from the legal realm allows the EHRC to focus on a broader set of issues, but it brings it 'back into a political domain, where it has to compete for attention and resources' (Mabbett 2008: 52) rather than utilising legal precedent.

Historically the CRE focused on promoting good relations between different ethnic and religious communities. The EHRC has a responsibility to promote good relations between all groups; this is likely to prove much harder, and highly controversial. For example what position should the commission take on conflicts between gay and religious groups? Tensions between these two groups were brought to the public's attention when the Catholic Church sought to halt the extension of the Equality Act of 2006 (which forbids various public bodies and private firms, such as hotels, from refusing services on the grounds of age, disability, race, gender or religion) to cover sexuality. The Church argued that providing adoption services for same-sex couples was contrary to its religious beliefs and practices and would undermine the work undertaken by catholic adoption agencies in Britain. Cardinal Cormac Murphy-O'Connor, the Archbishop of Westminster, wrote to every cabinet minister expressing his concerns about the new rules. Stonewall argued vehemently that no exemption from the law should be allowed for any organisation that is in receipt of public money and that there is no excuse for discrimination on the grounds of sexuality. The Equality Act (Sexual Orientation) Regulations 2007, which came into force on 30 April 2007, was seen as a victory for Stonewall and other equalities campaigners, but this example highlights the difficulties the EHRC is likely to face when trying to negotiate between groups when their interests do not coincide.

There has also been a renewed interest in social class. In a speech surveying the state of the nation in 2010 and future challenges, the chair of the EHRC, Trevor Phillips, drew attention to 'the importance of socioeconomic background' arguing that 'it matters more in our society who your parents are than in other societies' (2010: 5). The acknowledgement of socio-economic sources of inequality, as opposed to only focusing upon identity politics, was also a concern of the last Labour government with Harriet Harman referring to it in her role as Women and Equalities Minister when an influential report was produced, by Alan Milburn, that flagged up poor social mobility as one of the biggest challenges facing British society today. In the context of the financial crisis and spending cuts the Conservative–Liberal Democrat coalition has been at pains to stress that it will protect the most economically vulnerable members of society. Economic inequality has been a focus of the new Home Secretary and Equalities Minister Theresa May. In a letter to Operation Black Vote she claimed that a Conservative government would use its 'big society' agenda to push forward race equality and challenge economic disadvantage. She also said that a Conservative government would continue to use the EHRC to protect individual and group rights.

Despite May's public support for some aspects of the EHRC's work questions remain as to how long the new body will remain intact. The EHRC's budget was cut by 15 per cent in the 2010 spending review, a less drastic reduction than many predicted. However, the organisation's future may depend upon the results of the coalition government's 'red-tape challenge' where citizens and pressure groups are being asked to comment on the usefulness of the 2010 Equalities Act which sets out much of the EHRC's remit.

Conclusion

Public attitudes to race, gay rights and gender equality have shifted significantly in a progressive direction in recent years. At the same time the state has responded by introducing legislation that promotes individual equality and prohibits discrimination on the basis of race, sexuality, gender, age and disability. Momentous changes have been made in the lives of same-sex couples. The representation of women in parliament has gradually improved, although women are still under-represented. The Conservative party has significantly increased the number of women MPs, although Labour, through its use of equality guarantees, continues to be by far the most representative party of women in parliament. BME groups are now better represented at Westminster than ever before and the Conservatives have come some way towards catching up with the Labour party's advantage. On both counts the Liberal Democrats are still a long way behind.

Although the British public is now less colour prejudiced than ever before, it is more sensitive to immigration and concerned about religious diversity. This anxiety about religious diversity centres mainly on attitudes to Islam and Islamic extremism. The political parties have responded to these concerns by focusing on tightening immigration controls and the debate about how to integrate minority communities into the mainstream has become a central concern of the political elite. The state has developed legal mechanisms and public bodies to manage sometimes competing demands for the equality of individuals with those of religious groups to protect their beliefs and practices, although in the context of significant reductions in public spending no one can be sure what the future shape of these bodies will be.

Chapter 12

The Changing News Media Environment

ANDREW CHADWICK AND JAMES STANYER

Since the mid-2000s Britain's political communication environment has undergone rapid change. During the 2010 election campaign, television continued its dominance as the most important medium through which the British public acquires its political information, as Britain's first ever live televised party leaders' debates received saturation coverage for almost the entire campaign. But over the previous half-decade the growing mainstream popularity of the internet has started to undermine some broadcast-era assumptions regarding strategic news management, both in government, and on the campaign trail. This new, hybrid, environment, one characterised by a complex intermingling of the 'old', the 'new' and the 'renewed' creates particular uncertainty for 'old' news media, established politicians and political parties. The old media environment, dominated by media and political elites working in traditional television, radio and newspapers, remains significant for British politics, but politics is increasingly mediated online. The internet is creating a more open, fluid political opportunity structure – one that increasingly enables the British public to exert its influence and hold politicians and media to account. The origins of this current hybridity can be traced back over the last couple of decades, but since the mid-2000s, the pace of change has quickened. The stage on which the drama of British politics unfolds is in the process of being redesigned, partly by political and media elites, and partly by ordinary citizens.

Old, new and renewed media

Britain's political communication environment is now a hybrid, contradictory, mixture of old, new and what Hoskins and O'Loughlin term 'renewed' media (2007: 17). Old media, primarily television, radio and newspapers are still, given the size of their audiences and their centrality to the life of the nation, rightly referred to as 'mainstream', but the very nature of the mainstream is changing. While old media organisations are adapting, evolving and renewing their channels of delivery, working practices and audiences, genuinely new media outlets, driven primarily by the spread of the internet, are achieving popularity and becoming part of a new mainstream. Politicians, journalists and the British public are simultaneously creating and adapting to these complexities.

Despite declining audience share, traditional media organisations continue to play a pivotal role in British politics, as we saw, for example with the *Daily Telegraph*'s initiation of the MPs' expenses scandal during 2009. The media professionals at the heart of these organisations remain deeply embedded in the routines and insider networks of Westminster, Whitehall and the major metropolitan centres. They interact with politicians and senior civil servants on a daily basis. Politicians still stage their interventions to coincide with the rhythms of the newsrooms, which remain the main route to a large audience and maximum publicity, as Labour's minister for work and pensions, James Purnell, revealed when he resigned from the cabinet on the day of the European Parliament elections in June 2009. Purnell sent his resignation email to two national newspapers several hours before he called the prime minister, realising that this would have the biggest impact on the evening television news bulletins when it was published once the polls closed (Stratton and Wintour 2009).

Outside what is traditionally understood as the mainstream, genuinely new media players such as political bloggers make frequent interventions in the political arena (Dale 2008). They sometimes shape the political agenda through their commentary and, less frequently, their investigative 'scoops', but are still more often parasitical upon old media for their content. Even when a leading blog lands an exclusive it is dependent upon traditional news organisations for taking these stories to a truly mass audience. This dependency is mutual: news organisations increasingly capitalise on new media as a resource, tapping into the viral circulation of online content and weaving it into their news genres and production techniques. The new media outlets are in the process of being integrated into the mainstream digital political news system in a journey that is likely to continue for many years. In this hybridised system, the old media organisations are currently still king: they have the collective financial and organisational resources to 'outscoop' exclusively new media upstarts, and to leapfrog new media outlets with the launch of expensive new initiatives, such as online television delivery and ever more elaborate web environments, which combine editorial authority with popular participation.

An excellent example of how politics now plays out in this hybrid digital media environment is the furore over MPs' expenses in 2009 –

arguably parliament's most serious crisis since the emergence of British democracy. The huge quantities of data on expenses were leaked from parliament in digitised form on optical discs. The *Daily Telegraph* bought the discs and ran an extended series of revelations, both online and offline, spanning almost three weeks in May 2009. *Telegraph* researchers sifted through the data, extracting the most damaging items. Each day's new releases were carefully staged to cause the maximum impact on other media. Frequent television appearances by the paper's deputy editor, Benedict Brogan, were a key part of this. Broadcast news and political blogs engaged in a sustained feeding frenzy, as, day after day, MPs' expenses were the top story across all news outlets. This was an example of 'old-fashioned' investigative journalism, but with a difference: the hybrid media environment accelerated and amplified events and distributed the information across all platforms. As the *Telegraph* released information online and in printed form, other news organisations picked up the new revelations and ran their own stories. In a final twist, some weeks later, when parliament officially released the data, which ran to more than 458,000 pages, the *Guardian* published the entire database on its website and invited ordinary readers to identify, log and discuss claims. By July 2009, its readers had reviewed 201,000 pages (*Guardian* 2009). This reveals the growing importance of the internet, not just as a channel for the communication of information, but also as a mechanism of organisation and collective action in the creation of news.

New media use in Britain

By any measurement, the British public's use of the internet has grown at a remarkable rate. Households now have 70 per cent access, up from 58 per cent in 2003 and 96 per cent of all households with the internet use broadband (OXIS 2009: 4). The diversity of means by which individuals go online has also increased and the internet is no longer predominantly a static, computer-based medium. Mobile access has grown in popularity during recent years: some 20 per cent of internet users own a mobile smartphone (such as an Apple iPhone) or a mobile broadband device that they plug into their laptop computer (OXIS 2009: 9) and there were 74 million mobile phone accounts in a population of just 60 million in 2008 (UK Office of Communications 2008). This new diversity of opportunities for internet access also plays an important role in creating multitasking lifestyles in multi-connection households. Around a quarter of those with digital or cable television use it to access the internet, while 32 per cent use a mobile device while in the home – a figure that has trebled since 2005, reflecting the popularity of wireless handheld devices with built-in web browsers, email and messaging software. Seventy-one per cent of internet users now report 'doing more than one activity while online, such as listening to music, watching TV, or using the telephone' (OXIS 2009: 12, 36).

The changing face of news consumption

News consumption habits among the British electorate are shifting. In 2007 the number of internet users who reported that they read a 'newspaper or news service' online stood at 30 per cent. In the space of just two years, this number almost doubled, to reach 58 per cent (ibid.: 32). More generally, 75 per cent of internet users now report reading news online, including non-newspaper sources such as blogs (ibid.: 20). However, can we detect any audience preferences? Do internet users go to 'alternative' sources of news? The evidence suggests that the majority of those online tend to access the websites of the main news outlets, either directly or via news aggregators, such as Yahoo, AOL and Google (Stanyer 2008).

Figure 12.1   *Monthly unique readers of national newspaper websites, 2008–10 (millions)*

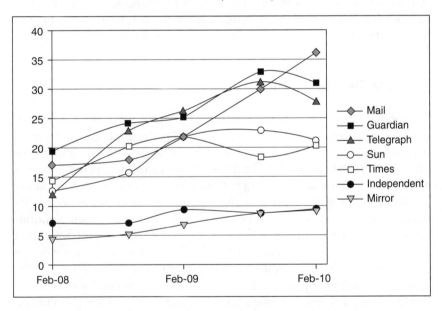

Note: data points are February and September of each year. *Independent* did not make ABCe figures public until May 2008; the February 2008 figure is therefore taken from May 2008. *Mirror* not part of ABCe until March 2008; the February 2008 figure is therefore taken from March 2008.
Data from: ABCe; Kiss (2007a, 2007b, 2009a, 2009b, 2010); Luft (2008)

Figure 12.2   *National newspaper print edition circulations, 2005–10*

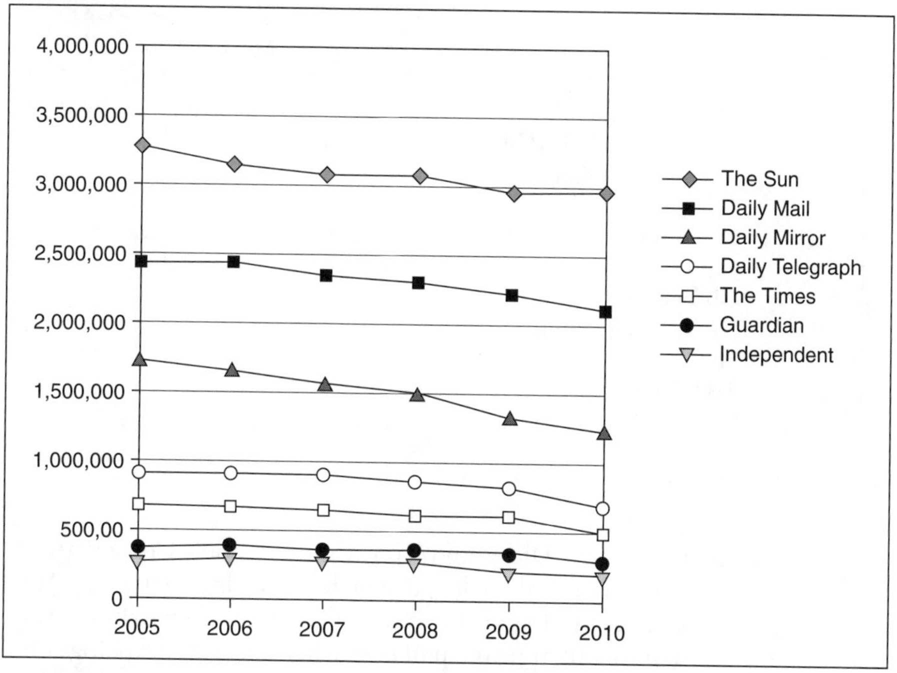

Note: includes bulk sales.
Data from: *Guardian* 2010, which uses data from ABC

Most strikingly, the growth in online news consumption contrasts starkly with the decline in print edition circulations of the same outlets. While it is difficult to determine precise levels of traffic, and it is clear that overseas readers are a huge presence in these data, figures provided by *ABCe* reveal overall growth in visitor numbers and show in 2010 that main newspaper organisations are a hugely important presence for news online see Figure 12.1).

Between 1987 and 2007 copies of national newspapers sold per year declined by about a third and between 1998 and 2007 sales fell for all the nationals, apart from the *Daily Star* and the *Daily Mail* (UK Office of Fair Trading 2008). The pace of change has accelerated since 2008 (see Figure 12.2).

While newspaper brands are big hitters online, alternative online news sites can still secure significant audiences. Some high-profile blogs attract a relatively large readership. For example, Paul Staines' Guido Fawkes blog attracted nearly 350,000 unique visitors in April 2009 and regularly averages 100,000 daily page views. Also popular are Conservative-supporting

Table 12.1   *Top ten British blogs by internet visits for May 2008*

Rank	Website	Market share (%)
1	BBC blog network	20.2
2	Guardian Unlimited blogs	12.7
3	Times Online Comment Central	3.5
4	Telegraph blogs	3.4
5	News of the World Extreme Showbiz blog	2.5
6	Guido Fawkes' blog	2.3
7	Gizmodo UK	2.2
8	Neave.com (computer games)	1.9
9	Iain Dale	1.9
10	Tech Digest	1.6

Data from: Goad (2008)

blogs such as Iain Dale's Diary and Tim Montgomerie's Conservative Home. In May 2008, Iain Dale (who gave up blogging in 2010) had a 1.9 per cent share of overall blog visitor numbers and Guido Fawkes a 2.3 per cent share. This might appear small beer when compared to blogs on the BBC and the *Guardian*, which had a combined 33 per cent share of blog traffic over the same period (see Table 12.1), but things are not as straightforward as they might seem. If we set aside the BBC and *Guardian* blogs, the presence of alternative online news looks remarkably competitive. Guido Fawkes is not too far behind the mainstream newspaper blogs of the *Times* and the *Telegraph*.

From consumers to producers?

Perhaps the most startling shift since the mid-2000s comes in the form of mass participation in the creation of online content. This has been fuelled by the growth of web 2.0 services such as blogs, online social network sites, such as Facebook, MySpace and Twitter, collaborative production sites such as Wikipedia, and news aggregators and discussion sites such as Digg, Yahoo Buzz and the BBC's Have Your Say sections (Chadwick 2009). Some 49 per cent of British internet users maintain a profile on an online social network site; 22 per cent update a blog; and 27 per cent participate in online chat rooms. Older online communication forms such as instant messaging (64 per cent of users) and email (97 per cent) are now ubiquitous in British society (OXIS 2009: and see Figure 12.3).

Figure 12.3 *Growth of online user-generated content in Britain, 2005–9*

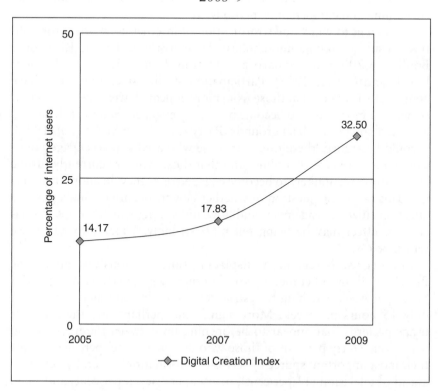

Note: the Digital Creation Index is a composite mean value generated by the authors from measures in OXIS (2009: 28). Questions were 'How often do you use the internet for the following purposes?; Update or create a profile on a social networking site; Post pictures or photos on the internet; Post messages on discussion or message boards; Use a distribution list for email; Write a weblog; Maintain a personal website' (2005: N=1,309; 2007: N=1,578; 2009: N=1,401)
Data from: authors' analysis and adaptation of data from OXIS (2009)

One nation, digitally divided

These trends are impressive, but equally important is the persistence of Britain's digital divide. Thirty per cent of the population are still without internet access in the home. In Britain the strongest predictors of not using the internet have remained constant: age, educational attainment, and socio-economic status (Chadwick 2006: 49–80; UK Office of Communications 2009: 3). Thus, while the internet has achieved mainstream popularity and is now an important source of political information for the British public, there is still a significant proportion for whom it is largely irrelevant. These individuals principally rely on broadcast media for their political information, and if they do participate in politics, they are compelled to do so through what can often be more time-consuming and cumbersome methods.

The extent to which the stratification of internet use matters for politics is a subject of ongoing scholarly debate (Brundridge and Rice 2008; Boulianne 2009; di Gennaro and Dutton 2006; Gibson *et al.* 2005; Norris and Curtice 2007). Participation studies since the 1960s have continually revealed that those from more educated, wealthier sections of society are more likely to become politically engaged than those from less educated and poorer backgrounds (Parry *et al.* 1992; Verba *et al.* 1995). It could be argued, therefore, that those who are likely to engage politically online are *already* online, and that those who are currently offline are, in any case, unlikely to become engaged once they do adopt the internet. This raises the question of whether new media are having a positive effect on citizen engagement, and how and among which groups in society that effect may be being felt most strongly, a theme to which we return below.

Internet use is seemingly displacing time previously spent by the British public on other media. Non-internet users spend an average of 25 hours per week watching terrestrial television, but internet users spend only 15 hours per week. More significant, perhaps, are the different usage patterns that appear to be opening up between the internet and television. Thirty per cent of those who use the internet perceive it to be their most important source of access to information, generally defined – ahead of television (11 per cent), newspapers (seven per cent) and radio (six per cent). At the same time, non-internet users naturally report that terrestrial television is their main media source of entertainment, but also report that television is much more *important* to them for entertainment content (OXIS 2009: 33). This may have implications for the future communication of politics. There may be a growing divide between those who use the internet for their 'hard' news and information (including, of course, political news) and those without the internet, whose media diets consist mostly of entertainment that they deem more important than informational content.

Old news and the new media environment: quality under pressure?

The rapidly changing media environment has generated difficulties for traditional news media organisations and this may well have consequences for the quality of political information available to the British public. Multi-channel digital television now reaches 80 per cent of British households and in several areas of the country, such as Scotland and the north west of England, penetration rates are much higher (UK Office for National Statistics 2009: 4). Television news channels continue to proliferate and a panoply of different news genres now exists in the television environment, from short bulletins and soft infotainment content on the entertainment channels (or at least those that run news), relatively detailed 'serious' coverage on BBC Radio 4, through to round-the-clock treatments on channels such as Sky News, the BBC News Channel, Euronews or even BBC Parliament. There is no shortage of political news but audiences are scattered across the channels, the schedules, and the non-scheduled 'time-shifting' environments of Sky Plus personal video recorders, the BBC's web-based iPlayer, or mobile video applications. This process of fragmentation has important implications for the business models of the large media organisations and it has serious consequences for news output.

Expensive, high-quality news is becoming increasingly difficult to produce because advertising revenue is now spread more thinly across multiple outlets and advertisers have been moving their money online. By the mid-2000s, the internet had eclipsed the printed press in terms of British advertising spend and it is now almost on a par with spending on television advertising. Local television news is in particular trouble, as was demonstrated in 2009, when ITV lobbied successfully to cut back on some of its public service obligations regarding local and regional content (Sweney 2008). Conditions are also tight at the BBC. The organisation was forced to shed 3000 jobs in 2008 as a result of a relatively stringent licence fee deal and it is fighting a proposed top-slicing of the licence fee to subsidise ITV local news. In early 2011, the BBC announced plans to radically reduce the number of pages on its websites.

Revenue earners such as premium-rate phone-ins have been adversely affected by a number of 'fakery' scandals in which shows were found to have been fabricating competition results (for example, ITV's *Richard and Judy* and the BBC's *Blue Peter*, among others). There have also been general concerns over the less regulated areas of satellite and cable TV, such as the numerous quiz channels that occupy the obscurer reaches of the channel listings. According to the OXIS survey of 2007, levels of trust in the internet as a source of information are now higher than they are for both television and the printed press.

Wither the British press?

Television viewing and radio listening both declined from the early to the mid-2000s (UK Office of Communications 2007), but nowhere have the pressures of Britain's changing media environment been felt more strongly than in its newspaper industry. The British press are in the middle of a painful transition towards new business models. Readership of print editions across all newspaper sectors has been in decline for several decades due to competition from television and now the internet. The period since 2008 has seen a precipitous decline in the circulation of newsprint. While Britain awaits the first major casualty of this new environment, the signs are that it may not be too far away. In 2010, Alexander Lebedev, the billionaire former Russian KGB spy, bought the struggling *Independent* and the *Independent on Sunday* for a nominal sum of £1 and a follow-on deal worth just £9.25 million to the paper's Irish parent company, INM (BBC News Online 2010b).

The press's initial reaction to the internet in the 1990s was to ignore it in the hope that it might prove to be a fad. This was followed by a strategy of placing the content of the printed version of a paper onto a website in the hope of attracting sufficient 'eyeballs' to generate advertising revenue. Some papers, such as the *Financial Times*, experimented early on with subscription based models, only to scale back due to a lack of subscribers and the lure of the advertising model during the economic boom of the 2000s, before once again attempting to make the pay-per-view model work in the late 2000s. Many local and regional papers either lacked the resources to develop their own websites or stayed out of the game entirely for fear that they would cannibalise their print offerings. The annual circulation of local and regional newspapers fell by almost 40 per cent between 1989 and 2009 (UK Office of Fair Trading 2009:, 12). It seems clear that the pay-per-view model can be made to work online where an outlet has a distinctive niche, as is the case with the *FT*. It remains to be seen whether more general news outlets can also make it work. In June 2010, two of Rupert Murdoch's News Corporation online news sites, the *Times* and the *Sunday Times* were placed behind a 'paywall'. At the time of writing, none of the other national newspapers have chosen to follow suit. Even the *Daily Mail*, whose online offerings have soared in popularity over the last few years, remains wedded to the advertising-and-eyeballs model – for now (DMGT 2010).

In common with the situation in other countries, particularly the United States, the British printed press are currently caught in a trap. Declining paper circulations, increasing online readerships, competition from free online news providers and blogs, shrinking and more thinly spread advertising revenues, and the economic recession of the late 2000s, have all taken their toll. Advertising and search company Google now dominates the online advertising market, but online revenues per reader are substantially smaller than the revenues per reader for traditional classified advertising, and ceding in-house control over advertising mechanisms to an external company with a quasi-monopoly is unattractive for newspaper proprietors. At the regional and local levels, where 80 per cent of papers' income comes from advertising, the press have long relied upon classified small ads to sustain themselves, but revenues from these have almost halved since the late-1990s, due to competition from online outlets such as eBay and Craigslist (UK Office of Fair Trading 2009: 10).

The main news organisations have responded to this changing environment by finding new ways to appeal to audience loyalty. A key development is online social interaction. During the last half decade, interactive commenting spaces have flourished online. Space for reader participation is now much less tightly restricted and audience messages are much less dependent on the decisions of editorial gatekeepers. All of the major British news sites now have well established interactive features, such as op-ed columns with comments, message boards, chat rooms and email, and receive hundreds of thousands of comments per month. Readers are encouraged, sometimes paid, to submit material to news sites. National news organisations are also attempting to position themselves as online social networking hubs, where, in addition to reporting and debating political developments, readers post pictures, socialise, choose a date and create their own material. The websites of the *Daily Express*, the *Star* and the *Daily Telegraph* now allow their readers to set up their own blogs. The *Daily Telegraph*'s 'My Telegraph' had an estimated 20,000 registered users in 2008 (Dodson 2008) – a reasonable success, though some way short of the 26 million UK users of Facebook (CheckFacebook 2010).

While the adaptation of news organisations to the digital media environment is creating new opportunities for citizens to engage in political debate and express their opinions, it has inevitably led to cost cutting. Timely, relevant and challenging political journalism is an expensive business, especially if it involves an investigative element. However, the revenues to support this kind of activity have been falling for several years. Almost all commercial news organisations have seen deep cuts and radical restructuring of staff and budgets (Davies 2008). Writers and editors, in what were once powerhouses of in-depth reporting and commentary (such as the *Observer* and the *Sunday Times*), now sit side by side with upstart individual or group blogs, most of which have a keen awareness of niche interests and very short news cycles. Top political bloggers regularly produce articles indistinguishable from those published in the op-ed sections of newspapers. With low overheads, large readerships and, in some cases, self-sustaining advertising revenues they are free from the bureaucracy of the professional newsroom (see Dale 2008). Some bloggers are also able to conduct background investigations. An example was

Paul Staines' long-running series of exposés about Peter Hain during 2007, culminating in damaging revelations about the origins of donations to Hain's campaign fund for the deputy leadership of the Labour party. These were partly instrumental in the Hain's decision to resign his ministerial post in January 2008 (even if he was to return to cabinet in 2009). This was widely reported as the British blogosphere's first political 'scalp'. Despite such developments, one of the key criticisms of bloggers is that they are 'amateurs' who lack the professional training of journalists (Keen 2007). They have also been accused of being less discerning in what they publish, and as likely to disseminate unsubstantiated political gossip as much as genuine political news.

Yet it now seems clear that television's monopoly on 'breaking news' is loosening, not only because online news sites are more prepared to take risks by publishing stories without the standards of verification usually required of professional journalists, but also because the viral nature of online communication makes it much more likely that news will spread across interpersonal networks often before official press releases. Some big political news stories now break first online and are picked up by television and print journalists who obsessively follow their email, Twitter and blog feeds in the hunt for new leads. At the same time, however, some television and newspaper journalists, for example, the BBC's political and business editors, Nick Robinson and Robert Peston, now often release their own 'scoops' online, well before they officially file their stories or record a broadcast package for the evening news. The large, dedicated news organisations, particularly the BBC, but also Sky News, share vast amounts of content internally across their web and television divisions. This provides them with an ongoing structural advantage when it comes to breaking news.

While the British press and commercial broadcasters are certainly under pressure, the BBC is in a stronger position, largely as a result of the licence fee. Despite complaints of unfair competition, the BBC continues to build a sophisticated web presence which regularly gains 18 to 19 million monthly unique visitors. It has adopted many of the features used by other news organisations, such as columns with comments, message boards, chat rooms and email, and it also seeks to integrate citizen produced video into its news narratives, especially during exceptional events, such as the London tube bombings of 2005 or the G20 protests during 2009. In an era of cost cutting and downsizing in commercial media, the BBC may well come to play an even more important role as a source of news.

Transforming media management

A top-down model of political communication has tended to predominate in the UK. Indeed, the communication operation of the Blair government could be seen as the apotheosis of such an approach, with its aggressive strategy to market government and its policies in the best possible light (Stanyer 2007). This model has been gradually undermined by a series of spin scandals, by a press disenchanted with it as a method of media control, and by an audience increasingly fragmented and distrustful of government and its messages. During the closing stages of the Blair premiership in 2007, the then prime minister sought to distance himself from accusations of spin and 'control freakery' and attempted to lay the blame on the news media's neglect of policy and its obsession with political gossip and 'feral' personal attacks (Blair 2007).

When he took over as prime minister, Gordon Brown, in an attempt to reconnect with voters, sought to capitalise on early momentum by seeking to establish what was heralded as a new communication strategy based upon the factual presentation of policy. Periodic attempts to publicly demonstrate that government communication had moved away from the era of spin were a key feature of the Brown premiership, as a series of high-profile new appointments were presented to a largely sceptical audience of journalists and citizens. This metacommunication concerning how Downing Street went about repackaging its media operation was combined with what appear to have been genuine attempts to harness the power of new media, largely in response to David Cameron's and the Conservatives' growing success in experimenting with online video and social networking. But the merciless way in which the news media, old and new, exposed what it saw as Gordon Brown's character flaws and the behind-the-scenes realities of the Number 10 media operation were constant themes.

The end of spin, or just more?

One of Brown's first acts on taking office was his announcement of a shake-up of government media operations (Oborne 2007). Under Blair, Downing Street news management was a long-running story, despite Blair's belated attempts to alter matters, and by the time Brown took office, government communications were seen as untrustworthy by press and public alike (Phillis 2004). Perhaps the most significant act in Brown's revamp concerned the Downing Street media operation itself. Overall control was placed in the hands of a civil servant, Michael Ellam, and not a political appointee, as Blair's spokespersons, Alastair Campbell and David Hill, had been (UK House of Lords Committee on

Communication 2009). Ellam's appointment performed an important symbolic function. With him at the helm, Downing Street could claim to have moved away from the worst excesses of the Blair years. However, the reality of Brown's media operation turned out to be rather different. During the spring of 2009, the leaking of an email exchange between Gordon Brown's staffer, Damian McBride, and former Labour insider turned Labour blogger, Derek Draper, shed an unflattering light on Downing Street's approach. In addition to the front-of-house widely publicised media management activities, there was a below stairs shadow operation, run by McBride. If the former was aimed at addressing the image of government communications, the latter was focused on ruthlessly attacking opponents in and outside government.

'Smeargate', as it became known, revealed a plan by McBride to establish an ostensibly independent website called Red Rag, which would contain personalised attacks on leading Conservatives and their families. The fallout from this revelation and the earlier 'Statsgate', when Number 10 and Home Office claims about falling knife crime were condemned by the UK Statistics Authority as misleading, merely served to reinforce the image of government communications as a continuation of the worst excesses of the Campbell years. In the aftermath of the McBride email scandal an ICM poll for the *Guardian* found that only 13 per cent of those surveyed said Brown had succeeded in restoring trust in government; 82 per cent thought that he had failed (Glover 2009). A poll for the *Sunday Telegraph* found that a majority of the public thought the Brown government 'more likely to resort to spin and dirty tricks than Blair's' (Hennessy 2009).

The Draper–McBride affair is another example of the interaction of old, new and renewed media. It was first reported by a right-wing blogger, Paul Staines, whose website, Guido Fawkes, by being predicated on innuendo, gossip and rumour, emulates tabloid journalism. Staines' 'scoop' led to his being fêted as a beacon of truth by more mainstream Conservative bloggers. Draper and McBride's misguided attempt to emulate the success of Staines' approach by seeking to establish the Red Rag gossip site refracted new media through the lens of 1990s-style sleaze attacks and spin. Both individuals, however, entirely neglected the broader point about right of centre blogs such as Conservative Home's success in engaging and mobilising the Tory grassroots. Finally, it is important to stress that Staines did not publish the contents of the emails on his blog, but instead handed them to journalists in national newspapers: it was the *Daily Telegraph* and the *Sunday Times* which publicly broke the stories, not the Guido Fawkes blog.

The Conservatives on the offensive: from communications to online social networks

David Cameron's election as Conservative leader in December 2005 heralded a new strategic approach to communication for the party. Though widely ridiculed by television and newspaper journalists when first launched in September 2006, the Webcameron website established Cameron's informal, conversational approach to media. It also signalled to a growing community of online Conservative activists that the new leader was attempting to move the party away from a membership model to a supporter network model. The Conservative blogging community continued to expand, and Conservative Home, founded in 2005, came to provide a space for party members to interact and is now an important venue enabling party members and the party elite to interact with one another.

Cameron's approach was not, however, solely focused on new media. On winning the leadership election, his team, headed by marketing professional, Steve Hilton, undertook a major public relations offensive, rebranding the Conservative party in order to demonstrate to the media that it had been transformed from an uncaring 'nasty party' as it was once described by former party chairman, Theresa May. The old party logo was ditched in favour of a green and blue oak tree to signify the party's new green credentials. The new policy agenda was promoted in a series of high-profile photo opportunities, including one which planted Cameron in the Arctic Circle to highlight the party's stand on global warming. The Cameron team also assiduously sought to promote the leader's personal characteristics to the British public. Talk shows have been a key plank in this strategy, as Table 12.2 reveals. While Cameron mostly featured on political talk shows, he also targeted popular entertainment formats, which reach far beyond the usual audiences for political programmes.

The press have been an important target for the Cameron team. In 2007, to boost existing media operations, Cameron employed former *News of the World* editor Andy Coulson. Coulson, once described as an 'old fashioned Fleet Street bully' (Oborne 2007), was hired for his popular news instincts and communication skills, as well as his contacts within the Murdoch empire. Stories of lavish Notting Hill dinner parties at which Cameron and Murdoch were guests hint at the Cameron team's attempts to gain the support of the Murdoch press (see Oborne 2007). The Cameron operation was helped by largely favourable coverage in the press, especially when compared with the treatment of previous Conservative leaders, William Hague, Iain Duncan Smith and Michael Howard.

Table 12.2 *Party leaders' appearances on television talk shows,*
2007–10

	Show	Type	Appear-ances	Year
David Cameron	Alan Titchmarsh Show	Entertainment	2	2009, 2010
	Parkinson	Entertainment	1	2007
	BBC Breakfast	Breakfast News	1	2008
	GMTV	Breakfast News	1	2009
	Various political talk shows	Political	10	2007–9
Gordon Brown	Piers Morgan's Life Stories	Entertainment	1	2010
	BBC Breakfast	Breakfast News	1	2008
	GMTV	Breakfast News	4	2008–9
	Various political talk shows	Political	8	2007–9

Data from: authors, compiled from Internet Movie Database and other sources

Cameron's assurance in both old and new media environments soon put Brown on the defensive. Number 10's response was to seek out new opportunities for promoting the prime minister's personal qualities. This partly involved the tried-and-tested chat-show 'sofa offensive' that had been perfected by Blair and, latterly, Cameron. Brown became a regular guest on GMTV, as well as on Andrew Marr's high-profile Sunday morning show, and he started to give longer, more personally revealing interviews to national newspapers and, in the run-up to the election, on television.

New media were also a key part of this personal rebranding. Internet marketing specialists were hired to upgrade the Number 10 website with a new range of web 2.0 features designed to allow visitors to keep in touch and interact with the prime minister and his senior staff. Visitors to the new site could now subscribe to Twitter and Flickr feeds, read a blog, watch short videos via YouTube, link to news stories through Delicious and Digg and to the Number 10 page on Facebook. Cameron and Brown regularly used YouTube to make announcements, including Brown's damaging unilateral proposal for the reform of MPs' expenses in 2009.

With politicians increasingly adopting digital communication initiatives, news management strategies at the very top of British politics are changing. The new approach would appear to involve the parties using online social networking techniques that are increasingly used by many media organisations and private companies, and adapting a range of interactive features in the hope of attracting engaged followers.

Brown versus the press

Brown's premiership was marred by his toxic relationship with the traditional press. Relations between the news media and all governments undergo well documented changes, but Brown's honeymoon was particularly short. Press goodwill evaporated three months into his premiership after his U-turn on calling an early general election in the autumn of 2007. Despite a series of reshuffles and relaunches this hostility persisted through his tenure in office. Much of the anger with the administration was channelled through attacks on Brown's personal characteristics and leadership style. Such attacks often amplified the utterances of Brown's intra-party critics, so sometimes helping encourage others to join in the criticism. The press were quick to highlight the awkwardness of the prime minister's public performances and often sought to draw conclusions about his private behaviour. In June 2008, a leaked email conversation in which cabinet minister Peter Mandelson described Gordon Brown as failing to successfully mask his insecurities received widespread coverage. This angle reached a crescendo just weeks before the general election campaign, however, when the *Observer* journalist, Andrew Rawnsley, published *The End of the Party*, revealing what were painted as Brown's personal failings, including his alleged 'bullying' of Number 10 staff (Rawnsley 2010). Against this background it is easy to see why direct communication via the internet became more attractive to Number 10. However, while the broadcasters were initially willing to recycle Brown's YouTube announcements, his performances were widely derided as inauthentic and increasingly became the focus of negative coverage. His use of YouTube, in short, backfired: it became another reason for both the news media and party dissidents to express criticism.

The period of the Brown premiership was replete with new innovations, new appointments and relaunches. There were various attempts to repackage the prime minister and he was eager to be seen to be breaking with the past. But in the end, he often fell back on the 'old' tried-and-tested means of media manipulation and he was constantly fending off attacks from within his own party. Rumours of leadership challenges by members of the cabinet, particularly the foreign secretary, David Miliband, were never far from the front pages and this speculation was fuelled by a largely critical, often hostile press, creating vicious circles of negative coverage. Media operations under Brown were characterised by their own hybridity: the highly visible narrative for public consumption, where Brown emerges as a quasi-populist, in-touch reformer, providing a fresh start, using the latest web 2.0 tools; and the hidden methods, in which spin doctors were used to launch personal attacks on opponents. It was the exposure of this latter practice during the 'Smeargate' affair that proved particularly damaging to Brown's reputation. This and its consequences for government credibility may prove to be the outgoing prime minister's long-term legacy for British political communication.

The Conservatives fared rather better in establishing a coherent media strategy, one based on a blend of tried-and-tested command-and-control methods, the targeting of mainstream journalists, televisual 'sofa offensives' but also well-integrated experiments with online engagement, such as Webcameron. The Conservatives were also much more successful in stimulating or simply aligning themselves with the growing number of grassroots activists engaged in mobilising for the party in online discussion forums and blogs. They also indirectly benefited from the damage inflicted by the influential right of centre Westminster gossip blogs (Iain Dale, Paul Staines), which professional journalists now monitor with religious dedication. After all, it was Labour's desperation at being outmanoeuvred in the blogosphere which led to the ill-fated email exchange between Number 10 and Derek Draper concerning the establishment of a left-wing version of Staines' site. Finally, it needs to be borne in mind that the Conservatives enjoyed a remarkably favourable press environment. This began with the selection of David Cameron as party leader but the watershed came in 2009 when, on the eve of the Labour party conference, the entire Murdoch press, including Britain's bestselling newspaper, the *Sun*, publicly ditched Labour and switched their support to the Conservatives. By the time of the 2010 general election, only one national newspaper, the *Mirror*, declared unequivocal support for Labour.

Following the change of government, Cameron was initially to rely heavily upon the communications team headed by Andy Coulson to brief and to spin on his behalf (and to speak on behalf of the government). Coulson, however, having been long dogged by the phone hacking scandal that took place at the *News of the World* during his time as editor, was forced to resign from Cameron's employ in January 2011. He was replaced by another media professional, Craig Oliver, who had extensive broadcasting experience working for Independent Television News and the BBC. Cameron, it seems, following Coulson's enforced departure, is slowly moving back to the Blair and Brown model of having a professional communications team composed both of Conservative special advisers such as Gabby Bertin, Alan Sendorek and Henry Macrory and civil servants led by Steve Field and Jenny Grey (Montgomerie 2011). This is very much in the mould of Gordon Brown's communications team and echoes the way Tony Blair tried to operate following the departure of the highly political – and often abrasive – Alistair Campbell.

The media and the 2010 general election campaign: the impact of the televised leaders' debates

The general election of 2010 was one of the most closely fought in living memory. It was, therefore, a campaign in which the media were always likely to play an important role. But few could have predicted just how important this role would turn out to be. The reason was Britain's first live televised party leaders' debates. These three events dominated media commentary across all platforms – television, press and online – for more than three weeks of the four-week campaign.

The terms of engagement for the debates emerged during the early part of 2010, after more than 70 individual rules had been hammered out in numerous meetings involving party strategists and broadcasters. The agreed format required that questions were not presented to candidates in advance of the debate, that audience members would not applaud, shout or heckle, that programme producers would not use cutaway shots explicitly focusing on the audience's reaction to statements, and that the debate moderator would not introduce material outside of the scope of the audience's questions (ITV *et al.* 2010). The format's design was therefore politicised. During the campaign itself the rules became the subject of 700 complaints by party activists to the British broadcasting regulator, OFCOM (Sweney 2010).

For each of the debates, which took place in Manchester, Bristol and Birmingham, the three candidates stood side by side behind lecterns and faced the presenter and a small, handpicked, studio audience. The candidates gave tightly scripted one-minute opening and closing statements, then responded to a range of questions from the audience. This was followed by periods of varying length during which the leaders directly engaged with each other. The first half of each debate was assigned a specific policy theme: home affairs, international affairs and the economy.

As occurs in the United States, broadcast media and the press heavily trailed the television debates during the opening stages of the campaign and coverage ratcheted up during the first week of the campaign proper, culminating in two days of preview features on television and in the press. The entire week following the first debate was decisively shaped by media reaction to those first 90 minutes in Manchester and this established a pattern for the reporting of the subsequent debates. Television's treatment was dominated by commentary from an assortment of 'body language experts', 'language experts' and opinion-polling companies. Broadcast media also made much of 'spin alley': a backstage space set aside for the post-debate huddles involving journalists, politicians and the parties' press officers. By the third debate, television news ran a great deal of behind-the-scenes material showing the parties' communications teams grouped with numerous journalists.

The scheduling of the debates had a crucial influence on their impact, creating the perfect conditions for a powerful cycle of coverage and commentary. All three ran on Thursday evenings, in television's hallowed 8 p.m. to 10 p.m. prime time. This ensured close integration with the rhythms of the British media's regular politics, commentary, and opinion cycle, which now reaches a crescendo with the weekend newspapers and the Sunday political television shows. The television audience for the first debate, hosted by ITV, was 9.4 million. The second was hosted by Sky News, a satellite and cable-only outlet, but it was also aired by the BBC News channel, ensuring a total audience of 4 million. The third, run by the BBC, was watched by 8.4 million (BBC News Online 2010a).

In keeping with Britain's hybrid media environment, live television coverage of the debates was accompanied by instant reaction based on snap online polls on the broadcasters' websites and small studio panels of citizens operating sentiment dials which generated real-time reaction 'worm' charts overlaid on top of the live streaming video. Overall, during the first 90-minute debate, 184,000 individual Twitter messages were produced, as users structured their commentary and conversations using shared hashtags. The messages flooded in at an average rate of 29 per second, as 36,000 individual Twitter users engaged in real-time discussion (Tweetminster 2010). This continued the emergent role played by Twitter and Facebook as backchannels adopted by the politically interested to form ad hoc discursive communities around major television events – a practice that first came to prominence during British National party leader Nick Griffin's controversial appearance on the BBC's *Question Time* in October 2009 (Anstead and O'Loughlin 2010).

Within a few minutes of the end of the first debate, polls from YouGov/*The Sun*, ComRes/ITV, Sky News, Angus Reid and Populus all showed Nick Clegg to be the clear winner. Conservative leader David Cameron came second in all but one poll (*Guardian*, 16 April 2010). Following a weekend of remarkably positive broadcast and press coverage from newspapers across the entire political spectrum, the Liberal Democrats started the third week of the campaign with a huge boost in the opinion polls. Some polls placed them on an almost equal footing with the Conservatives; in most, Labour were unexpectedly relegated to third place (Young 2010). Even the *Sun* carried Clegg's victory on its Monday morning front page (Dunn 2010). Broadcast journalists, too, began to exercise much greater scrutiny over the Liberal Democrats' policy platform. Suddenly, the election had become a genuine three-party contest.

The increase in support for the Liberal Democrats greatly unsettled the Conservative-supporting newspapers, especially the *Mail*, the *Times* and the *Daily Telegraph*, who were torn between reflecting the rise of Clegg – clearly a major political story with a popular grassroots narrative – or turning their fire on the Liberal Democrats. This tension was resolved in a couple of days. Once it became clear that 'Cleggmania' was not likely to dissolve in the short term, the right-wing press turned, producing torrents of critical coverage in the run-up to the second debate. The *Mail* ran an extraordinary series of stories on Clegg, one suggesting that the Liberal Democrats' leader had uttered a 'Nazi slur' on Britain in 2002 when he had suggested that victory in the Second World War had made it more difficult for the British to accept that other European countries enjoyed greater prosperity (Shipman 2010). The night before the second televised leaders' debate, the *Telegraph* announced that its debate-day front page would feature what it claimed was an investigative scoop: a report that Clegg, before he had become party leader, had received party donations from three businessmen directly into his personal bank account (Winnett and Swaine 2010). The *Telegraph* had trawled through the archive of documents it had bought in order to run its months-long series of exposés on MPs' expenses in mid-2009. Clegg was given a chance to respond to the story before it published and he issued a statement saying that he had used the money to pay for a member of staff and that these donations were reported in the parliamentary register of members' interests.

But during the morning of the second debate there unfolded an extra-ordinary series of events. As news of the *Telegraph*'s 'scoop' reverberated through media and online networks, it became obvious that a large proportion of journalists – on both right and left – were sceptical of the *Telegraph*'s front-page story. By mid-morning, a satirical online flash campaign had emerged. Tens of thousands of Twitter users sardonically added the hashtag '#nickcleggsfault' to their status updates. These messages ranged from political observations to ludicrous statements such as 'We've run out of houmous #nickcleggsfault,' 'Lunch meeting was cancelled at the last minute. So obviously #nickcleggsfault'. By the middle of the day this had become the third most popular shared hash-tag, not just among the 7.5 million Twitter users in the UK, but the entirety of the service's 105 million registered global users. Suddenly the *Telegraph* was thrown on the defensive. Sensing that the Clegg donations story was not being as well received as he had perhaps hoped, its deputy editor, Benedict Brogan, took the highly unusual step of issuing a defence on the paper's political blog. The story was dead.

Arguably the most important single development in the British media's treatment of politics since the arrival of television during the 1959 election race, the televised leaders' debates altered the course of the campaign, propelling Liberal Democrat leader, Nick Clegg, into the media spotlight as his party rose in the opinion polls immediately following a 'winning' performance in the first debate. While the surge fell away during the final week of the campaign and did not directly translate into seats gained for the party on polling day, 'Cleggmania' arguably had three important effects. First, the Manchester debate established that precious commodity – campaign momentum – for the Liberal Democrats. The Conservatives and Labour were on the back foot until very late in the race. Brown was a consistent loser in the media commentary and the snap polls following all three debates. Cameron was widely perceived to have disappointed during the first two events. He staged a strong recovery during the third, but this came just a few full campaigning days before polling day. Second, because the Liberal Democrats ended the campaign with a 3 or 4 percentage point increase in their share of the popular vote, when compared with their position in the pre-election opinion polls, they avoided being wiped out in some seats by the powerful electoral swing to the Conservatives. Their total of 57 seats could easily have been substantially lower had they not benefited from the boost provided by the debates. Third, Clegg's strong performance enhanced his overall credibility with the media and the public, smoothing the Liberal Democrats' transition into coalition government with the Conservatives on May 11.

Conclusion

As this chapter has shown, the political communication environment in Britain is in transition. While broadcasting still remains at the heart of national political life, the nature of mediated politics is evolving rapidly and in directions that are sometimes contradictory, sometimes complementary. The election leaders' debates reinforced television's predominance, though as we saw above, even those events were accompanied by a panoply of online activism, some of it facilitated by the broadcasters themselves.

The way citizens consume political information is changing in the new digital environment. As use of the internet and mobile technologies has grown, so they have become an important port of call for those seeking political news. Audiences have never had access to so much political information through such a variety of news outlets. At the same time, these technologies provide new opportunities for audiences to engage in political activities, express their opinions and contribute content in historically unprecedented ways. The evidence suggests that growth in the numbers taking advantage of these interactive opportunities is likely to continue.

There are, however, cautionary themes. Concerns about the stratified nature of the digitised public sphere remain. Those that take advantage of new technologies to participate in politics remain a minority and still tend to be wealthy, well educated and younger. Second, this new communicative digital space has also impacted upon politicians and media organisations, creating opportunities, but at the same time new uncertainties. Established news outlets remain a visible presence but face financial pressures. While news organisations have responded innovatively, competition, shrinking audiences and lower revenues – especially from advertising – have negatively affected their resource bases. There have often been no alternatives to cost cutting. The public service provider, the BBC, has fared well up to now, but it too is likely to face future financial constraints, and this may well have implications for the quality of news citizens receive.

Politicians and their strategists have been forced to adapt to a rapidly pluralising digital sphere. Party leaders have promoted themselves using a range of interactive features to try and connect with citizens, albeit with varying degrees of success. While the internet has opened up new ways for politicians to interact with the public, it has also posed a series of challenges. Some aspects of the online information environment have proved difficult to control. The fast-moving news cycles require constant monitoring and are significantly more difficult to direct. The public spread of gossip and rumour is perhaps more common place. While political elites have been keen to be seen embracing new media, they are understandably less keen to be seen reverting to necessary but dubious methods of control. The leaked emails that led to 'Smeargate' reveal, not only that some old command-and-control techniques of the broadcast era are still hugely important, but also that the new media environment is inherently porous. Understanding the complex new political communication environment in the twenty-first century remains a challenge, but one to which students of politics must rise if they are to fully comprehend the nature of British democracy.

Chapter 13

Britain and the Global Financial Crisis: The Return of Boom and Bust

COLIN HAY

The political salience of economic policy, and the economy more generally, rises and falls as growth rates fluctuate. For almost a decade and a half from 1992 to 2007, and particularly once New Labour took office in 1997, sustained economic growth served in effect to reduce the political significance of the economy in Britain – as an unspoken economic policy consensus emerged between the parties and as a low inflation–low interest rate equilibrium served to produce stable growth, cheap credit, a buoyant housing market and high levels of consumer demand. This undoubtedly contributed to New Labour's longevity in office and the almost palpable sense of economic competence and confidence that it exuded.

That was then ... As is so often the case in politics, just when all appears tranquil and calm the hurricane strikes. In a little over two years the political salience of the economy has returned with a vengeance, pitching the British economy into its longest and deepest recession since the 1930s and shattering the illusions of those who had became increasingly wedded to the convenient fiction that sustained economic growth signalled an 'end to boom and bust'.

Though the global financial crisis provided more the background than the focus of the 2010 General Election, the advent of the Cameron–Clegg coalition may well come to be seen as marking the dawn of a new age of British austerity. Thus, while all three of the principal parties committed themselves during the election campaign to a halving of the public deficit in a single parliamentary term, it is the Conservative–Liberal Democrat coalition that has the perhaps unenviable task of being the first to attempt to put this into practice. Their first ('Emergency') Budget, promised in the Conservative manifesto and delivered within fifty days of taking office, and the Comprehensive Spending Review concluded in October 2010, give an early indication of what the future might hold –

though the devil will undoubtedly lie in the details of implementation. For the coalition, deficit reduction is the most pressing and urgent priority; and there can be no waiting for the recovery to be established before this takes effect. This puts them significantly at odds with their Labour predecessors in office. Indeed, before and during the election campaign both Labour and the Liberal Democrats had committed themselves to the broadly Keynesian view that cuts in public spending and/or raising taxes in the absence of evidence of a sustained economic recovery would guarantee, at best, a 'double-dip recession' and, at worst, threaten to precipitate a decade or more of economic decline – in short, a depression. Labour remains the sole party wedded publicly to such a view. Yet this is not the only significant difference between the new government and the opposition on the handling of the recession. For improving the state of the public finances is always a juggling act, requiring a balance to be struck between raising increased revenue through tax increases on the one hand and cutting public spending on the other. And the point is that this balance would be struck very differently by the opposition than by the government. For the Conservatives and their Liberal Democrat coalition partners, the proposed ratio between tax rises and spending cuts is one to four (i.e.: for every £1 raised in new taxation there will be £4 of public spending cuts). For Labour, the ratio would have been very different – probably around to one to two. The significance of this difference in emphasis is seen when we consider the June 2010 Emergency Budget. Through increases in VAT (from 17.5 to 20 per cent from January 2011), capital gains tax (from 18 to 28 per cent for higher earners) and a balance sheet levy on banks and building societies, the Budget raised an estimated £8.2 billion per annum (HM Treasury 2010). But at a ratio of tax rises to spending cuts of one to four this committed the government to finding almost £35 billion per annum in public spending cuts – equivalent to a cut of around one quarter in the budget of unprotected government departments. These figures were largely confirmed by the Comprehensive Spending Review. Such spending cuts have not been seen in Britain outside of wartime emergency planning.

From boom to bust

So how did the growth prospects of the British economy and the associated state of the public finance turn quite so sour quite so quickly? To begin to answer that question it is useful first to return to the idea, prevalent in policy-making circles for almost a decade, that the era of boom and bust was over.

However naïve such a view might now seem, those who held it had been in very good company. Nobel Laureate Robert Lucas was merely capturing the mood of the times when, in his 2003 presidential address to the American Economic Association, he suggested that 'for all practical purposes...the central problem of depression prevention has been solved' (2003: 1). How wrong he now turns out to have been. But the point is that Lucas from was far from alone in presuming that the business cycle was dead so long as central banks were independent of political influence and policy makers observed a few basic principles of sound economic management. Indeed, crucially, the new economy orthodoxy that he was articulating had already extended to policy makers, with ideas like his own influencing decisively the course of macro and microeconomics policy. This meant that British policy makers entered what we now tend to call the 'global financial crisis' committed to a set of economic policies, a supporting economic policy paradigm and, indeed, a set of institutions for economic governance predicated on the assumption that such events simply couldn't happen. In short, they were not well prepared for what was happening.

What makes this all the more remarkable (and all the more depressing) is that although the precise chain of events was, of course, almost impossible to foresee, that something like this would happen was far less difficult to predict. Indeed, and if only to show just how easy it was to anticipate 'the great recession' as it is now being termed, consider the final lines of the equivalent chapter to this in *Developments in British Politics 8*, written in the wake of the 2005 general election.

> New Labour's third consecutive electoral victory is a major, and historically unprecedented, achievement...Yet, as in 1974 and 1992, this may not be a terribly good election to have won...The economic prospects look, for the first time in a long time, far from benign...[and] New Labour's political economy is rather better equipped to deal with phases of the business cycle that may now have passed. In short, its economic policy record...is flattered by the phase of the business cycle in which it has thus far been achieved. The real test is yet to come. (Hay 2006: 271)

That test, arguably, it failed. But the point is that it is a test that any of the major political parties in Britain was almost bound to fail, since all of them were committed – as, in effect, they remain – to a set of economic orthodoxies which neither prepared them for what was to happen nor provided much guidance on what to do in such an (unanticipated) scenario.

In this chapter I examine how this came to pass, considering the advent and consequences of the great recession, assessing the origins of the growth dynamic that the British economy enjoyed between 1992 and 2007, its systemic vulnerabilities and its exposure to financial instability in particular, and the nature, causes and likely consequences (economic and political) of the recession itself. In the process, I seek to gauge the character, significance and effectiveness of the interventions made in the attempt to shore up Britain's growth model during the recession and the prospects for the resumption of growth in the years ahead. I argue that the Anglo-liberal or 'privatised Keynesian' growth model that Britain stumbled across somewhat fortuitously after 1992 is, indeed, fatally flawed and that, in the absence of a new growth model, it is difficult to see how sustained economic growth can be achieved. This may well make 2010 no better an election to win than 2005, 1992 or 1974. And in so far as that proves to be the case, the heightened salience of the economy is likely to endure until sometime after the *next* election.

The great moderation and the emergence of the Anglo-liberal growth model

To see why, it is necessary to retrace our steps, examining first the impressive economic performance of the British economy throughout the 1990s and for most of the first decade of the new millennium. Figure 13.1 places recent economic performance in a longer-term historical context, showing the government's own data on unemployment, long-term interest rates and inflation since the mid-1980s until just before the onset of the global credit crunch (which began first in the US in late 2006).

It tells a simple and, on the face of it, an encouraging story – of consistently falling unemployment (from a peak in 1992 to 1993), of consistently falling long-term interest rates (from a peak in 1990) and of inflation falling rapidly following Britain's ejection from the European Exchange Rate Mechanism in September 1992 (on 'Black Wednesday') to stabilise at around the 2 per cent official target (as set for the Monetary Policy Committee of the Bank of England by the government). Indeed, it is difficult to imagine a more benign macroeconomic context.

Figure 13.2 compares Britain's rate of economic growth over the same period with that for the G7 leading economies. After a mini-recession in 1990 the British economy recovered well and, from 1994 to 2006, enjoyed a period of impressively consistent economic growth of around 3 per cent per annum. Moreover, its growth rate over this period of time was both higher than that for the G7 economies together and, more significantly perhaps, less volatile. Again, the picture was encouraging and it offered no hint of what was to follow.

What data like do show, however, is that New Labour was fortunate

Figure 13.1   *British economic performance 1986–2006*

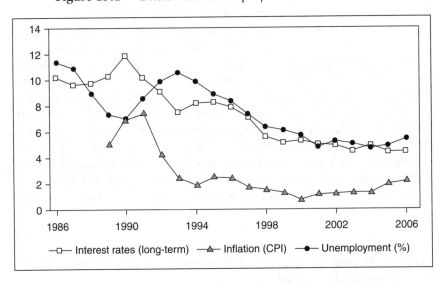

Data from: HM Treasury, Pocket Book Data Series (various years)

Figure 13.2   *Economic growth in Britain and the G7, 1985–2006
(% annual increases in GDP)*

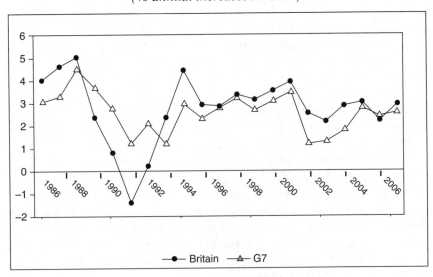

Data from: HM Treasury, Pocket Book Data Series (various years)

in the economic legacy bequeathed to it by the outgoing Conservative administration of John Major in 1997. Whatever else it is, this is not a story of an economic transformation that postdates New Labour's election. For the low inflation–low interest rate equilibrium from which it benefited for so long once in office was already established when it took office in 1997. Indeed, the key moment here is undoubtedly September 1992 – the key factor being the devaluation of sterling that occurred with its forcible ejection from the European Exchange Rate Mechanism (the precursor to Monetary Union). From this moment onwards the government and Bank of England no longer had to use interest rates to defend an overvalued currency on foreign exchanges – they could, in short, use monetary policy to manage demand in the economy and allow the exchange rate to float. The result was that interest rates fell, consolidating the recovery from the mini-recession that had begun in 1990. The devaluation served additionally to reduce the effective size of the public deficit – and certainly the payments required to service it – while also providing a much needed boost to the (cost) competitiveness of British exporters.

This was New Labour's economic inheritance and pretty favourable it was too. But although the new government did little to establish the low inflation-low interest rate equilibrium in the first place, its actions once in office certainly served to consolidate this – albeit arguably more by luck than judgement. For while still in opposition the party had committed itself to matching the stringent spending targets set by the outgoing Major government (arguably, at a point when the latter had already discounted the prospect of its re-election). Though this was almost certainly more the product of perceived electoral expediency rather than economic foresight, it led the new Blair government to run a substantial budget surplus between 1997 and 1999. This in turn led to quite a significant reduction in national debt and, in the process, served to increase the sensitivity of demand in the economy to interest rate variations. In other words it allowed the newly independent Bank of England to control inflationary pressures as they arose without pushing interest rates back to anything like the levels they had reached in the 1980s and early 1990s. As such it served further to institutionalise the developing low interest rate–low inflation equilibrium (see also Hay 2007). And that in turn reinforced growth and with it the rising taxation receipts out of which a significant investment in the public sector – particularly the NHS – was funded.

'Privatised Keynesianism' – the new growth model

But what, you might well ask, is so fantastic about a low inflation-low interest rate equilibrium anyway? To answer that question we need to turn our attentions more directly to the character of the new growth model that Britain inadvertently stumbled across from 1992 onwards. Various labels have been attached to it in the academic literature. Andrew Gamble (2009a) refers to the 'new financial' growth model, Colin Crouch (2008) to 'privatised Keynesianism', Matthew Watson (2010) to 'house price Keynesianism', whereas in my own work I have tended more simply to refer to it as the 'Anglo-liberal' growth model (Hay 2011). Yet, while such authors are divided, as it were, by the absence of a common language, the account that each provide of the determinants of growth is essentially the same. But before considering that account directly, it is important to sound a couple of notes of caution. First, there is a danger that in appealing to the language of growth models, too much conscious choice and agency is attributed to the largely unwitting architects of such a growth strategy. As already noted, in so far as it is useful to suggest that Britain developed in the 1990s a coherent and distinctive model of growth, that model was stumbled across serendipitously – it was not a product of conscious choice, far less of design or planning. Second, memorable, striking and useful though they undoubtedly are, terms such as 'privatised' and 'house price Keynesianism' are potentially misleading – certainly if they are not used carefully. For, strictly speaking, there is nothing at all Keynesian about the new British growth model; in a sense that is the point, as we shall see presently. Indeed, Keynes is no more the inspiration for 'privatised Keynesian' growth than he was the architect of monetarism. It is thus important to emphasise from the outset that the concept is based on an analogy (and a pretty loose one at that); and, like all analogies, it should not be stretched too far.

Terminological difficulties and differences notwithstanding, the literature is united in seeing the growth model that sustained the British economy from Black Wednesday until the great recession as consumer-led and financed from private (rather than public) debt. Its most basic precondition was easy access to personal credit, much of it secured against a rising housing market. And that, in turn, was made possible by the simultaneous combination of low interest rates and low inflation – or, more precisely, inflationary pressures that could be ameliorated without posing any threat to historically low interest rate settings. For as long as this persisted, credit was easily accessible on favourable terms. This served to broaden access to – and to improve affordability within – the housing market, driving up prices and leading to both a developing house price bubble and, on the back of that, a consumer boom. Once inflated this was sustained and, increasingly, nurtured, by interest rates which remained historically low throughout the boom.

To all intents and purposes it appeared that a virtuous circle had been established in which growth would pretty much take care of itself – the basis of a distinctively British (or, at least Anglo-liberal) growth model (one also evident in the US and a number of other anglophone liberal market economies). Stable low interest rates allied to substantial capital inflows from China and South-East Asia allowed the British and US economies to grow despite their large and widening trade deficits (their rapid consumer growth led them to import far more than they exported and this could only be balanced by large capital inflows). Low interest rates and a highly competitive market for credit provided both the incentive and the opportunity for first- time buyers to enter a rising market and for established home owners to extend themselves financially, by either moving up the housing ladder, or releasing the equity in their property to fuel consumption. There was now little incentive to save, as reflected in the dwindling household savings ratio (the value of new household savings expressed as a proportion of gross household disposable income). This fell precipitously from around 12 per cent in 1992 to an all time low of less than 3 per cent by 2007 (HM Treasury Pocket Book Data 2010).

Indeed, this switch savings to investment in appreciating asset classes (including property) was consciously promoted by the government, with consumers increasingly encouraged to think of their asset purchases as investments which they might cash in to fuel their consumption – in retirement, or as the state withdrew from pension provision, or in times of economic difficulty or unemployment. Such 'asset-based welfare' was, in effect, the social policy corollary of the new growth model (see Finlayson 2009). That it became a conscious social policy strategy in itself, actively promoted by the New Labour government, was a clear indication that, despite its accidental origins, the growth model was now becoming quite a conscious part of its economic thinking.

It is at this point that the Keynesian analogy becomes helpful. For what it serves to highlight is both the delightful simplicity of this growth model and, more significantly perhaps, its fundamental fragility. In particular, what it draws our attention to is the key relationship at the heart of the model between private debt, domestic demand and consumption. In so doing, it arguably strips the growth model to its core.

If we are to understand privatised Keynesianism it is first important that we remind ourselves of the essence of Keynesianism itself. A rather stylised account will suffice – indeed, arguably the analogy really only works if we treat Keynesianism in stylised terms. Genuine Keynesianism (the Keynesianism of Keynes, for instance) sees public expenditure as key to the management of demand within the domestic economy. In particular, when demand and hence growth falls in the economy, it sees it as the responsibility of the state to intervene by engaging in public spending (sustained, where necessary, by borrowing). In this conception, public debt is no bad thing if such debt is used to inject demand into the economy in the service of stimulating growth. Thus, at the heart of traditional Keynesianism is a link between public debt, demand and growth – and it is this relationship that authors like Colin Crouch are pointing to when they label the new growth model 'privatised Keynesianism'.

For privatised Keynesianism also sees debt as crucial to demand and hence growth. But the role that traditional Keynesianism assigns to *public* debt, privatised Keynesianism assigns to *private* (and, invariably, personal) debt, typically secured against a rising housing market. If credit is cheap and access to credit is widespread, then there is a powerful incentive for consumers to borrow – either to acquire property or, indeed, to fuel their consumption. Debt, in other words, generates demand which would not otherwise be there – driving up property prices and drip feeding the consumer economy. And, if interest rates remain low or even fall while property prices are rising then a further set of incentives take hold. For consumers who do not fully stretch themselves in the housing market are missing out on the potential return on their investment that property offers. Moreover, with house prices rising, consumers are able to remortgage their property, releasing the equity built up in their homes to fuel additional consumption. For as long as inflation is manageable without compromising the low interest rate regime, growth in consumer demand (serviced by rising private debt) is almost guaranteed. As this suggests, the state need no longer take responsibility for managing demand through public debt and the public expenditure such borrowing makes possible, since personal and hence private debt made possible by a credit glut is now capable of taking care of that function – so long as interest rates remain stable. In other words, the borrowing function previously performed by the state has, in effect, been privatised – hence privatised Keynesianism.

In theory at least, this sounds all very attractive. In so far as – or, more realistically perhaps, only for so long as – the low inflation–low interest rate equilibrium persists, demand is likely to be fuelled by private debt secured against a rising housing market. Such demand is likely to generate a consumer boom. And that, in turn, is likely to sustain a growing, profitable and highly labour-intensive services sector whose expansion might both mask and compensate for the ongoing decline of the manufacturing base (a decline reinforced by low levels of productive investment as credit lines to business are crowded out by the supply of personal credit). A final factor completes the growth model. It relates to the incentives, not for consumers, but for financial institutions, investors and intermediaries. With credit cheap, demand for credit is likely to be high – a set of market conditions which strongly favour the banks and other financial intermediaries. They are well placed to benefit, in such a model, from the somewhat higher transactions fees they can charge for issuing and renewing credit lines, particularly for those – like sub-prime mortgage holders – at the fringes of the system. In a rapidly rising property market they are also well placed to benefit from repackaging and selling on mortgage debt to international investors – by issuing mortgage-backed securities (MBSs), for instance. In the process they pass the debt associated with their mortgage lending 'downstream' and, in theory at least, off their own balance sheets – ostensibly reducing their exposure to default on mortgage repayments in the process (for a more detailed account of the complexity of mortgage securitisation, see Hay 2011). But the key point is that the financial incentives of privatised Keynesianism, however complex they may have been, clearly encouraged the demand for and supply of sub-prime lending, high loan-to-value ratios and, crucially, equity release which might fuel consumption.

For as long as it lasted, this was all well and good. But arguably, it is precisely where the Keynesian analogy breaks down that that problems begin. The whole point of Keynesianism was, of course, to manage the business cycle (the periodic alternation between growth and recession, boom and bust). By borrowing to injecting demand into the economy when economic growth was falling, it was argued, the business cycle could be softened, such that 'bust' did not inevitably follow 'boom'. But privatised Keynesianism, in effect, takes no account of the business cycle. Indeed arguably, in so doing, it tends to accentuate it, contributing to the inflation of bubbles in the housing market for instance, but being incapable of providing any macroeconomic stabiliser when such bubbles burst.

Thus, if perhaps as a result of an inflationary shock, the low interest rate–low inflation equilibrium is disturbed, then mortgage repayments and ultimately default rates rise, housing prices fall, equity is diminished and, crucially, consumption falls – as disposable income is squeezed by the higher cost of servicing outstanding debt and as the prospects for equity release to top up consumption diminish. Lack of demand translates into unemployment with consequent effects on mortgage default rates, house prices and so forth. The virtuous circle rapidly turns vicious. Arguably this is precisely what happened in the heartlands of Anglo-liberal growth, the US and Britain, from 2006 and 2007 respectively. It is to the details of this process and to their lasting implications that we can now eventually turn.

The bursting of the bubble: the re-nationalisation of 'Privatised Keynesianism'?

The housing bubble burst first, as is widely known, in the US. Indeed, it is tempting – if, ultimately, wrong – to see the British recession of 2007 to 2009 as a product solely of contagion from the US. In fact the British economy would almost certainly have endured a deep and damaging recession even in the absence of contagion effects from the US. Yet, chronologically, the story starts with the bursting of the US housing bubble in late 2006 as interest rates soared in response to the sliding value of the dollar on international markets, a build up of domestic inflationary pressures as the economy eventually recovered from the bursting of the dot.com bubble and 9/11 and, crucially, a sharp rise in oil prices. Of these three factors it is the third, the doubling of the price of oil in a little over two years, that is the most important – not least because the threat of oil price rises reinforced by speculation is likely to return.

In response to this inauspicious combination of factors, the Federal Reserve raised US interest rates almost fivefold between mid-2004 and early 2006. The shock to mortgage holders was palpable, with mortgage default rates predictably soaring. No less predictable was that default rates would prove highest among sub-prime mortgagees, whose mortgage terms were typically punitive in the first place to compensate for the greater financial risk they posed and who could scarcely afford the repayments even when interest rates had been at their lowest. The result was a housing crash which radiated outwards from areas of greatest sub-prime density eventually to encompass the entire US housing market.

But the ripple effects would not stop there. Because of the highly securitised character of the US mortgage market, a breathtaking variety of international financial institutions that had been siphoning up whatever US MBSs they could get hold of now found themselves exposed to major losses – as these previously high-yielding securities were rapidly reclassified as 'toxic assets'. Major banks, insurance companies and other financial institutions around the world starting toppling like dominoes, prompting the largest ever bailout of the financial sector as the world economy slumped into its longest and deepest recession since the 1930s and as inter-bank lending – and hence the global supply of credit – seized up altogether. In the process private debt was, in effect, re-nationalised with horrendous consequences for the state of public finances around the world and the credit lines which had lubricated the world economy dried up altogether, cutting off at the point of supply the principle source of consumer demand in economies like Britain.

This is the context in which we now need to insert the British economy. Consider first the contagion effects associated directly from the bursting of the US housing bubble. The first thing perhaps to note here is that the British economy would have been exposed to such contagion effects regardless of its growth model – but the magnitude of such effects was all the greater because of the sheer size and character of its financial services sector and the reliance of its growth model on access to personal credit. That said, simply by virtue of the highly securitised nature of the US mortgage market and the international diffusion of such securities, any bursting of the US housing bubble was always going to result in significant losses for British financial institutions. But what compounded matters was the freezing up of both international and domestic interbank lending that followed as financial institutions licked their wounds, counted their losses and re-scaled (downwards) their expectations as to whom they might profitably lend. The brutal reality was that, given its levels of consumer debt and the dependence of growth on access to more of the same, the British economy was always going to be more exposed to such a credit crunch than almost any other leading economy. No less significantly, the size and significance of financial services to the economy left the government with little option other than to underwrite the entire sector with public funds. The total funds committed were estimated by the National Audit Office, in December 2009, at £850 billion, destroying at a stroke the state of the public finances – and, in all likelihood, condemning the public sector to at least a decade of retrenchment. Yet the rationale for a bailout of the banking sector on this scale was clear – to insure depositors and, rather more significantly, to re-secure the supply of credit on which the growth of the consumer economy for over a decade had been predicated.

As this suggests, contagion borne of financial interdependence can account for much of the damage inflicted on the Britain economy since 2007. But it cannot account for it all – and, no less significantly, it cannot explain the timing of the onset of the British recession. To explain that we need to turn to rather more domestic considerations.

Crucial, once again, is the link between trends in oil prices (driven at least as much by speculative dynamics as by the laws of supply and demand) and domestic interest rates.

As Figure 13.3 shows clearly, from the second quarter of 2006 oil prices, inflation and British interest rates rose in parallel. Interest rate rises were, of course, much less pronounced than they were in the US. Yet, unremarkably, the increases in mortgage repayments to which they gave rise combined with a reduction in disposable income associated with rising prices led to a squeeze on consumer demand and an increasingly sharp fall in the number of housing transactions prices – followed soon thereafter by a no less sharp and accelerating depreciation in house prices. Having grown at around 12 per cent per annum since 1992

Figure 13.3   *Interest rates, the price of oil, inflation and the housing market*

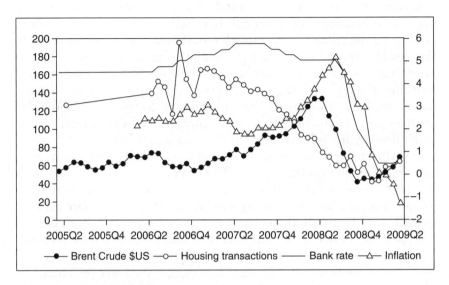

Data from: HM Treasury Pocket Book Data Series (various years); HM Revenue and Customs Annual Receipts (monthly values, 1,000s)
Note: inflation and interest rates are plotted on the right-hand axes

residential property prices were, in the final quarter of 2008, falling at around 20 per cent per annum. This brought about a quick staggering change in personal fortunes. In late 2006 the average earner living in the average home was seeing a wealth effect associated with house price inflation equivalent to three quarters of their pre-tax annual average earnings. In other words, were they to release all the equity in their home they could effectively double their spending power. Yet two years later, with property prices in freefall, annual house price deflation on the same property was equivalent to over 120 per cent of the pre-tax earnings of the average citizen (Hay 2009: 471). Any residual equity was seeping away at a very alarming rate.

As this suggests, privatised Keynesianism had now become, not a source of growth, but an impediment to growth – because the low-inflation–low interest rate equilibrium upon which it depended had been disrupted, reducing demand in the housing market and hence cutting off at source the equity which had drip-fed consumption for a decade and a half. The result was a highly corrosive combination of falling house prices and equity depreciation which, in combination with high interest rates and high and rising commodity prices, led directly to falling demand and, in due course, to rising unemployment. The close link

Figure 13.4 *The link between the housing market and British growth, 1990–2010*

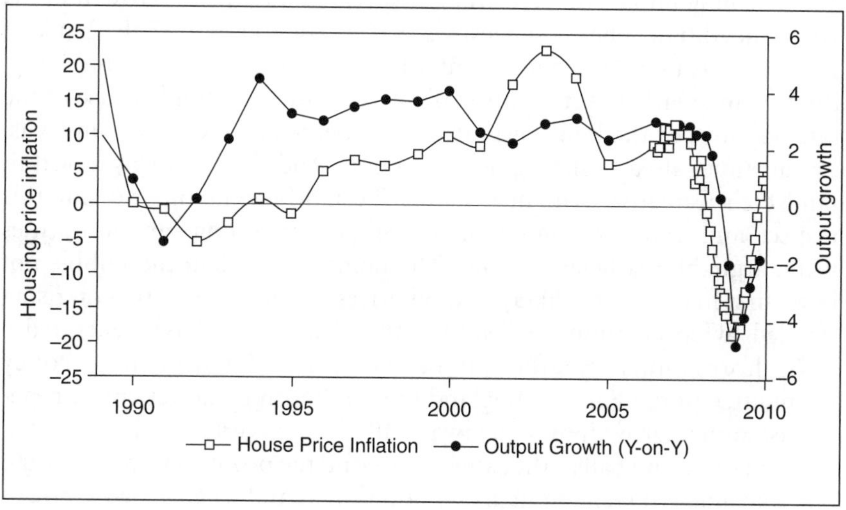

Data from: HM Treasury, Pocket Book Data Series (various years)

between the housing market and the fortunes of the domestic economy is clear to see from Figure 13.4.

What it also suggests is that although Britain's economic problems were reinforced by the credit crunch (in that it is difficult to see steady growth returning to the economy in the absence of the resumption of lending), Britain would almost certainly have experienced a deep and painful recession without out. The unavailability of credit to consumers throughout 2008 and 2009 undoubtedly deepened the recession. But it cannot hide the fact that, by this point, there was very little demand for personal credit anyway.

Having differentiated between the domestic and external sources of Britain's slide into recession in 2007, we are now in a position to take stock of the damage that has been inflicted on the British economy by the bursting of the housing bubble and the ensuing credit crunch and to turn to the likely implications of this for any return to growth in the years ahead. But before doing so, there is one key factor which we need to note. It refers back to Figure 13.3 and relates to the Bank of England's interest rate settings in response to rising oil prices and other inflationary pressures. What the data show very clearly is that, although the Bank of England initially acted swiftly and decisively in raising interest rates as inflationary pressures built in the economy, it stopped doing so as soon as the housing market stalled – despite the fact that, if anything, inflation and the price of oil rose even more steeply once interest rates had reached their ceiling. This is very interesting – and it has potentially significant and alarming implications for the prospects of a return to growth in the years ahead. For what it suggests is that in 2006 and 2007 the Bank of England was unable to control inflation without bursting the bubble in the housing market. Yet inflation did eventually fall – not because of the interventions of the Bank of England but because the US economy was, by this time, already sliding into recession. And that, in turn, served to tame the speculative dynamics that has been driving up oil prices. In this respect, and strange though it might seem, Britain's monetary authorities were, arguably, rather fortunate. The point is that, had the bubble not burst first in the US it is likely that oil prices would have carried on rising (fuelled by speculation) well into 2009. That would have generated a quite horrendous 'stagflation' headache for the Monetary Policy Committee of the Bank of England (with a housing market crash, negative economic growth and runaway inflation exacerbated, presumably, by a run on sterling all at the same time). And the problem is that it would not take much to recreate such conditions if, as and when growth returns to the world economy – an alarming prospect to which we return presently.

The political fallout and the prospects for the return to growth

So where does leave the British economy and the privatised Keynesian model of growth on which it has relied since the devaluation of sterling in 1992? It is to this question that we can now turn directly, considering in turn the character and effectiveness of the interventions made by the government of Gordon Brown to shore up the growth model, the likely political legacy of the recession, and the prospects for the resumption of growth in the years ahead.

Brown's recession

Perverse though it might seem in the immediate wake of its electoral defeat, the government of Gordon Brown arguably had a good recession (see especially Thain 2009; and, for similar judgements, Gamble 2009a: 108; Pemberton 2009; for a contrasting view see Coates 2009). It acted swiftly, decisively and with some degree of creativity in responding to a set of challenges that they had not anticipated in any way and which cut to the heart of the growth model on which they had come to rely. Brown in particular played a key role in setting the tone and temper of what proved a perhaps surprisingly coordinated international response. Indeed, that it is even possible to suggest the public rescue of the global banking system from the precipice marks the return to an era of Keynesian economics owes much to the influence of Brown himself (Krugman 2008: 185). But that does not make it true.

Though we did not see the return of the Keynesian economic paradigm, we did see something very interesting – and strangely reminiscent of economic policy making, at least in Britain, in the mid to late 1970s. For just as just as the Labour government of Jim Callaghan sought to deploy monetarist techniques in an attempt to consolidate the prevailing Keynesian growth model, so that of Gordon Brown engaged in a bout of inter-paradigm borrowing – in using a repertoire of at least quasi-Keynesian techniques to shore up the existing growth model. But the point is that both episodes of inter-paradigm borrowing were characterised by the attempt to stabilise, rather than to replace, the existing model; as such, neither marked a paradigm shift (Gamble 2009a: 459). In so far as this was Keynesian at all, it was a form of 'foul weather Keynesianism' – a dipping into the repertoire of Keynesian techniques in recession only for such instruments to be abandoned as and when growth resumed. Indeed, a legitimate concern of many was that in a perhaps understandable desire to signal to international markets the intention to restore balance to the public accounts, such techniques would be abandoned well before any recovery were firmly established. Those concerns have not gone away.

Indeed, that Cameron's Conservatives emerged as the largest party in the 2010 general election almost guaranteed such an outcome – an impression only confirmed by their Emergency Budget in June 2010. For, as they repeatedly emphasised before, during and after the election campaign, their priority in office would be to make immediate cuts in public expenditure to appease market sentiment. In this respect, as in many others, Cameron's Conservatives and their coalition partners are no more carriers of an alternative economic paradigm than the government of Gordon Brown they replace – nor do they offer an alternative growth model. But there were during the election campaign – as there remain today – significant differences in emphasis between the parties on economic policy. Although they did not explicitly deny that they would have engaged in the same public underwriting of the banking sector, the Conservatives were clearly much more uneasy about deficit financing and the associated ratcheting up of public debt.

In this context it is interesting that they did, and still do, refer to the recession as a crisis, but they do so in a very particular way. The crisis, for them, is a debt crisis, 'Labour's debt crisis' – and that, of course, implies that the solution to the crisis is to restore balance to the public finances through a combination of tax raising and unprecedented cuts in public spending. Yet it is by no means the only significant difference between the parties. Interestingly in their 2010 election manifesto, the Conservatives were far more sanguine about the degree to which the British growth model was broken than Labour. Its economic chapter opened with a stark question: 'where is the growth to come from?' What is less clear is that either party offered much of an answer. For Labour, it seems growth rested, as it still rests, on resuscitating the old growth model. But for the Conservatives, it is very clear that this will not suffice. As they boldly state:

> we cannot go on with the old [growth] model...built on debt. An irresponsible public spending boom, an overblown banking sector and unsustainable consumer borrowing on the back of a housing bubble were the features of an age of irresponsibility that left Britain so exposed to this economic crisis. They cannot be the source of sustainable growth for the future. (Conservative Party 2010)

Yet this does not lead to a clear sense of what is to be done. Instead we are simply told that Britain must make the transition to a new growth model based on saving rather than borrowing, investment rather than conspicuous consumption, and a balance of trade surplus in place of an existing deficit – as well as a greatly reduced role for financial services. The problem here is that the new coalition government simply disavows the kind of intervention and, indeed, the degree of public investment, necessary to secure any such transformation and it also seems to believe that this transition can be achieved in a single parliamentary term when, in all likelihood, it would take several decades. While this remains the case, the new growth model remains almost entirely aspirational – and, in all likelihood, elusive.

Conclusion

So what are the prospects for the resumption of growth in the years ahead? The preceding analysis suggests three key impediments to growth, each of which would need to be overcome before it is credible to think that the British economy might grow again at anything like the rate to which it became accustomed in the 1990s and the first five years of the 2000s.

The first of these relates to the confidence invested by all of the major parties in the prospects for a manufacturing and export-led rebalancing of the economy in the years to come. Here, one might think, the very depth of the recession might offer some crumbs of comfort – for it has seen a significant depreciation of sterling in key export markets. This, it might be thought, would have led to a marked improvement in British competitiveness, the economy's balance of trade position and a strong platform from which to move to a more conscious export-led growth strategy. Yet the data show this not to have been the case, with the balance of trade position in fact worsening since the height of the recession.

Two further factors compound this already depressing state of affairs. Second, the global nature of the recession has led to a sharp decrease in the level of world trade as a percentage of global GDP. This makes it very difficult even to think of the British economy retaining, let alone expanding, its global market share. And third, this is merely reinforced by alarmingly low levels of productive investment in the economy in recent years – during a period of easy credit. With the very significant tightening of credit that has occurred since the recession and with a 40 per cent or so drop in the value of the commercial property against which most small businesses secure their credit, it is difficult to envisage the transition to an export-led growth strategy built on the back of private investment – and the parlous condition of the public finances would seem to preclude a programme of public investment to stimulate export growth.

So much for export-led economic growth. What about the prospects for a resumption of consumer-led and private debt-financed growth – a return to privatised Keynesianism in effect? The problem here is Britain's fragility in the face of any inflationary shock – and the likelihood of such a shock in a context of significant speculation in oil markets. As we have seen, by mid-2007 British interest rate settings were sufficient to burst the housing bubble *without controlling inflation*. What ultimately brought inflation down was the onset of the American recession and the fall in oil prices that followed.

If this is true, then it is deeply worrying. For arguably the Bank of England's Monetary Policy Committee still lacks the capacity to control inflation without crashing the housing market (at the time of writing, inflation is well above target and rising, yet interest rates remain at 0.5 per cent). This would be fine if the low inflation–low interest rate equilibrium of the 1990s and early 2000s could be restored. But the speculative character of oil price dynamics today makes that most unlikely. The point is that it would not even take the resumption of growth in the British economy to see the price of oil rise steeply, bringing with it similar inflationary pressures to those which have already taken us to the edge of the precipice once. Almost certainly all that is required is the resumption of growth in the US and that now seems established.

Oil prices quadrupled in the years before the global recession and they have already doubled since their floor in late 2008. Indeed, perhaps most worrying of all, their rate of growth in 2009 was as high as that from late 2006 until their peak in the second quarter of 2008.

This leaves just one significant factor which we need to consider. The British economy has endured the longest and deepest recession since the 1930s; but it is surely credible to think that it is far from over. At best, the private sector recession is over; but the public sector recession has scarcely begun. In a sense Britain has experienced something of a pre-election lull before the post-election storm. When it comes, as the consequences of deficit reduction start to become manifest in the second half of 2011, unemployment will rise steeply, demand will falter, and in all likelihood, house prices will fall once again. That is not an enticing prospect and it suggests that, rather like 1992 and 1974, 2010 may well be remembered as not a very good election to win. Britain's coalition government is likely to be sorely tested.

Chapter 14

Britain's Place in the European Union

LORI THORLAKSON

British membership in the European Union (EU) is striking for the high degree of Euroscepticism that shapes domestic public debate and internally divides party politics. In the 2009 Eurobarometer opinion polls, the British public reported the lowest levels of trust in EU institutions compared to all other member states. Less than 33 per cent of the public agree that British membership of the EU is a good thing, compared to an average of over 50 per cent across the EU as a whole. More respondents believe EU membership has *not* benefited the UK than believe that the UK has benefited from membership. This means there are few gains to be made in the domestic political arena by parties and the government from high-profile engagement with Europe. The Labour governments of Blair and Brown sought to manage this public Euroscepticism through an approach that has been described as one of 'utilitarian supranationalism': constructive engagement with the EU in order to achieve its policy goals, accompanied by efforts to depoliticise its EU policies and reduce the salience of the EU issue (Bulmer 2008). This can perhaps explain the low profile of EU issues during the 2010 election campaign.

Accompanying its public Euroscepticism, the UK has often held a reputation as an 'awkward partner' in the EU (George 1998) and a country that 'often punches well below its weight, for lack of sustained political engagement at the highest level' (Wallace 2005: 62). Britain's historical transatlantic and commonwealth ties curtailed the development of a strong European identity and its liberal market traditions have been at odds with continental forms of corporatist and social market models. The UK has opted out of some highly visible policy areas, such as the single currency and the Schengen area. Some key UK policy positions, on the budgetary rebate and Common Agricultural Policy (CAP) reform, have pitted it against powerful member states such as France and Germany and in the arena of intergovernmental relations, it often finds itself marginalised outside the Berlin–Paris axis. Finally, British engagement in Europe is hampered by a political culture engrained in the

Table 14.1   *Public attitudes towards the EU*

Generally speaking, do you think that [our country's] membership of the European Union is...

	UK	EU 27
A good thing	30 %	53 %
A bad thing	30 %	15 %
Neither good nor bad	34 %	28 %
Don't know	6 %	4 %

Would you say that [our country] has on balance benefited or not from being a member of the European Union?

	UK	EU 27
Benefited	36 %	57 %
Not benefited	49 %	31 %
Don't know	15 %	12 %

Data from: Standard Eurobarometer 72, autumn 2009

Westminster system that does not cultivate the skills of compromise and conciliation that are effective in EU politics.

The EU and domestic party politics

The Liberal Democrats, now part of the coalition government with the Conservatives, have long been the most pro-European of the major political parties in the UK. Party leader Nick Clegg, now deputy prime minister, was a former European Commission official and an MEP before entering national politics. The Liberal Democrat 2010 election manifesto called for Britain to be 'at the heart of Europe', and to 'ensure that Britain maximizes its influence through a strong and positive commitment' (Liberal Democrat 2010: 66). While the party is critical of some European policies, calling for reform of the budget and CAP, it supports closer cooperation with the EU in order to achieve British policy goals. This includes support for tighter EU regulation of banking and financial services. While committed to eventual membership of the euro, the party ruled out membership in the current economic situation, and has called for a referendum in the event of British membership. The party also supports a referendum on the UK's membership of the EU when there is a 'fundamental change in the relationship between the UK and EU' (Liberal Democrat 2010: 67). In such an event, the party has committed to campaigning for continued membership of the EU.

The issue of Europe has been complicated for both Labour and the Conservatives. The Labour party has developed from its anti-integrationist origins into a party that, in government, often cloaked its European policies in the rhetoric of national interest to stave off competition from the Eurosceptic right as well as from sceptical factions in its own party. The Conservatives, meanwhile, have evolved from the party of Europe in the 1970s, to a party that today is dominated by Eurosceptics. Evolution in the positions on Europe of both parties is a consequence of how far the EU has developed since the 1970s. Labour, originally hostile to Europe and the single market project of the EU, became much more pro-EU from the late 1980s, due in part to the centrist shift of Labour's 'third way' policies that were friendlier to market liberalism. Meanwhile, the Labour left, long sceptical of the EU's pro-market bent, has welcomed the development of the EU's social dimension. Labour's anti-integrationist wing was evidenced by the fact that the parliamentary ratification of the Lisbon Treaty led to a number of backbench Labour rebellions, more than had occurred on votes on Europe under Tony Blair's leadership (Cowley and Stuart 2008: 3). Both Blair and his successor, Gordon Brown, pursued the same European policy, but Brown was often seen to be less enthusiastically pro-European than Tony Blair, and his personal style was less well suited to the politics of summitry in the EU (Bulmer 2008; O'Donnell and Whitman 2007). Brown's EU agenda focused on growth and employment through market deregulation, a social dimension characterised by promotion of labour market flexibility and skills training, climate change and energy security, combating security and organised crime, promoting regional security and stability, including support for enlargement, tackling global poverty and EU budget reform (Cabinet Office 2007). These policy priorities reflect Brown's past commitment, as chancellor of the exchequer, to strongly promoting an economic liberalisation agenda in the EU. Also, these policy goals reflect a commitment to using the EU to more effectively achieve global policy goals, such as the Millennium Development Goals and climate change policy.

The Conservative party has moved further towards Euroscepticism as integration has encompassed an increasing number of policy areas traditionally viewed as national competences, such as social policy or justice and home affairs. Its Eurosceptic faction now dominates the party. By 2005, over 91 per cent of parliamentary Conservative party members identified themselves as Eurosceptic (Heppell and Hill 2009: 399). The Conservative party represents 'soft Euroscepticism' which combines general support for membership with either opposition to specific aspects of integration or a general rhetorical strategy of defending the national interest against Europe (Taggart and Szczerbiak 2004: 4). While in opposition, the Conservative party pursued a hard-line stance on Europe. After the 2009 European Parliament (EP) elections the UK Conservatives left the parliamentary grouping of the centre-right European People's party–European Democrats (EPP), the largest and therefore highly influential party grouping in the European Parliament, to form a new right-wing Eurosceptic party grouping called the European Conservatives and Reformists Group (ECR). This move cost the Conservative party influence in the European Parliament. The ECR group has just over 7 per cent of seats in the European Parliament, compared to the EPP's 36 per cent, which puts it at a disadvantage in terms of influencing legislation and securing parliamentary resources such as committee rapporteurships. The Conservative 2010 election manifesto called for a repatriation of powers related to social and employment policy, criminal justice, and the Charter of Fundamental Rights. The Tories had also called for legislation that would require a referendum on any further transfer of competences to the EU. David Cameron was forced to retreat on an earlier promise to hold a referendum on the Treaty of Lisbon after its 2009 ratification made this impractical. He promised instead to hold a referendum on any future transfer of powers to the EU.

Among other, smaller parties, the United Kingdom Independence party (UKIP), a single-issue Eurosceptic party, has achieved significant success in European parliamentary elections. It represents 'hard' Euroscepticism in the UK, which rejects not only further integration, but also EU membership (Taggart and Szczerbiak 2004: 3). While UKIP have as yet won no seats in general elections, they fare well in elections to the European Parliament, returning 13 MEPs in 2009 and securing a larger share of the vote than Labour (16.5 per cent for UKIP compared to 15.7 per cent for Labour), marginally increased their seat share from the 2004 EP election. UKIP has benefited from the tendency of the British public to use EP elections as a chance to lodge a protest vote.

Overall, however, UKIP aside, there is a surprising degree of cross-party consensus on major British policy aims in the EU. While in opposition, the Conservatives called for reform of the CAP, maintaining momentum on enlargement, fundamental budgetary reform and pursuit of the deregulatory programme of the Lisbon Agenda. They have called for the EU to take action on cross-border challenges that the UK faces due to globalisation, such as climate change and energy security. All of these were policy priorities identified by Labour and the Liberal Democrats. Many are areas of intergovernmental policy-making that employ non-binding modes of governance. Cross-party consensus on policy goals is countered by deep disagreement on the integration process and the UK's method of engagement with the EU, including institutional reform. While areas of consensus represent important contemporary policy developments in the EU, they garner a relatively low profile in comparison to debates on integration and sovereignty. Intra-party tensions often lead parties to adopt 'rhetorical negativism' to strategically contain anti-integrationists in their party (Aspinwall 2004: 20) while more quietly pursuing constructive engagement out of the glare of the media.

The coalition government and European policy

As part of its agreement the Conservative–Liberal Democrat coalition government issued the declaration that 'Britain should play a leading role in an enlarged European Union, but that no further powers should be transferred to Brussels without a referendum' and claims to be a 'positive participant...playing a strong and positive role with our partners' (Cabinet Office 2010b: 19). The coalition government's policies on Europe have many points of continuity with the policy of the Blair and Brown governments. These include support for enlargement and the coalition government's priorities of addressing through EU membership the challenges of global competitiveness, global warming and global poverty.

Notably, however, the 2010 governing programme does not include Conservative manifesto pledges to repatriate policy competence in social and employment legislation, criminal justice and the Charter of Fundamental Rights – demands which would have required treaty renegotiation at the European level and the unanimous agreement of the other member states. Instead of seeking repatriation of social policy in broad terms, the coalition government has called for action to limit the application of 48-hour maximum work week in the Working Time Directive. This is a pragmatic stance, as the Working Time Directive currently contains a provision, negotiated by the UK and used by several member states, to allow member states to opt out of the 48 hour work week. Reform of this directive (and the opt-out) is on the EU policy agenda and so the British government essentially is committing to defending ground already won. This policy moderation reflects compromise with the pro-European Liberal Democrats. It also reflects the payoff structure of the party's new environment in government. The party's Euroscepticism was less costly in opposition than in government, whereas it now finds itself directly involved in iterative negotiations with other member states in an environment where consensual bargaining and compromise prevails. While a combative stance plays well to a domestic audience with little appetite for further integration, it runs the risk of alienating the other member states and marginalising the UK in the Council, thus jeopardising the UK's longer term European policy goals. With critical policy challenges facing the government in the wake of the global financial crisis, Foreign Secretary William Hague has called the government's policy of constructive engagement with Europe a 'strategic decision' (Parker 2010).

Three Conservative manifesto commitments preserved in the governing programme mark a shift towards a more critical stance on Europe. Three measures are designed to prevent the further transfer of national competences to the EU:

1   The government plans to introduce a United Kingdom Sovereignty Bill to establish that 'ultimate authority remains with Parliament' (Cabinet Office 2010b: 19). Proponents of the bill compare this to principles established by Germany's Federal Constitutional Court that hold that the German constitution is sovereign and EU treaties cannot conflict with it.

2   The government plans to amend the European Communities Act 1972 so that the use of the passerelle, a legislative device that allows the Council of Ministers to speed up decision-making by agreeing to change decision rules to qualified majority voting (QMV), will require approval of the EP through primary legislation. Currently, use of the passerelle requires unanimous consent from member states and national parliaments can prevent the passerelle from being used by launching an objection within six months. Under the new proposal, use of the passerelle would require active endorsement by the UK parliament.

3   The government plans to introduce a 'referendum lock'. This would require that any further treaty that transfers power or competences to the EU would trigger a national referendum, similar to constitutional requirements found in Ireland or Denmark. The Conservatives have found some natural compatibility with the Liberal Democrats on this issue: the Liberal Democrats have called for a referendum on British membership of the EU when treaty reform results in a 'fundamental change in the relationship between the UK and the EU' (Liberal Democrat 2010: 67). The impact of a referendum lock will depend on the details of the proposed legislation – there is a great deal of difference between a referendum triggered by a 'fundamental change' – as sought by the Liberal Democrats – and one triggered by any shift in national and EU competences.

Since forming their coalition, then, the Conservatives have moderated their policies on Europe and toned down their Eurosceptic rhetoric; the

Liberal Democrats have reciprocated by not being so stridently European. Of course, it remains to be seen if the coalition agreement on Europe will hold in the long term. It seems likely to stick, however, in the short to medium term, not least because there is no possibility of the UK moving towards euro membership, there are very few pan-European pressures for further integration in the immediate future, and little if any appetite among the European class for further European institutional reform. The present EU status quo, around which the Conservative–Liberal Democrat coalition is prepared to huddle, is likely to remain the status quo for the medium term.

The UK and the euro

A decade ago, UK membership of the euro seemed a distinct possibility. It is now ruled out for the current parliament and the push for membership is unlikely to be resurrected while the Conservatives remain in power. The government's coalition agreement states that the government will ensure Britain 'does not join or prepare to join the euro in this Parliament' (Cabinet Office 2010: 12). This is in line with the Conservative party's campaign position opposing euro membership, but takes opposition further for the Liberal Democrats, who had ruled out membership in the current parliament on economic grounds yet supported continued preparations for eventual membership. Both parties sought a referendum in the event of British membership of the single currency. The European Union Bill, introduced in parliament in November 2010, would make it necessary for future transfers of sovereignty – such as giving up the British opt-out of the final stage of monetary union and adopting the single currency – to be subject to referendum.

With a Eurosceptic Conservative party in power, even as part of a coalition government, there is little drive for deeper British participation in monetary union. Moreover, economic and political developments now make euro membership less attractive for Britain. Sovereign debt crises have threatened the stability of eurozone economies and have raised questions about the future of the currency itself. Germany has called for treaty reform to strengthen the institutional framework of monetary union, creating a new economic governance framework that would bring closer economic and political integration to the eurozone. Such a framework, which would constrain economic policy-making in the UK, would be difficult to sell to the British public.

Ten years ago, the prospect of British membership of the euro did not seem as distant as it does today. The Blair government came into office in 1997 supportive of membership once the Treasury's five economic tests (convergence, flexibility, investment, preparedness of the financial sector and prospects for growth and employment) were met. In June 2003 the Treasury determined that only one test – the preparedness of and potential benefit to the financial sector – had been met. Events soon overtook the euro debate in the UK. The failed ratification of the Constitutional Treaty and criticism of the government's decision not to hold a referendum on the Lisbon treaty made the prospect of a referendum on euro membership politically unattractive. During Brown's leadership of the Labour government, economic crisis pushed euro membership off the agenda.

The UK and the Lisbon Treaty

The negotiation and ratification of the Treaty of Lisbon, signed by member states in December 2007 and ratified by parliamentary vote in the UK in July 2008, was one of the most contentious developments in European integration in the UK since the Treaty of Maastricht. The Lisbon Treaty, also known as the Reform Treaty, contains institutional and policy reforms designed to streamline the Union's decision-making processes and make an EU of 27 member states more democratic and effective in response to new policy challenges such as internal security, crime and terrorism, globalisation, climate and energy security and foreign policy (see Box 14.1). It replaces the failed Constitutional Treaty, which was stalled by the Dutch and French 'no' votes in ratification referendums in 2005. It is very similar in substance to the Constitutional Treaty, but avoids the language of a constitution. As an amending treaty, it amends but does not replace the existing treaties of the EU. After overcoming its final hurdles of Czech and Irish ratification, the Treaty came into force in December 2009.

Despite cross-party consensus on many of the UK's EU policy objectives, the fierce debate over the Lisbon Treaty illustrates the deep divides in British domestic politics about the *process* of European integration. Debate has cantered on issues of institutional reform, deepening of supranational control, British sovereignty, the protection of UK 'red lines' and the question of whether to put the treaty to a referendum. Britain's support for integration to achieve policy aims – such as completion of the single market – has traditionally been tempered by its reluctance to accept as a necessary trade-off the strengthening of supranational institutions such as the European Parliament or European Commission. The UK prefers an intergovernmental approach, where national governments retain as much control as possible over integration. During debates on the Treaty, the Labour government emphasised the need for reform of EU institutions in order to make them function

---

Box 14.1   The key provisions of the Lisbon Treaty

Extends QMV to over 40 new policy areas, including immigration, asylum and energy policy. This replaces unanimity voting rules, making decision-making more efficient.

The extension of co-decision rules to new policy areas increases the power of the European Parliament.

A simplified QMV formula, to be introduced after 2014, will require a double majority of 55% of member states representing 65% of the EU's population.

A full-time President of the European Union (Herman Van Rompuy) leads the European Council.

Creates a High Representative for Foreign Affairs and Security Policy (Catherine Ashton) and a foreign service.

A Citizens' Initiative will allow citizens to request a policy proposal from the European Commission upon the collection of one million signatures.

National parliaments are given the role of monitoring subsidiarity.

The Charter of Fundamental Rights gains legally binding status.

---

more effectively. It framed its support for the Lisbon Treaty in terms of ensuring the EU is able to pursue policy goals that have some broader support across parties in the UK, particularly intergovernmental policies that arise from the challenges of globalisation. These include migration, climate change, security and defence and counter-terrorism (FCO 2008). Meanwhile, ministers played down the impact of the Lisbon Treaty on institutional reform and the depth of integration, insisting that the treaty was an amending treaty, arguing that the impact of further integration, in the form of extension of QMV, will be 'significantly less' than that under the Single European Act or the Treaty of Maastricht, treaties ratified by previous Conservative governments.

During treaty negotiations, the UK strongly supported institutional reforms that strengthened the intergovernmental leadership of the Union, specifically through the creation of a 'semi-permanent' president of the European Council, appointed for a renewable two and a half year term. This plan, originally developed by Spain, the UK and France, was intended to strengthen the leadership capacity of the intergovernmental Council and was originally opposed by member states who saw this as upsetting the institutional balance in the Union, weakening the supranational Commission and undermining the Community method. The UK also supported the Lisbon Treaty's creation of a High Representative of the Union for Foreign Affairs and Security Policy, appointed by and answerable to the European Council. This reform – in which the more neutral term of 'representative' replaced the state-based language of 'minister' – was one that the British regarded as strengthening the EU capacity for conducting effective Common Foreign and Security Policy, while keeping this role rooted in an intergovernmental institution. By replacing the existing position of Commissioner for External Affairs, it represents a shift of influence away from the Commission to the European Council. Britain's influence in the intergovernmental arena of the Council of Ministers was preserved, if not enhanced by the reweighting of votes in the treaty's QMV formula, which more closely reflects population size than that in the Treaty of Nice.

The Lisbon Treaty debate in the UK: sovereignty and British constitutional tradition

The debate in the UK over the Lisbon Treaty – and the Constitutional Treaty before it – focused on the British government's protection of its so-called 'red-lines', policy areas in which it was keen to preserve national autonomy, as well as the extent to which the treaty creates a 'constitution' that threatens the sovereignty of British parliament. While the UK was generally supportive of a treaty that would enhance the EU's policy effectiveness in areas such as energy security and fighting organised crime, it also defended traditional British 'red lines', seeking and maintaining national control in key areas, including justice and home affairs, tax, foreign policy and defence, and social security. The UK has also retained its special opt-out related to freedom, security and justice policies. This allows the UK, along with Denmark and Ireland, to continue to opt in or opt out of elements of policy in this area.

The centrality of the principle of parliamentary sovereignty in the British political system has heightened concerns that further integration would erode both national sovereignty and the role of parliament. The language of a 'constitution', used for the defunct Constitutional Treaty, played upon fears that the treaty was constructing a European superstate – a legal order comparable to that of a nation-state. The Constitutional Treaty was called a 'constitution' because it replaced previous treaties with a single text. The Lisbon Treaty, by contrast, is an amending treaty, referring to and amending previous treaties but not replacing them.

Dropping the symbolically powerful language of 'constitution' was important for securing support for the Lisbon Treaty. This debate is more semantic than substantive. Legal scholars note that the process of constitutionalisation of the European legal order has been decades in the making, driven by the development of legal doctrine by the European Court of Justice (Weiler 1999). The introduction of a legally binding Charter of Fundamental Rights raised additional concerns about the impact on British parliamentary sovereignty. In response, the UK sought and obtained a special protocol on the Charter of Fundamental Rights to guarantee that the Charter will not be used to strike down UK legislation.

Critics of the reform treaty, ironically, sought to overturn a central feature of British constitutional tradition through calls for ratification of EU treaties by referendum rather than through parliament. This undermines parliamentary sovereignty by creating a competing channel of influence to parliament. The Conservatives called for the Labour government to hold a referendum on the Lisbon Treaty, as the Blair government had pledged for the Constitutional Treaty before the Treaty's failure left the government off the hook for its referendum promise. The Brown government, like most other member state governments, opted instead for parliamentary ratification. The Labour government justified its decision to ratify the Treaty by parliament rather than referendum by arguing that the Lisbon Treaty is a minor amending treaty that is significantly different from the Constitutional Treaty. The UK government ratified the Lisbon Treaty on July 16 2008 after the EU (Amendment) Bill was approved by both houses of parliament. Despite a backbench rebellion by Labour MPs, the government defeated Conservative amendments that called for a referendum on the Treaty. The Liberal Democrats were split on the issue of a referendum. Party leader Nick Clegg used a three-line whip to order MPs to abstain from a vote in the Commons on a Conservative amendment to the bill that would require the government to hold a referendum on the Lisbon Treaty. Clegg argued that the referendum question should be on whether the UK should be in or out of the EU, not on the Treaty, which he argued resulted in minor amendments and not fundamental changes. Fifteen Liberal Democrat MPs rebelled and voted for a referendum. In the Lords, Liberal Democrat peers defied Clegg by voting against a referendum in order to prevent the passage of the Conservative proposal. David Cameron pledged to hold a referendum on ratification of the Lisbon Treaty should the Conservatives win office, but was forced to abandon this pledge (which he had described as a 'cast iron guarantee') when the Treaty was ratified by all member states in November 2009.

The post-ratification implementation of the Treaty led to disappointment for the UK when Tony Blair's candidacy for the new top post of

European Union President was rejected. His candidacy was doomed by his controversial role in the Iraq war and concerns from the Benelux countries that that UK was not sufficiently pro-European to hold the presidency. Instead, the European Council chose former Belgian Prime Minister Herman Van Rompuy. The selection was a result of a deal struck between the two major political groupings in the EU, the social democrats and the centre right, to split the posts between them. The presidency was to go to a candidate from the centre right. Van Rompuy, a low-profile candidate, who was known for effective consensus building in Belgium. Lady Catherine Ashton, a UK Labour Peer, EU Trade Commissioner and an equally low-profile choice, was named as the EU High Representative for Foreign Affairs and Security Policy. Ashton's selection was a consolation prize for the UK, heralded by Gordon Brown as a victory for the UK. Brown was criticised for not switching strategies when support for Blair's candidacy first waned, which could have enabled the UK to lobby for a highly influential economic portfolio in the Commission. David Miliband, Brown's foreign secretary, was mentioned as a possible High Representative in preference to Blair, but chose not to put his name up for consideration. Both Van Rompuy and Ashton were such surprising choices, striking for having a relatively low-profile, that their appointment contrasted with arguments that had been made during negotiations over institutional reforms that the EU needed strong and visible leadership.

Economic crisis, EU budgetary and the Lisbon Strategy for growth

The UK has long been one of the strongest advocates of EU budgetary reform, calling for full reform of the CAP and structural funds and a shift in spending priorities to reflect emerging needs and new policy goals: economic growth, innovation and job creation, climate change policy, free trade and flexible regulation. This budgetary reform agenda is presently very similar to that of the European Commission. This policy leadership role marks a shift from the UK's traditional position as an isolated 'awkward partner' in its fight to secure and retain a budgetary rebate. When the UK joined the EC in 1973, it was the second largest contributor to the EC budget after Germany due to its relatively low level of CAP receipts, despite the fact that at the time, it was one of the least prosperous member states. This led Margaret Thatcher to demand a British budget rebate at Fontainebleau in 1984 worth roughly 66 per cent of the UK's net contribution.

The UK has fought through successive budgetary negotiations to retain its rebate. Changing circumstances have made this increasingly difficult. The UK's relative prosperity in the EU has increased, especially with the accession of central and East European member states. Other countries, including the Netherlands, Sweden, Finland and Austria have joined the group of net budgetary contributors, as the level of CAP expenditures has fallen to about 40 per cent of the EU budget. At the conclusion of the UK presidency of the EU in December 2005, the UK agreed to give up £10.5 billion of its rebate in the 2007–13 budgetary period, putting it at parity with France and Italy in terms of net contributions. The rebate does not apply to EU expenditures on development in Central and Eastern Europe, and so the deal supported economic development in the newer member states and upheld the principle that the EU budget should transfer funding to the poorest member states.

The UK used negotiations over the British rebate as a bargaining tool in a broader effort to secure fundamental reform of the EU's finances. It agreed to renegotiate its rebate in return for a commitment by the Commission to hold a 2008 budgetary review on the 2007–13 financial framework, with the goal of shifting budgetary priorities away from the agricultural spending and towards the Lisbon priorities. Fundamental budgetary reform is crucial for the success of the UK's EU policy agenda, including enlargement, the Lisbon process, economic development in Central and East Europe and reform of the CAP, a policy it views as wasteful and potentially threatening to its free trade agenda through trade-distorting subsidies.

In the budget review the UK called for radical reform of the budget to reflect current priorities, including the Lisbon Agenda for growth and development, climate change and the Millennium Development Goals; reform of the CAP and cohesion spending to reduce 'wasted' subsidies that chiefly benefit rich member states, and the application of more stringent principles of budgetary oversight (HM Treasury 2008). While the significance and practical impact of the budget review has been downplayed by member states such as France, the UK presented it as an important step towards fundamental reform of EU budgetary priorities and of the CAP (Begg 2007: 1).

The global financial crisis, regulatory reform and eurozone debt

The global financial crisis, triggered in 2006 to 2008 by the collapse of the real estate bubble and subsequent failure of financial institutions saddled with toxic assets, has pushed regulation of the financial services industry high on the EU's agenda. This policy is of great importance for the UK, as a global financial services centre, but also one with a high potential for intra-EU division. Responses to the financial crisis have highlighted divisions between the UK, who, together with the US, urged greater fiscal stimulus spending and other member states, especially France and Germany, who instead called for tighter global financial regulation. The UK's position on financial services regulation differs widely from its European partners. Labour was – and now the Conservative–Liberal Democrat coalition is – determined to prevent such regulation from undermining its financial services industry. The European Commission has proposed a package of reforms that would tighten financial supervision in Europe and the regulation of banks, financial markets – including hedge funds and private equity – and insurance companies. The UK wants to see stronger safeguards to prevent EU interference in national financial affairs and assurance that national governments will not be forced to spend taxpayer money on bailouts.

The Greek, Portuguese and Irish debt crisis – which also threatened Spain and Italy – has also revitalised a longstanding policy tension between the UK and other member states (notably France). As a member state outside the eurozone, the UK's contribution to the 750 billion euros stabilisation package agreed by the EU and the International Monetary Fund (IMF) is limited. However, the debt crisis also led to demands for a tightening of fiscal discipline, stricter supervision of adherence to stability and growth pact requirements for eurozone members and closer economic coordination among all member states. This has reignited old tensions between the British version of voluntary economic coordination through economic 'governance' and the French approach of more interventionist economic 'government' (see Hopkin and Wincott 2006). The UK has rejected binding measures in economic coordination and will continue to object to peer review of national budgets before budgets are submitted to national parliaments and binding measures that would force national budget revisions.

The Lisbon Strategy and social policy

The UK has emerged as an influential policy leader in the Lisbon Strategy for growth (no relation to the Lisbon Treaty) and is no longer isolated and excluded in social policy. In these areas the EU employs non-binding, intergovernmental methods, a mode of governance favoured by the UK. These policy areas also illustrate the argument that there is more cross-party agreement on Europe than first appears. While sharp disagreement persists between (and sometimes within) parties on EU constitutional matters, method of engagement, institutional reform, symbolic politics, institutional reform and sovereignty, there is general consensus on many major policy priorities.

The 2000 Lisbon Strategy, which emphasises economic growth, flexibility and competitiveness, and its successor, the EU 2020 strategy for jobs and growth, launched in 2010, are major EU policy initiatives that have received strong British support. They are representative of the UK's long-time pursuit of gains from market integration and the general British preference for non-binding 'soft law' policy tools. While there is a general degree of cross-party consensus in the UK on the deregulatory agenda of the Lisbon Strategy, there is disagreement about how to balance this with social market elements. On the left, trade unions and social non-governmental organisations (NGOs) are critical of the 'hollow core' of EU social policy and of the British government's attempts to curtail the application of binding EU social policy measures, for example through its opt-out of the Working Time Directive. On the right, Eurosceptics are critical of European-level social policy.

The Lisbon Strategy (also known as the Lisbon Agenda), set the aim of making Europe 'the most dynamic and competitive knowledge-based economy in the world' by 2010 (see Box 14.2).

The Lisbon Strategy focused on growth, flexibility and competitiveness and emphasised investment in research and development and the information society. It also incorporated a social policy dimension, with a focus on social exclusion, addressed through an emphasis on training and employment. In March 2010 the EU adopted a new statement, EU

Box 14.2   The Lisbon Strategy

This ten-year programme, aimed at revitalising growth and sustainable development, identified a 'new strategic goal for the next decade' enabling the EU 'to become the most competitive and dynamic knowledge-based economy in the world, capable of sustainable economic growth with more and better jobs and greater social cohesion'. Lisbon embraced the following specific targets:

- an overall employment rate of 70% by 2010;
- an employment rate for women of over 60%;
- an employment rate of 50% among older workers; and
- annual economic growth around 3%.

Through a range of policies, including a sound macroeconomic policy mix conducive to high growth, completing the internal market, investing in people and combating social exclusion, the EU pledged to aim for high growth and full employment within the European single market in a society accommodating the personal choices of women and men.

Box 14.3   The EU 2020 Strategy

In March 2010, the European Council agreed the EU 2020 to update the Lisbon Strategy. Developed in the wake of the global financial crisis, it focuses on debt reduction, macroeconomic stability, growth and employment. The member states adopted the following 'headline goals' for the year 2020:

- an employment rate of 75% for women and men aged 20–64;
- an increase in research and development to 3% of GDP;
- a reduction of greenhouse gas emissions by 20% of 1990 levels (and possibly by 30% of 1990 levels in the event of commitment by other developed countries), an increase in the share of renewable energy to 20% of consumption levels and an increase in overall energy efficiency by 20% ; and
- a reduction in secondary education drop-out rates and an increase in tertiary education.

Member states adopt their own targets in line with these EU goals and create peer-reviewed National Reform Programmes.

2020 (see Box 14.3), which updated Lisbon and set out a framework for Europe's social market economy for the twenty-first century demonstrating how the EU thought Europe would emerge stronger from the economic crisis by producing a smart, sustainable and inclusive economy delivering high levels of employment, productivity and social cohesion.

Social policy under Lisbon and EU 2020 is framed in terms of social integration and is closely related to goals of labour market participation and skills training. To achieve these objectives, which are areas of national competence, the strategy uses a non-binding governance method that involves the development of peer-reviewed national action plans. This results in national-level measures with a limited EU role. EU 2020 proposals have sought to improve national coordination measures in response to disappointing economic growth outcomes.

With its emphasis on economic growth and competitiveness, the Lisbon Strategy is market centred and broadly compatible with a deregulatory neo-liberal model. Its project of non-binding policy coordination has occurred alongside a deregulatory project in the EU to create freer markets in goods and services, labour and capital using binding legislation. This market emphasis was strengthened in March 2005, when a mid-term review of the Lisbon process by the European Commission led to a reorientation of Lisbon to growth and employment. Opponents of this, including the European Parliament, social NGOs and trade unions, argued that the social policy component became secondary to market integration policy goals (Daly 2006: 471).

The British position on the Lisbon Strategy and social policy

The UK has long supported the market-creating activities that underpin the economic agenda of the Lisbon Strategy. In contrast, British support for its social policy component represents a gradual change in the UK's engagement with EU social policy. While the UK initially opted out of key EU social policy provisions in the early 1990s, the Lisbon Strategy represents an EU social policy initiative in which it has exercised policy-shaping influence.

Its policies have focused on training and education rather than social integration and redistributive activities. Its policy aims of targeting poverty and social exclusion were compatible with those of the Labour government, which in 1997 had introduced a Social Exclusion Unit to tackle these issues (Armstrong 2006). Tony Blair introduced talks on the European social model during the British presidency, arguing that the single market must be accompanied by social policy. The Lisbon Strategy created a non-threatening European social policy model because it was market-supporting, employed non-binding methods of governance and left the national level as the primary site of policy formulation.

The movement of the UK from a marginalised outsider to active participant in EU social policy under the Lisbon Strategy does not reflect a radical shift in the British position on EU social policy so much as it indicates that social policy as developed in the Lisbon Strategy was more compatible with British policy aims than social policy developed during the Delors era. The UK has continued to oppose binding social policy measures that it views as constraining national social policy formulation. In negotiations on the Lisbon Treaty, the government fought to retain its 'red lines' on labour, social legislation, social security and taxation. When selling the treaty to the British public, the government emphasised that the social policy 'emergency brake' in the Lisbon Treaty effectively gives the UK a veto on legislation that could potentially affect the social security system. In the spring of 2009, the government fought to retain its opt-out on the Working Time Directive, arguing that preserving flexibility for businesses and workers was crucial during a recession, and that the directive was unworkable for the NHS. British trade unions, the European Parliament and Commission hoped to see an end to the Working Time opt-out.

Such support for the market liberalising reforms of the Lisbon Strategy and its emphasis on competition and growth pit the UK against European pressure and interest groups, the European Parliament and those member states, such as France, who favour a stronger social market orientation in the EU. This political cleavage has emerged in debates over the future direction of the EU. The 'no' vote in the 2005 referendum in France on the Constitutional Treaty was partly due to fears by French voters that the Treaty represented a neo-liberal turn for the EU. The Lisbon Treaty represents a swing of the pendulum in the other direction. At the request of French president Nicolas Sarkozy, the reference to 'free and undistorted competition' in the EU was removed from the main treaty text on the objectives of the EU and relegated to a protocol on the internal market. Meanwhile, the treaty still contains 'full employment and social progress' as objectives in its main text. The impact of this development on competition policy may be minimal as the protocol is a legally binding instrument, but it represents a symbolic victory for the French and for those who seek to forge a stronger social element in the EU. This could pose a challenge for Britain in the future and provoke stronger domestic debate on EU social policy.

EU enlargement

The UK has been a traditional supporter of enlargement and was, together with Germany, Austria and the Nordic countries, one of the strongest drivers of eastward enlargement in 2004 and 2007 and is one of the strongest proponents of enlargement to include Turkey and the Western Balkans. Enlargement is also a policy area in which we find a broad consensus across political parties in the UK. The UK's support for enlargement has been based on a general preference for 'widening' over 'deepening'. Resistance to 'widening', enlarging the EU, which has often come from France, is linked to concerns that enlarging the Union will prevent 'deepening' or further integration, due to a wider and more diverse membership, which makes unanimous agreement more difficult to secure. For the UK, a member state that has long been sceptical about further deepening of integration, this has been a welcome impact of enlargement. Widening also makes internal coalitions more complex, introducing opportunities for the UK's role in the EU. The eastern accession brought a number of new member states into the Union that embrace market liberal ideologies. As the number of member states has increased (whose working language is English rather than French) it brings both a culture shift to the workings of EU institutions and a dilution of French leadership of the Union, enhancing the potential role for the United Kingdom. It also brings the possibility of new policy coalitions favourable to the UK. In a speech on the future of Europe in Oxford in February 2006, Tony Blair said 'the new members are themselves the product of a history that impels them towards a Europe that is open, free, Atlanticist and ready, willing and able to compete. Not for nothing have they been Britain's allies in the political and economic arguments'. This support for enlargement is found across party lines in the UK.

The UK has welcomed enlargement for its economic benefits of increased trade and market access, and promotion of liberalising economic reforms. Another major benefit of enlargement for the UK is its security benefits. The accession process and eventual membership promotes regional stability, political and economic transformation. (The government argues that the 2004/7 enlargements, as with the accessions of Greece, Spain and Portugal, have promoted political transformation.) The Foreign Office refers to enlargement as the 'EU's most effective "soft" power to foster political and economic reform in candidate countries' (FCO 2007). For the UK, both Labour, the Conservatives and the Liberal Democrats regard enlargement as an important political tool to secure democratic stability, security and economic growth in the region, as well as to maximise the gains from UK membership through access to a larger market. The UK has linked its budgetary reform strategy to its support for an effective enlargement policy through its call to focus cohesion funds on the least-prosperous states.

Despite broad British support for enlargement, the resulting free movement of workers with the EU has created tension in the UK. Workers from other EU member states working in the UK outnumber British workers in other EU member states. The UK received an influx of workers from the new member states, particularly Poland, following the eastward enlargement of 2004. While Gordon Brown pledged at the 2007 Labour party conference to create 'British jobs for British workers', firms operating in the UK have exercised their right to recruit workers from other member states. In January 2009 a series of wildcat strikes spread across refineries and power stations in Britain as workers protested the awarding of a construction contract at a North Lincolnshire oil refinery to an Italian firm, which used its predominantly Italian and Portuguese workforce for the job.

British support for future enlargement in Turkey, Croatia, West Balkans

Enlargement, and particularly getting accession negotiations under way with Turkey was a key priority of the UK Presidency of the European Union in the latter part of 2005. However, French and Dutch 'no' votes on the constitutional treaty in May 2005 placed constraints on pursuit of these aims – stalling institutional reforms to the Union also stalled enlargement prospects. The EU was left in a 'period of reflection'. 'Enlargement fatigue' and turning of public opinion in other member states slowed down momentum for enlargement to Turkey and the Western Balkans.

Nevertheless, the UK played an important leadership role advancing the enlargement agenda. During its presidency, membership negotiations with Turkey and Croatia were opened in October 2005 and Macedonia was granted candidate status. Accession negotiations with Croatia are now at an advanced stage and are expected to be completed by the end of 2009 or early 2010. The UK is also a strong supporter of enlargement in the Western Balkans, where prospective candidate countries include Albania, Bosnia and Herzegovina, Montenegro, Serbia, Kosovo (under UN Security Council resolution 1244). Enlargement is viewed as a logical complement to the policy goals served by EU involvement in peacekeeping in the region (peacekeeping was transferred from NATO to the EU in Bosnia Herzegovina in 2005). The UK public is generally favourable towards Turkish membership of the EU if it complies with accession conditions. Support in the UK is higher than average support across the EU25. Prime minister Cameron fully supports Turkey's accession. Similarly, the British public is more supportive of enlargement to the Western Balkans than their counterparts in other large member states such as Germany, Italy and Austria. While not sharing the strong support of the major political parties for enlargement, a greater percentage of the British public supports Western Balkan enlargement than opposes it (Eurobarometer 255).

British policy is to maintain momentum in the enlargement process, which it argues is important for achieving political and economic reform and regional security. This includes the pre-accession policy framework. The Stabilisation and Association Process is an EU policy framework designed to help these countries make the necessary economic and political reforms for Union membership. The UK also maintains bilateral aid programs to support the enlargement process. The Foreign and Commonwealth Office operates a Global Opportunities Fund and Twinning projects that aim to prepare candidate countries for enlargement. The UK–Croatia Strategic Partnership provides £600,000 funding.

Britain's enlargement agenda has been frustrated by growing 'enlargement fatigue' among the other member states. Germany, a strong supporter of the eastward enlargement, now questions the EU's capacity to absorb new member states. With unanimity required from member states for accession to occur, it is looking increasingly unlikely that enlargement will proceed smoothly beyond the accession of Croatia. The

UK position, of ensuring an enlargement process in which the EU main- tains a credible promise of membership – is becoming more margin- alised. German Chancellor Angela Merkel has called for the EU to offer a 'privileged partnership' instead of full membership status to the Western Balkan states. The Austrian government and its public – once champions of eastward enlargement – are now firmly opposed to allowing more members in the club, especially Turkey. French President Nicolas Sarkozy is opposed to Turkish membership of the Union and unless the French constitution is amended, French voters will have to approve its membership in a referendum.

While the British government scored a major victory during the UK presidency through launching membership talks with Turkey, it also conceded some ground on the terms of further enlargement in the Western Balkans where the presidency conclusions called for the 'absorption capacity' of the Union to be taken into account when considering future enlargement. This represents a significant shift in the terms of the enlargement debate. In the past, enlargement has been justified on the basis of candidate states meeting the accession criteria and not on the willingness of the EU to absorb their membership. Compared with the Copenhagen Criteria set out in Article 49 of the Treaty on European Union (the Maastricht Treaty), which outline the political and economic conditions and adoption of the *acquis commu- nautaire* that candidate countries must meet, the 'absorption capacity' of the Union is rather vague and makes enlargement a much more subjective and political decision. The UK has been critical of this policy development, arguing that it threatens the credibility of the promise of future membership, which in turn may jeopardise the effectiveness of the enlargement strategy for securing real political and economic reforms. In its 2007 strategy for European policy, the Foreign Office has called for these accession negotiations to continue and warned that failure of the EU to maintain a credible offer of eventual membership would damage the EU and hinder regional stability.

British support for EU neighbourhood policy

The British government has been a strong supporter of the develop- ment of the European Neighbourhood Policy (ENP), a framework for strengthening political and economic relationships with neighbouring countries. These include the Euromed countries (Algeria, Egypt, Israel, Jordan, Lebanon, Libya, Morocco, Palestinian Authority, Syria, Tunisia) and Eastern regions (Armenia, Azerbaijan, Belarus, Georgia, Moldova and Ukraine). For the EU, the neighbourhood policy is a capacity-building project used to promote dialogue and advance democracy, human rights and good governance. It contributes to a larger goal of promoting peace and stability in the region. Following the crisis in Georgia in summer 2008 and gas crisis in winter 2008/9, the EU introduced the 'Eastern Partnership' to bring neighbouring Eastern countries closer to the EU. In opposition the Conservatives supported the neighbourhood policy and in the House of Commons then Shadow Foreign Secretary William Hague has called for the EU to go even further and not only extend ties on the condition of democratic reforms, but to also accept the eventual 'European aspirations' of the Eastern regions (Hansard, 9 December 2008).

Conclusion

While Tony Blair may not have succeeded in placing Britain at the 'heart' of Europe, the UK has emerged as influential in shaping both institutional reforms and policy development. Despite its strident Euroscepticism and policy positions, particularly on budgetary issues, which often put it at odds with other member states, the UK is no longer an awkward isolationist. While unable to deliver the fundamental CAP and budgetary reform it sought, the UK has been notably influential on a number of other fronts. Over the past decade, the UK has been influential in promoting institutional reforms to strengthen the intergovernmental framework of the Union, and forming effective alliances with France and Spain to do so. These reforms, reflected in the provisions of the Constitutional and Lisbon Treaties, allow the UK to engage with the EU in the intergovernmental governance mode that it prefers.

Finally, at that same time as domestic political opposition to further integration intensified, the Labour government pursued a set of policy aims that enjoyed a relatively high degree of consensus across party lines. The Conservatives may sometimes loudly speak up for Euroscepticism (and have opposed the Reform Treaty), but under Labour the UK remained a powerful but sometimes reluctant EU member, one preferring an intergovernmental approach which emphasised a strong role for national governments in European-level decision-making and opposing a 'federalist' vision for Europe, which seeks closer political union and a more powerful role for European institutions. This established UK approach, in spite of the pro-European Liberal Democrats having formed a coalition with the less European Conservatives, can be expected to continue, particularly when the EU lacks the political will and, presently, the economic means to pursue a more integrationist agenda. It may well be that, as EU pressures for 'ever closer union' have ebbed, the UK's coalition government will not need to make use of its proposed 'referendum lock' – a mechanism triggering a UK national referendum should any further treaty transfer more power or competences to the EU. If that proves to be the case, a status quo may well have been achieved.

Chapter 15

Security and Surveillance in Britain

RICHARD J. ALDRICH AND ANTONY FIELD

Major events, such as the terrorist attacks of 11 September 2001 (9/11) and 7 July 2005 (7/7), have had significant implications for the deployment of both military power and what Michael Herman has called 'intelligence power' (Herman 1996). In common with other states, the UK has been confronted by threats from terrorism, nuclear proliferation, intrastate war and transnational organised crime that stretch across national borders to undermine the stability of the international system. The interplay between the local and the global has become increasingly apparent in recent years. Seemingly distant global security threats have required a focused local response, whilst emerging domestic security problems have necessitated international action. Indeed, we now live in an era in which we can talk, perhaps for the first time, of 'the global politics of domestic security'. The ability to identify and pre-empt security threats through the careful collection and analysis of intelligence, together with 'forward borders', has assumed increasing importance.

Over the last few years, new strategies, policies and capabilities have been developed in pursuit of this goal. However, in the process of adjusting to the new security environment, uncomfortable questions have been raised about the legitimacy of intelligence activity. The distinction between lightly regulated foreign intelligence gathering and more constrained domestic activity has become increasingly thin. A great deal of attention has been paid by MPs and human rights organisations to the overseas actions of UK security and intelligence agencies, together with their allies, in the pursuit of achieving security at home. There is an active and ongoing debate about norms and traditions governing intelligence activity in a liberal democratic setting. Globalisation ensures that there are innumerable points at which current political debates about domestic security intersect with foreign and defence policy. One of the trends this chapter will focus on is the way in which globalised threats tend to encourage a convergence of practices among allied intelligence and security agencies (Svendsen 2009). For over a decade, the United States pondered whether it should develop a UK-style domestic intelligence organisation (MI5). Here we argue that the UK is actually adopting something that looks not unlike the FBI. We are seeing the emergence of a national counter-terrorism force that overlaps with 'special operations' against organised crime. Those attempting to manage a rapidly expanding UK security apparatus have produced a new form of 'high policing' that is somewhat detached from traditional modes of local police accountability, raising complex constitutional issues. Rapidly technological development has also been an important driver of change. Accordingly, the new Cameron government that began its work in May 2010 faces significant choices in the realm of security and surveillance over the next five years. Striking a balance between security, liberty and accountability will continue to present a major challenge for the UK government.

Terrorism and international security

The attacks on America on 9/11 pushed terrorism to the top of the security agenda on both sides of the Atlantic. In the course of a single morning, a group of Al Qaeda terrorists executed a series of audacious airline hijackings inside US borders and turned the planes into guided weapons. The available intelligence at the time indicated that the leadership of the Al Qaeda organisation were based in Afghanistan. Within weeks the USA and its allies had launched strikes against Al Qaeda strongholds in the country, then launched a full-blown invasion with the aim of eliminating Al Qaeda and removing the Taliban regime that was harbouring the organisation. This military invasion of Afghanistan was accompanied by a plethora of covert actions against Al Qaeda across the globe with the aim of reducing the capacity of the organisation to develop further plots. Despite these efforts a large number of Al Qaeda members remained active in many different countries. In the years that followed, the remnants of the network reconstituted and managed to execute several high-profile attacks, including a double bombing in Istanbul on 20 November 2003 that targeted a leading British bank and the British Consulate-General. The senior British diplomat in the city, Roger Short, was killed along with 30 other people. The following year, the bombing of Madrid killed 191 people and wounded 1,800.

In light of these events, anxieties grew about the possibility of attacks in the UK. On 7/7, these concerns proved well founded when a group of British nationals with links to the Al Qaeda organisation perpetrated attacks against the London transport infrastructure. Three of the men succeeded in detonating suicide bombs on the London underground and a fourth triggered his device on a London bus. In the biggest attack on UK soil, 52 people were killed and over 700 were injured. A fortnight later, an almost identical plot by another home-grown group was only foiled when their home-made explosives failed to detonate. Security professionals were stunned by how little they apparently knew about the terrorist plots that were being fermented within the UK. The intelligence agencies had to confront the fact that there were conspiracies developing amongst UK nationals of which they had no knowledge and that the scale of threat was to some extent unknown. This would lead to a step-change in security activity, especially covert surveillance and intelligence gathering.

Subsequent investigations into the 7/7 bombings in London revealed the involvement of both domestic and foreign terrorists. Although the group had received a certain degree of support from extremists outside the country, much of the preparation for the attack had taken place at a local level. The leaders of the group were British citizens who had been raised and educated in Yorkshire and their radicalisation seems to have occurred mainly within the UK. The attacks were financed by a loan from a local bank and the money was used to purchase the components for improvised explosive devices. These were assembled in a flat in Leeds. Yet there was also an international component to the plot. The leadership of the cell had travelled abroad to meet with extremist groups in Pakistan and had spent time in terrorist training camps in the region. They had apparently maintained contact with overseas figures via the internet and had researched bomb-making techniques on the web. Significantly, after the attacks took place, a foreign terrorist group released video footage of the bombers justifying their actions in the context of the British presence in Iraq and calling on others to take up the fight. The attacks showed that it was becoming increasingly tenuous to speak of 'domestic' terrorism as if it was isolated from overseas groups, global security problems or indeed UK foreign policy.

A similar pattern was revealed by the 'airline plot' targeted on Heathrow in August 2006. This was a failed attempt to detonate improvised liquid-based explosive devices onboard several United Airlines aircraft travelling from London to the east coast of the United States. Again, these plots involved local extremists linking up with overseas terrorist groups. Whilst much of the preparation for the attacks had again taken place on a local level, there was also some external support and encouragement. Crucially, some of the main players in the plot had made visits to overseas camps and they had apparently maintained contact with foreign extremists via the internet. The connection between the local and global was apparent for all to see, with particular countries, including Pakistan and the Yemen, emerging as areas of special concern.

UK counter-terrorism strategy

The United Kingdom's overarching counter-terrorism strategy is referred to as 'CONTEST' and it clearly reflects the changing security landscape of the post 9/11 world. It was developed in the wake of the 9/11 terrorist attacks and was first made public during 2003. The main architect of the CONTEST strategy was Sir David Omand, the Intelligence and Security Coordinator in the Cabinet Office at the time. Its importance redoubled in 2005 when the European Union drew heavily on CONTEST in designing its own counter-terrorism strategy. Despite being revised and expanded in both 2006 and 2009, its overall purpose has remained largely unchanged. Now referred to as CONTEST II, it seeks to develop a fourfold approach that simultaneously contributes to reducing the threat to the UK from international terrorism and also allows life to continue normally – an aspiration often articulated to the British public as 'be alert not alarmed' (see Box 15.1). The strategy is designed to gain purchase on all aspects of the terrorist cycle and the main pillars of this approach are 'Prevent', 'Pursue', 'Protect' and 'Prepare'. The CONTEST II strategy aims to 'prevent' people from becoming radicalised; 'pursue' terrorist groups and disrupt their operations; 'protect' vulnerable locations from attack; and 'prepare' the emergency response to terrorist incidents (Hennessy 2007).

Significantly, CONTEST II has an explicitly global orientation. The overall purpose of the strategy is to reduce the risk to the United Kingdom and its interests overseas from international terrorism (Ormond 2009). It recognises that terrorism is both a domestic and international problem that requires an appropriately joined up response. The confluence of foreign and domestic security eventually manifested itself in the vast new Office of Security and Counter-Terrorism (OSCT) that was created within the Home Office in March 2007. OSCT has taken over the traditional role of the Cabinet Office as the primary coordinating mechanism for counter-terrorism policy. In the immediate aftermath of the 9/11 attacks this task had initially been taken up by Sir David Omand, who occupied the long-standing post of Coordinator of Intelligence and Security within the Cabinet Office – a role that had been expanded to include Resilience (Omand 2004). Following his departure in April 2005, there was a gradual shift of gravity in favour of the Home Office. Dr John Reid, briefly Home Secretary between May 2006 and May 2007, was determined that the Home Office would take ownership of UK counter-terrorism. New opportunities for this emerged with the radical restructuring of the Home Office, which became re-focused on security issues after the removal of many of its legal functions to constitute the newly created Ministry of Justice. Senior ministers now

Box 15.1   The four strands of the CONTEST II Strategy 2009

- **Prevent: to stop people becoming terrorists or violent extremists**
  Attempting to reduce the threat of international terrorism by reducing radicalisation of individuals. This encompasses deterring those who incite and organise terrorism and waging a campaign to counter ideologies that are thought to incite terrorism.
- **Pursue: to stop terrorist attacks**
  The active pursuit of terrorists posing a threat to the UK and its interests through intelligence collection and analysis, and disruption (especially through prosecutions). A key aspect of this is increased international cooperation.
- **Protect: to strengthen protection against terrorist attacks**
  This involves the improvement of physical security and procedures. This means not only the strengthening of borders and the protection of government buildings and public places, but also increased resilience for all kinds of national infrastructure.
- **Prepare: where an attack cannot be stopped to mitigate impact**
  This requires a constant horizon scanning activity designed to evaluate vulnerability, investment to improve response capabilities by the emergency services along with regular exercises to normalise reaction to emergency.

portrayed the Home Office as the natural place for UK's core counter-terrorism capacity. Within Whitehall the new OSCT was put forward as the lynchpin of the British response and its size was quickly expanded to over 500 permanent staff. If CONTEST II was the overarching counter-terrorism strategy of the UK, then the OSCT was viewed as the primary vehicle for managing that strategy. Accordingly, the new OSCT was organised into a number of different directorates, each with responsibility for a particular aspect of CONTEST. OSCT is headed by Charles Farr, a diplomat with considerable experience of intelligence and counter-terrorism (see Box 15.2).

Crucially, the OSCT was not only given responsibility for domestic counter-terrorism matters, but has also been accorded a major role in developing overseas counter-terrorism policy. In this respect, partnership between the Home Office and the Foreign and Commonwealth Office is seen as essential. The main channel for this cooperative working is the Overseas CONTEST Group (OCG), which has assumed primary responsibility for guiding counter-terrorism efforts abroad. The OSG is chaired by the Foreign and Commonwealth Office and includes a number of other government departments that contribute to the fight against terrorism overseas, including the Ministry of Defence, the Department for International Development, the Department for Transport and the Metropolitan Police Service. It aims to improve the UK's international response to the global terrorist problem and promote cooperation with counter-terrorism partners across the world. In this task the OCG prioritises resources for capacity building, security sector reform and the sharing of best practice in particular countries. Its work is diverse and ranges from attempting to diffuse radicalisation through public diplomacy to monitoring international cooperation on Chemical Biological Radiological and Nuclear (CBRN) problems. The Overseas CONTEST Group acts as a visible symbol of the merging of the domestic and foreign security agenda within Whitehall.

Despite the significant efforts to unify the UK's counter-terrorism strategy there are still some disconnects to be addressed. The most notable of these can be found in the realm of counter-terrorism intelligence. Without question, underpinning the four separate strands of the CONTEST strategy is a reliance on an expanded counter-terrorism intelligence capability. If the government does not receive timely and accurate intelligence, then it will be unable to develop appropriate responses to the terrorism threat. Such intelligence is required not only to identify and disrupt terrorist plots, but also to understand strategic issues such as the sources and drivers of radicalisation. Similarly, the process of securing vulnerable targets and preparing the emergency services to respond to attacks requires a detailed appreciation of the aspirations and capabilities of different terrorist actors. In this context, the overarching challenge for government has been to ensure that there is an adequate connection between intelligence inputs and policy outputs. The successful implementation of CONTEST not only requires the policy making branches of government to be brought together, but it also necessitates effective integration with the wider intelligence community. Unfortunately, recent reforms may actually have served to make the relationship between intelligence producers and policy-makers more complex and problematic.

The intelligence reforms since the 9/11 attacks have led to a plethora of different assessments staffs emerging across Whitehall. While the Cabinet Office has retained the lead in the development of counter-terrorism intelligence, it has seen its influence diminish as a number of additional assessment bodies have been created to supplement its work. The Cabinet Office still houses the community's Intelligence Coordinator and the Central Intelligence Machinery, including the Joint Intelligence Committee (JIC), which continues to carry out the overall assessment of the terrorist threat. However, new assessment institutions have arisen to

---

Box 15.2   The Six Directorates of OSCT in 2010

Director-General: Charles Farr CBE

1 Prevent & RICU (the Research, Information and Communications Unit)
   Responsible for implementing strategies to stop people becoming terrorists or supporting violent extremism; and for the strategic communications to support this. Much of its work is focused on the Internet.
2 Strategy, Planning & Change
   Responsible for setting strategic direction; programme and project management services; corporate services; strategic oversight of Police CT capability and close links with ACPO TAM; and OSCT's secretariat capability.
3 Prepare, Protect, & CBRNE (Chemical, Biological, Radiological, Nuclear Explosives)
   Responsible for implementing strategies on the Protect and Prepare work strands, as well as ensuring that science supports the delivery of counter-terrorism.
4 Law, Security and International
   Responsible for the 'Pursue' policy. It handles OSCT's international engagement with allied security efforts. It also superintends interception and surveillance policy and casework; and oversight of the Security Service.
5 Interception Modernisation Programme (IMP)
   Works with GCHQ and Internet Service Providers to develop a large-scale cross-government programme being delivered out of OSCT. The government claims that IMP will maintain the UK's lawful Interception and Communications Data capability, but the Internet Service Providers claim that it will extend it considerably.
6 OSCT Olympic Safety and Security
   Responsible for producing an integrated security strategy and costed plan with the police, London 2012 organisers and other security providers, which will deliver a safe, secure and resilient Olympics in 2012. This latter function suggests that OSCT will continue to grow in size.

---

challenge the previously dominant voice of the JIC. The two main players are the Joint Terrorism Analysis Centre (JTAC) and the Research Information and Communications Units (RICU), both of which have close ties to the Home Office and the OSCT. These new organisations are solely focused on matters of counter-terrorism, dealing with operational and tactical concerns, along with the broader causes of radicalisation and terrorist recruitment. On a positive note, these bodies have improved intelligence sharing by reaching out to a wider range of government partners. Unfortunately, it is not clear how effectively the Cabinet Office, the JIC, JTAC, RICU and the OSCT have been in encouraging joint working among themselves. Paradoxically, efforts to improve counter-terrorism intelligence may have actually led to a more fractured intelligence community at the highest levels. It is hard to escape the conclusion that the Cabinet Office is losing much of its tradition intelligence coordination function. This is a time-honoured role that stretches back to the pre-war period when the lynch-pin for intelligence community coordination was the Cabinet Secretary. Since 2005 this role has been in decline. The Cabinet Office has suffered the embarrassing failure of SCOPE II, an IT project which it managed, and which was designed to connect up Whitehall and the intelligence agencies providing seamless multilevel access to intelligence in real time. A replacement project is underway, but now managed by SIS and GCHQ rather than the Cabinet Office. Arguably, OSCT now 'owns' much of the UK's security and intelligence activity, having responsibility for MI5, elite police counter-terrorism units and also overseeing the controversial Interception Modernisation Programme. It remains to be seen whether the OSCT will manage to perform any better in this respect and engage effectively with the wider intelligence community

In the field: UK counter-terrorism operations

The problems of coordinating and integrating counter-terrorism operations has been no less taxing than developing strategic policy. As demonstrated by the 7/7 terrorist attacks, the threat of terrorism was dynamic and transnational, incorporating both domestic and international elements. The mantra was moving from the culture of 'Need to Know' that had become embedded during the Cold War, towards a culture of 'Need to Share'. Vigorous shake-ups have not been attractive, since they raise the possibility of the intelligence community going 'offline' while it reforms itself, and thereby losing track of current threats. Accordingly, while some – including Nick Clegg – have suggested merging the UK's three intelligence and security agencies, MI5, GCHQ and the Secret Intelligence Service (SIS) this has not proved to be a practical option. The heads of the three secret services have also stressed the need to maintain their own security through compartmentalisation between the three agencies.

Instead, the British government has opted for the development of an inter-agency 'national counter-terrorism network'. This programme of change had been initiated after the events of 9/11, but was accelerated after the 7/7 terrorist attacks. The expansion and coordination of the intelligence community came to be seen as an essential component of delivering the CONTEST strategy on the ground. It was considered particularly important for the 'Pursue' agenda that was aimed at disrupting terrorist groups and pre-empting their operations. Anxiety about another 7/7 attack ensured that 'Pursue' was given a high priority, while officials puzzled over exactly how to implement the longer-term 'Prevent' strand. The overarching aim was to enable intelligence agencies to share data more effectively and coordinate their operations more closely. Whilst there had always been some degree of cooperation between the main intelligence agencies within the UK, attention was now turned away from London and focused more on the regions. There was also a desire to widen the relationship to encompass private entities such as banks and airlines that hitherto had not considered themselves intelligence gatherers.

Within the UK, the responsibility for domestic counter-terrorism operations has traditionally been shared jointly by the Security Service (MI5) and the Police Service. Over the years, a division of labour has developed between the two organisations, with the Security Service taking primary ownership of intelligence gathering, while the police have focused more on evidence collection. This separation of responsibilities reflects that fact that terrorism is conceptualised throughout Europe as a criminal activity – it is the police who retain the power of arrest, and who respond to intelligence provided by MI5 and other specialist units. This reflects a carefully crafted compromise that any Whitehall official questions at their peril (Kochan 2006). However, while in theory there is a clear separation of functions, in practice there is often a substantial overlap between the roles the two services. Furthermore, at a strategic level, there is considerable coordination between MI5 and the Police Service, particularly regarding the progress of high-profile investigations. Consequently, although MI5 and the Police Service exist as separate entities, the success of counter-terrorism operations often depends on their ability to work together.

Perhaps the most high-profile change within UK security structures has been its massive expansion. MI5 has almost doubled in size over the last decade. In 2008, half their personnel had been with organisation for less than two years. The MI5 headquarters at Thames House near Lambeth Bridge now houses JTAC, along with numerous other joint centres that are run in cooperation with the police, including the National Security Counter-Terrorism Office and the Centre for the Protection of National Infrastructure. These entities are focused on 'hardening' possible targets such as businesses or crowded public places. They also offer advice on the secure storage of chemicals that might be used to make explosives together with pathogens and toxins, and sources of radiation. Many of these activities require significant public engagement and this outward-facing approach is in marked distinction to what went on before (JTAC 2006). Similar increases in personnel have been occurring within the Police Service. In October 2006 then Metropolitan Police Commissioner, Sir Ian Blair, decided to create a unified Counter-Terrorism Command by combining London's Special Branch and Counter-Terrorism elements. Across the UK, there are now some 3,000 police officers involved in counter-terrorism, about half of whom are in the London area. This new national counter-terrorist machinery is run by the Assistant Commissioner for Specialist Operations and the Senior National Coordinator Counter-Terrorism. The Association of Chief Police Officers (ACPO) has taken an important role in the development and funding of Counter-Terrorism Units that correspond to each ACPO region. It gained a new Counter-Terrorist Coordination Centre in 2009 and four of its senior officers work as national coordinators for the police components of CONTEST.

Closer working between MI5 and the Police Service has been encouraged through the development of six shared counter-terrorism hubs in the regions. High-profile terrorist plots in places such as Birmingham and Manchester have underlined the need to enhance the sharing of counter-terrorism intelligence on a regional level and improve the coordination of operations outside of London. To this end, the Security Service has introduced new Regional Stations (RGs) that include representatives from MI5, the military and other intelligence agencies. In a similar fashion, the Police have created a number of elite regional organisations called 'Counter Terrorism Units'. These cover six constabularies in each ACPO region and are in effect directed by the Counter Terrorism Command in London. The RGs and the CTUs have been deliberately collocated, with the aim of promoting inter-agency cooperation. Numbering over a hundred staff, these regional counter-terrorism hubs have been developed in Leeds, Manchester, Birmingham and Reading. There are similar units in Scotland, Wales and Northern Ireland. In addition, slightly smaller Counter Terrorism Intelligence Units (CTIUs), with more emphasis on intelligence rather than investigation, are located near Bristol, Welwyn and Hucknall. Whether the oversight of these mixed regional centres is a matter for Police Authorities or the UK Intelligence and Security Committee is not at all clear.

The deepening level of cooperation been MI5 and the police has raised important questions about the separation of normal policing and national security functions. Recent reforms have seen the gradual emergence of an elite national force engaged in 'high policing' that is quite revolutionary in British terms. Indeed, there is a level of routine cooperation and coordination between intelligence officers, the police and the military that goes beyond anything previously encountered on the UK mainland. This has raised the issue of whether there is a fundamental conflict between the policing expectations of local communities and national government. In recent years, there have been increasing concerns that local policing is being shaped more by the demands of the national counter-terrorism strategy than the interests of local police authorities and police constabularies. Alongside this, there is the worry that deepening the relationship between the police and intelligence agencies will serve to undermine local trust in neighbourhood policing. There is the clear potential for police to become further alienated from ethnic communities if they are simply perceived as 'spies' for intelligence agencies.

In 2009, Parliament's Home Affairs Committee expressed the view that the national counter-terrorism network might amount to an elite police command in its own right. They also wondered whether it was operating without reference to chief constables or indeed the long-standing local police authority mechanism of accountability (HC 212, 2009). These concerns were illustrated by Operation Overt in autumn 2006. This was the counter terrorism operation focused on the Thames Valley Police area following the 'liquid bomb plot' designed to bring down several airliners heading to the United States. The police investigation involved searching 803 acres of woodland near High Wycombe, in an area known as 'The Booker'. Although this was in the Thames Valley Police area, the operation was coordinated by the Counter-Terrorism Command of the Metropolitan Police and MI5. The result was five raids and 24 arrests nationwide. The investigation started in August 2006, and was expected to take around three weeks, but in fact it ran until the end of the year. The scale of the operation was so great that assistance was requested from virtually every force in the country. ACPO itself admits that Operation Overt 'revealed significant areas of weakness'. Even the most senior officers in Thames Valley Police knew little about what was going on 'due to restrictions on information supplied to the Chief Constable by the security services and the MPS [Metropolitan Police Service]'. The vast search initially left Thames Valley to foot a surprise bill of some £7 million out of their routine police authority budget. Meanwhile Thames Valley Police was reduced to subsidiary roles, such as 'scene security' and 'community management'. London officers from Counter-Terrorism Command conducted the raids and arrests, but left Thames Valley to deal with the concern generated within the Muslim community in High Wycombe. Indeed, Thames Valley was given so little information by the counter-terrorist police, that the chief constable had real difficulty in reassuring the local community or responding to media enquiries. Apparently, during the early stages of the operation, Thames Valley police 'received more information from the press and media than from those leading the events' (ACPO 2008: 38–40). Such incidents have done little to reassure critics of the national counter-terrorism network.

Alongside the deepening relationship between the Security Service and the police, there has also been a widening of the domestic counter-terrorism community to encompass new partners. The traditional counter-terrorism relationship between the Security Service and the Police Service has been expanded to include a range of other governmental bodies, such as transport coordinators, local authorities and the NHS. More important has been the effort to connect with private bodies, in many cases by laying a legal duty upon them to cooperate. The most obvious example is Suspicious Activity Reports (SARs) for financial institutions. Banks and building societies are required to report any financial activity over £10,000 that is considered to be unorthodox. This generated over 500,000 SARs in 2009. Although this data needs to be processed, it is an extraordinary windfall of free intelligence collection for the security agencies. Increasingly, the data that security services are interested in is less old-fashioned 'intelligence' and more protected private information to do with travel, finance and other mundane aspects of our lives – all of which is increasingly warehoused by service providers (Omand 2009). As a result, a range of political, social, economic and cultural institutions, both public and private, have to some degree become part-time outworkers of the intelligence services.

Alongside the widening of domestic intelligence cooperation, has been the expansion of international partnerships. The presence of both the CIA and the FBI in the UK has increased in the last decade. Across Europe, security agencies have created a Counter-Terrorist Group to share new expertise and training. Time-honoured traditional intelligence partnerships with intelligence agencies on the continent and across the Atlantic have been supplemented by new relationships with a host of other organisations. The shared threat of terrorism has fostered better intelligence sharing with unlikely partners such as Pakistan, Russia and China. Investigations have revealed that the UK has received intelligence that has been gathered by foreign powers through prohibited methods, such as torture and harsh interrogation. Many feel that the UK government should maintain intelligence sharing arrangements with countries that are known to violate human rights in the collection of intelligence. In these difficult areas, traditional modes of political oversight are increasingly being overtaken by issues of law and regulation.

Surveillance and the Intercept Modernisation Programme

The evolution of the global terrorist threat has led to a fundamental reconsideration of attitudes towards surveillance practices in the United Kingdom. Proposals have been brought forward that enhance the capabilities of intelligence agencies to monitor the domestic population, which considerably blur the established boundaries between foreign and domestic intelligence activity. Traditionally, there have been relatively few limitations placed on the collection of intelligence overseas. Intelligence agencies, such as GCHQ, have been entitled to monitor the communications of foreign governments and people living abroad without much hindrance. The exact opposite can be said of the surveillance of people living within the UK. In the past, domestic monitoring has been constrained by legal restrictions and systems of oversight that prevent the widespread surveillance of the population. Activities like the interception of telephone conversations have had to be justified on a case-by-case basis and this has meant that surveillance operations have normally been targeted at specific suspects or groups, rather than the population at large. However, changes to communications technology – combined with the rise of the global terrorist threat – have led to calls for 'modernisation'. The arguments for this are threefold.

First, the globalisation of communications has created new opportunities for terrorist groups to communicate and interact on a transnational level. Technological advances in mobile phones and the internet have fostered a global communications infrastructure that has made it much easier for terrorists to contact their associates in other countries. Such developments pose new problems for intelligence agencies. For one, the exponential increase in international communications means that the intelligence agencies are literally swamped. Moreover, internet communications are simply much harder to intercept on a technical level. The information that constitutes phone calls and emails is broken into 'packets' and sent across the network by different routes, which makes it very hard to collect actual telephone call content known as an 'intercept'. The problems associated with voice over ISP are particularly worrisome, as it is anticipated that over the next ten years most telephone traffic will move to the internet. Watching internet activity is a growing priority for UK security agencies, since the internet is now thought to be a major vehicle for both radicalisation and for the dissemination of terrorist training. The overarching goal is the seamless tracking and surveillance of terrorist suspects across borders.

Second, there has apparently been a substantial increase in the number of potential terrorist suspects living in the UK and has caused a surge in the demand for targeted surveillance operations against these individuals. It is claimed that there are over 2,000 people who are part of terrorist networks operating in the UK. With each target requiring perhaps 20 people to keep them under 24-hour surveillance, the resources of MI5 and the police have become massively overstretched. Simply put, there are not enough people to do the job adequately, meaning that many suspects cannot be monitored by the conventional methods of human surveillance – following and observing. This has led to demands for the greater use technical methods of intelligence collection, particularly interception and bugging. This type of technical surveillance has helped to plug the intelligence gap surrounding many terrorist suspects. It is argued that this technical approach can enable the intelligence agencies to passively monitor much larger numbers of people and enable them to target their scarce human surveillance teams more effectively the most dangerous individuals.

Third, as a result of high-profile terrorist attacks such as 7/7, the government has become much more risk averse in its approach to surveillance. In the past terrorist suspects would often be left 'in play' with the aim of maximising opportunities to gather intelligence. Active terrorists tend to give off vast amounts of useful information – they contact other associates by telephone and email, transfer money, move about from place to place, and unwittingly reveal safe houses and supply dumps. Once in custody, this flow of intelligence comes to an abrupt end. Even if suspects are successfully interrogated and disclose information, everything they know is soon out of date. Unfortunately, since the 7/7 terrorist attacks it has become increasingly difficult for intelligence agencies to adopt this long-term approach. British operations have moved away from this 'watch and wait' approach towards a regime of 'see and strike' (Svendsen 2009). Once suspects are identified it is now more common to arrest them and raid their premises quickly. There is an increased emphasis on intervening early in order to prevent terrorist plots from developing. More effort has been placed on identifying 'acts preparatory' to terrorism, coupled with taking swift action against those who may be planning violence. Counter-terrorism agencies have become more interested in precursor indications that that someone is heading down the path of violence. This entails monitoring larger groups of people, as opposed to focusing surveillance operations against specific known terrorists.

Over the last decade the government has made a number of key proposals that demonstrate a clear shift towards greater surveillance of the population. Following the 9/11 attacks, the UK attempted to persuade the rest of Europe to shoulder more of the odious burden of legislation to permit wider electronic surveillance of its own citizens. British ministers urged Europe to pass legislation that would require mobile phone companies and internet service providers to retain vast amounts of records relating to personal emails, details of web pages accessed and telephone calls for ten years. This 'communications data' would be made accessible to the police and intelligence services on request. The proposals were denounced by privacy campaigners as one of the most wide-ranging extensions of government security surveillance over private individuals ever contemplated. The main opponent was in fact the internet industry itself, who resisted the plans vehemently, again stressing issues of privacy and business confidentiality. The material in question here is not the content of the call or communication, but the names and addresses of customers, the source and destination of their emails and the addresses of web sites visited. All of this would be available freely to the authorities, since only access to the actual content of emails and telephone calls requires a warrant. In 2006, this measure finally passed into European law and has since become an essential resource for counter-terrorism agencies (Mathieson 2005).

For some UK ministers, this mass retention of data by internet service providers (ISPs) did not go far enough. In 2008 the British government unveiled a new domestic intercept plan of unprecedented proportions. The then Home Secretary Jacqui Smith announced the British government's remarkable Intercept Modernisation Programme (IMP). Costing an estimated £12 billion pounds, this project amounted to a vast surveillance concept that was quite beyond the bounds of anything previously been seen in the UK. Despite the fact that Europe had finally agreed to compel ISPs to retain everyone's past communications data within their own companies, the UK nevertheless proposed to build a vast government-run silo to duplicate essentially the same function. Simply put, the government wished to hold all the data itself. This would entail the recording and storing the details of every telephone call, email, text and instance of web access by each person in the UK. The scheme was initially associated with the innocuously titled Communications Data Bill scheduled for 2009. The stated purpose was bland – to 'allow communications data capabilities for the prevention and detection of crime and protection of national security to keep up with changing technology'. However, Lord Carlile of Berriew, QC, the UK's then independent reviewer of anti-terrorist legislation immediately expressed anxiety about the new government-run database, asserting that: 'As a raw idea it is awful'. He added that it would lead to the authorities undertaking searches 'willy-nilly' and without review (Verkaik and Morris 2008).

In late 2008, growing public hostility to IMP prompted the government to withdraw the bill at the last minute. Instead, government has resolved to advance the plan by stealth. Remarkably, and without any legislation, a pilot scheme at an estimated cost of £2 billion pounds was launched. Indeed, sample 'probes' were established at the facilities of one major fixed line telecom operator and one major mobile phone provider. The British government had always insisted that IMP was merely about maintaining an existing and traditional capability to do interception in a world of rapidly changing technology. However, the reality looked rather different. In April 2009 GCHQ advertised for new senior staff to direct an ambitious programme which it called 'Mastering the Internet'. The sinister title of this project caused alarm and GCHQ was soon forced to issue a public statement denying that it was developing technology to enable the monitoring of all internet use and phone calls, or to target everyone in the UK.

However, in August 2009 government denials that it had ambitions for expanded surveillance met a direct challenge. Britain's own telecommunications firms and ISPs, including British Telecom and Virgin, condemned these plans as an unwarranted intrusion into people's privacy. The very companies that the British government was depending upon to help it to implement the scheme asserted strongly that government officials were not being honest with the public about the vast scale of monitoring that they were planning. It told the government that:

> We view the description of the government's proposals as 'maintaining' the capability as disingenuous: the volume of data the government now proposes [we] should collect and retain will be unprecedented, as is the overall level of intrusion into the privacy of citizenry ... This is a purely political description that serves to win consent by hiding the extent of the proposed extension of powers for the state. (London Internet Exchange 2009)

The UK's ISPs also boggled at the mammoth scale of the private information they were being asked to retain themselves on the telephone and internet use of British citizens. Indeed, they complained that they were 'not aware of any existing equipment' that even would enable them to 'acquire and retain such a wide range of data (Leppard 2009).

What does government want with all this detail? And why did they want to hold it in one place? The answer is quite simply 'data-mining', a practice which now constitutes the most insidious threat to personal liberty. What makes surveillance different in the age of ubiquitous computing and the mobile phone is that our data is never thrown away. Machines routinely store millions of details about our everyday lives and, at some distant point in the future, this can be brought together and searched in the hope of finding patterns. Devices which were introduced to make life more convenient, such as the mobile phone, are also generating a detailed electronic narrative of our lives. In 2009, the British public sent 60 billion text messages, a microscopic account of our personal interactions. A decade ago, such data was discarded by many companies, but with the cost of warehousing data halving every two years – many now choose to retain it. What many governments now wish to do is take this data over and use it to produce a wholly new kind of intelligence (Sommer and Hosein 2009).

Data-mining is the use of computers to comb through unimaginable amounts of information looking for patterns and statistical relationships. It allows governments to search for individuals or groups of people with particular types of behaviour and to profile them as suspicious. Data-mining is as powerful as it is dangerous. It is powerful, because it allows the sifting of titanic amounts of private information, and it is dangerous because it often throws up 'false positives'. In other words, some people will look suspicious because a number of chance activities have coalesced to generate something which a computer thinks is a problem. It also permits social profiling. At present, data-mining is limited because government can only access so much information. However, the appetite is clearly there. Under the Regulation of Investigatory Powers Act 2000 (RIPA), the authorities can go to ISPs or mobile phone companies and ask them to hand over details of the phone, email and internet habits of specific individuals without seeking a warrant. A staggering 504,073 requests were made by the authorities in 2008. Although this is too many requests, it is still 'retail surveillance' because it relates to individual persons. Data-mining is the next step and means wholesale surveillance. For the state, vast reservoirs of person data such as Facebook and Google are now the great prize (Aldrich 2010).

Strangely, while the UK government wants more intelligence from technical sources, it remains reluctant to use this material as 'evidence'. Unlike America, the use of 'intercept' evidence has not historically been deployed in UK courts. Over the last decade a controversy has raged over the controversial matter of 'intercept evidence' – in other words using intelligence derived from eavesdropping on telephone communications in criminal cases. When confronted with the detention without trial of sixteen persons denied asylum on national security grounds in 2002, a committee of privy counsellors reviewed the problem. One of the solutions it recommended was more aggressive criminal prosecution, aided by the use of electronic intercept evidence from telephone calls to secure convictions (Walker 2006). Over the last decade, countless commissions and review boards have sought to change the British convention that forbids the use of telephone intercepts as evidence in court. Each time, the prime minister, home secretary and director of public prosecutions has been in favour, but ultimately the intelligence services have exercised a veto. The major concern has been that the use of intercepts in criminal trials would reveal too much about intelligence collection techniques, potentially nullifying their effectiveness. The Director of GCHQ asserted in 2009 that its use would result in 'a very, very serious blow back to our capability' (ISC 2009: para. 171). Despite the possibility that this sort of evidence might resolve a number of cases that are troubling from a human rights perspective, we are unlikely to see the widespread use of intercept evidence in courts in the UK. This is a paradoxical situation since communications data is playing a growing role in counter-terrorism operations, yet its ability to resolve some of the troubling legal problems and human rights dilemmas associated with counter-terrorism remains weak.

Security and the Cameron government in 2010

In May 2010, UK security policy was confronted with the prospect of radical change. Unexpectedly, the result of the general election was a coalition between the Conservatives and the Liberal Democrats. On many broad aspects of defence and foreign policy there were obvious areas of disagreement that required negotiation, including nuclear weapons and policy toward the European Union. Other subjects, such as Afghanistan, presented a conundrum of a high order, given its direct connection to Anglo-American relations. However, narrower issues of intelligence and counter-terrorism were more straightforward. Over the course of the preceding parliament, both the Conservatives and the Liberal Democrats parties had displayed marked of scepticism when confronted with some of the more elaborate praetorian measures proposed by the Labour government of Gordon Brown. They had been especially critical of what they perceived as expensive technological panaceas that were unlikely to deliver. Both parties had been vocal opponents of emblematic Labour security programmes, including ID cards and the Intercept Modernisation Programme. All this was highlighted in June 2008 by the personal decision of the opposition spokesman on Home Affairs, David Davis, to resign and re-fight his seat on the issue of extended detention for terrorism suspects. In July 2009, David Davis revealed new evidence on the treatment of suspects and accused the government of effectively outsourcing torture by the Pakistani intelligence service, the ISI.

The new Cameron government of 2010 wasted no time in convening a meeting of newly established National Security Council, which it hoped would help to achieve joined-up security. It also confirmed its commitment to civil liberties by appointing Dame Pauline Neville Jones as Minister for Security. A former senior diplomat who had served as chair of the JIC, Neville-Jones was both a seasoned Whitehall operator and also a persistent critic of what she regarded as the Labour government's moral panic and overreaction in the face of terrorism. She had served as Shadow Security Minister since July 2007. Underpinning this was the wider economic context of impending retrenchment. Many new ministers, including the Home Secretary Theresa May, were not convinced that the baroque mechanism of counter-terrorism in the UK was delivering results commensurate with its costs. As if to underline this, the government announced the early scrapping of the ID card programme.

Although the new government was broadly impressed by CONTEST II as an overall counter-terrorism strategy, they pressed Whitehall officials for more emphasis upon coordination between the 'Pursue' and 'Prevent' strands. The incoming Cameron government were convinced that these different activities had often collided in the past, creating public suspicion and mistrust as a result. The previous administration, they insisted, had not only confused tackling violent extremism with other softer activities designed to discourage radicalisation, they had also prioritised the more aggressive 'Pursue' strand by emphasising raids and arrests. From May 2010 there was to be less emphasis on radicalisation as a form of criminality and more stress on addressing community grievances and developing common values. The new policy was to refocus 'Prevent' on supporting those most vulnerable to radicalisation. This meant more resources for counter-radicalisation and de-radicalisation methods. However, exactly what form this intensified 'Prevent' strand would take was not clear, since finding meaningful projects that offered measurable impact had historically proved difficult. Some civil servants were openly sceptical, regarding 'Prevent' as an especially challenging area, not least because many local authorities are wary of it. Counter-terrorism chiefs asked pointed questions about just how many terrorists the new government wanted them to stop watching.

In the summer of 2010 the new government requested a thorough review of counter-terrorism powers by Lord Macdonald of River Glaven, formerly Director of Public Prosecutions. On 27 January 2011, after considering his report, the Home Secretary Theresa May outlined a number of policy changes, including:

- An end to 28 day detention – reverting to 14 days as the standard maximum period that a terrorist suspect can be detained before they are charged or released;
- A reduction in the use of terrorism stop and search powers provided under Section 44 of the Terrorism Act 2000.
- The end to the use of the more intrusive surveillance (RIPA) powers used by local authorities to investigate low level offences and new oversight by magistrates.

- A stronger effort to deport foreign nationals involved in terrorist activities in this country – insofar as this was congruent with human rights obligations;
- The repeal of Control Orders and their replacement with a more focused regime to be known as Terrorism Prevention and Investigation Measures or 'T-PIMs'.

The latter measure was the most controversial. The new T-PIMS quickly became known as 'Control Orders-lite' and were denounced by many as a compromise, although in effect the revised restrictions on movement were similar to those used in the civil justice system. While the police and security agencies were promised greater resources for surveillance to offset the relaxing of detention orders, they have since claimed that they do not have enough personnel to do this. The T-PIMs regime illuminated the awkward trade-off between detention and surveillance.

The other major change planned by the Cameron government was 'a shift in focus to community intelligence'. The new emphasis was upon information from the local community that would allow intervention before law enforcement was needed. There was more emphasis on sharing information about the vulnerability of individuals with community leaders. This sat awkwardly with the established regional CTU hub approach into which so much resource had been poured. The calls of Pauline Neville-Jones for the information in Counter Terrorism Local Profiles to be 'more local' suggested the possibility of a shift back towards the old constabulary-based Special Branches and a decline for the shiny aluminium buildings on remote industrial estates. The new style was to be an avuncular one, based on trust that sought to integrate counter terrorism with neighbourhood policing. The new Security Minister was on record as saying that: 'It is this bottom-up information which will develop truly rich Counter Terrorism Local Profiles' (Neville-Jones 2010). The overall concept was now community-led, allowing individuals to participate in their own security and contribute to it. All these new ideas betokened an administration that was less risk-averse than the last and which asserted that a certain amount of terrorism was perhaps the tariff that a society paid for robust civil liberties. To what extent this phlegmatic approach survives the next major terrorist attack has yet to be seen.

The security agenda of the Cameron government was not only constrained by ideals, but by necessity. The UK intelligence and security community had broadly doubled in size in the decade after the 9/11 attacks in America. Secret intelligence, whether driven by technical activities or human sources is eye-wateringly expensive. Active security measures, such as large numbers of armed police or control orders are even more costly. At the very least, the enthusiasm of the previous administration for large surveillance databases and biometric projects is likely to be curbed because of the consistent failure of IT consultants to deliver. However, Cameron had already signalled his strong support for improving defences against cyber-attacks from countries such as China, and so the new Cyber Security Operations Centre at GCHQ in Cheltenham, which was stood up in September 2009, is one of the few areas likely to see more resources. In October 2010, the government's new Strategic Defence and Security Review used the word 'Cyber' no less than 79 times in just 75 pages. While the value of ongoing activities in Afghanistan and Pakistan was a matter for ongoing revaluation, the chance of further military interventions, for example in the Yemen, was now close to non-existent.

Conclusion

In 2010, the new government embarked on the early stages of a retrenchment of counter-terrorism measures, particularly those centralised in the established intelligence community. Over the last ten years an increasingly global terrorist problem had necessitated a response that crosses the traditional divide between foreign and domestic counter-terrorism. Indeed, at the heart of the UK CONTEST II strategy was an expansive approach towards combating terrorism that envisaged both internal and external efforts. To facilitate this global approach, the UK has pursued the development of joined up policy at a strategic level, stronger physical controls on suspect individuals and the introduction of greatly enhanced surveillance. Whilst such reforms strengthened the United Kingdom's ability to manage the terrorist threat, they also challenged many of the conventions regarding the nature of legitimate intelligence activity. Efforts to join up government departments, improve intelligence cooperation and bring in new partners had brought into question the appropriateness of an expanded security architecture. Similarly, crossing the divide between foreign and domestic intelligence activities has raised the issue of what methods could be tolerated in the pursuit of security at home. The overarching task for the new Cameron government at the end of the decade is to reconcile the demands for greater security with the expectations people have regarding civil rights in a liberal democracy. Admittedly, these are not new issues, but they nevertheless continue to resonate in the current security climate.

Questions remain to be asked about whether the preceding Labour administration successfully managed to strike the right balance in its counter-terrorism agenda. It is not only academics and privacy lobbyists who have been uneasy about the growth of the new counter-terrorism leviathan. In October 2008, the retiring Director of Public Prosecutions, Sir Ken Macdonald, QC (later Lord Macdonald of River Glaven) gave a lecture entitled 'Coming out of the Shadows'. He called for common sense and 'legislative restraint' in the UK approach to security. His concern was less the growth of police powers and more the acceleration of new types of surveillance. He warned that the internet had extended to immense riches of information, knowledge and interconnectivity to individual citizens making our lives immeasurably richer. However, by equal turns, the same technology extends enormous powers to the state which can collect and store a great deal of information about individuals. Understandably, governments will always be under pressure to take action in response to terrorism events. However, it is crucial that policies and approaches to counter-terrorism, intelligence and surveillance are not developed in a vacuum, devoid of engagement with wider political values except 'security'. Otherwise, as Ken Macdonald warns, 'We might end up living with something we can't bear' (CPS 2008).

Macdonald's comments were perceptive, since they identify the two contending explanations for the acceleration of surveillance in our society. The UK security sector has grown at remarkable speed, but what were the drivers? It is hard to ignore the argument for agency here, since so often ministers asserted the need for greater powers, despite the vocal scepticism of both serving and recently retired intelligence and security chiefs (Russell 2008). Others would point to deeper structural explanations that relate to globalisation and technology. The very business of surveillance has changed radically. We have witnessed a dramatic shift away from a world in which a few specialised government agencies handled intelligence towards one in which all of government is involved in a new process of what might be called 'knowledge-intensive security'. Most government departments and most forms of regional and local government have developed security sections and responsibilities. Large companies such as banks and airlines are substantial producers and consumers of intelligence. Even individual citizens are both intelligence producers and consumers since they receive alert states and asked to report suspicious behaviour by their neighbours. Security now involves everybody in a new intelligence ecology within which the basic currency is huge volumes of personal data. The engine of surveillance is not longer the secret state but all of society. The puzzling question for the Cameron government is how this leviathan might deliver accountability and rights, as well as safety and protection (Leigh 2005).

Chapter 16

Britain in the World

ANDREW GAMBLE

In the course of a speech at Fulton, Missouri, in 1946, during which he declared that an iron curtain had descended across the continent of Europe, Winston Churchill set out his view of Britain's place in the world after the convulsions of the Second World War. Britain, he argued, was at the centre of three circles of interest, influence and sentiment: the circle of the Empire, the circle of the English-speaking peoples, and the circle of Europe. In March 2009 Gordon Brown addressed the US Congress in Washington, one of only very few British prime ministers to do so. In the 63 years which had elapsed since Churchill's speech, the Empire had all but disappeared; only a few rocky outposts, mostly in distant oceans, remained. The total population of the remaining British colonies was less than 300,000. In 1946 it had been 700 million. In contrast the other two circles were alive and well, and Britain was ever more deeply embedded in them, but in very different ways. The relationship with the rest of Europe had been transformed by the steady progress towards European integration, and Britain had finally joined the European Community (today's EU) in 1973. The special relationship with the United States had also survived and in spite of ups and downs had flourished as never before, first under Margaret Thatcher and then under Tony Blair. Underlining its importance, Gordon Brown spoke in glowing terms about the special relationship and the importance of the Atlantic relationship to Britain:

> Alliances can wither or be destroyed, but partnerships of purpose are indestructible. Friendships can be shaken, but our friendship is unshakeable. Treaties can be broken, but our partnership is unbreakable and I know there is no power on earth that can ever drive us apart. (Brown 2009)

These sentiments were shared by the new Prime Minister, David Cameron, and his Foreign Secretary, William Hague, who took office in May 2010. These two remaining circles of Europe and Anglo-America increasingly defined Britain's place in the world in 2010, despite some remaining Commonwealth ties. But both were troubled relationships, and Britain was not at ease with either of them, although for different reasons. At the end of three consecutive terms of Labour government Britain seemed no nearer to making relations with Europe its top priority, or with working out a less dependent relationship with the United States. The Iraq war of 2003 still cast its shadow in 2009, with the final withdrawal of British troops making possible the announcement of a full inquiry into the war, when the Chilcot Iraq Inquiry, which opposition parties had long been demanding, was first convened (it is, in early 2011, still in session). Europe remained a difficult issue for leaders of all parties. Scepticism towards the European Union remained strong among MPs, in the media, and in the electorate, and this was reinforced by the eurozone crisis in 2010. In Britain, in the 2009 European Parliament elections, a substantial minority of voters backed parties which were in favour of complete withdrawal. The reasons for this ambivalence towards the two traditional circles in Britain's political class will be explored later in this chapter. First, the changing context of the international state system and world politics in the period since the end of the cold war in 1991 will be outlined. The new Conservative–Liberal Democrat coalition has taken office at a time of great uncertainty in world politics, framed by the financial crash of 2008 and its aftermath, the challenges to the position of the United States, the decline of Europe, and the rise of India and China (Hutton 2008).

From liberal peace to liberal war

For more than 40 years, until the opening of the Berlin Wall in 1989 and the collapse of the Soviet Union in 1991, the key context for thinking about Britain's place in the world was provided by the cold war. The long confrontation between the United States and the Soviet Union shaped everything else. The perception that the Soviet Union constituted a threat to the vital interests of the United States and that it had to be contained became the dominant assumptions in Washington. It finally persuaded the American political class that it had to play a leading role within the world by becoming the global leader for the West, building military alliances, establishing a worldwide military presence, and providing economic and political and ideological support to all countries threatened by communism. During the cold war the international state system had a peculiar bipolar shape, with two superpowers, and their satellites and allies confronting one another. All other questions in international politics tended to become subordinate to this. The two great blocs, the First World of the West and the Second World of the East, competed for the allegiance of other parts of the world, mainly the less developed and underdeveloped, which became known as the Third World.

The end of the cold war and the 'new world order'

The cold war ended with the collapse of the Soviet Union in 1991 (Halliday 2000). Suddenly there was a unipolar world; the other pole had simply imploded. The United States had a military and political dominance which was without parallel. For a moment it faced no significant challenger. There was understandably a feeling of triumphalism that such a complete political and ideological victory had been won over communism, and without a major war being fought. Francis Fukuyama, following Hegel, called it the 'end of history', by which he meant that there no longer any serious alternatives to liberal democracy and free market capitalism as organising principles for modern societies. The values and institutions which the United States and its allies had championed were now universal, and could not be improved upon (Fukuyama 1992). George H. W. Bush, US President between 1989 and 1993, declared that the end of communism meant the creation of a 'new world order'. An era of peace and prosperity was confidently expected.

This euphoria was not to last, but in important respects the period since 1991 has been shaped by the end of the cold war, and the unipolar nature of the international system which succeeded it. The events following September 11, 2001, especially the interventions in Afghanistan and Iraq, those of 2007–8 in the financial markets, and their profound consequences for world politics and the world economy, mean that this period has now ended (Gamble 2009b). The period 1991–2008 increasingly looks like being transitional, between a bipolar international state system and a multipolar one (Anderson *et al.* 2008). To understand those developments correctly, the deeper shifts in the balance of power, and the wider contexts need to be recognised.

The new order which was proclaimed after 1991 was to be an order which was based on the spread of economic globalisation and democracy. It was to be an era of liberal peace, in which the nations of the world would enjoy a peace dividend, and which would celebrate interdependence and the soft power of cultural and ideological persuasion, rather than national sovereignty and the hard power of military and economic coercion. There were many who spoke of the end of the era of the nation-state and the rise of new forms of global and regional governance. As the 1990s progressed however it became clear that many problems, such as the stalemate in the Middle East, were no easier to resolve and that there were new challenges for the international state system, for which it was unprepared. There were numerous local wars, as well as internal conflicts and civil wars, and the breakdown of legitimate government (Kaldor 2007). Failed states and rogue states were identified, the first unable to provide basic security for their citizens, and the second challenging the norms of the new world order established by the United States. The civil war in some of the states of the former Yugoslavia, particularly in Bosnia and in Kosovo, together with the genocide in Rwanda, and the continuing confrontation between Iraq and the United States, created a different mood, and a different policy agenda, in which the case for intervention under certain conditions in the affairs of other nations began to be openly canvassed, to prevent gross abuses of human rights. In this way liberal peace merged imperceptibly into liberal war. The new world order had to be enforced, and those states which flouted its rules, either through intent or incompetence, justified intervention. They had lost the right to preserve their independence (Duffield 2001).

Many people agreed on the principle of intervention to prevent major abuses of human rights. But there was strong disagreement on who had the right to intervene. The Americans and the British increasingly took the view that the UN was too weak in many instances to take the required action, and that partnerships between allies, or 'coalitions of the willing' as it became known under the Bush administration, were necessary in order to carry out UN mandates, even if not precisely authorised by the UN. It was argued strongly by Tony Blair among others that the interdependence of all nations had increased to the point where new rules of engagement were necessary, and the old principle of non-interference in the internal affairs of other sovereign states were no longer sufficient (Cooper 2007).

September 11 and its international impacts

What drove liberal war forward and gave huge momentum to these new doctrines of international engagement was September 11, 2001. The response by the United States to this attack upon its own territory was to announce that the country was once more at war. The enemy however was not another nation-state but a transnational organisation – al-Qaeda – a loose network of terrorist groups united in the opposition to the United States and the West and to most of the ruling governments of the Islamic world (Burke 2007). Most of George Bush's time as president between 2001 and 2009 was dominated by this war on terror and by the interventions in Afghanistan and Iraq, and all the consequences which flowed from them. Throughout this period Britain proved a stalwart ally, more reliable and more committed than any of America's other NATO allies.

September 11, 2001 woke the world from a ten-year reverie, in which for a brief moment the normal security concerns of states had abated somewhat, and dreams of perpetual peace had re-emerged. After that fateful day, continuing up to the present, security has come back to trump other priorities, at the same time exposing the fragility of the new world order of the early 1990s. The international mood perceptibly darkened during the first decade of the twenty-first century, and this was then compounded by the financial crash of 2008. By the end of the decade the talk was not of the end of history, but of the return of history (Kagan 2009), and of the shifting balance of power in international politics. The rise of China, India and Brazil, the new assertiveness of Russia, the continuing enlargement and weakness of the EU, the still powerful Japanese economy, made the return to a multipolar world increasingly probable. The limits of US capacity and will in several fields had become clear, and a renewal of American global leadership required a different approach to the predominantly unilateralist path of the Bush years.

Blair's legacy: foreign and external policy to 2007

Labour won a third consecutive election victory in May 2005, the first time this had happened in the party's history. The majority was considerably reduced, as was the share of the vote, but given the unpopularity of Tony Blair's government, particularly over its foreign policy, and its support for the United States in the invasion of Iraq in 2003, it was remarkable that Labour was still able to win. There have been few post-war British general elections where foreign policy issues played such a large role. The impact of Iraq in particular was substantial. It had already had a major impact on British domestic politics, because the fallout from the invasion had significantly weakened the position of Tony Blair as prime minister, so much so that before the election he had been obliged to announce that if Labour was re-elected he would stand down as party leader and prime minister before the next election (Seldon 2008).

The Iraq war had been popular at first with the public, despite the fact that some 1.5 million people had demonstrated against it in 2003, but the support was not sustained. Once the invasion had triggered a civil war and the collapse of effective government in the country support for Blair's policy rapidly diminished. The failure to find any weapons of mass destruction which for Britain, if not the United States, was the ostensible reason for invading, was deeply damaging to the legitimacy of the war, and led to accusations that the country had been deliberately deceived (Kampfner 2003). Although a number of official enquiries set up by the government indicated otherwise, a large part of the public, and a large part of the Labour party was not convinced. Liberal intellectuals and the liberal media in particular turned against Blair, and this meant that his position steadily grew weaker, enabling his enemies in the party to undermine him, obliging Blair to stand down earlier than he had intended and to be replaced by Gordon Brown in 2007.

Blair's position was also made more difficult by the London bombings in July 2005. Although this was an issue of internal security it was widely associated with foreign policy, and the way in which under Blair Britain had become the leading supporter of the United States in its war on terror, and had, in a number of instances, Kosovo, Sierra Leone, Afghanistan, put the principles of liberal interventionism into practice. It was suggested by some that British foreign policy made Britain a terrorist target, both from external terrorist groups and from the radicalisation of parts of the British Muslim community. The obvious disaffection of a large number of British citizens with the foreign policy of their own government was a development with many implications for the future; especially when a handful of them were prepared to contemplate expressing their alienation through murder and treason.

Blair's legacy for Britain's place in the world can be analysed along three dimensions; the relationship with the US; the relationship with the EU; and the initiatives on world poverty and Africa.

Britain's relationship with the US

The impact on the relationship with the US is perhaps the most striking. Blair performed the remarkable feat of establishing a strong relationship with not just one but two American Presidents, Bill Clinton and George Bush, from different parties and with very different ideological perspectives (Riddell 2003). At the beginning of his premiership Blair had appeared to want to give equal priority to the US and to the EU, and he was considered by many the most pro-European Prime Minister since Edward Heath. Although he significantly pushed forward European defence cooperation, when hard choices in the security field had to be made, Blair sided unequivocally with the United States. In contrast, Harold Wilson, when faced with the Vietnam war in the 1960s, had sided equivocally with the United States, which lost him friends on all sides. Blair gave unwavering support to Bush after September 11. In doing so he returned to the default position of British foreign policy since 1945, that Britain's primary national interest was to ensure that the United States remained committed through NATO to the defence of Britain and the rest of Europe, and therefore to support the United States in carrying out its role as the global hegemonic power in governing the international state system and the world economy (van der Pijl 2006).

The choices Blair made were broadly supported by the Conservatives, which since Thatcher had been predominantly Atlanticist in its thinking. Under Iain Duncan Smith the bulk of the party had voted for the Iraq war in 2003, giving Blair a parliamentary majority for his decision to go to war. Under Duncan Smith's successors, Michael Howard and then David Cameron, support had become more equivocal, as the party sensed how unpopular both the war and George Bush personally had become in Britain. Of the major parties only the Liberal Democrats were committed to a different order of priorities than the one Blair chose. Although they too supported the interventions in Kosovo, Sierra Leone and Afghanistan, they strongly opposed the Iraq intervention. Iraq proved hugely divisive, and in the anti-American feeling it provoked, fuelled by issues such as the detention of suspects at Guantánamo Bay, the employment of abusive interrogation techniques, and the practice of extraordinary rendition, it raised questions over whether permanent damage was being done to the Anglo-American relationship, and whether a future British government would be able to commit British troops to an American-led intervention which was not sanctioned by the United Nations.

Yet despite the level of passionate opposition to Blair's US-focused foreign policy it was still substantially in place when he left office, and was continued by his successor, Gordon Brown, and Brown's successor, David Cameron. The intervention in Iraq has few public defenders in Britain any more, but this has not changed British foreign policy. The war in Afghanistan, which began in 2001, continues, and Britain remains committed to the long haul, in alliance with the Americans. Other NATO members are involved in Afghanistan, but the bulk of the fighting is being borne by the Americans, the British and the Afghans themselves. Tony Blair's policies have not led to a re-evaluation of Britain's role in the world. By reminding the world, and the American public, of the strength of the special relationship, Blair helped to reinvigorate that relationship and distance himself from Europe.

Much has been written about the illusory character of the special relationship and how it is special only for Britain, but this can be overstated. It ignores the extent of the cooperation between the two states at many different levels, and the willingness of the United States to equip Britain with nuclear technology, something it has not done for other allies. The degree to which the British state has an Atlanticist perspective when it considers British interests across a range of policy areas remains considerable. Sometimes the special relationship is reduced to the particular personal chemistry, or lack of it, between leaders, or to specific institutional relationships. But most important of all has been the perception in Britain, articulated most memorably by Churchill, that Britain's fundamental interest lies in preserving the liberal world economic and political order which it helped create in the nineteenth century, but which after 1918 and even more so after 1945 it no longer had the capacity to maintain (Gamble 2003). Britain will continue to support the United States, with occasional periods of friction, so long as the United States continues to offer itself as the global leader and sustainer of a liberal world order. This is a theme which ran through all Blair's speeches, and which he became more committed to the longer he remained prime minister. Atlanticism for the British political class has been primarily a matter of strategic interest, and certainly not a question of Britain being a poodle to the Americans. The charge of being the Americans' poodle was first hurled at Margaret Thatcher by Denis Healey, and was then revived by Blair's critics. But it misses the target.

Britain's European relations

Blair, despite his initial intentions, failed to change the direction of British European policy. Despite his desire to pursue a much more positive pro-European policy he only achieved limited success. The divisions in the EU over Iraq were symptomatic of this failure, but an even more significant was Blair's inability to commit Britain to joining the euro, because of the opposition he encountered within his cabinet and particularly from Gordon Brown. Entering the eurozone was indispensable to Blair's desire to see Britain at the heart of Europe, able to influence the key decisions of the Union (Dyson 2008). Staying outside the euro may have made short-term economic sense (and, given the public hostility to joining, political sense), and when the eurozone crisis erupted in 2010, many opponents of adopting the euro considered themselves vindicated. But the decision also displayed once again Britain's fundamental lack of commitment to the European project as it was understood by many of its partners. It accelerated the move to a variable geometry, multi-speed differentiated Europe (Dyson and Sepos 2010). Already outside the Schengen Agreement on border controls, Britain was now outside the monetary union. It meant that Britain was unlikely to play much part in the deepening of European integration, or in the debate over the creation of a common European economic policy which would make the EU independent of the United States (Cafruny and Ryner 2007).

Another side of Blair's European legacy was more positive. He strongly favoured the traditional British position on enlargement, and was an advocate of the admission not just of the East European and Balkan states but also of Turkey (Cameron, too, favours Turkish entry). The continual widening of the community, however, made deeper integration more difficult to achieve, and made the forming of a common European will on any practical issue harder. The British support for enlargement was sometimes seen by advocates of deeper integration as a ploy to make deeper integration more difficult. The Blair government did not take this position and, at the same time as supporting enlargement endorsed the new Constitutional Treaty, aimed at consolidating the existing treaties and streamlining the decision-making procedures of the Union to cope with the larger number of member states (Duff 2009). The earlier EU Constitution had also been supported, and Labour had been committed to holding a referendum on it, which it was not expected to win. Once France and the Netherlands had voted against the EU constitution in their referendums in 2005, the British government suspended plans to hold its own referendum. When the EU constitutional treaty was put forward, which critics alleged contained the same content as the EU Constitution, the British government declared that a treaty as opposed to a constitution would not require a referendum but could be ratified by the royal prerogative in the normal way. Ireland's failure to endorse the constitutional treaty in its referendum in June 2008 for a time threw the process of ratification into disarray. It was put back on track by a second Irish vote in October 2009 which this time approved the treaty, and allowed it to be ratified by all member states. The divisions within Europe and within Britain over the constitutional treaty indicated how many obstacles now existed to making Europe an effective global player. It appeared to be losing cohesion rather than gaining it. Britain's continued semi-detachment contributed to the malaise (Hutton 2003; Wall 2008).

Initiatives on world poverty and Africa

The third legacy from the Blair years to his successors was the progress made on a different aspect of internationalism – the fight against global poverty and third world debt, as well as the taking up of other international issues where international cooperation was needed, such as climate change. This was the other side of Blair's liberal internationalism, although it also had its critics, who saw it as operating within the limits of the neo-liberal policy framework as interpreted by international agencies such as the IMF and the World Bank. Nevertheless Blair, in conjunction with Gordon Brown, did put a great deal of effort into getting international action on poverty, aid and climate change issues. The Bush administration blocked action on climate change, refusing to sign the Kyoto protocol, but there was more international action on plans to tackle poverty and debt, most notably at the 2005 summit of the G8 held at Gleneagles, where all the member states signed up to ambitious targets for aid and debt relief. Fulfilment of the pledges was, however, subsequently patchy, but it became a distinctive part of British foreign policy and the British conception of their place in the world. It was to be continued by Gordon Brown, and the new coalition government under David Cameron pledged that the aid budget would be protected from public spending cuts.

From Blair to Gordon Brown: foreign and external policy from 2007

Gordon Brown finally achieved his ambition to succeed Tony Blair in June 2007. His supporters had suggested that there would be some substantial changes of policy, direction and style once Brown took over, but the first two did not materialise. In foreign policy Brown continued all of Blair's main policies. There was no quick withdrawal from Iraq; instead the reduction in troop numbers proceeded as planned, and the final exit did not occur until June 2009. Brown defended the continued presence of British troops in Iraq in terms indistinguishable from his predecessor. He also, as mentioned above, renewed and extended the British commitment in Afghanistan, and this war now took on greater importance as Britain's main external military engagement. Brown also affirmed his full support for the special relationship and the Atlantic Alliance. He confirmed the plans to renew the Trident nuclear deterrent, tying Britain for a long time ahead to American technology. He contrived to appear unenthusiastic in his relations with George Bush, and miscalculated by at first privately backing Hillary Clinton rather than Barack Obama in the race for the Democratic nomination. But no one was in any doubt about his very strong Atlanticism, which had become more pronounced during his time at the Treasury (Lee 2007).

The other side of his strong Atlanticism was that Brown was noticeably cooler towards Europe than Blair had been. He became prime minister at a time when the EU was in disarray because of its problems in ratifying the European constitution, and although Brown made no move to offer a referendum on the constitutional treaty for British voters, he also made it clear that he did not see a case for deeper integration in Europe. Brown was also lukewarm on greater European cooperation on defence, preferring to put effort into NATO, and in pushing forward international agreements on poverty, aid and climate change. He was not an instinctive Europeanist, and saw no need to develop common European policies, as opposed to common international policies. His efforts tended to go into the latter.

An example of this was his reaction to the financial crisis in September and October 2008. Brown worked closely with the American authorities in brokering deals and proposing rescue packages for the world economy

(Seldon and Lodge 2010). It was Anglo-American finance, and the Anglo-American financial model which were in such serious trouble, and he sought to deal with them through Anglo-American networks. European networks were separate. At no time did he seek to broker a common European policy towards the crisis: Rather he attempted to set out a distinctive British line of action, which other states were commended to follow. Since Britain was not a member of the eurozone, in large part because of Brown's earlier refusal to support membership, this was hardly very surprising. But it accentuated Britain's differences with the rest of the EU, and its closeness to the United States. Many eurozone countries were quick to blame the crisis on the 'Anglo-Saxons'. It was Anglo-American finance and its associated doctrines of neo-liberalism and globalisation which had brought the world's financial system down, and so damaged the world economy.

Brown's government supported European initiatives over issues such as Iran and the Middle East, and these have been continued by David Cameron and William Hague. The EU has pursued negotiations with Iran over its nuclear programme, and the possibility that it is seeking to acquire nuclear weapons, culminating in new sanctions imposed by the UN in June 2010. It has also been an important mediator in the Israel–Palestine dispute, and part of the Quartet, together with the US, Russia and the UN. The Quartet was first established in 2002, and after he left office Tony Blair was appointed its special envoy. This caused some disquiet at the time, since in office Blair had been associated with a marked pro-Israeli policy, most notably in 2006, when he refused to condemn the Israeli incursion into Lebanon. It was argued that Blair would have no credibility in negotiating with the Palestinians. Those who supported the appointment believed that Blair's role in bringing the peace process in Northern Ireland to a successful conclusion made him especially qualified about world leaders to perform a mediating role in the Middle East.

There has been increasing recognition that Britain, as in the Middle East, can only exercise influence in conjunction with its European partners, but this is a slow development, and on crucial issues such as the reform of the governance of international institutions Britain does not take a lead. A prime example is Britain and France refusing to contemplate giving up their seats on the UN Security Council in favour of a single EU representative. Members of the EU are overrepresented in many international forums, including the G8 and now the G20. This could be easily corrected if the EU itself became the representative for all its members. But the most powerful member states are mostly reluctant for this to happen, and Britain is no exception.

Brown appointed David Miliband as his foreign secretary, replacing

Margaret Beckett. Miliband had been Head of Blair's Policy Unit at Number 10, and had never been close to Brown, but his obvious ability marked him out for promotion to a senior Cabinet position. As foreign secretary he was noticeably keen to pursue a more pro-European course and delivered a number of very strong pro-European speeches, but given the general stance of the government he was never able to shift policy very much in a pro-European direction. He was also eager to broaden the scope of foreign policy in line with the claims of a number of think tanks such as the Foreign Policy Centre. As a former environment secretary Miliband was keen to expand foreign policy to include discussions on climate change, to identify what needs to be done to create lasting agreements that can make a difference. He sought to take further many of the ideas propounded within the Blair circle by Robert Cooper and others about responsible sovereignty, and developing foreign policy for an interdependent world (Cooper 2007). Following Brown's resignation some of the contestants for the Labour leadership in 2010, including David Miliband, were instinctively European in a way which many in the older generation, including Gordon Brown, are not. But for all his advocacy of a stronger pro-European policy, people like David Miliband have yet to find a way to convince a sceptical public of the benefits of EU membership. The EU remains deeply unpopular with the British electorate, and is regularly attacked and ridiculed in many parts of the media. The pro-Europeans in the political class have not yet found a way of overcoming this.

Relations beyond the US and Europe

Other issues which David Miliband had (and now William Hague has) to deal with as foreign secretary included relations with China, India, Russia and with some former parts of the Empire, most notably Zimbabwe. The increasing importance of the BRICs (Brazil, Russia, India and China) and the increasing dependence of European trade and consumption upon them, has made them an increasing focus of British diplomacy. Relationships with India are relatively easy, because of the historic ties and the high proportion of the Indian elite which speaks English. China continues to grow at a very rapid rate, and has emerged as a crucial player in the global economy, as well as a rising power which is developing interests in many parts of the world including Africa, in pursuit of reliable sources of energy and raw materials for its industries (Halper 2010). The overriding concern of Western countries is to ensure that China continues its growth within the structures of the global economy. At the same time there are many aspects of China's policies, for example on Tibet and on Taiwan, and its attitudes towards internal dissent, and its support for regimes like those of Sudan and Burma, which Britain opposes. Finding the best way to engage with a re-emerging China has become a preoccupation for all Western governments including Britain. China is moving only slowly towards opening its political system and making itself more democratic, and still relies heavily on nationalism to unify the country. The huge imbalances between surplus and deficit countries which emerged during the boom reflect the determination of the Chinese leadership to keep its currency low and to boost exports. China has delivered low-cost goods to be consumed in North America and Europe, so keeping inflation lower in those countries and creating vast surpluses. These imbalances cannot continue for ever, as the financial crisis revealed, but how a more stable world order can be negotiated is a difficult question, without major changes to the financial and currency arrangements currently in place. As an architect of the liberal world order Britain in particular has a key role to play in finding a way to accommodate China. But the speed of its rise makes this hard, and as China grows more powerful, so it will seek to exercise its power in pursuit of its legitimate interests, and this may bring conflict with Western countries (Hutton 2008; Jacques 2009; Nolan 2003).

Russia is a rather different case. Its resurgent power is based largely on its huge oil and gas reserves. Relations with Britain were poor for a time, partly because of the refusal of Russia to agree to the extradition of a suspect wanted for questioning in London in relation to the murder of a Russian dissident, Alexander Litvinenko. There have also been disputes over joint ventures between Russian and British countries, and accusations in both countries about spies. The Russians have expelled British diplomats and placed restrictions on the operation of some British organisations, like the British Council. Relations have also grown worse because of Russian attitudes to its neighbours and its unwillingness to see any more of them join NATO or the EU. The Russian incursion into Georgia to protect two breakaway Russian speaking enclaves in 2008 greatly alarmed the West. The Russians justified it as no different from what the West did in Kosovo. Russia's use of its military and economic muscle was applauded at home, but although it alarmed its neighbours, the threat was not on the same scale as in the past. In general Russia remained too dependent on the West to threaten it unduly. The confrontation with Britain was almost as if the Russians chose to use Britain as a proxy for the United States. Confronting the United States was not something the Russians sought.

A final problem for British foreign policy was the worsening plight of Zimbabwe. As a former British colony Britain felt a special responsibility, but was also hampered by its colonial past in the extent of the pressure it could apply. The Mugabe regime depicted Britain as its leading enemy, banned the BBC from reporting in the country, and accused Britain of siding with the white farmers and seeking to subvert the Zimbabwean government. The abuse of human rights in Zimbabwe and the huge suffering of its people was much clearer than in many other cases where Britain had intervened militarily, but the military option in Zimbabwe was never considered. Instead Britain worked with other Commonwealth countries, and in particular with neighbouring African states, especially South Africa, to put pressure on the Mugabe regime to change course. Eventually in 2008 a power-sharing agreement was put in place, which made the opposition leader, Morgan Tsvangirai, Prime Minister, but with very restricted powers. The inability of Britain to force the pace was demonstrated very clearly, and indicated the limits of Britain's effective influence in Africa.

Conservative policy under Cameron

The election of David Cameron as Conservative leader in December 2005 brought some changes of emphasis in Conservative policy on Britain's place in the world, but no major change of direction. As suggested earlier, the Conservatives continued their strong Atlanticist position, but began to use the unpopularity of some of Labour's foreign wars, particularly Iraq, to distance themselves from the government. At one point this earned Cameron a magisterial rebuke from the *Wall Street Journal*, which accused him of playing politics with the Atlantic relationship. But there was never much doubt that the Conservatives in government would pursue very similar policies to those of Labour. The circle of Anglo-America was for Cameron, as it had been for Thatcher, the lynchpin of Britain's relationship with the rest of the world, and this view was shared by those around him, including close associates such as his chancellor and education secretaries, George Osborne and Michael Gove, and also by the foreign and defence secretaries, William Hague and Liam Fox.

Cameron inherited a party that for 20 years had been fighting a vicious civil war over Britain's involvement with the European Union. But by 2005 this war was over and the pro-Europeans had largely disappeared from the party, which was now overwhelmingly Eurosceptic. Cameron even felt able in 2008 to invite Ken Clarke, one of the last remaining major pro-Europeans in the party to rejoin the shadow cabinet, on condition that he accepted that the European issue was settled; Clarke, a *bête noire* of the Conservative right, was appointed to the cabinet in May 2010. The argument now was between those few who wanted to leave the European Union altogether and those who thought Britain could remain so long as it vetoed any further moves to integration. Cameron sought to deal with the issue by playing it down, trying quite successfully to get the party to stop talking about Europe. What Cameron and William Hague did not seek to do was to adopt a new positive pro-European narrative, extolling a vision of the kind of Europe they wanted to see. It was easier, given the reflexes of much of the British media, to go on presenting the European Union as a malign bureaucracy against which the British government needed to be forever vigilant.

The depth of Conservative disquiet about Europe was shown at every European Parliament election when large numbers of Conservative voters defected to the UK Independence party (UKIP), which campaigned on the issue of withdrawing Britain from Europe. In 2009 UKIP again polled well and retained a sizeable number of seats in the European Parliament even though in 2010 it was again to fail to win a single seat at Westminster. Norman Tebbit, a former chairman of the Conservative party, has often hinted that Conservative voters should consider voting for a party that promised to take Britain out of Europe. That party was not the Conservatives. A leading Conservative donor, Stuart Wheeler, was expelled from the party for funding UKIP candidates. Cameron could deal with these frictions in opposition, but it raised interesting questions as to how the Conservatives would deal with the issue in government.

The capacity of the European issue to embarrass the Conservatives was shown by the row over which grouping the party should join in the European Parliament. David Cameron had promised in his election campaign for the leadership that he would take the Conservatives out of the main centre-right grouping in the Parliament, the European People's party, because many of the parties within it supported a federal Europe. But he had great difficulty in finding suitable anti-federalist partners in the Parliament. Nevertheless the plan was pursued, and after the elections in 2009 the Conservatives did announce the formation of a new group, mostly consisting of parties from Eastern Europe. Critics were quick to point out that it contained some politicians with far right views, some of which appeared to be anti-Semitic and homophobic, which sat oddly with David Cameron's desire to give the Conservatives a liberal, centrist image. Nevertheless despite the public disapproval of his fellow centre-right leaders, including Angela Merkel and Nicolas Sarkozy, the Conservatives did not reconsider, even after they had formed a coalition government with the Liberal Democrats.

The Conservatives considered the European Parliament not to matter very much, but the more serious issue for them was that they fought the 2009 European Parliament election on a very negative EU platform in order to try and minimise the UKIP vote. They promised that a Conservative government would not sign any further European treaty without a referendum, and they reiterated their opposition to the euro and to any closer common foreign and defence policy. They found it hard to find anything positive to say about Europe at all. With elements of the party still flirting with the idea of withdrawal, and of negotiating European Economic Area status for Britain, the party leadership was anxious as to how in government it might deliver its anti-European policy without conceding at some stage a referendum which could quickly become a demand for withdrawal. In previous Conservative governments many ministers accepted pragmatically the benefits of European cooperation.

The Conservative attitude to Europe often baffled the Americans, and not just the Obama administration. Even those Americans who are supporters of the Anglosphere find the attitude of the Conservatives to the European Union anachronistic (Mead 2008). They think the Conservatives see Europe as though it were the recrudescence of the continental system, of Napoleon or the Kaiser. Americans regard it in less threatening terms. The Union is occasionally an irritant, but not a substantial threat to American interests. The exaggerated fear that many British Conservatives now have of it they find hard to understand. Those Americans who do sympathise with this position think the Anglosphere, which comprises the main English-speaking members and some honorary members, might be welded together into a network Commonwealth, a permanent coalition of the willing supporting American foreign policy aim (Bennett 2004). But the Obama administration has made it clear that it wants a much more inclusive relationship with all members of the Western alliance, and not just with a small subset of it.

Conclusion: foreign policy and the Conservative Liberal–Democrat coalition

The surprising outcome of the 2010 general election, which saw the formation of a Conservative Liberal Democrat coalition government, raised interesting questions for Britain's place in the world, since the Conservatives were much closer to Labour on many foreign policy and defence questions than they were to the Liberal Democrats. The latter in opposition had voted against the Iraq war, terming it an illegal war; they had been opposed to the renewal of Trident; and they were fierce critics of the special relationship and the strongest pro-European party in British politics, still declaring in their manifesto in 2010 that Britain should consider joining the euro.

In the negotiation of the coalition agreement, the Conservatives were prepared to abandon many of their manifesto commitments on tax and spending priorities, and agree to many Liberal Democrat commitments on civil liberties and constitutional reform. What the Conservatives were not prepared to concede was any real movement on what they called their red lines, many of which were defence and foreign policy related. The agreement pledged to maintain Britain's nuclear deterrent and to renew Trident, subject only to the demand that it be scrutinised to ensure value for money. The Liberal Democrats are allowed to continue to make the case for alternatives (HM Government 2010: 15). Similarly on Europe, while avowing that the British government will be a 'positive participant' in the European Union and supports its further enlargement, the agreement also states that there will be no further transfer of sovereignty or powers over the course of the next Parliament, no attempt to join the euro, and legislation to ensure that any future treaty which transfers power is subject to a referendum (ibid.: 19). On the special relationship the agreement merely states 'We will maintain a strong, close and frank relationship with the United States' (ibid.: 20).

The foreign policy of the coalition government is, as a result, likely to maintain substantial continuity with its Labour predecessor, and no dramatic shifts are expected. The stances which William Hague took on issues which arose in the first month of the coalition taking office, such as the death of the campaigners on a Turkish ship seized by Israel off Gaza, or the support for the new sanctions against Iran, did not deviate from the policy established by Labour. The coalition declared its commitment to Britain's continued participation in the war in Afghanistan, and although it has criticisms of the previous strategy, and of the resourcing of the war effort, there is no indication that much is likely to change. Government rhetoric about the conflict and justification for it is remarkably similar to the previous government. David Cameron spoke in opposition about the undesirability of Western countries trying to 'impose democracy from 30,000 feet', but although Liam Fox the Defence Secretary did characterise Afghanistan as 'a broken thirteenth century country' and argued that the only reason British troops were there was to hunt down Islamic militants and keep the streets of Britain safe, he quickly backtracked. The only prospect of an early withdrawal from Afghanistan is if the situation is stabilised sufficiently for the Afghan government to take control of its own security. This, in January 2011, still looked a distant prospect, and the war was still not going well for NATO: The British were deploying just under 10,000 troops and had lost 350 soldiers killed, more than in the Iraq war. In spite of some progress, winning the political battle in Afghanistan, and installing a government which enjoyed real legitimacy and was free of corruption, one likely to be able to hold the Taliban at bay, was not much nearer being achieved.

In 2009, shortly before the general election, the IPPR Commission on National Security in the 21st Century published its final report *Shared Responsibilities* (IPPR 2009). The report examined five options for Britain's future alliance relationships:

1   Continuing to rely on American capabilities and resources, with Britain trying to retain full-spectrum defence capabilities but on a much smaller scale.
2   Strengthening European defence and security cooperation through NATO as a means to reducing dependence on the US.
3   Building other intergovernmental groupings, such as the Commonwealth.
4   Going it alone.
5   Making no choice, but keeping all the above options in play.

The view of the Commission was unambiguously for option 2, and followed through in the rest of the report the implications for this in great detail. The Cameron-led government will have, in time, to consider similar options but presently ministers claim that commitments such as Afghanistan have not been properly resourced, and that, because the government's financial problems prompt the need to make deep cuts in public spending, Britain will have to re-examine its military capacity. The government promises in making such cuts to ask searching questions about what the state should and should not be doing. Rethinking Britain's role in the world could obviously make a major contribution to this. It is, however, too early to assess the implications of the coalition's Strategic Defence and Security Review, published in October 2010, so it remains to be seen if Cameron's government will consider this the moment to make a major change in Britain's place in the world, as significant as the decisions in the 1940s to begin the withdrawal from the Empire, and in the 1960s to authorise the end of Britain's east of Suez commitments.

In public the special relationship between Britain and the US is still warm, although it is noticeable that it is not a priority for Barack Obama as it became for George Bush or Ronald Reagan. The strong rhetoric used by Barack Obama and White House staff against British Petroleum in the summer of 2010 after the oil spill in the Gulf, had a strong anti-British tone, and aroused protest in Britain, but Britain made no public protest, following the usual conventions of the special relationship (at least on the British side). Britain and Europe have a lower priority for the Obama administration, and a further cooling in the relationship can be expected, especially when the Afghan campaign finally ends. It will be much harder in future for any British government to commit troops to foreign wars launched by the United States. The era of liberal interventionism may have passed, and Britain may soon no longer have the will or the capacity to project its power both militarily and diplomatically to the rest of the world as it has been accustomed to do.

Further Reading

Constitutional politics

There are many good-quality texts looking back on the legacy of Labour's constitutional reforms. The most complete analyses can be found in King (2007) and Bogdanor (2009). Johnson (2004) provides a conservative critique of the early years, while McLean (2009) is a more radical critic, and more up to date, but covers fewer reforms. For a historical analysis of the British constitution, Bogdanor (2003) is an excellent starting point, while Hazell (2008b) takes a forward look at how things may develop over the next 10 years or more. Both he and Flinders (2009) attempt to assess the overall impact of reform to date, drawing rather different conclusions. There are many articles on the subject, too numerous to mention, but one by Norton (2007) is worth singling out as a readable overview. The series of Oxford University Press books edited by Jowell and Oliver under the title *The Changing Constitution* contain many useful contributions. For up-to-date analyses, including reports, short articles and a regular newsletter (the *Monitor*) the website of the Constitution Unit at University College London also has much to offer.

Changing patterns of executive governance

There is no single contribution around which debates on either the British political tradition or the Westminster model are organised, but notable contributions are Birch (1964), Beer (1965) and Greenleaf (1983a, b and 1987), Tant (1993) and Flinders (2009). Two alternatives challenging the Westminster model are the differentiated polity model (see Rhodes 1997) and the asymmetric power model (see Marsh *et al.* 2001). Michael Barber (2007) provides a useful 'insider' commentary on New Labour's approach to governance, while Peter Mandelson's memoirs (2010) reveal the extensive personality clashes at the heart of the New Labour project. Tony Blair tells his own story (2010) and stories about Gordon Brown's style of government are recounted to good effect in Rawnsley (2010) and Seldon and Lodge (2010). Four weighty reports on Labour's governing legacy are Better Government Institute (2010 – www.civilservant.org.uk/bgigoodgovernment.pdf), House of Lords Select Committee on the Constitution (2010 – www.publications.

parliament.uk/pa/ld200910/ldselect/ldconst/30/30.pdf), Institute for Government (2010 – www.instituteforgovernment.org.uk/pdfs/shaping-up-a-whitehall-for-the-future.pdf). Elsewhere, informative commentaries on Labour's approach to governing are Evans (2003), Bevir and Rhodes (2003) and Richards (2008). For the prime minister, see Heffernan (2003, 2005). Some useful, initials guides to understanding the current coalition government's governance strategy include Blond (2010), Cabinet Office (2010a – www.number10.gov.uk/wp-content/uploads/srp-cabinet-office.pdf) and Conservative–Liberal Coalition (2010 – www.conservatives.com/News/News_stories/2010/05/Coalition_Agreement_published.aspx).

Changing parliamentary landscapes

Good introductory overviews of the Westminster parliament may be found in Norton (2010), Kelso (2009c) and Rogers and Walters (2006), although not all the recent changes explored here will necessarily be fully covered. A survey of parliamentary developments during Blair's premiership is provided by Cowley (2007). A historical background to House of Lords reform, only tangentially touched on here, is offered by Dorey and Kelso (2011) and Russell (2010) provides an analysis of the impact on reform on the impact of the second chamber. The Hansard Society regularly produces pamphlets and research about parliament and its website is a very useful resource (www.hansardsociety.org.uk). For up-to-date overviews of ongoing debates about and developments in Westminster practice and reform, the House of Commons Library Parliament and Constitution Centre is an excellent starting point (search www.parliament.uk). An introduction to the Scottish parliament can be found in McGarvey and Cairney (2008).

Political parties and the British party system

The ongoing fragmentation of the British party system has been variously discussed – Dunleavy (2005) is one useful account – although the historical account in Searle (1995) emphasises just how the British political system has long been used to coalition and its various relatives. For an overview of the changing form of political parties, see Webb (2002) and Heffernan (2009). The British general election of 2010 is covered in detail in Kavanagh and Cowley (2010); see especially Appendix 2 by Curtice *et al.*, which examines the results. The resulting process of coalition formation has already generated a series of books (with no doubt many more to follow), of which Wilson (2010) is perhaps the best to date. The Conservatives' path back from the electoral wilderness is well covered in Bale (2010) and Snowden (2010), although the polling evidence discussed in Ashcroft (2010) demonstrates the extent to which the party did not fully succeed in transforming itself. Labour's fall from grace is outlined (through the prism of Gordon Brown) in Seldon and Lodge (2010) and in similar fashion (this time focusing on Tony Blair and Brown) by Rawnsley (2010).

Elections and voting

The standard introductory text on voting in Britain is Denver (2007) and a third edition is to be published in 2011. More advanced treatments are to be found in the last two British Election Study reports (Clarke *et al.* 2004, 2009). For a detailed study of voting in the 2007 Scottish parliament elections, see Johns *et al.* (2010). After each general election a number of books appear analysing the campaign, the results, the role of the mass media, and so on. Those focusing on the 2010 election include Kavanagh and Cowley (2010), Geddes and Tonge (2010) and Allen and Bartle (2010).

Territorial politics in post-devolution Britain

Bogdanor (2009) places devolution in the wider context of constitutional change, as does King (2007), and revisits many of his arguments in his earlier text exploring the history and meaning of Scottish and Welsh devolution (2001). An edited collection by Hazell (2006) also explores the impacts of devolution on Britain's hitherto strictly unitary, majoritarian state as does the monographs by Mitchell (2009) and Trench (2007) and the edited collections by Stolz (2010), Trench (2007) and Trench and Hazell (2004, 2008). Alan Trench also blogs on devolution matters at Devolution Matters (http://devolutionmatters. wordpress.com). The findings of the Economic and Social Research Council's Devolution and Constitutional Change Programme can be browsed at www.devolution.ac.uk/final_report.htm. The Scottish parliament has produced a number of briefings on the history and working of devolved government, which can be found at www.scottish.parliament.uk/vli/ publicInfo/hspw/index.htm. The Welsh assembly offers similar basic briefings which can be explored at http://wales.gov.uk/about/?lang=en.

Power sharing in Northern Ireland

Those interested in the conflict should read McGarry and O'Leary (1995), which examines internal and external explanations of the roots of the conflict. The peace process has been superbly covered in Darby and MacGinty (2002). Extensive information and source material on 'the Troubles' and politics in Northern Ireland from 1968 to the present are available on CAIN (Conflict Archive on the Internet – http://cain. ulster.ac.uk). See also Aughey (2005) for a post-agreement analysis. The most up-to-date records and analysis of devolution in Northern Ireland are found in *Northern Ireland Devolution Monitoring Reports* (at: www.ucl.ac.uk/constitution-unit/nations). Published three times per years, they cover the peace process, devolved government, the Assembly, the media, public attitudes, intergovernmental relations, relations with the EU, relations with local government, finance, political parties and elections and public policies. Finally, the *Northern Ireland Life and Times Survey* (www.ark.ac. uk/nilt) record the attitudes, values and beliefs of people in Northern Ireland annually and is a valuable source for reviewing the political attitudes of the general public and changes over the last 10 years.

Anti-politics in Britain

The starting point should be the classic study of political culture by Almond and Verba (1963) because it is only then possible to realistically judge the nature of Britain's political culture at the start of the twenty-first century. The Power Commission report (2006) captures the critical but mainstream understanding of the problems with our politics. More in depth analysis comes from Stoker (2006) and Hay (2007a), with the former perhaps being more focused on citizens and their failings and the latter more focused on politicians and the way they are presented and present themselves as the key driver of anti-politics. The work of Hibbing and Theiss-Morse (2001, 2002) although focused on the United States, empirically opens up an important range of theoretical understandings and insights. To picture how politics can be different, read the discussion of democratic innovation in G. Smith (2010).

Pressure group politics

Grant (2000), while old now, provides an accessible introduction to the study of pressure groups in British politics and it may be usefully supplemented by Coxall (2001), Grant (2005, 2008) and Jordan and Maloney (2007). The collection edited by Crowson *et al.* (2009) looks at the historical role and functions of non-governmental organisations in Britain, Lent (2001) and Drache (2008) variously – but differently – discuss social movements, and the Oxford handbook edited by Coen *et al.* (2010) considers the relationship of business and government. Hay (2007) and Stoker (2006) separately – and collectively Hay and Stoker (2009) – explore why and how (and with what impacts) citizens are alienated from politics, while Keane (2009), in offering his notion of 'monitory democracy', suggests that group politics, together with other forms of civil society engagement, play an increasingly important role in helping hold the state accountable for its actions.

The politics of diversity

Lovenduski's (2005) and Childs (2008) provide a good basis for understanding the politics of gender equality. Campbell (2006) analyses to what extent men and women vote differently. For an analysis of how attitudes to gender equality have changed internationally see Inglehart and Norris (2003). Eatwell and Goodwin's edited collection (2010) includes a range of essays providing an insight into the impact of religious, ethnic and cultural diversity on British politics. For an analysis of how BME voters cast their ballots, see Saggar (1998). Much of the literature on BME voters is out of date but a new study, *The Ethnic Minorities British Election Study 2010*, funded by the Economic and Social Research Council and conducted by Heath *et al.* (forthcoming) will provide an important source of new data.

Political communication and the changing media environment

There is a growing body of literature on the changing political communication environment in Britain. Kuhn (2007) is a well-informed, up-to-date and accessible text on the news media in general. Other broad overviews on the new media environment can be found in books by Coleman and Blumler (2009), Chadwick (2006), Stanyer (2007) and in edited collections by Chadwick and Howard (2008) and Corner and Pels (2003). All these works are easily accessible to the non-specialist reader. In addition to the general overviews, there are studies with a more specific focus, for example, examinations of the impact of the internet on the profession of journalism, such as Keen (2007). A useful regularly updated source of information on the online environment is provided by Ofcom (at: www.ofcom.org.uk).

Britain and the global financial crisis: the return of boom and bust

The literature on the 'great recession' is still very much in its infancy. Gamble (2009a) offers an excellent portrait of the events themselves and their implications, despite being written as those events were still unfolding. The first and final chapters are particularly valuable. Crouch (2008) and Watson (2010) provide helpful overviews of 'privatised' and 'house price Keynesianism' respectively, whilst Finlayson (2009) gives an excellent account of 'asset based welfare' and the assumptions on which it is based. Hay (2009, 2011) and Pemberton (2009) provide more detail on the economic and political implications of the bursting of the housing bubble. Thain (2009) and Coates (2009) provide diametrically opposed judgements of New Labour's handling of the recession.

Britain's place in an Enlarging European Union

For excellent historical general overviews of the relationship between the UK and the European Union, see Wall (2008) Young (1999) and George (1998). Aspinwall (2004) offers a theoretical examination of how British electoral institutions shape party and public attitudes towards integration. On British political parties and the issue of Europe during the 2005 election see Sherrington (2006). Taggart and Szczerbiak (2004) provide a comparative theoretical framework for understanding Euroscepticism in political parties. For a detailed discussion of the British case see George (2000), Wall (2008) or Gifford (2010). Many of the British positions on EU policies discussed in this chapter are covered in detail in Treasury, FCO and Cabinet Office publications and can be accessed online. British responses to the EU 2020 policy proposals can be viewed online at: http://ec.europa.eu/dgs/ secretariat_general/eu2020/contrib_ member_ states_en.htm.

Security and surveillance in Britain

Much has been written on Britain and terrorism since 9/11, but somewhat surprisingly, surveillance and the secret state have received less attention. Hewitt's study of the British war on terror (2008) provides a concise and current overview of the main events. Omand's *Securing the State* (2010) offers an advanced conceptual framework and elegantly combines both academic and practitioner insights. Hennessy's *New Protective State* (2007) captures a unique blend of work from the admirable Mile End Institute programme. The recent work of MI5 is examined by Andrew (2009) and the work of GCHQ by Aldrich (2010). Field's article on tracking terrorist networks (2009) provides an up-to-date analysis of the problems of sharing within the UK intelligence community. A recent article by Croft and Moore (2010) provides a good overview of the narratives of radicalisation in Britain. The inquiry by the House of Commons Select Committee into Counter-Terrorism (2009), especially the minutes of evidence, allows detailed introspection into the major issues.

Britain in the world

On the theme of liberal peace and its replacement by liberal war see Fukuyama (1992) and Kagan (2009), also Halliday (2000) and Kaldor (2007). The complex international environment after the end of the cold war is explored from different perspectives by Cooper (2007) and Duffield (2001). The liberal interventionism of the Blair government is surveyed critically by Kampfner (2003) and the relationship of Britain to the United States by Riddell (2003), Gamble (2003a), Mead (2008) and van der Pijl (2006). The uneasy relationship between Britain and the European Union is explored in Wall (2008), Dyson (2008), Dyson and Sepos (2010) and Cafruny and Ryner (2007). The implications of the rise of China are analysed from different perspectives by Hutton (2008), Jacques (2009), Nolan (2003) and Halper (2010). For the strategic choices facing the coalition government about Britain's role in the world, see IPPR (2009), the party manifestos at the 2010 election, and the Coalition Agreement (HM Government 2010). See also the websites of Chatham House, RUSI and the Foreign Policy Centre.

Bibliography

Aaronovitch, D. (2010) 'There's too much old in this new politics', *The Times*, 20 May.

Aaronovitch, D. (2010a) *Voodoo Histories: The Role of the Conspiracy Theory in Shaping Modern History*, London: Vintage.

Abramson, P. and Inglehart, R. (1995) *Value Change in Global Perspective*, Michigan: Michigan University Press.

ACPO (2008), Guidance for police authorities on the performance monitoring and scrutiny of protective services, November 2008 Version 1.0, Appendix 2: Case Study: Thames Valley – Operation Overt (at: http://nd.durham.gov.uk/durhamcc/etech/PAMinutes.nsf/ad3cf9af81b6890a80256d56002d0c76/941D9F176C9A766480257546005659BE/$FILE/Item+7+Appendix+2+-+APA+Guidance.pdf; accessed 20 December 2009).

Aldrich, R. J. (2009) 'Beyond the vigilant state? Globalization and intelligence', *Review of International Studies*, 35(4): 889–904.

Aldrich, R. J. (2010) GCHQ: *The Uncensored Story of Britain's Most Secret Intelligence Agency*, London: HarperCollins.

All Wales Convention (2009) *All Wales Convention Report*. Cardiff: All Wales Convention.

Allen, N. and Bartle, J. (2010) *Britain at the Polls 2010*, London: Sage.

Almond, G. and Verba, S. (1963) *The Civic Culture*, Princeton: Princeton University Press.

Anderson, J., Ikenberry, J. and Risse-Kappen, T. (2008) *The End of the West? Crisis and Change in the Atlantic Order*, Ithaca, NY: Cornell University Press.

Andrew, C. (2009) *The Defence of the Realm: The Authorised History of MI5*, London: Penguin Books.

Anstead, N. and O'Loughlin, B. (2010) 'The emerging viewertariat: explaining Twitter responses to Nick Griffin's appearance on BBC *Question Time*', University of East Anglia School of Political, Social and International Studies Working Paper. Norwich: University of East Anglia.

Armstrong, K. (2006) 'The "Europeanisation" of social exclusion: British adaptation to EU coordination', *British Journal of Politics and International Relations*, 8(1): 79–100.

Ashcroft, M. (2005) 'Smell the coffee: a wake-up call for the Conservative party', London.

Ashcroft, M. (2010) 'Minority verdict: the conservative party, the voters and the 2010 election', London.

Aspinwall, M. (2004) *Rethinking Britain and Europe*, Manchester: Manchester University Press.

Aughey, A. (2005) *The Politics of Northern Ireland: Beyond the Belfast Agreement*, London: Routledge.

Axelrod, R. (1970) *Conflict of Interest*, Chicago: Markham.

Bache, I. and Jordan, A. (eds) (2006) *The Europeanization of British Politics*, London: Palgrave Macmillan.

Bale, T. (2010) *The Conservative Party from Thatcher to Cameron*, Cambridge: Polity.

Barber, M. (2007) *Instruction to Deliver: Tony Blair, Public Services and the Challenge of Achieving Targets*, London: Politico's.

BBC News Online (2000) 'Sanctions against DUP ministers', 8 June (at: http://news.bbc.co.uk/1/hi/northern_ireland/783228.stm).

BBC News Online (2009) 'Robinson rejects "swish" pay tag', 6 April (at: http://news.bbc.co.uk/1/hi/northern_ireland/7986031.stm).

BBC News Online (2010a) '8.4 million watch final prime ministerial debate', 30 April (at: http://news.bbc.co.uk/1/hi/uk_politics/election_2010/8653551.stm; accessed 10 May 2010).

BBC News Online (2010b) '*The Independent* bought by Lebedev for £1', 25 March (at: http://news.bbc.co.uk/1/hi/business/8587469.stm; accessed 10 May 2010).

Beer, S. (1965) *Modern British Politics*, London: Faber & Faber.

Begg, I. (2007) 'The 2008/9 EU budget review' EU-CONSENT EU-Budget Working Paper No. 3, March.

Bell, M. (2008) 'The implementation of European anti-discrimination directives: converging towards a common model?', *Political Quarterly* 79(1): 36–44.

Bell, S. and Hindmoor, A. (2009) *Rethinking Governance: The Centrality of the State in Modern Society*, Cambridge: Cambridge University Press.

Bellamy, R. (2007) *Political Constitutionalism: A Republican Defence of the Constitutionality of Democracy*, Cambridge: Cambridge University Press.

Bennett, J. (2004) *The Anglosphere Challenge: Why the English-Speaking Countries Will Lead the Way in the Twenty-first Century*, Lanham, MD: Rowman & Littlefield.

Better Government Institute (2010) *Good Government Reforming Parliament and the Executive: Recommendations from the Executive Committee of the Better Government Initiative* (at: www.civilservant.org.uk/bgigood government.pdf).

Bevir, M. and Rhodes, R. A. W. (2003) *Interpreting British Governance*, London: Routledge.

Bevir, M. and Rhodes, R. A. W. (2006) *Governance Stories*, London: Routledge.

Bevir, M. and Rhodes, R. A. W. (2006) 'Prime ministers, presidentialism and Westminster smokescreens', *Political Studies*, 54(4): 671–90.

Bew, P. (2007) *The Making and Remaking of the Good Friday Agreement*, Dublin: Liffey Press.

Bew, P. (2009) 'Terrorism is back in Northern Ireland', *The Spectator*, 9 September.

Birch, A. H (1964) *Representative and Responsible Government*, London: George Allen & Unwin.

Birch, S. and Allen, N. (2009) 'How honest do politicians need to be?', *Political Quarterly*, 81(1): 49–56.

Birrell, D. (2009) 'The restoration of devolution in Northern Ireland: policy making without consensus', paper presented to the Political Studies Association Conference, University of Manchester, 7–9 April.

Birrell, D. (2009) *Direct Rule and the Governance of Northern Ireland*, Manchester: Manchester University Press.

Blackburn, R. and Kennon, A. (2003) *Parliament: Functions, Practice and Procedures*, London: Sweet & Maxwell.

Blair, T. (1996) *New Britain, My Vision of a Young Country*, London: Fourth Estate.

Blair, T. (2007) 'Blair on the media', BBC News Online, 12 June (at: http://news.bbc.co.uk/1/hi/uk_politics/6744581.stm; accessed 7 July 2009).

Blair, T. (2010) *A Journey*, London: Hutchinson.

Blick, A. and Jones, G. W. (2010) *Premiership: The Development, Nature and Power of the Office of the British Prime Minister*, London: Imprint Academic.

Blond, P. (2010) *Red Tory: How Left and Right Have Broken Britain and How We Can Fix It*, London: Faber.

Bochel, H. and Denver, D. (2007) 'A quiet revolution: STV and the Scottish Council elections of 2007', *Scottish Affairs*, 61(4): 1–17.

Bogdanor, V. (2001) 'Constitutional reform', in A. Seldon (ed.), *The Blair Effect: The Blair Government 1997–2001*, London: Little, Brown and Company.

Bogdanor, V. (ed.) (2003) *The British Constitution in the Twentieth Century*, Oxford: Oxford University Press.

Bogdanor, V. (2009) *The New British Constitution*, Oxford: Hart Publishing.

Boles, N. (2010) *Which Way's Up?* London: Biteback.

Boulianne, S. (2009) 'Does internet use affect engagement? A meta-analysis of research', *Political Communication*, 26(2): 193–211.

Boulton, A. and Jones, J. (2010) *Hung Together: The 2010 Election and the Coalition Government*, London, Simon & Schuster.

Brown, G. (2009) speech to the US Congress, 4 March.

Brundidge, J. and Rice, R. E. (2008) 'Political engagement online: do the information rich get richer and the like-minded more similar?', in Chadwick, A. and Howard, P. N. (eds), *The Handbook of Internet Politics*, London: Routledge.

Bulmer, S. (2008) 'New Labour, New European policy? Blair, Brown and utilitarian supranationalism', *Parliamentary Affairs*, 61(4): 597–620.

Burke, J. (2007) *Al-Qaeda: The True Story of Radical Islam*, Harmondsworth: Penguin.

Butler, D. (1998) 'Reflections on British elections and their study', *Annual Review of Political Science*, 1(2): 451–64.

Butler, D. and Stokes, D. (1969) *Political Change in Britain*, London, Macmillan.

Butler, R. (2004) *Review of Intelligence on Weapons of Mass Destruction: Report of a Committee of Privy Counsellors*, HC Papers 898, London: TSO.

Cabinet Office (2007) *Global Europe: Meeting the Economic and Security and Challenges*, London: TSO.

Cabinet Office (2010a) Cabinet Office Structural Reform Plan (at: www.number10.gov.uk/wp-content/uploads/srp-cabinet-office.pdf).

Cabinet Office (2010b) *The Coalition: Our Programme for Government*, London: TSO.

Cafruny, A. and Ryner, M. (2007) *Europe at Bay: In the Shadow of US Hegemony*, London: Lynne Rienner.

Cameron, D. (2010a) 'Big society versus big government', speech, 19 April (at: www.conservatives.com/News/Speeches/2010/04/David_Cameron_Big_Society_versus_Big_Government.aspx).

Cameron, D. (2010b) 'Big society speech Liverpool', 19 July (at: www.number10.gov.uk/news/speeches-and-transcripts/2010/07/big-society-speech-53572).

Cameron, D. (2010c) 'Speech by the prime minister on structural reform plans, given at the Civil Service Live event', 8 July (at: www.number10.gov.uk/news/speeches-and-transcripts/2010/07/pms-speech-at-civil-service-live-53064).

Campbell, R. and Childs, S. (2010) '"Wags", "wives" and "mothers"... but what about "women politicians"?', in Geddes, A. and Tonge, J. (eds), *Britain Votes 2010*, Oxford: Oxford University Press.

Campbell, R., Childs, S. and Lovenduski, J. (2010) 'Do women need women representatives?', *British Journal of Political Science*, 40(4): 171–94.

Carman, C. (2005) *The Assessment of the Scottish Parliament's Public Petitions System 1999–2006*, Edinburgh: Scottish Parliament Information Centre.

Chadwick, A. (2006) *Internet Politics: States, Citizens, and New Communication Technologies*, New York: Oxford University Press.

Chadwick, A. (2009) 'Web 2.0: new challenges for the study of e-democracy in an era of informational exuberance, I/S', *Journal of Law and Policy for the Information Society*, 5(1): 9–41.

Chadwick, A. and Howard, P. N. (eds) (2008), *The Handbook of Internet Politics*, London: Routledge.

CheckFacebook (2010) 'CheckFacebook: Facebook marketing statistics, demographics, reports, and news', CheckFacebook website, 24 May (at: www.checkfacebook.com; accessed 24 May 2010).

Childs, S. (2008) *Women and British Party Politics: Descriptive, Substantive and Symbolic Representation*, London: Routledge.

Clarke, H., Sanders, D., Stewart, M. and Whiteley, P. (2004) *Political Choice in Britain*, Oxford: Oxford University Press.

Clarke, H., Sanders, D., Stewart, M. and Whiteley, P. (2009) *Performance Politics and the British Voter*, Cambridge, Cambridge University Press.

Clegg, N. (2010) 'The new politics: Nick Clegg's speech on constitutional reform', 19 May 2010, City & Islington College Centre for Business, Arts and Technology, London (at: www.cabinetoffice.gov.uk/media/408354/new-politics.pdf).

Cm 7170 (2007) *The Governance of Britain*, London: TSO.

Coates, D. (2009) 'Chickens coming home to roost? New Labour at the eleventh hour', *British Politics*, 4(4): 421–33.

Cockett, R. (1995) *Thinking the Unthinkable: Think-Tanks and the Economic Counter-Revolution, 1931–83*, London: Fontana.

Coen, D. and Richardson, J. (2009) *Lobbying the European Union: Institutions, Actors, and Issues*, Oxford: Oxford University Press.

Coen, D., Grant, W. and Wilson, G. (2010) *The Oxford Handbook of Business and Government*, Oxford: Oxford University Press.

Coleman, S. and Blumer, J. (2009) *The Internet and Democratic Citizenship*, Cambridge University Press.

Commission on Scottish Devolution (2009) *Serving Scotland Better: Scotland and the United Kingdom in the 21st Century*, Edinburgh: Commission on Scottish Devolution.

Common Cause (2009) 'Legislating under the influence' (at: www.common-cause.org/site/pp.asp?c=dkLNK1MQIwG&b=5281465).

Conservative Party (2010) *The Conservative Party Manifesto 2010: Invitation to Join the Government of Britain*, London: Conservative Party.

Conservative–Liberal Coalition (2010) Conservative–Liberal Democrat Coalition Negotiations Agreements Reached 11 May 2010 (at: www.conservatives.com/News/News_stories/2010/05/Coalition_Agreement_published.aspx).

Cook, R. (2003) *The Point of Departure*, London: Simon & Schuster.

Cooper, R. (2007) *The Breaking of Nations: Order and Chaos in the Twenty-first World*, London: Atlantic Books.

Corner, J. and Pels, D. (2003) *Media and the Restyling of Politics: Consumerism, Celebrity and Cynicism*, London: Sage.

Cowley, P. (2002) *Revolts and Rebellions*, London: Politico's.

Cowley, P. (2005) *The Rebels: How Blair Mislaid His Majority*, London: Politicos.

Cowley, P. (2006) 'Making parliament matter?', in Dunleavy, P., Heffernan, R., Cowley, P. and Hay, C. (eds), *Developments in British Politics 8*, London: Palgrave Macmillan.

Cowley, P. (2007) 'Parliament', in Seldon, A. (ed.), *Blair's Britain*, Cambridge: Cambridge University Press.

Cowley, P. (2009) 'The parliamentary party', *Political Quarterly*, 80(2): 214–21.

Cowley, P. and Stuart, M. (2009) *Browned off? Dissension amongst the Parliamentary Labour Party, 2007–8: A Data Handbook* (at: www.revolts.co.uk).

Cowley, P. and Stuart, M. (2009) 'There was a doctor, a journalist and two Welshmen: the voting behaviour of independent MPs in the United Kingdom House of Commons, 1997–2007', *Parliamentary Affairs*, 62(1): 19–31.

Coxall, B. (2001) *Pressure Groups in the UK*, London: Longman.

CPS 2008, Ken Macdonald, CPS lecture, 'Coming out of the shadows', 20 October (at: www.cps.gov.uk/news/nationalnews/comi).

Crick, B. (2000) *In Defence of Politics*, 5th edn, London: Continuum.

Criddle, B. (2010) 'More diverse, yet more uniform: MPs and candidates', in Kavanagh, D. and Cowley, P. (eds), *The British General Election of 2010*, London: Palgrave Macmillan.

Croft, S. and Moore, C. (2010) 'The evolution of threat narratives in the age of terror: understanding terrorist attacks in Britain', *International Affairs*, 86(4): 821–35.

Crouch, C. (2004) *Post Democracy*, Cambridge: Cambridge University Press.

Crouch, C. (2008) 'What will follow the demise of privatised Keynesianism?', *Political Quarterly*, 79(4): 476–87.

Crowson, J., Hilton, N. and McKay, M. (2009) *NGOs in Contemporary Britain: Non State Actors in Society and Politics since 1945*, Basingstoke: Palgrave Macmillan.

Curtice, J. (2005) 'Public Opinion and the Future of Devolution', in Trench, A. (ed.), *The Dynamics of Devolution: The State of the Nations 2005*, London: Imprint Academic.

Curtice, J. (2008) 'How firm are the foundations? Public attitudes towards the Union in 2007', in Devine, T. (ed.), *Scotland and the Union 1707–2007*, Edinburgh: Edinburgh University Press.

Curtice, J., Fisher, S. and Ford, R. (2010) 'Appendix 2: an analysis of the results', in Kavanagh, D. and Cowley, P., *The British General Election of 2010*, Basingstoke: Palgrave Macmillan.

Curtice, J. and Heath, A. (2009) 'England awakes? Trends in national identity in England', in Bechhofer, F. and McCrone, D. (eds), *National Identity, Nationalism and Constitutional Change*, Basingstoke: Palgrave Macmillan.

Dahlgren, P. (2009) *Media and Political Engagement: Citizens, Communication and Democracy*, Cambridge: Cambridge University Press.

Dale, I. (2008) 'Mining for gold in the blogosphere', *British Journalism Review*, 19(4): 31–6.

Dalton, R. (1996) *Citizen Politics in Western Democracies: Public Opinion and Political Parties in the US, UK, Germany and France*, Chatham NJ: Chatham House.

Dalton, R. (2007) *The Good Citizen: How a Younger Generation is Reshaping American Politics*, Washington, DC: CQ Press.

Dalton, R. and Waltenberg, M. P. (2002) *Parties without Partisans*, Cambridge: Cambridge University Press.

Daly, M. (2006) 'EU social policy after Lisbon', *Journal of Common Market Studies*, 44(3): 461–81.

Davies, N. (2008) *Flat Earth News: An Award-Winning Reporter Exposes Falsehood, Distortion and Propaganda in the Global Media*, London: Chatto & Windus.

Davies, R. (1999) *Devolution: A Process, Not an Event*, Cardiff: Institute of Welsh Affairs.

Denver, D. (2007) *Elections and Voters in Britain*, 2nd edn, Basingstoke, Palgrave Macmillan.

Denver, D. and Hands, G. (2004) 'Exploring variations in turnout: constituencies and wards in the Scottish parliament elections of 1999 and 2003', *British Journal of Politics and International Relations*, 6(4): 527–42.

di Gennaro, C. and Dutton, W. H. (2006) 'The internet and the public: online and offline political participation in the United Kingdom', *Parliamentary Affairs*, 59(2): 299–313.

Diamond, P. and Radice, G. (2010) *Southern Discomfort Again*, London: Policy Network.

DMGT (2010) Investor Day presentation. DMGT website, 29 April (at: www.dmgt.co.uk/events/investor-day; accessed 25 May 2010).

Dodson, S. (2008) 'Platform for free speech... or hate?', Guardian website, 19 May (at: www.guardian.co.uk/media/2008/may/19/pressandpublishing. telegraphmediagroup; accessed 10 May 2010).

Dorey, P. and Kelso, A. (2011) *House of Lords Reform Since 1911: Must the Lords Go?* London: Palgrave Macmillan.

Drache, D. (2008) *Defiant Publics: The Unprecedented Reach of the Global Citizen*, Cambridge: Polity Press

Duff, A. (2009) *Saving the European Union*, London: Shoehorn.

Duffield, M. (2001) *Global Governance and the New Wars: The Merging of Development and Security*, London: Zed Books.

Dunleavy, P. (2005) 'Facing up to multi-party politics: how partisan de-alignment and PR voting have fundamentally changed Britain's party systems', *Parliamentary Affairs*, 58(3): 503–32.

Dunleavy, P. (2006) 'The Westminster model and the distinctiveness of British politics', in Dunleavy, P., Heffernan, R., Cowley, R. and Hay, C. (eds), *Developments in British Politics 8*, London: Palgrave Macmillan.

Dunn, T. N. (2010) 'It's Lib Dems in front', *The Sun*, April 19.

Durkan, M. (2008) Speech by Mark Durkan, then leader of the Social Democratic and Labour Party (SDLP), at the British Irish Association Conference in New College, Oxford, 5 September (at: http://cain.ulst.ac.uk/issues/politics/docs/sdlp/md050908.htm).

Dyson, K. (ed.) (2008) *The Euro at Ten: Europeanization, Power and Convergence*, Oxford: Oxford University Press.

Dyson, K. and Sepos, A. (eds) (2010) *Which Europe? The Politics of Differentiated Integration*, London: Palgrave Macmillan.

Eatwell, R. and Goodwin, M. (eds) (2010) *The New Extremism in 21st Century Britain*, London: Routledge.

Eijk van der, C. and Franklin, M. (2009) *Elections and Voters*, Basingstoke: Palgrave.

Electoral Commission (2006) Election spending at the 2005 general election (at: www.electoralcommission.org.uk/elections/election-spending).

Electoral Reform Society (2010) 'STV and the parliament that might have been' (at: www.electoral-reform.org.uk/news.php?ex=0&nid=469).

Erdos, D. (2009) 'Charter 88 and the constitutional reform movement: a retrospective', *Parliamentary Affairs*, 62(4): 537–51.

Eurobarometer (2009) Standard Eurobarometer 72, autumn.

Evans, E. (2011) Gender *and the Liberal Democrats: Representing Women?*, Manchester: Manchester University Press.

Evans, G. and Andersen, R. (2005) 'The impact of the party leaders: how Blair lost Labour votes', in Norris, P. and Wlezien, C. (eds), *Britain Votes 2005*, Oxford: Oxford University Press, pp. 162–80.

Evans, M. (2003) *Constitution-Making and the Labour Party*, Palgrave: Macmillan.

Evans, M., Webster, P. and Sharrock, D. (2009) 'Northern Ireland shootings: MI5's response', *The Times*, 11 March (at: www.timesonline.co.uk/tol/news/uk/article5884288.ece).

Ewing, K. (2010) *Bonfire of the Liberties: New Labour, Human Rights, and the Rule of Law*, Oxford: Oxford University Press.

Ewing, K. M. and Tham, J. C. (2008), 'The continuing futility of the Human Rights Act', *Public Law*, winter: 668–93.

Field, A. (2009) 'Tracking terrorist networks: problems of intelligence sharing within the UK intelligence community', *Review of International Studies*, 35(4): 997–1009.

Finlayson, A. (2009) 'Financialisation, financial literacy and asset-based welfare', *British Journal of Politics and International Relations*, 11(3): 400–21.

Flinders, M. V. (2005) 'Majoritarian democracy in Britain: New Labour and the constitution', *West European Politics*, 28(1): 61–93.

Flinders, M. V. (2006) 'Volcanic politics: executive–legislative relations in Britain, 1997–2005', *Australian Journal of Political Science*, 41(3): 385–406.

Flinders, M. V. (2009) *Democratic Drift: Majoritarian Modification and Democratic Anomie in the United Kingdom*, Oxford: Oxford University Press.

Flinders, M. V. (2010) 'In defence of politics', inaugural lecture, University of Sheffield.

Flinders, M. V. and Kelso, A. (2011) 'Mind the gap: political analysis, public expectations and the parliamentary decline thesis', *British Journal of Politics and International Relations* (forthcoming).

Foley, M. (2000) *The British Presidency*, Manchester: Manchester University Press.

Foley, M. (2002) *John Major, Tony Blair and a Conflict of Leadership*, Manchester: University of Manchester Press.

Ford, R. (2006) 'Prejudice and white majority welfare attitudes in the UK', *Journal of Elections, Public Opinion and Parties*,16(2): 141–56.

Ford, R. (2008) 'Is racial prejudice declining in Britain?', *British Journal of Sociology*, 59(4): 609–34.

Ford, R. (2009) 'Who might vote for the BNP? Survey evidence on the electoral potential of the extreme right in Britain', in Eatwell, R. and Goodwin, M. (eds), *The New Extremism in 21st Century Britain*, London: Routledge.

Ford, R. (2010) 'Angry white men: individual and contextual predictors of support for the British National party', *Political Studies*, 58(1): 1–25.

Foreign and Commonwealth Office (2007) *Global Europe: Meeting the Economic and Security Challenges*, London: TSO.

Foreign and Commonwealth Office (2008) *Global Europe: Vision for a 21st Century Budget*, London TSO.

Franklin, M. (2004) *Voter Turnout and the Dynamics of Electoral Competition in Established Democracies since 1945*, Cambridge: Cambridge University Press.

Fukuyama, F. (1992) *The End of History and the Last Man*, London: Hamish Hamilton.

Gamble, A. (2000) *Politics and Fate*, Cambridge: Polity.

Gamble, A. (2003a) *Between Europe and America: The Future of British Politics*, London: Palgrave Macmillan.

Gamble, A. (2003b), 'Remaking the constitution', in Dunleavy, P., Gamble, A., Heffernan, R. and Peele, G. (eds), *Developments in British Politics 7*, London: Palgrave Macmillan.

Gamble, A. (2008) 'Gordon Brown and the re-invention of Britishness', paper presented at the Annual Meeting of the American Political Science Association (at: www.allacademic.com/meta/p281278_index.html).

Gamble, A. (2009a) 'British politics and the financial crisis', *British Politics*, 41(1): 450–62.

Gamble, A. (2009b) *The Spectre at the Feast: Capitalist Crisis and the Politics of Recession*, London: Palgrave Macmillan.

Gearty, C. (2007) *Civil Liberties*, Oxford: Oxford University Press.

Geddes, A. and Tonge, J. (2010) *Britain Votes 2010*, Oxford: Oxford University Press.

George, S. (1998) *An Awkward Partner: Britain in the European Community*, 3rd edn, Oxford: Oxford University Press.

George, S. (2000) 'Britain: anatomy of a Eurosceptic state', *European Integration*, 22(1): 15–33.

Gibson, R. (2009) 'New media and the revitalisation of politics', *Representation*, 45(3): 289–300.

Gibson, R. K, Lusoli, W. and Ward, S. J. (2005) 'Online participation in the UK: testing a contextualised model of internet effects', *British Journal of Politics and International Relations*, 7(4): 561–83.

Gifford, C. (2010) 'The UK and the European Union: dimensions of sovereignty and the problem of Eurosceptic Britishness', *Parliamentary Affairs*, 63(2): 321–38.

Glover, J. (2009) 'Tories winning the battle for economic credibility, poll suggests', Guardian, 20 April (at: www.guardian.co.uk/politics/2009/apr/20/icm-poll-conservatives-ahead-on-economy; accessed 25 May 2010).

Goad, R. (2008) 'Blog traffic reaches all time high', Hitwise website, 10 June (at: http://weblogs.hitwise.com/robin-goad/2008/06/uk_blog_traffic_reaches_all_time_high.html; accessed 24 May 2010).

Gould, P. (1998) *The Unfinished Revolution: How the Modernisers Saved the Labour Party*, London: Little Brown.

Gove, M. (2010) 'Speech to the Scottish Conservative Conference', 12 February (at: www.scottishconservatives.com/news/speeches/223; accessed 24 May 2010).

Grant, W. (2000) *Pressure Groups and British Politics*, London: Palgrave Macmillan.

Grant, W. (2005) 'Pressure politics: a politics of collective consumption?', *Parliamentary Affairs*, 58(2): 366–79.

Grant, W. (2008) 'The changing patterns of group politics in Britain', *British Politics*, 3(2): 204–22.

Greenleaf, W. (1983a) *The British Political Tradition: The Rise of Collectivism*, vol. 1, London: Methuen.

Greenleaf, W. (1983b) *The British Political Tradition: The Ideological Heritage*, vol. 2, London: Methuen.

Greenleaf, W. (1987) *The British Political Tradition: A Much Governed Nation*, vol. 3 (parts 1 and 2), London: Methuen.

Guardian, the (2009) 'Investigate your MP's expenses', Guardian website (at: http://mps-expenses.guardian.co.uk; accessed 21 July 2009).

Guardian, the (2010) 'ABCs', Guardian website (at: www.guardian.co.uk/media/abcs; accessed 24 May 2010).

Hall, B. and Barber, T. (2010). 'Europe agrees rescue package', *Financial Times*, 9 May (at: www.ft.com/cms/s/0/f96a6c14-4-5b48-8-11df-85a3-3-00144 feab49a.html; accessed 31 May 2010).

Halliday, F. (2000) *The World at 2000*, London: Palgrave Macmillan.

Halper, S. (2010) *The Beijing Consensus*, New York: Basic Books.

Hansard Society (2006) *Members Only? Parliament in the Public Eye*, London: Hansard Society.

Hansard Society (2007) *Friend or Foe? Lobbying in British Democracy*, London: Hansard Society (at: www.hansardsociety.org.uk/blogs/downloads/archive/2007/09/24/friend-or-foe-lobbying-in-british-democracy-jan-2007. asp).

Hansard Society (2008) House of Commons Debate, 485, Col. 432 (9 December).

Hansard Society (2009) Audit of Political Engagement 6, London: Hansard Society.

Harfield, C. (2006) 'SOCA: a paradigm shift in British policing', *British Journal of Criminology*, 46(4): 743–61.

Harfield, C. (2008) 'Paradigms, pathologies, and practicalities: policing organized crime in England and Wales', *Policing*, 2(1): 633–73.

Hay, C. (2006) 'Managing economic interdependence: the political economy of New Labour', in Dunleavy, P., Heffernan, R., Cowley, P. and Hay, C. (eds), *Developments in British Politics 8*, London: Palgrave Macmillan.

Hay, C. (2007a) *Why We Hate Politics*, Cambridge: Polity Press.

Hay, C. (2007b) 'What's in a name? New Labour's putative Keynesianism', *British Journal of Political Science*, 37(1): 187–92.

Hay, C. (2009) 'Good Inflation, bad inflation: the housing boom, economic growth and the disaggregation of inflationary preferences in the UK and Ireland', *British Journal of Politics and International Relations*, 11(3): 382–99.

Hay, C. (2011) 'The 2010 Leonard Schapiro Lecture: pathology without crisis? The strange demise of the Anglo-Liberal growth model', *Government and Opposition*, 46(1) forthcoming.

Hay, C. and Stoker, G. (2009) 'Revitalising politics: have we lost the plot?', *Representation*, 45(3): 225–36.

Hazell, R. (2006) *The English Question*, Manchester: Manchester University Press.

Hazell, R. (2008a) 'Conclusion: Where will the Westminster Model End Up?', in Hazell, R. (ed.), *Constitutional Futures Revisited: Britain's Constitution to 2020*, London: Palgrave Macmillan.

Hazell, R. (ed.) (2008b) *Constitutional Futures Revisited: Britain's Constitution to 2020*, London: Palgrave Macmillan.

Hazell, R., Worthy, B. and Glover, M. (2010) *Does FoI Work? The Impact of the Freedom of Information Act on Central Government in the UK*, London: Palgrave Macmillan.

HC 1097 (2005–6) *The Legislative Process: First Report from the Modernisation Committee*, London: TSO.

HC 1117 (2008–9) *Rebuilding the House: First Report from the Select Committee on Reform of the House of Commons*, London: TSO.

HC 1248 (2003–4) *Public Petitions: Fifth Report from the Procedure Committee*, London: TSO.

HC 136 (2007–8) *e-Petitions: First Report from the Procedure Committee*, London: TSO.

HC 144-4-I (2008–9) *Banking Crisis: Oral Evidence to the Treasury Select Committee*, London: TSO.

HC 368 (2003–4) *Connecting Parliament with the Public: First Report from the Modernisation Committee*, London: TSO.

HC 513 (2006–7) *Public Petitions and Early Day Motions: First Report from the Procedure Committee*, London: TSO.

Heffernan, R. (2003) 'Prime ministerial predominance? Core executive politics in the UK', *British Journal of Politics and International Relations*, 5(3): 347–72.

Heffernan, R. (2005) 'Why the prime minister cannot be a president: comparing institutional imperatives in Britain and the US', *Parliamentary Affairs*, 58(1): 533–70.

Heffernan, R. (2009) 'British political parties', in Flinders, M. V., Gamble, A., Hay, C. and Kenny, M. (eds), *The Oxford Handbook of British Politics*, Oxford: Oxford University Press.

Held, D. (2006) *Models of Democracy*, Cambridge: Polity.

Hennessy, P. (2000) *The Prime Minister: The Office and Its Holders since 1945*, London: Penguin.

Hennessy, P. (2009) 'Damian McBride email smears: Gordon Brown pays the price', *Daily Telegraph*, 18 April.

Hennessy, P. (ed.) (2007) *The New Protective State*, London: Continuum.

Heppell, T. and Hill, M. (2009) 'Transcending Thatcherism? Ideology and the Conservative party leadership mandate of David Cameron', *Political Quarterly*, 80(3): 388–99.

Herman, M. (1996) *Intelligence Power in Peace and War*, Cambridge: Cambridge University Press.

Hewitt, S. (2008) *The British War on Terror: Terrorism on the Home Front since 9/11*, London: Continuum.

HM Government (2006) *Countering International Terrorism: The United Kingdom's Strategy*, London: TSO.

HM Government (2009) *Pursue, Prevent, Protect, Prepare: The United Kingdom's Strategy for Countering International Terrorism*, London: TSO.

HM Government (2010) *The Coalition: Our Programme for Government*, London, TSO.

HM Treasury (2008) *Global Europe: Vision for a 21st Century Budget*, London: TSO.

HM Treasury (2010) *Budget 2010: Economic and Fiscal Strategy Report, Financial Statement and Budget Report*, London: TSO.

Holliday, I (2000) 'Is the British state hollowing out?', *Political Quarterly*, 71(2): 167–76.

hooks, b. (1982) *Ain't I a Woman?* London: Pluto Publishing.

Hopkin, J. and Wincott, D. (2006) 'New Labour, economic reform and the European social model', *British Journal of Politics and International Relations*, 8(1): 50–68.

Hoskins, A. and O'Loughlin, N. (2007) *Television and Terror: Conflicting Times and the Crisis of News Discourse*, London: Palgrave Macmillan.

House of Commons (2009) *House of Commons Home Affairs Committee, Project CONTEST: The Government's Counter-terrorism Strategy, Ninth Report of Session 2008–9*, London: TSO.

House of Commons Library (2009) *Proposals for an e-petitions System for the House of Commons: Standard Note SN/PC/4725*, London: TSO.

House of Lords Select Committee on the Constitution (2010) *The Cabinet Office and the Centre of Government Report, 4th Report of Session 2009–10*, London: TSO.

Hutton, W. (2003) *The World We're In*, London: Abacus.

Hutton, W. (2008) *The Writing on the Wall: China and the West in the Twenty-first Century*, London: Abacus.

Inglehart, R. (1990) *Culture Shift in Advanced Industrial Society*, Princeton, NJ: Princeton University Press.

Inglehart, R. and Norris, P. (2000) 'The developmental theory of the gender gap: women and men's voting behaviour in global perspective', *International Political Science Review*, 21(4): 441–62.

Inglehart, R. and Norris, P. (2003) *Rising Tide: Gender Equality and Cultural Change Around the World*, Cambridge: Cambridge University Press.

Institute for Government (2010) *Shaping-Up: A Whitehall for the Future*, London: Institute for Government.

Intelligence and Security Committee (2009) *Annual Report 2007–8*, Cmnd. 7542, London: TSO.

IPPR (2009) *Shared Responsibilities: A National Security Strategy for the United Kingdom*, London: IPPR.

Isaby, J. (2010) 'Brown trailing in the post-debate polls', Conservativehome website, 15 April (at: http://conservativehome.blogs.com/thetorydiary/2010/04/brown-trailing-in-first-two-postdebate-opinion-polls-.html; accessed 15 April 2010).

ITV, Sky and BBC (2010) 'Programme format agreed by all parties 1st March 2010', ITV website. 15 April (at: www.itv.com/utils/cached/common/ProgrammeFormat2.pdf).

Jacques, M. (2009) *When China Rules the World: The Rise of the Middle Kingdom and the End of the Western World*, London: Allen Lane.

Jessop, B. (2004) 'Multi-level governance and multi-level metagovernance', in Bache, I. and Flinders, M. V. (eds), *Multi-Level Governance*, Oxford: Oxford University Press.

Johns, R., Denver, D., Mitchell, J. and Pattie, C. (2009) 'Valence politics in Scotland: towards an explanation of the 2007 election', *Political Studies*, 57(1): 207–33.

Johns, R., Denver, D., Mitchell, J. and Pattie, C. (2010) *Voting for a Scottish Government*, Manchester, Manchester University Press.

Johnson, N. (2004) *Reshaping the British Constitution: Essays in Political Interpretation*, London: Palgrave Macmillan.

Jordan, G. and Maloney, W. (2007) *Democracy and Interest Groups: Enhancing Participation?*, London: Palgrave Macmillan.

JTAC (2006) *Countering International Terrorism: The United Kingdom's Strategy* (at: www.intelligence.gov.uk/upload/assets/www.intelligence.gov.uk/countering.pdf).

Judge, D. (1993) *The Parliamentary State*, London: Sage.

Judge, D. (2006) '"This is what democracy looks like": New Labour's blind spot and peripheral vision', *British Politics*, 1(3): 367–96.

Kagan, R. (2009) *The Return of History and the End of Dreams*, London: Atlantic.

Kaldor, M. (2007) *New and Old Wars: Organized Violence in a Global Era*, Stanford: Stanford University Press.

Kampfner, J. (2003) *Blair's Wars: A Liberal Imperialism in Action*, London: Free Press.

Kavanagh, D. (1980) 'Political culture in Britain: the decline of the civic culture', in G. Almond and S. Verba (eds), *The Civic Culture Revisited*, Boston: Little Brown and Co.

Kavanagh, D. and Cowley, P. (2010), *The British General Election of 2010*, London: Palgrave Macmillan.

Keane, J. (2009) *The Life and Death of Democracy*, London: Simon & Schuster.

Keane, J. (2010) Bridget Cotter interviews John Keane (at: www.johnkeane.net/pdf_docs/others/CSD%20Bulletin%20Volume%2017-Jk_15%20qxd.pdf).

Keaney, E. and Rogers, B. (2006) *A Citizen's Duty: Voter Inequality and the Case for Compulsory Turnout*, London: IRRP.

Keating, M. (ed.) (2007) *Scottish Social Democracy: Progressive Ideas for Public Policy*, Brussels: Peter Lang.

Keen, A. (2007) *The Cult of the Amateur: How Today's Internet Is Killing Our Culture and Assaulting Our Economy*, London: Nicholas Brealey.

Kelso, A. (2003) 'Where were the massed ranks of parliamentary reformers? Attitudinal and contextual approaches to parliamentary reform', *Journal of Legislative Studies*, 9(1): 57–76.

Kelso, A. (2006) 'Reforming the House of Lords: navigating representation, democracy and legitimacy at Westminster', *Parliamentary Affairs*, 59(4): 563–81.

Kelso, A. (2007a) 'Parliament and political disengagement: neither waving nor drowning', *Political Quarterly*, 78(3): 364–73.

Kelso, A. (2007b), 'The House of Commons Modernisation Committee: who needs it?', *British Journal of Politics and International Relations*, 9(1): 138–57.

Kelso, A. (2009a) 'Parliament on its knees: MPs expenses and the crisis of transparency at Westminster', *Political Quarterly*, 80(2): 165–7.

Kelso, A. (2009b) *Parliamentary Reform at Westminster*, Manchester: Manchester University Press.

Kelso, A. (2009c) 'Parliament', in M. V. Flinders, A. Gamble, C. Hay and M. Kenny (eds), *The Oxford Handbook of British Politics*, Oxford: Oxford University Press.

Kettell, S. (2006) *Dirty Politics: New Labour, British Democracy and the Invasion of Iraq*, London, Zed Books.

King, A. (1976) 'Modes of executive–legislative relations: Great Britain, France and West Germany', *Legislative Studies Quarterly*, 1(1): 11–36.

King, A. (2007) *The British Constitution*, Oxford: Oxford University Press.

Kisby, B. and Sloam, J. (2009) 'Revitalising politics: the role of citizenship education', *Representation*, 45(3), 313–24.

Kiss, J. (2007a) 'Guardian Unlimited extends lead', Guardian website, 22 November (at: www.guardian.co.uk/media/2007/nov/22/abcs.digitalmedia; accessed 25 May 2010).

Kiss, J. (2007b) 'Sun website draws record traffic', Guardian website, 27 September (at: www.guardian.co.uk/media/2007/sep/27/digitalmedia. pressandpublishing).

Kiss, J. (2009a) 'ABCe: Guardian.co.uk, Telegraph.co.uk and Mail Online top 30 million users', Guardian website, 22 October (at: www.guardian.co.uk/ media/2009/oct/22/abce-guardian-telegraph-mail-online; accessed 24 May 2010).

Kiss, J. (2009b) 'Sun Online overtakes four rivals to become the most popular newspaper website', Guardian website, 26 March (at: www.guardian.co.uk/ media/2009/mar/26/sun-online-most-popular-newspaper-website; accessed 25 March 2010).

Kiss, J. (2010) 'ABCe: Mail holds on to UK newspaper website lead', Guardian website, 25 March (at: www.guardian.co.uk/media/2010/mar/25/abce-february-2010; accessed 24 May 2010).

Klug, F. and Starmer, K. (2005) 'Standing back from the Human Rights Act: how effective is it five years on?', *Public Law*, (winter): 716–28.

Kochan, N. ((2006) 'Interview with Sir Stephen Lander and David Armond', 19 October (at: www.nickkochan.com/docs/printerfriendly_m-l/lander.html)

Krugman, P. (2008) *The Return of Depression Economics and the Crisis of 2008*, London: Penguin.

Kuhn, R. (2007) *Politics and the Media in Britain*, London: Palgrave Macmillan.

Laver, M. and Schofield, N. (1990) *Multi-Party Government*, Oxford: Oxford University Press.

Laver, M., Rallings, C. and Thrasher, M. (1987) 'Coalition theory and local government payoffs in Britain', *British Journal of Political Science*, 17(4): 501–9.

Laws, D. (2010) *22 Days in May*, London: Biteback.

Lee, S. (2007) *Best for Britain? The Politics and Legacy of Gordon Brown*, London: Oneworld Publications.

Leigh, I. (2005) 'Accountability of security and intelligence in the United Kingdom', in Born, H., Johnson L. K. and Leigh, I. (eds), *Who's Watching the Spies: Establish Intelligence Service Accountability*, Washington DC: Potomac.

Lent, A. (2001) *British Social Movements since 1945: Sex, Colour, Peace and Power*, London: Palgrave Macmillan.

Leppard, D. (2009) 'Internet firms resist minster's plan to spy on every e-mail', *Sunday Times*, 1 August.

Levy, J. (2009) *Strengthening Parliament's Powers of Scrutiny? An Assessment of the introduction of Public Bill Committees*, London: Constitution Unit.

Levy, J. (2010) 'Public bill committees, an assessment: Scrutiny sought, scrutiny gained', *Parliamentary Affairs*, 63(3): 534–44.

Liaison Committee (2002) *Minutes of Evidence, Tuesday 16 July 2002, Session 2001–2*, London: TSO

Liberal Democratic Party (2010) *General Election Manifesto*, London: Liberal Democratic Party.

Lijphart, A. (1977) *Democracy in Plural Societies: A Comparative Exploration*, New Haven, CT: Yale University Press.

Lijphart, A. (1999) *Patterns of Democracy: Government Forms and Performance in Thirty-Six Countries*, New Haven, CT: Yale University Press.

London Internet Exchange (2009) 'Submission to the Home Office', private document, August.

Lovenduski, J. (2005) *Feminizing Politics*, Cambridge: Polity Press.

Lovenduski, J. (2008) 'A standing commission on social justice?', *Political Quarterly*, 79(1): 3–5.

Lucas, R. E. (2003) 'Macroeconomic priorities', *American Economic Review*, 93(1): 1–14.

Luft, O. (2008) 'ABCe: credit crunch boosts quality newspapers websites', Guardian website, 23 October (at: www.guardian.co.uk/media/2008/oct/23/abcs-digitalmedia; accessed 25 May 2010).

Mabbett, D. (2008) 'Aspirational legalism and the role of the Equality and Human Rights Commission in equality policy', *Political Quarterly*, 79(1): 45–52.

Madano Partnership (2010) 'The elected class of 2010' (at: www.theclassof2010.co.uk).

Maloney, W., Grant, W. and McLaughlin, A. (1994) 'Interest groups and public policy: the insider/outsider model revisited', *Journal of Public Policy*, 14(1): 17–38.

Mandelson, P. (2010) *The Third Man: Life at the Heart of New Labour*, London: Harper Press.

Mandelson, P. and Liddle, R. (1996) *The Blair Revolution: Can New Labour Deliver*, London: Faber & Faber.

Margetts, H., John, P. and Weir, S. (2004) 'Latent support for the far right in British Politics: the BNP and UKIP in the 2004 European and London elections', paper delivered to the EPOP Conference, September.

Marinetto, M. (2003) 'Governing beyond the centre: a critique of the Anglo-Governance School', *Political Studies*, 51(3): 592–608.

Marsh, D., Richards, D. and Smith, M. J. (2001) *Changing Patterns of Governance*, London: Palgrave Macmillan.

Mathieson, S. (2005) 'UK seeks all-EU traffic data retention', *Computer Fraud and Security*, 7(July): 1–2.

Mattinson, D. (2010) *Talking to a Brick Wall: How New Labour Stopped Listening to the Voter and Why We Need a New Politics*, London: Biteback.

McGarry, J. and O'Leary, B. (2004) *The Northern Ireland Conflict: Consociational Engagements*, Oxford: Oxford University Press.

McGarry, J. and O'Leary, B. (2006) 'Consociational theory, Northern Ireland's conflict and its agreement: Part I. What consociationalists can learn from Northern Ireland', *Government and Opposition*, 41(1): 43–63.

McGarry, J. and O'Leary, B. (2006a) 'Consociational theory, Northern Ireland's conflict and its agreement: Part II. What critics of consociation can learn from Northern Ireland', *Government and Opposition*, 41(2): 249–77.

McGarvey, N. and Cairney, P. (2008) *Scottish Politics*, London: Palgrave Macmillan.

McKay, J. and Hilton, N. (2009) 'Introduction', in Crowson, J., Hilton, N. and McKay, M. (2009) *NGOs in Contemporary Britain: Non State Actors in Society and Politics since 1945*, London: Palgrave Macmillan.

McKittirck, D., Kelters, S., Feeney, B. and Thornton, C. (1999) *Lost Lives: The Stories of the Men, Women and Children Who Died Through the Northern Ireland Troubles*, Edinburgh: Mainstream Press.

McLean, I. (1987) *Public Choice*, Oxford: Blackwell.

McLean, I. (2009) *What's Wrong with the British Constitution?*, Oxford: Oxford University Press.

Mead, W. R. (2008) *God and Gold: Britain, America and the Making of the Modern World*, London: Atlantic Books.

Melding, D. (2009) *Will Britain Survive Beyond 2020?*, Cardiff: Institute of Welsh Affairs.

Mellors, C. (1989) 'Non-majority British local authorities in a majority setting', in Mellors, C. and Pijenburg, B. (eds), *Political Parties and Coalitions in European Local Government*, London, Routledge.

Miliband, D. (2010) 'Blair–Brown is over: no more living in the past', *The Times*, 18 May.

Mitchell, J. (2009) *Devolution in the UK*, Manchester: Manchester University Press.

Mitchell, J. (2010) 'The narcissism of small differences: Scotland and Westminster', *Parliamentary Affairs*, 63(1): 98–116.

Morgan, R. (2002) 'Clear red water', speech to the National Centre for Public Policy, Swansea.

Mowlam, M. (2002) *Momentum: The Struggle for Peace, Politics and the People*, London: Hodder & Stoughton.

Muslim Council of Britain (2010) 'About us' (at: www.mcb.org.uk/index.php).

National Assembly for Wales (2009) *Getting it right for Wales: An independent review of the current arrangements for the financial support of Assembly Members*, Cardiff: National Assembly for Wales.

Neville-Jones, P. (2010) 'Evolving threats and responses', speech given at RUSI on 17 March (at: www.conservatives.com/News/Speeches/2010/03/Pauline_Neville-Jones_Evolving_Threats_and_Responses.aspx).

Nicol, D. (2004) 'The Human Rights Act and the politicians', *Legal Studies*, 24(3): 451–79.

NILT (2008) Northern Ireland Life and Times Survey (at: www.art.ac.uk/nilt/2008).

Niven, B. (2008) 'The EHRC: transformational, progressively incremental or a disappointment?', *Political Quarterly*, 79(1): 17–26.

Nolan, P. (2003) *China at the Crossroads*, Cambridge: Polity Press.

Norris, P. (1999a) *Critical Citizens*, Oxford: Oxford University Press.

Norris, P. (1999b) 'Gender: a gender-generation gap?', in Evans, G. and Norris,

P. (eds), *Critical Elections: British Parties and Voters in Long-Term Perspective*, London: Sage.

Norris, P. (2002) *Democratic Phoenix: Reinventing Political Activism*, Cambridge: Cambridge University Press.

Norris, P. (2008) 'Political activism', in Heywood, P., Jones, E., Rhodes, M. and Sedelmeier, U. (eds), *Developments in European Politics 2*, London: Palgrave Macmillan.

Norris, P. (2009) 'The impact of the internet on political activism', in C. Romm and K. Setzekorn (eds), *Social Networking Communities and E-Dating Service*, I-Global.

Norris, P. and Curtice, J. (2007) 'Getting the message out: a two-step model of the role of the internet in campaign communication flows during the 2005 British general election', *Journal of Information Technology and Politics*, 4(4): 3–13.

Norris, P., Lovenduski, J. and Campbell, R. (2004) *Gender and Political Participation*, London: Electoral Commission.

Norton, P. (2005) *Parliament in British Politics*, London: Palgrave Macmillan.

Norton, P. (2007) 'Tony Blair and the constitution', *British Politics*, 2(2): 269–81.

Norton, P. (2010) 'The House of Commons', in Jones, B. and Norton, P. (eds), *Politics UK*, 7th edn, Harlow: Pearson.

O'Brien, N. (2008) 'Equality and human rights: foundations of a common culture?', *Political Quarterly*, 79(1): 27–35.

O'Donnell, C. M. and Whitman, R. (2007) 'European policy under Gordon Brown: Perspectives on a future prime minister', *International Affairs*, 83(2): 253–72.

O'Toole, S. (2007) 'Let no one interfere with that' (at: www.sluggerotoole. com/2007/03/28/let-no-one-interfere-with-that).

Oborne, P. (2007) 'Clean-up in Spin City', *British Journalism Review*, 18(4): 111–18.

Oliver, D. (2009) 'The United Kingdom constitution in transition: from where to where?', in Andenæs, M. T. *et al.* (eds), *Tom Bingham and the Transformation of the Law: A Liber Amicorum*, Oxford: Oxford University Press.

Omand, D. (2004). 'Emergency planning, security and business continuity', *RUSI Journal*, 149(4): 26–33.

Omand, D. (2009) *The National Security Strategy: Implications for the UK Intelligence Community*, London: Institute for Public Policy Research.

Omand D. (2010) *Securing the State*, London: Hurst.

Osmond, J. (ed.) (2008) *Unpacking the Progressive Consensus*, Cardiff: Institute of Welsh Affairs/Wales Governance Centre.

OXIS (2009) *The Internet in Britain: 2009*, Oxford: Oxford Internet Institute.

Parker, G. (2010) 'EU relief as Osborne treads softly', *Financial Times*, 18 May.

Parker, G. (2010) 'We will have a mandate for cuts, says Osborne', *Financial Times*, 5 May (at: www.ft.com/cms/s/0/49a23c26-6-57dd-11df-855b-00144 feab49a.html).

Parris, M. (2009) 'Are we over the rainbow?', *The Times*, 27 June.

Parry, G., Moyser, G. and Day, N. (1992) *Political Participation and Democracy in Britain*, Cambridge: Cambridge University Press.

Pattie, C., Seyd, P. and Whiteley, P. (2003) 'Citizenship and civic engagement: attitudes and behaviour in Britain', *Political Studies*, 51(3): 443–68.

Pemberton, H. (2009) 'Macroeconomic crisis and policy revolution', *Renewal*, 17(4): 46–56.

Peters, B. G., Pierre, J. and Stoker, G. (2009) *Debating Institutionalism*, Manchester: Manchester University Press.

Pharr, S. and Putnam, R. (2000) *Disaffected Democracies*, Princeton: Princeton University Press.

Phillips, M. (2006) *Londonistan: How Britain Has Created a Terror State Within*, London: Gibson Square.

Phillips, T. (2010) 'The future of equalities' (at: www.equalityhumanrights.com/uploaded_files/speeches/tpspeeches_2402210.pdf).

Phillis, B. (2004) *An Independent Review of Government Communications*, London: TSO.

Pierre, J. and Peters, B. G. (2000) *Governance, Politics and the State*, London: Palgrave Macmillan.

Platform for Change. Available at: http://platformforchange.net

Political Studies Association (2007) *Failing Politics? A Response to the Government's Green Paper*, Newcastle, PSA (at: www.psa.ac.uk/PSAPubs/PSA%20Response%20to%20Governance%20Green%20Paper.pdf).

Power Commission (2006) *Power to the People*, London: Power Inquiry.

Prince, R. (2008) 'Gordon Brown starts YouTube question time', Daily Telegraph website 19 May (at: www.telegraph.co.uk/news/1986581/Gordon-Brown-starts-YouTube-Question-Time.html?source=rss).

PSNI (2010) 'Statistics relating to the security situation 1st April 2009–31st March 2010', PSNI Annual Statistical Report 6, Belfast: Central Statistics Branch.

Putnam, R. (1993) *Making Democracy Work: Civic Traditions in Modern Italy*, London: Princeton University Press.

Putnam, R. (2000) *Bowling Alone: The Collapse and Revival of American Community*, New York: Simon and Schuster.

Quinlan, M. (2004) 'Lessons for governmental process', in Runciman, W. G. (ed.), *Hutton and Butler Lifting the Lid on the Workings of Power*, Oxford: Oxford University Press.

Rake, K. (2009) 'Are women bearing the brunt of the recession?', London: Fawcett Society.

Rallings, C. and Thrasher, M. (1990) 'Turnout in Local Elections: an aggregate data analysis with electoral and contextual data', *Electoral Studies*, 9 (2): 79–90.

Ram V. (2006) 'Public attitudes to politics, politicians and parliament', *Parliamentary Affairs*, 59(1): 188–97.

Rawlings, R. (1998) 'The new model Wales', *Journal of Law and Society*, 25(4): 461–509.

Rawnsley, A. (2010) *The End of the Party: The Rise and Fall of New Labour*, London: Viking.

Rees, W. (2006) *Transatlantic Security Cooperation: Drugs, Crime and Terrorism in the Twenty-first Century*, London: Routledge.

Rees, W. and Aldrich, R. J. (2005) 'Contending cultures of counter-terrorism: divergence or convergence?', *International Affairs*, 81(4): 905–24.

Regulatory Policy Institute (2009) *Trust in the System: Restoring Trust in our System of Government and Regulation*, Oxford: Regulatory Policy Institute.

Reif, K. and Schmitt, H. (1980) 'Nine second-order elections', *European Journal of Political Research*, 8(1): 3–45.

Reprieve (2010) *About us* (at: www.reprieve.org.uk).

Rhodes, R. A. W. (1997) *Understanding Governance: Policy Networks, Governance, Reflexivity and Accountability*, Buckingham: Open University Press.

Rhodes, RAW (2006) 'Executive government in Parliamentary Systems', in R. A. W. Rhodes, S. Binder and B. Rockman (eds), *The Oxford Handbook of Political Institutions*, Oxford: Oxford University Press.

Richard Commission (2004) *Report of the Richard Commission*, Cardiff: Stationary Office.

Richards, D. (2008) *New Labour and the Civil Service: Reconstituting the Westminster Model*, London: Palgrave Macmillan

Richards, D., Blunkett, D. and Mathers, H. (2008) 'Old and New Labour narratives of Whitehall: radicals, reactionaries and defenders of the Westminster model', *Political Quarterly*, 79(4): 488–98.

Riddell, P. (2003) *Hug Them Close: Blair, Clinton and the 'Special Relationship'*, London: Politico's.

Riker, W. (1962) *The Theory of Political Coalitions*, New Haven, CT: Yale University Press.

Rogers, R. and Walters, R. (2006) *How Parliament Works*, Harlow: Pearson Longman.

Russell, B. (2008) 'Former head of MI5 says 42-day detention plan is "unworkable"', *Independent*, 9 July.

Russell, M. (2008) 'Parliament: emasculated or emancipated?', in Hazell, R. (ed.), *Constitutional Futures Revisited*, Basingstoke: Palgrave Macmillan.

Russell, M. (2009) 'House of Lords Reform: are we nearly there yet?', *Political Quarterly*, 80(1): 119–25.

Russell, M. (2010) 'A stronger second chamber? Assessing the impact of House of Lords reform in 1999 and lessons for bicameralism', *Political Studies*, 58(5): 866–85.

Russell, M. and Sciara, M. (2008) 'The policy impact of defeats in the House of Lords', *British Journal of Politics and International Relations*, 10 (4): 571–89.

Saggar, S. (1998) *Race and British Electoral Politics*, London: Routledge.

Saward, M. (1997) 'In search of the hollow crown', in Weller, P., Bakvis, H. and Rhodes, R. A. W. (eds), *The Hollow Crown: Countervailing Trends in Core Executives*, London: Palgrave Macmillan.

Scottish Government (2010) *Scotland's Future: Draft Referendum (Scotland) Bill Consultation Paper*, Edinburgh: Scottish Government.

Scottish Labour Party (2007) *Building Scotland*, Glasgow: Scottish Labour Party.

Scottish Parliament (2008) *How to Submit a Public Petition*, Edinburgh: Scottish Parliament Public Information Service.

Scully, R., Wyn Jones, R. and Trystan, D. (2004) 'Turnout, participation and legitimacy in post-devolution Wales', *British Journal of Political Science*, 34(3): 519–37.

Searle, G. (1995) *Country Before Party*, London: Longman.

Seldon, A. (2008) *Blair Unbound*, London: Pocket Books.

Seldon, A. and Lodge, G. (2010) *Brown at 10*, London: Biteback.

Shapley, L. S. and Shubik, M. (1954) 'A method for evaluating the distribution of power in a committee system', *American Political Science Review*, 48(3): 787–92.

Sherrington, P. (2006) 'Confronting Europe: UK political parties and the EU 2000–2005', *British Journal of Politics and International Relations*, 8(1): 69–78.

Shipman, T. (2010) 'Nick Clegg's Nazi slur on Britain', Daily Mail website, 22 April (at: www.dailymail.co.uk/news/election/article-1267921/GENERAL-ELECTION-2010-0-Nick-Clegg-Nazi-slur-Britain.html; accessed 22 April 2010).

Short, C. (2004) *An Honourable Deception? New Labour, Iraq and the Misuse of Power*, London: Free Press

Smith, A. (2009) 'New man or son of the manse? Gordon Brown as reluctant celebrity father', *British Politics*, 3(4): 566–75.

Smith, G. (2010) *Democratic Innovations*, Cambridge: Cambridge University Press.

Snowden, P. (2010) *Back from the Brink: The Inside Story of the Tory Resurrection*, London: Harper Press.

Sobolewska, M. (2010) 'Religious extremism in Britain and British Muslims', in Eatwell, R. and Goodwin, M. (eds), *The New Extremism in 21st Century Britain*, London: Routledge.

Sommer, P. and Hosein, G. (2009) Briefing on the Internet Modernisation Programme, PEN Paper 5, LSE (at: www.lse.ac.uk/collections/information Systems/research/policyEngagement/IMP_Briefing.pdf).

SP 300 (2009) *Inquiry into the Public Petitions Process*, 3rd report from the Public Petitions Committee, Session 3.

Squires, J. (2007) The New Politics of Gender Equality, London: Palgrave Macmillan

Stanyer, J. (2007) *Modern Political Communication: Mediated Politics in Uncertain Times*. Cambridge: Polity.

Stanyer, J. (2008) 'Web 2.0 and the transformation of news and journalism', in Chadwick, A. and Howard, P. N. (eds), *The Handbook of Internet Politics*, New York: Routledge.

Stoker, G. (2006) *Why Politics Matters: Making Democracy Work*, London: Palgrave Macmillan.

Stoker, G. (2006a) 'Explaining political disenchantment: finding pathways to democratic renewal', *Political Quarterly*, 77(2): 184–94.

Stoker, G. (2010) 'The rise of political disenchantment', in C. Hay (ed.), *New Directions in Political Science*, Basingstoke: Palgrave Macmillan.

Stolz, K. (ed.) (2010), *Ten Years of Devolution in the United Kingdom: Snapshots at a Moving Target*, Augsburg: Wissner Verlag.

Stratton, A. and Wintour, P. (2009) 'James Purnell quits Cabinet and calls on Gordon Brown to stand aside now', Guardian website, 5 June (at: www.guardian.co.uk/politics/2009/jun/04/james-purnell-resigns-gordon-brown-cabinet; accessed 24 May 2010).

Strom, K. (1990) *Minority Government and Majority Rule*, Cambridge: Cambridge University Press.

Summerskill, B. (2009) 'Why I quit the new human rights and equality watch-dog', *The Times*, 27 July.

Sunstein, C. (2009) *Republic.com 2.0*, Princeton: Princeton University Press.

Svendsen, A. (2009) 'The globalization of intelligence since 9/11: frameworks and operational parameters', *Cambridge Review of International Affairs*, 21(1): 129–44.

Sweney, M. (2008) 'Ofcom backs ITV plans for regional news cuts', Guardian website, 25 September (at: www.guardian.co.uk/media/2008/sep/25/ofcom.itv; accessed 7 July 2009).

Sweney, M. (2010) 'Leaders' debate: nearly 700 complain to OFCOM over Treatment of Nick Clegg', Guardian website, 28 April (at: www.guardian.co.uk/media/2010/apr/28/leaders-debate-complaints; accessed 13 May 2010).

Taggart, P. and Szczerbiak, A. (2004) 'Contemporary Euroscepticism in the party systems of the European Union candidate states of Central and Eastern Europe', *European Journal of Political Research*, 43(1): 1–27.

Tant, A. (1993) *British Government: The Triumph of Elitism*, Dartmouth: Dartmouth Press.

Taylor, R. (ed.) (2009) *Consociational Theory: McGarry and O'Leary and the Northern Ireland Conflict*, London: Routledge.

Thain, C. (2009) 'A very peculiar British crisis? Institutions, ideas and policy responses to the credit crunch', *British Politics*, 4(4): 434–9.

Theiss-Morse, E. and Hibbing, J. R. (2001) *What is it about Government that Americans Dislike?*, Cambridge: Cambridge University Press.

Theiss-Morse, E. and Hibbing, J. R. (2002) *Stealth Democracy*, Cambridge: Cambridge University Press.

Theiss-Morse, E. and Hibbing, J. R. (2005) 'Citizenship and political engagement', *Annual Review of Political Science*, 8: 227–49.

Tomkins, A (2002) 'In defence of the political constitution', *Oxford Journal of Legal Studies*, 22(1): 157–75.

Trench, A. (ed.) (2007) *Devolution and Power in the United Kingdom*, Manchester: Manchester University Press.

Trench, A. (ed.) (2008) *The State of the Nations 2008: Into the Third Term of Devolution in the UK*, London: Imprint Academic.

Trench, A. and Hazell, R. (eds), (2004) *Has Devolution Made a Difference? The State of the Nations 2004*, London: Imprint Academic.

Tweetminster (2010) 'The leaders' debate', Tweetminster website, 15 April (at: http://tweetminster.co.uk/posts/index/page:3; accessed 30 April 2010).

UK House of Lords Select Committee on Communication (2009) Communication Committee First Report: Government Communications, 10

December (at: www.publications.parliament.uk/pa/ld200809/ldselect/ldcomuni/7/702.htm; accessed 25 May 2010).

UK Office for National Statistics (2009) *Internet Access 2008: Households and Individuals*, Cardiff: Office for National Statistics (at: www.statistics.gov.uk/pdfdir/iahi0808.pdf; accessed 11 May 2009).

UK Office of Communications (2005) *Viewers and Voters: Attitudes to Television Coverage of the 2005 General Election*, London: TSO.

UK Office of Communications (2007) *The Communications Market 2007*, London: TSO.

UK Office of Communications (2008) *The Communications Market 2008*, London: TSO.

UK Office of Communications (2009) *Citizens' Digital Participation*, London: TSO (at: www.ofcom.org.uk/advice/media_literacy/medlitpub/medlitpubrss/cdp/main.pdf; accessed 11 May 2009).

UK Office of Fair Trading (2008) *Newspaper and Magazine Distribution in the United Kingdom*, London: TSO.

UK Office of Fair Trading (2009) *Review of the Local and Regional Media Merger Regime: Final Report*, London: TSO.

UK Prime Minister's Office (2008a) 'E-petitions: facts, figures and progress', UK Prime Minister's website, 6 March (at: www.number10.gov.uk/Page11051; accessed 10 October 2008).

UK Prime Minister's Office (2008b) 'Ask the PM: answered!', UK Prime Minister's website, 10 July (at: www.number10.gov.uk/Page16293; accessed 10 October 2008).

van der Pijl, K (2006) *Global Rivalries from the Cold War to Iraq*, London: Verso.

Verba, S., Schlozman, K. L. and Brady, H. E. (1995) *Voice and Equality: Civic Voluntarism in American Politics*, Cambridge, MA: Harvard University Press.

Verkaik, R. and Morris, N. (2008) 'Exclusive: storm over Big Brother database', *The Independent*, 15 October .

Vibert, F. (2007) *The Rise of the Unelected: Democracy and the New Separation of Powers*, Cambridge: Cambridge University Press.

von Neumann, J. and Morgenstern, O. (1947) *Theory of Games and Economic Behaviour*, Princeton: Princeton University Press.

Walker, C. (2006) 'Clamping down on terrorism in the United Kingdom', *Journal of International Criminal Justice*, 4(5): 1137–51.

Wall, S. (2008) *A Stranger in Europe*, Oxford: Oxford University Press.

Wallace, W. (2005) 'The collapse of British foreign policy', *International Affairs*, 82(1): 53–68.

Watson, M. (2010) 'House price Keynesianism and the contradictions of the modern investor subject', *Housing Studies*, 25(3): 413–26.

Webb, P. (2000) *The Modern British Party System*, London: Sage.

Webb, P. (2002) 'Political parties in Britain', in Webb, P., Farrell, D. and Holliday, I. (eds), *Political Parties in Advanced Industrial Societies*, Oxford, Oxford University Press.

Webb, P. (2004) 'Party responses to the changing electoral market in Britain', in

Mair, P., Muller, W. C. and Plasser, F. (eds), *Political Parties and Electoral Change*, London: Sage.

Weiler, J. (1999) *The Constitution of Europe*, Cambridge: Cambridge University Press.

Wilford, R. (2007) 'Inside Stormont: the assembly and the executive', in Carmichael, P., Knox, C. and Osborne, R. (eds), *Devolution and Constitutional Change in Northern Ireland*, Manchester: Manchester University Press.

Wilford, R. (2008) 'St Andrews – the long Good Friday Agreement', in Bradbury, J. and Mawson, J. (eds), *Devolution, Regionalism and Regional Development: The UK Experience*, London: Routledge.

Wilford, R. and Wilson, R. (2009) 'The assembly', in Wilford, R. and Wilson, R. (eds), *Northern Ireland Devolution Monitoring Report – May 2009*, London: UCL, Constitution Unit.

Wilson, R. (2002) 'Portrait of a profession revisited' (at: www.civilservant.org.uk/srwspeech0302.pdf).

Wilson, R. (2008) 'Devolved government', in Wilford, R. and Wilson, R. (eds), *Northern Ireland Devolution Monitoring Report – September 2008*, London: UCL, Constitution Unit.

Wilson, R. (2010) *5 Days to Power*, London: Biteback.

Winnett, R. and Swaine, J. (2010) 'Nick Clegg, the Lib Dem donors and payments into his private account; exclusive donor cash mystery', *Daily Telegraph*, 22 April.

Wyn Jones, R. (2001) 'On process, events and unintended consequences: national identity and the politics of Welsh devolution', *Scottish Affairs*, 37 (autumn): 34–57.

Wyn Jones, R. and Scully, R. (2008) 'The legitimacy of devolved government in Scotland and Wales', paper presented to the Annual Conference of the American Political Science Association, Boston.

Wyn Jones, R. and Scully, R. (2010) 'Devolution and the people of Wales', in Stolz, K. (ed.), *Ten Years of Devolution in the United Kingdom: Snapshots at a Moving Target*, Augsburg: Wissner Verlag.

Young, H. (1999) *This Blessed Plot*, London: Macmillan.

Young, T. (2010) 'Tonight's polls: Lib Dem surge holds up', Daily Telegraph website, 19 April (at: http://blogs.telegraph.co.uk/news/tobyyoung/100035455/tonights-polls-lib-dem- surge-holds-up; accessed 19 April 2010).

Index